P9-APA-011

Lewis Wetzel – Indian Fighter
West Virginia University
West Virginia
Wesleyan College
Scale of miles
0 10 20 30 40
State Capital
County Seats
State Capitol
Coal Fields
HANCOCK
Chester
NEW CUMBERLAND
BROOKE
WELLSBURG
Bethany
West Liberty
OHIO
WHEELING
MOUNDSVILLE
MARSHALL
Cameron
NEW MARTINSVILLE
WETZEL
Sistersville
MIDDLEBOURNE
TYLER
Smithfield
Williamstown
ST. MARYS
PLEASANTS
PARKERSBURG
WOOD
Pennsboro
Ellenboro
HARRISVILLE
RITCHIE
WEST UNION
DODDRIDGE
Salem
West Milford
ELIZABETH
WIRT
Ravenswood
GRANTSVILLE
CALHOUN
GLENVILLE
GILMER
Normantown
WESTON
POINT PLEASANT
MASON
JACKSON
RIPLEY
SPENCER
ROANE
Walton
BRAXTON
Gassaway
SUTTON
WINFIELD
PUTNAM
Clendenin
CLAY
Lesage
CABELL
HUNTINGTON
Kebova
CHARLESTON
KANAWHA
Malden
Marmet
SUMMERSVILLE
NICHOLAS
Richwood
Camden on Gauley
WAYNE
HAMLIN
LINCOLN
Montgomery
Kanawha Falls
Hawks Nest
MADISON
BOONE
FAYETTEVILLE
FAYETTE
Whitesville
Oak Hill
LOGAN
MINGO
WILLIAMSON
BECKLEY
RALEIGH
Oceana
WYOMING
PINEVILLE
HINTON
SUMMERS
LEWISBURG
White Sulphur Sp
UNION
MONROE
WELCH
North Fork
MC DOWELL
Athens
MERCER
PRINCETON
Bluefield
OHIO RIVER
Kanawha River
Elk River
Gauley River
Guyandot River
Tug Fork
New River
Middle Island Cr.
Little Kanawha River

Anna Jarvis
Founder of Mother's Day
Fort Ashby
Tygart Dam
Seneca Trail
Old Stone Face
White Sulphur Springs
n
S
POTOMAC RIVER
BERKELEY SPRINGS
Great Cacapon
MORGAN
Pawpaw
Hedgesville
BERKELEY
MARTINSBURG
Shepherdstown
Bunker Hill
Harpers Ferry
JEFFERSON
CHARLESTOWN
Shenandoah
Green Spring
KEYSER
MINERAL
Elk Garden
Burlington
ROMNEY
HAMPSHIRE
Gormania
Mt. Storm
Capon Sprs.
Wardensville
MOOREFIELD
GRANT
PETERSBURG
HARDY
Cacapon
Lost City
South Branch
Clifton Mills
Monongahela R.
Masontown
KINGWOOD
PRESTON
Rowlesburg
Aurora
Kasson
PHILIPPI
St. George
PARSONS
Cheat R.
TUCKER
Red Creek
Belington
ELKINS
RANDOLPH
Mill Creek
Mouth of Seneca
Ft. Seybert
PENDLETON
FRANKLIN
North Fork
South Fork
Greenbank
Tygart
Shavers
River

West Virginia and Its Government

West Virginia
AND ITS GOVERNMENT

Oscar Doane Lambert
PROFESSOR OF HISTORY IN WEST VIRGINIA UNIVERSITY

GREENWOOD PRESS, PUBLISHERS
WESTPORT, CONNECTICUT

The Library of Congress has catalogued this publication as follows:

Library of Congress Cataloging in Publication Data

Lambert, Oscar Doane, 1888-1959.
West Virginia and its government.

Bibliography: p.
1. West Virginia--Politics and government.
[JK4025 1951.L32] 320.4'754 77-142859
ISBN 0-8371-5958-X

Originally published in 1951
by D. C. Heath and Company, Boston

Reprint by permission of D. C. Heath and Company,
Lexington, Massachusetts

First Greenwood Reprinting 1972

Library of Congress Catalogue Card Number 77-142859

ISBN 0-8371-5958-X

Printed in the United States of America

TO THE MEMORY OF

My Mother

ALICE JANE (BONNER) LAMBERT

PREFACE

THE WRITING of a book on the constitutional history of West Virginia is long overdue. For many years the lack of such a work has left a gap in the sources of information needed by the citizens of this commonwealth, especially by teachers and pupils of the public schools and colleges. To the end of filling this need, the following pages are now presented.

Following an introductory chapter on the physical aspects of West Virginia, it has seemed fitting to include a brief survey of the early political history of the Virginia territory. Organized civil administration in America had its beginning in Virginia, out of whose territory West Virginia eventually emerged. Hence the two states not only have the same colonial history but they remained one and the same commonwealth until separation was finally consummated in 1863. The manners and institutions of both states thus spring from the same root.

After the account of colonial developments, the text explains how variations appeared and expanded between the eastern part of the state and that other part lying west of the Allegheny Mountains. As time went on these dissimilarities resulted in social, economic, and political disagreements. The contest between the two regions was waged with such asperity and vehemence that separation, long threatened, eventually became an actual fact.

From this point the government of West Virginia is followed in detail to the present time. A full description is given of the political organization of the people, ever changing, moving, advancing, acting, and reacting. The will of the people in action is seen as their government in the process of functioning.

For help rendered in the preparation of this work grateful acknowledgment is made to Dr. Festus P. Summers, head of the Department of History of West Virginia University; Dr. Roy Bird Cook, author, Charleston, West Virginia; Mr. H. B. Lambert, attorney-at-law, Charleston, West Virginia; Dr. W. D. Barns of the Department of History of West Virginia University; and Dr. D. D.

Johnson, Professor Emeritus, Morgantown, West Virginia. Dr. Summers read the manuscript and offered valuable suggestions with respect to its content and arrangement. Dr. Cook also made a complete review of the work and presented constructive criticism of material and style. Mr. Lambert gave particular attention to Chapter 17, for which he suggested not only many revisions but also numerous valuable additions. Dr. Barns and Dr. Johnson critically read the entire manuscript.

Finally, the writer has learned much from the students enrolled in his classes in West Virginia History. The keen and intelligent interest of students in this subject was a genuine inspiration to their teacher.

To all other persons who assisted in any way in the completion of this work the author extends his grateful thanks.

Oscar Doane Lambert
Morgantown, West Virginia

CONTENTS

MAPS 

West Virginia and Its Government

CHAPTER 1

The Physical Setting

Location

All of West Virginia except the northern half of the Northern Panhandle lies between the thirty-seventh and fortieth degrees north parallel, and between the seventy-seventh and eighty-third degrees west from Greenwich. Across the country this latitude maintains a common parallel with the southern parts of Ohio, Indiana, and Illinois, with Missouri, Kansas, Utah, and Nevada, and with central California. On the east, Virginia, Maryland, and Delaware intervene between West Virginia and the Atlantic Ocean.

West Virginia occupies a vantage position in that region of our country which lies east of the Mississippi River. If one will place a map before him he will see that a motorist traveling from the northern section of the state covers about the same distance in reaching either Maine or Florida. He will also observe that New York City and Chicago are about equidistant from Sutton, the most centrally located town in West Virginia. The Eastern Panhandle is bordered by the Potomac, which flows into Chesapeake Bay, while the western division of the state is drained by the Ohio, whose waters reach the Gulf of Mexico by way of the Mississippi. Harpers Ferry, the most eastern town in West Virginia, is only seventy miles from Washington. A straight line drawn from Chester to Bluefield intersects the main channels of commerce between the upper Mississippi Valley and the populous East.

Size and Boundary

Among the states of the Union, West Virginia is fortieth in size, having a total area of 24,242 square miles. About 150 square miles of this total are water surface; and the area of the water increases yearly through the building of ponds, dams, and reservoirs.

The length of the irregular boundary of the state is reckoned as 1,170 miles. Rivers form 609 miles of this distance,[1] along the Maryland, Ohio, and Kentucky borders. In addition to these natural boundary lines, the boundaries between Preston County and Maryland, and between Pennsylvania and Virginia, had been established long before the division of Virginia; consequently the new state inherited more than half of its territorial limits. The eastern extent was fixed according to county lines when West Virginia came into the Union in 1863.

Topography

In consideration of its surface West Virginia may be divided into three main parts, the Potomac basin, the Allegheny highland, and the Ohio basin.

By far the largest of these sections is the one farthest west, drained by the Ohio River. The eastern section, drained by the Potomac and its affluents, consists of eight counties; this portion contains the lowest elevation in the state, at the point where the Potomac crosses the boundary line. The mountain section, which runs from the northern to the southern boundaries, contains great hollows through uplifted and warped surfaces. Here the plateaus, known locally as plains (e.g. the Roaring Plains, the Flat Rock Run Plains, and the Rohrbaugh Plains), maintain an elevation of more than 4000 feet. By virtue of this fact West Virginia has a mean altitude of 1500 feet, exceeding that of any other state east of the Mississippi River. The natural beauty of the valleys, as the Canaan, the awe-inspiring canyons, as the Black Water, and the majesty of the mountains, as the Gauley, can scarcely be excelled anywhere on the continent.

Most of the rivers of West Virginia rise in the Alleghenies and flow westward into the Ohio. In traversing the western piedmont

---

1 The Potomac River forms 218 miles of the distance, the Ohio 277 miles, and the Tug-Big Sandy 114 miles.

hills these main waterways have cut deep channels and thus attracted to them numerous smaller streams whose devious courses drain the regions both to the north and the south of the rivers. This area is the part of the Ohio basin which is located in West Virginia, and which comprises most of its surface. In the geographic description below, due attention has been paid to the basins of several rivers that have important influences on the topography of the basin located between the Ohio River and the Allegheny Mountains.

THE APPALACHIAN HIGHLANDS

The territory of the state lies as an irregular belt across the central Appalachian Mountains. Here row after row of highlands whose summits are long stretch straight as far as one can see unless the view is interrupted by a deep gorge or watergap that cuts transversely across the heights. These ranges rise more than 4000 feet and are ribbed by bold ridges at the bases of which rush torrential streams, eventually passing through the notches in the mountains to join their currents with the Potomac or Ohio, the two large rivers that drain nearly all the surface of West Virginia. Beautiful waterfalls decorate the flow of the rivers, and between the mountains and ridges rest the lowland valleys of great fertility. On a clear day, a person standing on a West Virginia mountain top may discern the wave-like appearance of the succeeding ranges, each blending more nearly with the colors of the sky as the distance increases until the subdued green has completely merged with softened blue.

The Allegheny plateau varies in width. From Aurora to Mt. Storm on route No. 50 the distance is approximately twenty miles from the western to the eastern brows of the mountain. At other places the distance across is not so great. But the plateau is not level. It has rises and depressions, ridges and valleys. In many places there are glades of swamp lands, but the streams are small, never reaching the flow of rivers. In olden days travelers occasionally became bewildered by the sameness of the landscape on the Allegheny plateau, and some are known to have perished. Here rise all the main watercourses of the state except the New River, whose fountainhead is in Watauga County, North Carolina. Spruce Knob, Pendleton County, pitched high on the mountain's crest, reaches 4860 feet, the apex of the West Virginia highland. Davis, Tucker County, is known to have the greatest elevation, being 3101 feet above sea level. Bluefield in the extreme southern part is 2558 feet high.

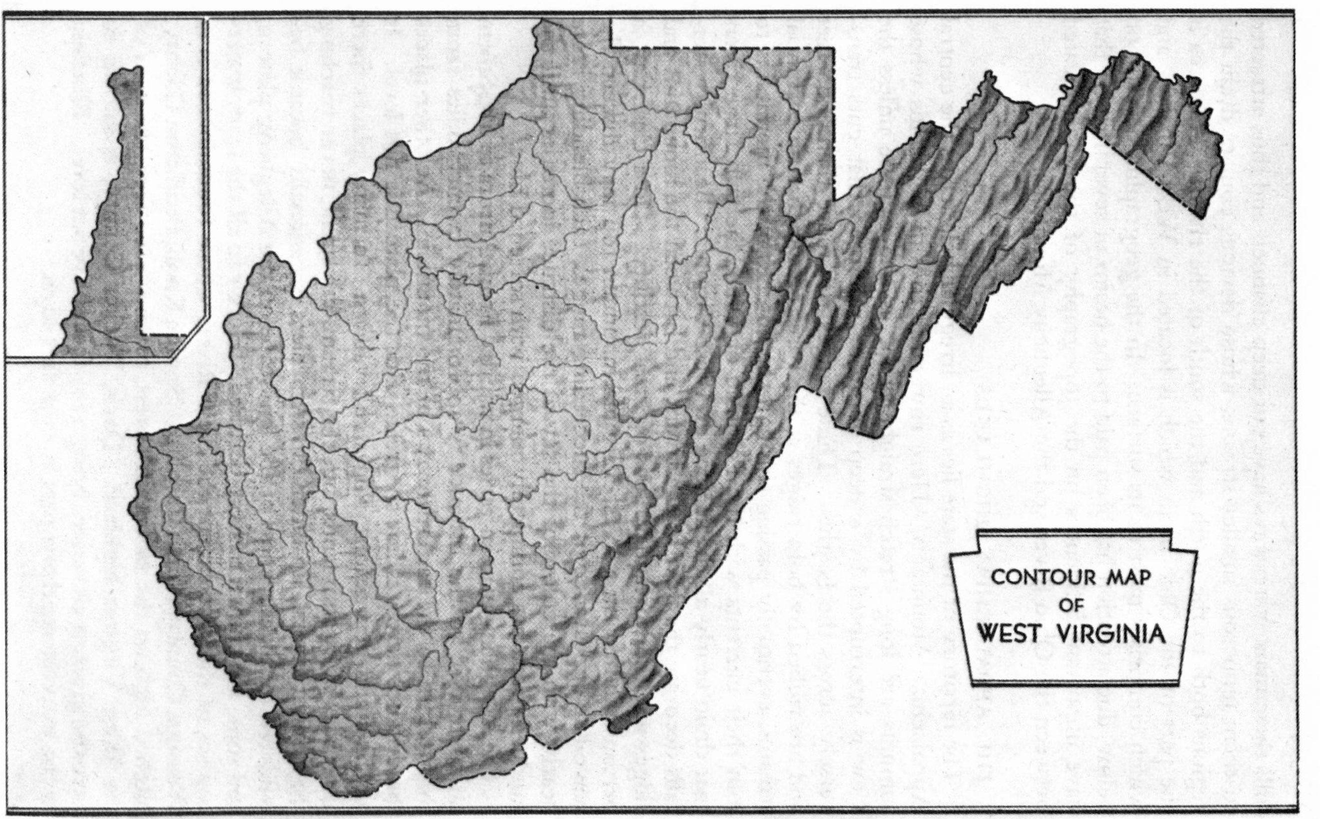
CONTOUR MAP
OF
WEST VIRGINIA

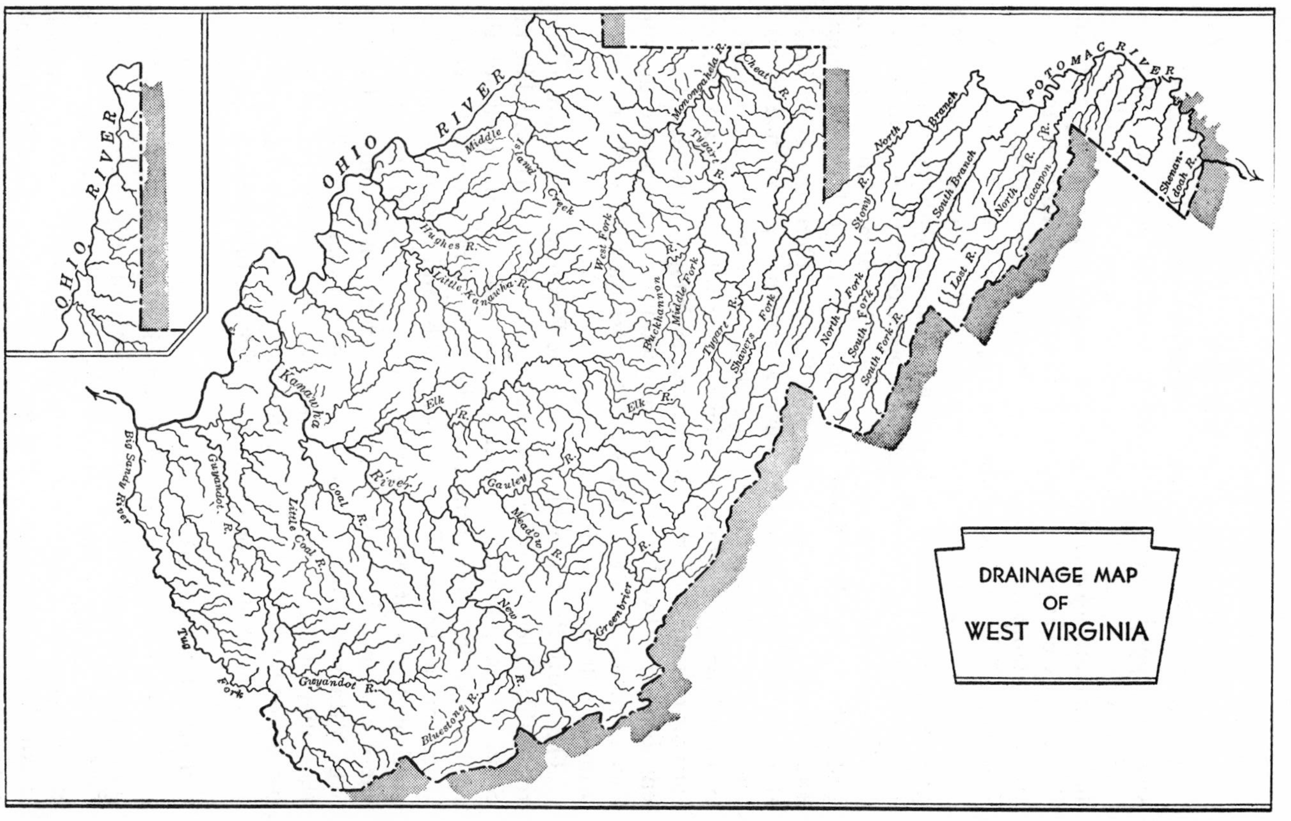
DRAINAGE MAP
OF
WEST VIRGINIA
OHIO RIVER
OHIO RIVER
POTOMAC RIVER
Shenan-doah R.
Cacapon R.
North R.
Lost R.
South Branch
North Branch
South Fork R.
South Fork
North Fork
Stony R.
Cheat R.
Monongahela R.
Tygart R.
Shavers Fork
Tygart R.
Middle Fork
Buckhannon R.
West Fork
Elk R.
Greenbrier R.
Gauley R.
Meadow R.
New R.
Bluestone R.
Middle
Island Creek
Hughes R.
Little Kanawha R.
Elk R.
Kanawha River
Coal R.
Little Coal R.
Guyandot R.
Guyandot R.
Tug Fork
Big Sandy River

THE EASTERN PIEDMONT REGION

A piedmont belt lies on either side of the mountain range. On the east the rugged mountains gradually lose their austere heights and recede to ridges and spurs which in turn level off to gently rolling hills. Looking east from the heights near Davis one may note the decline in elevation. Franklin, in Pendleton County, is 1730 feet; Romney, Hampshire County, is 731, while Harpers Ferry, Jefferson County, is only 274, being the lowest point in West Virginia.

The eastern piedmont belt is drained by the Potomac River, whose general direction is east. The South Branch, with its innumerable tributaries coming down from the slopes, contains in its basin most of the trans-Allegheny region of West Virginia. On the extreme east is the Shenandoah River, which flows through Jefferson County and joins the Potomac at Harpers Ferry. Here the river breaks through the Blue Ridge, forming a watergap of unusual majesty and beauty. The age-old erosion cut through the resistant rock formation, leaving on either side the exposed folds of strata, while the current of the broad river is diverted, swirling in a thousand different directions, by the limestone projections that jut above the surface of the blue water. One who observes the beauty of this natural wonder will not soon forget it.

The North Branch, which is the true Potomac, comes down from the highland in a swift current, leaving the valley narrow, while the South Branch, although walled on both sides by the uplift of the land, is gentle. Along the river the broad strath terraces reach in places more than a mile in width. This land is smooth and easily cultivated and produces ample yields of corn, wheat, and fruit. Here erosion is in constant process, carried on by rills and creeks which transport fertility from the mountains and the hills down to the valley of the river. The South Branch Valley is one of the regions first settled in West Virginia and is widely known to this day for the culture of its people and the richness of its soil.

THE SHENANDOAH VALLEY

The lower section of the Shenandoah River traverses West Virginia soil. Though it touches the territory of only one county (Jefferson) in the state, both Jefferson and Berkeley counties are within the Shenandoah Valley, and the topography of the two counties is strikingly similar to that of the rest of the valley. The Shenandoah enters the Potomac nearly at right angles, and the northern counties of the valley in Virginia, Frederick and Clarke, border the two counties of West Virginia on the south. Martinsburg, the county seat of Berkeley County, has an elevation of 456 feet above sea level.

The width of the valley from North Mountain to the Blue Ridge is approximately twenty-five miles. Its orange-colored soil is fertile and has a sub-layer of limestone strata that the rivers have incised, leaving many bold cliffs facing the stream. The surface is generally smooth and undulating; and fields of corn and wheat, square miles of elm and oak, white and brick colonial homes attractively intersperse the broad landscape.

THE WESTERN PIEDMONT REGION

West of the Alleghenies the topography of the piedmont is strikingly similar to the land on the east. The Cheat River flows close by and nearly parallel with the highland range and empties into the Monongahela just north of the state boundary at Point Marion, Pennsylvania. The Cheat is formed by the confluence of the Dry Fork and Shavers Fork at Parsons.

Black Water, a tributary of the Dry Fork, drains the Canaan Valley, known for its lofty altitude, serenity, and beauty. The point where the Black Water rises has an elevation of 3250 feet. All through the valley the river appears sluggish and almost completely base-leveled, but below the mouth of Beaver Creek the slow current changes into tumultuous rapids, its rate of fall being 136 feet per mile.[2] At the bottom of the deep and narrow gorge huge boulders litter the bed of the stream, making human passage very difficult. The falls make one of the most magnificent scenes in America.

The dark reddish-brown color of the Black Water is thought to come from tannic acid common to the hemlock and spruce that once grew in great abundance in the Canaan Valley. This tableland, consisting of wide bottoms and glades broken by low, flat hills, is about thirteen miles long and varies in width from two to four miles; it embraces the land lying on either side of the river. To the east stands Bald Knob, like the face of a giant, eternally gazing on the whole surrounding region.

THE CHEAT RIVER VALLEY

The main branch of the Cheat rises at the sources of Gandy Creek, which flows through a limestone spur of the mountain forming the Sinks in Randolph County, a short distance beyond which it takes

---

[2] *West Virginia Geological Survey*, 1923, p. 64.

the name of Dry Fork. The river continues in rapid current until it unites with the Shavers Fork.

The valleys of the branches of the Cheat are narrow and composed of a sandy soil, a situation that proves the comparative youth of the formation. On the east the streams flow along the foothills of the Alleghenies, but to the west erosion has carved the mountains — Rich, Middle, Shavers, and Green — which stand out in high relief like the fingers of a hand. Between these highlands flow Laurel, Glady, and Otter forks, all turbulent streams. On the sides of the ranges are steep and successive slopes, small upland V-shaped valleys, and turretlike hillocks.

At no place along Cheat River does the water reach a slow and meandering flow. As the stream continues in its northern course, its volume is increased by numerous tributaries. Through its entire length of 149 miles it is flanked on either side by rugged mountains. Its valley, however, widens toward the north. Dunkard Bottom along the Cheat in Preston County, and the Horse Shoe in Tucker County, have become resorts as a result of their singular seclusion and rare beauty.

The tablelands reaching out from the river vary greatly in contour. They stand too near the mountains to be continuous in smoothness. But the plateaus on some of the highland are smooth, fertile, and very productive.

THE MONONGAHELA VALLEY

This river also flows northward. It lies west of the Cheat in West Virginia. At Fairmont the Tygart Valley and the West Fork unite to form the Monongahela, which continues to Pittsburgh and there makes a junction with the Allegheny to cause the beginning of the Ohio River. Rich Mountain and Laurel Hill largely form the divide in West Virginia between the Cheat and the Monongahela.

Only thirty-seven miles of this historic river is in West Virginia but its main tributaries have a length of three hundred and seventy-four miles. Along the upper Tygart Valley, the eastern branch, the land along the river is anticlinal and deeply eroded into the soft Upper Devonian shales, while to the east Laurel Ridge and Rich Mountain exhibit an escarpment of Pottsville strata that is broken where the river cuts through the highland just north of Elkins.[3] Steep wooded slopes mark the sides of the mountains and the ridges that radiate out from the main chain. The upper valley is a base-

[3] *West Virginia Geological Survey*, 1931, p. 43.

level region occupied by farms and ranges for sheep and cattle. The river and the main affluent creeks have become sluggish and meander through the wide valley.

North of Elkins and beyond the gap in the mountain, the Tygart Valley River is generally swift; its valley is narrow and the rough, steep slopes recede in altitude until they reach the Pennsylvania boundary. Passing beyond Rich Mountain to the West Fork, the uneven, precipitous slopes of the highland gradually flatten out into smooth, low hills that were readily adapted to farming and cattle ranges. All through this attractive region, which was an allurement to the early settlers, the streams are sluggish and maintain most of the year a muddy cast. The common altitude of the basin of the West Fork has only a slight variation from one thousand feet.

The main Monongahela River flows through Marion and Monongalia counties. It is about the half-way point between the Allegheny Mountains and the Ohio River, draining most of the piedmont hills in north-central West Virginia. Although the banks of this river are abrupt, to the west the tableland consists of smooth hills that grow lower as they near the Ohio.

In the early American period of history the Monongahela furnished an outlet for the people who lived in north-central western Virginia, and likewise it served as a way of entry from western Pennsylvania. The recent development of the rich coal deposits in this river basin has made the Monongahela one of the busiest rivers of the world. It has been reliably reckoned that the annual commerce it carries exceeds that transported through the Panama Canal. To increase its commercial value the United States Government built locks in the river in 1886, and at the present time bigger and better locks that will increase the water depth about ten feet are well toward completion.

THE GREENBRIER VALLEY

Randolph County has been truly called the mother of rivers in West Virginia. The Greenbrier rises here and flows south, joining the New River at Hinton. It may be observed that the current of this river flows in an opposite direction from the Cheat and the Monongahela. The sources of these streams are not far apart.

This river, whose clear waters flow uncontaminated by coal mine or factory, has a length of one hundred and sixty-seven miles, and drains Pocahontas and Greenbrier counties. Its valley varies from rough, precipitous mountains on the north to low, smooth hills in the south. Its elevation is generally high, varying from about 4000 feet at the source to 1382 feet at Hinton, where it joins the New.

Early settlers sought an abode in the Greenbrier Valley. From east of the mountains Jacob Marlin and Stephen Sewell came as early as 1750, and after the trail had been blazed an increasing number of pioneers followed, making the Greenbrier Valley one of the first regions settled in the state. By 1774 General Andrew Lewis rendezvoused eleven hundred frontiersmen at Fort Union to march against the Indians on the Ohio.

The Greenbrier Valley still remains a region devoted to agriculture and stock raising. Locks have not been built across the river, but when the virgin timber was being harvested millions of feet of cherry, oak, and poplar logs floated down the stream to Ronceverte and Hinton, where the mills manufactured them into lumber. Ever-flowing springs, bursting from the limestone strata, keep the valley fresh and green. White Sulphur Springs, situated deep in the valley, has become one of the most luxurious resorts in the East.

THE OHIO VALLEY

The Ohio, the Nile of West Virginia, is the longest river in the state, being two hundred and seventy-seven miles in length. When Virginia granted its claim to the Northwest Territory to the National Government it reserved the boundary line on the northern bank of the Ohio, and when West Virginia became a state it inherited the original western boundary from Pennsylvania to Kentucky. For this reason West Virginia owns the bed of this river as far as it flows along the border of the state.

As the distance lengthens from the piedmont hills to the west, the topography gradually changes to a low, wide valley through which the Ohio flows. This river drains about seven-eighths, or 21,000 square miles, of the surface of the state, and receives the flow of all the large rivers west of the Allegheny Mountains. Also the turbid waters of numerous small streams which emerge from the hills and wind their devious courses through low valleys finally empty into the Ohio. From the western piedmont to the river this smooth, undulating surface occupies a belt of territory about one hundred miles wide and two hundred miles in length.

The Ohio served as an early gateway to the West. Boats, built at Pittsburgh and Wheeling, floated with the current of the river, bearing settlers bound for Indiana, Illinois, and Missouri. When the old East migrated to the new West, in the early part of the nineteenth century, the emigrants took to the Ohio as the shortest and easiest way to reach their destination. The history of the Ohio Valley is the history of the western part of this state, for life on the river was inseparable from life on the land.

With respect to elevation the river is low. Wheeling on the north is only 678 feet above sea level, while Huntington, near the Kentucky border and about two hundred miles to the southwest, has an elevation of 563. This means a drop of less than one foot per mile. Owing to this smoothness of surface and the nature of the region through which the river flows, the Ohio has become one of the most valuable inland waterways in the country.

THE LITTLE KANAWHA VALLEY

This stream drains the central western hills of the state. It rises in Upshur County and flows through Gilmer, Calhoun, Wirt, and Wood counties. The topography of the area drained by this stream is not different from that which has already been described. Before the coming of the hard-surfaced roads, freight boats regularly ran between Glenville and Parkersburg, not encountering rapids or falls.

Along this stream the first oil wells were drilled in West Virginia, and the river provided a means for the shipment of the product. From the interior early industrialists also shipped great quantities of lumber, cattle, and other products by way of the Little Kanawha to Parkersburg on the Ohio. In return they received merchandise suitable to the needs of the people.

To facilitate the commercial use of the Little Kanawha, four dams deepen its channel. But is has largely fallen into disuse within recent years. Now, however, a project has been set on foot to build five fixed dams to give the river a navigable depth of four feet for a distance of forty-eight miles. It is hoped that this improvement, when completed, will renew the commercial use of the river.

THE GREAT KANAWHA VALLEY

The Great Kanawha is the largest tributary of the Ohio in West Virginia. The junction of the Gauley and New rivers at Gauley Bridge forms this river, which has a flow of only ninety-seven miles before reaching the Ohio at Point Pleasant. Its general course follows the flow of the New, whose headwaters rise in the southern region of the Blue Ridge. In view of the fact that the New River cuts across the Allegheny highland, it flows swiftly, and its valley is narrow and bordered by high, steep mountains. Its deep gorge at

Hawks Nest is representative of the work of Nature where the elevation of a highland comes into conflict with the persistent flow of a river. The deep, rough channel of the New is generally continuous from the point where it enters West Virginia. It is fed by short, rapid creeks that rush down V-shaped valleys in Mercer, Raleigh, and Fayette counties. At places the tableland stretching back from the river is smooth and adapted to farming.

The New-Kanawha completely spans southern West Virginia. Two miles below the mouth of the Gauley is located Kanawha Falls, which, although only twenty-two feet high, is in volume the largest cataract in the state. But from the point where the Elk joins this river at Charleston its fall is gradual and the slopes on either side are smooth and gentle.

The quiet flow of this stream has invited commerce. It has been related how General Andrew Lewis widened an Indian trail from Fort Union to march his colonial army against the Indians at Point Pleasant. From that time onward, this military road and the river served the people migrating from the Greenbrier to the Ohio. On account of recent commercial developments, provision has been made for the building of three dams at London, Marmet, and Winfield. When completed they will furnish a navigable depth of nine feet from the Ohio ninety miles inland.

The Kanawha Valley has become a center of manufacturing. At Charleston, South Charleston, Belle, and Nitro huge steel and chemical factories turn out enormous quantities of goods, and their output continues to grow. Thanks to almost inexhaustible supplies of coal, natural gas, and salt brines, and with the help of river navigation, the Kanawha Valley is approaching the point of becoming the greatest chemical manufacturing center in the world.

THE BIG SANDY VALLEY

When Kentucky was formed in 1792, the Big Sandy marked the boundary between the new state and the territory later to become West Virginia. At that time the line along Tug River, the main branch of the Big Sandy, had not been surveyed, and the boundary remained vague until 1799. In that year a joint commission representing the two states met at Louisa and fixed the northern bank of the Tug as the proper boundary. For this reason the Big Sandy-Tug is a Kentucky river, the territory of West Virginia extending only to the northern bank.

The Tug River rises high in the hills of McDowell County, the southern extremity of the state. It flows north, flanked by narrow valleys and high, steep hills. Back from the river the tableland is rolling and at places cut by deep gorges. Its tributaries come down through deep defiles in swift currents, making the contour of the region very irregular.

At Louisa, Kentucky, the West Fork and Tug join to form the Big Sandy. From that point to the Ohio, about twenty-six miles, the tendency of the topography is to become more gentle. Like other streams in the state, this river furnished an outlet from the interior to the Ohio, both in travel and in commerce. The abundant virgin timber that grew in this region caused the opening of the lumber enterprise, which first used water transportation; but when the rich coal deposits in southern West Virginia were opened, railroads replaced the river in the handling of freight. However, three locks and dams now furnish a slack water depth of six feet for seven miles from the Ohio.

Climate

West Virginia lies in the north temperate zone, but its climate is subject to considerable variation because of the irregularity of its surface. On the lower Potomac, which is not far from the ocean, the temperature takes on the warmth of the Atlantic slope, being comparable to that of Washington, D.C. Here the summers are long and warm while the winters are short and cool. Rarely does the temperature rise above 100° or fall as low as zero. During the long warm seasons agricultural crops have suitable temperature in which to develop, and frosts infrequently injure first plantings or freeze the bloom of the orchards. Now and then snows fall to the extent of hindering traffic on the highways, and on one occasion the writer witnessed the Potomac frozen safe enough for skating from bank to bank at Shepherdstown.

In the southwestern part the temperature does not vary sharply from that in the southeast. However, there is a change from the warmth, rainfall and winds common to the Atlantic coastal region to those typical of the Mississippi Valley. The mean annual temperature in these regions averages about 56°.

As the high altitudes are approached the temperature becomes cooler, and by the time the tops of the mountains are reached there is a variation of about 10° from the lowlands along the Ohio and the Potomac. In February, 1899, there was a recording of 36° below zero at Davis. Zero weather may be expected each winter in the mountain counties, but rarely does the thermometer register below 15°. However, on the high mountains and plateaus, varying from 3500 to 4500 feet above sea level, winters become severe and the summer seasons are perceptibly shorter than they are in the lower altitudes. Sometimes drifts of snow on the Alleghenies reach a depth of thirty feet and do not disappear until the coming of the warm sun of May. One who has not seen a winter storm on the Allegheny plateau can scarcely imagine its severity. The normal mean temperature in the whole state in January varies from 30° to 35° while in July it is about 75°. The variation of altitude makes a seasonal difference of about two weeks.

The winds in West Virginia blow prevailingly from the southwest, though occasionally from the east. As the wind currents move across the state and approach the highlands, they cool and lose their moisture, and for this reason the western counties have a greater rainfall than the east. The average precipitation in West Virginia is about forty-five inches.

A feature worthy of notice is the abundant rainfall in the mountains. The Weather Bureau at Elkins reports an annual average of 47.68 inches, while at Pickens, near the crest of the highland, it is 64.85 inches. This high average of precipitation is largely responsible for the extensive stands of timber that once stood all along the Allegheny range and for the rapid growth that is now taking the place of the virgin forests. The protection and tree planting now fostered by the national and state governments encourage the growth of timber in all sections of the state.

Animal Life

Animal life in West Virginia is common to that of the north central temperate zone, but the variation of altitude in the state produces regional differences. Good authorities have stated that there are fifty-six species and sub-species of mammals in West Virginia, and as many as two hundred and sixty-eight classifications of birds.

The first white men who came to the region found the land crisscrossed by buffalo trails, some of which crossed the Allegheny Mountains from the basin of the Cheat and the Greenbrier to the Shenandoah Valley. In his *Border Warfare*, Withers speaks of the Indians hunting buffalo along Elk Creek, Harrison County, along the Ohio and the Great Kanawha. By the deep-worn trails the hunter, with drawn bow and set arrow, heard the tramp of the heavy, black hoofs of the buffalo, and as its low-swung head, covered with brown wool and set on high ponderous shoulders, approached he gauged for a fair shot. About 1824, it is reckoned by Hu Maxwell, the last wild buffalo in West Virginia was killed near Valley Head, Randolph County. But this native beast has left its name on the creeks, mountains, and hills of this region.

Elk in great number frequented the same region as the buffalo, and on account of the choice flavor of its flesh it was largely sought by the pioneers. According to our best authority the elk became extinct in western Virginia in 1843 when three of them were brought down by a company of hunters in Canaan Valley, Tucker County. The name of this wild beast is perpetuated in the state in the designation of certain localities, as Elk Lick, Elk River, and Elk village.

Like the buffalo and elk, the timber wolf and panther have become extinct. The last record of a wild wolf in the state was in 1896, when one was trapped on the Allegheny Mountains in Randolph County.

Some of the other large mammals, as the black bear, the deer, and the bay lynx (wildcat), have by hard struggle withstood the onslaught of civilization. Their haunts have been in the darkest recesses of the mountains. Fur-bearing animals, as the beaver, otter, and marten, were for a time near the point of extinction, but they, like the deer, are now being restored under the protection of law and the shades of the second-growth forest. The white or snowshoe rabbit that frequented the loftiest mountains became dangerously reduced in numbers until recently, when the season on them was totally closed.

Other fur bearers, as the raccoon, mink, skunk, opossum, gray and red fox, and rabbit, diminished until new forests grew that gave them safe cover, and game wardens administered more rigidly protective laws. Smaller animals, as the several species of squirrels and woodchuck, are protected by closed seasons, more extensive forests, and game reservations.

Mice, rats, moles, and shrews frequent the cliffs and fields in all sections of the state. The flying squirrel, which keeps its den in hollow trees, is one of our common nocturnal rodents. Several species of bats, in the cool seasons, hang in clusters against the limestone walls of caverns and flap their leathery wings in the twilight sky of summer evenings.

In the early history of settlement the streams of West Virginia contained great numbers of various species of fish. The brook trout inhabited the black pools in the rushing mountain streams from which it challenged the skill of the angler. As the creeks widened into rivers bass, pike, sunfish, several species of suckers, eels, and catfish were found. The brown and rainbow trout, that now attract the trained line of the fisherman, are aliens in the waters of West Virginia. In the larger streams and sluggish creeks the elusive gar may be seen warming his bony back in the sunlight.

From the coldest spring that flows from the brow of the mountain to the mouth of the river along the Ohio, numerous amphibia inhabit the streams. Newts of various sizes and colors challenge the curiosity of the inquiring naturalist, and the salamander, the largest of this group, often annoys the fisherman by swallowing both hook and bait. Species of frogs, toads, and turtles inhabit every stream and marsh in the state. Of the reptiles only two are classified as poisonous, the copperhead and the rattlesnake. The former is the more numerous, being found generally in nearly all the counties, and perhaps the more dangerous on account of its stealth. The rattlesnake, often called the timber rattlesnake, lurks in the high plateaus and along the mountain slopes. The nonpoisonous reptiles are not numerous; among the most common are the garter snake, house snake, water snake, black snake, and green snake.

Perhaps the only bird once common in West Virginia that has become extinct is the passenger pigeon. It went the way of the virgin forests. The number of other species has been greatly reduced, but the teaching in our schools of the value of birdlife has renewed interest in protection and preservation. Bulletins have been published by our Department of Agriculture to emphasize the fact that man cannot live without birds.

The game birds common to West Virginia are the wild turkey, ruffed grouse, and bobwhite. The woodcock and mourning dove live on the borderline. Those of a migratory nature, as the Canadian goose, species of ducks, and brant, are only here while passing from one climate to another. Strict protective game laws have been enacted to forbid the further slaughtering of both the indigenous and migratory game species. The rivers, ponds, and dams also attract grebes, loons, and swans as they rest on their migratory journey, while swamps and marshlands are frequented by wading birds, as the white ibis, the blue and buff-colored bitterns, and the great blue heron. Sometimes storms along the seacoast drive terns, gulls, and herons across the mountains. They linger here only long enough to find their way back to the waves and salt marshes.

Birds of prey, as the great horned owl, the barred owl, several species of hawks, and the northern shrike, frequent the wooded hills and the fields. On infrequent occasions the bald eagle has been known to rob the poultry yard, and the vicious golden eagle sometimes makes it a habit to live on lambs from flocks that graze on the Allegheny Mountains. It is not uncommon to see the turkey vulture eating the carrion of rabbits and squirrels that have been killed along the highway.

Of the two hundred and sixty-eight species of birds, by far the greatest number may be classified in the group of songsters. By a vote of the school children and various organizations the cardinal has been named the state bird. The tufted titmouse and the robin also made a creditable showing in the balloting.

During the migratory spring season the woods ring with the melody of the wood thrush, the brown thrasher, the red-eyed vireo, the scarlet tanager, and a hundred other songsters. The red-winged blackbird, the field sparrow, and the catbird are among the first to arrive on the scene, but the march continues with warblers, grackles, swallows, and wrens until the host of visitors has arrived. Some of those which remain through the year and may be found in the deep winter woods, if one should venture so far, are the nuthatch, bluebird, chickadee, titmouse, jay, and song sparrow. Among the West Virginia birds rarely seen may be named the mockingbird, the grosbeak, the horned lark, and the bobolink. The rainfall, the varied slopes, and the warm summer sun make West Virginia a favorite feeding place for the feathered hosts that come here in great numbers to live.

Plant Life

The irregular topography of the state causes the growth of a varied plant life. This variation embraces vegetation which grows as far north as Maine and New Brunswick and as far south as the Carolinas. There is no part of West Virginia that has an altitude towering above the tree-line, such as may be found in the Rocky Mountains, but one may observe a marked difference in the plant life growing at Harpers Ferry from that native to Spruce Knob. The plant life may be classified according to our three belts of elevations already described, the mountains, the piedmont, and the river valley. The abundant rainfall both on the highlands and in the valleys, and the short cool seasons, are conducive to a luxuriant growth of vegetation in all sections of the state, even on the highest mountains where precipitation is greatest.

According to A. B. Brooks, who was a specialist in forestry, West Virginia has about one hundred and twenty-five native trees and an indeterminate number brought here for transplanting.[4] Some expert botanists have classified the plant life in approximately 3400 different species. Perhaps the most authoritative work written on this subject is that of Joseph E. Harned, *Wild Flowers of the Alleghenies*. Dr. Harned has searched the V-shaped mountain coves to their apexes and the crevices in the rocks from base to summit for new plants. His list still grows.

Reaching down the summits of the highland from north to south, evergreens covered the long, straight region like one continuous green belt. Giant forests of hemlock, pine, spruce and fir densely covered the plateaus and fringed the hollows like a great green carpet. Rhododendron, mountain laurel, and different species of ferns spread an undercover harmonizing in color with the canopy of branches. In the glades and swamps grew clusters of cranberries, alders, chokecherries, and evening primroses, while deep mosses, mountain huckleberry, and small ferns covered the rocks and crevices. On the faces of ledges may be found tufts of lichens that are reminders of regions far north of West Virginia, and the quaking Cranberry Glades, in Nicholas County, are not unlike the tundras near Hudson Bay.

Out on the benches of the mountains, but below the crest, grew sugar maple, shellbark hickory, and stands of the round, smooth beech whose silver-colored bark could be seen from a great distance. But these are deciduous trees, the falling of whose leaves, after the coming of frost, opens the view between earth and sky, which is closed again soon after the buds burst in spring.

Coming farther down the slope one reaches level benches once part of the old flood plains. Here the most usual tree was the rough-barked sugar maple, but also common at this elevation were the ash, black walnut, aspen, linden, buckeye, and butternut. Here once grew the chestnut that succumbed to a fatal blight, perhaps the greatest tragedy that ever befell the American forests. Stands of the huge yellow poplar, the white oak, and the red oak began at this elevation and reached down to the lowland valleys. In addition to the forest trees already mentioned, the ironwood, the gum, and the dappled sycamore in whose huge, cavernous trunks the Pringle

[4] *West Virginia Trees* (Morgantown, W. Va., 1920), p. 3.

brothers, Marlin and Sewell, took refuge, covered the river valleys. Although a terrific waste has been experienced in the destruction of the virgin trees, the forests still cover about half the area of this state.

The flowering trees, conspicuous for their beauty, decorate the hills of West Virginia with their color and fragrance in the springtime. The pink banks of the wild crabapple spread over the slopes and along the roadsides; the little laurel, or calico bush, covers rocky ridges with its delicate hues of pink; the flowering dogwood dapples the hillsides with white in May; the spectacular flaming azalea comes late in April and May, with its riot of red, yellow, white, and pink, throwing its beauty on bank and ledge and even in shaded ravine; the white hawthorn covers the dry grass in the old meadow and the brown leaves heaped in the corners of fence rows, with a fresh blanket of flowers that spread a delicate fragrance; and the redbud early unfurls its strands along brown ledges and by the borders of fields.

In West Virginia the flowering plants are legion; it is a haven for the botanist. The arbutus and hepatica awake at the first dawn of spring, and the meadows and hills are bedecked from that time until the coming of killing frosts that freeze the goldenrod, the meadow daisy, and the bottle gentian. All through the long warm season scores of plants, entirely too numerous to name here, take their turns in unfolding their beauty and challenging the watchful discernment of those who chance to see each one for its brief day.

Transportation

INDIAN TRAILS

The native human population and wild animals marked the surface of West Virginia so perfectly with roads that the grades of our modern highways often follow hard by the old trails. When the white people came into this region they found it interlaced with worn paths that led from one river valley to another where luscious pasture grew, or from the lowlands to the glades on the plateaus where the succulent grass covered an opening in the wilderness, walled around by deep, dark forests. After the region was colonized many of the old paths fell into disuse; others were widened into roads. Here we shall make reference to only a few of the most important; but it is worth remembering that the wild, roaming tribes trod these ways for centuries, and that when the possession of the land was contested by the aggressive white man the discerning eye and ear of the native guarded his wilderness road until his power was finally broken. Afterward the ways over which danger had approached and vanished for a hundred years were in many cases discontinued and grew dim, and the locations of some of them have faded into the unrecorded past.

The trails of the Indians generally followed the valleys and crossed the mountains through the gaps or from the source of one river to another. Along the Shenandoah River ran the Warrior's path, ascending the valley and eventually turning west through the Cumberland Gap near the western corner between Virginia and North Carolina. This path caused the great valley to be frequented by the natives, and pointed the way for early settlers who migrated south from Pennsylvania and Maryland. It also served the colonists who left Virginia and North Carolina to transfer to Kentucky and Tennessee.

Another important road lay along the Potomac to the point where Cumberland is now located. From this place the Nemacolin trail followed Wills Creek through the great notch and crossed the highland to the forks of the Ohio. The bewildered Braddock led his ill-fated legions over this way to the mouth of Turtle Creek in 1755.

Leaving the Potomac at Green Spring, the Seneca trail followed the South Branch to the mouth of Seneca Creek; from there it turned west and crossed the Alleghenies to a point near the present location of Beverly, Randolph County. Thence one branch turned south, crossed the divide, and passed down the Greenbrier Valley, while another branch took a northward course up Leading Creek, crossed Pheasant Mountain and followed the Cheat down to the Horse Shoe, where it intersected the McCulloch trail. Some good authorities think that a third branch of the Seneca trail proceeded west across Rich Mountain to the headwaters of the Little Kanawha and thence to the Ohio. The McCulloch trail followed from the South Branch through Greenland Gap, across the mountains, and down Horse Shoe Run to the Cheat, from which point it took the valley of Clover Run and crossed the divide to the Tygart Valley.

The Great Kanawha did not remain undisturbed by the natives. From the Ohio an important trail followed that river to the mouth of the Elk River, where Charleston now stands. One branch kept close to the Elk and continued nearly to its source, where it crossed the divide to the Tygart Valley. Another trail led up Kelley Creek, across the heights of the Gauley, and eventually down Muddy Creek to the Greenbrier. Over this circuitous path Gen. Andrew Lewis led his eleven hundred colonial veterans from Fort Union to the mouth of the Kanawha in 1774.

South of the Kanawha a well-worn trail followed the crests of the ridges from the present site of Lewisburg west until it joined the Kanawha near the mouth of Paint Creek. This road became one of the most famous ways of travel by foot and packhorse from the Greenbrier to the Ohio. Other trails followed by Indians and early settlers are known to have been along the Little Kanawha, the Guyandot, and the Big Sandy-Tug River Valley. Still other worn paths, less important than those named, crisscrossed the hills and streams of the Potomac and Ohio valleys and furnished direction and worn, narrow roads by which the pioneers reached the West.

Concerning Indian tribes which frequented this region, reasonably accurate information has been handed down to us. The identification of famous chiefs with their tribes has been made matter of record from which the historians have drawn information. Who has not heard of Killbuck, the famous chief of the Shawnees, who commanded his braves while besieging Fort Cumberland? His feigned friendship toward the imprisoned garrison was dissolved by Major Livingston, whose strategem led the deceptive Killbuck into captivity; there the colonists stripped him of his proud feathers and divested him of his hunting shirt, leggings, and moccasins.

Another noted chief of the Shawnees was Cornstalk, sachem of his tribe and king of the confederation composed of Wyandottes, Mingoes, Delawares, and Cayugas. He bravely commanded the warriors of the united tribes at the celebrated battle of Point Pleasant, which made his name famous in the annals of American history. Later he courageously met an inglorious death brought about by white "friends," and a fitting monument marks his grave hard by the renowned battlefield. Red Hawk, the Delaware, fought beside his comrade, Cornstalk, and suffered a common fate with him.

Of all the noted chiefs perhaps Logan, the Mingo, possessed the greatest intellect. His name is inseparably associated with the history of the upper Ohio Valley. His celebrated speech sent to Lord Dunmore at Camp Charlotte is a model of eloquence that has seldom, if ever, been excelled. Logan lived for many years at Shamokin, Pennsylvania, having been sent there by the great Iroquois nation to rule over the tribes of other Indians. While stationed at that point he frequently visited the Ohio and the new villages that fringed its banks. To the list of tribes herein mentioned may be added the Cherokees, Tuscaroras and Catawbas; and of other chiefs let us not omit the names of Red Jacket, Ellenipsico and Tanacharison, or Half King, the counsellor of George Washington.

OTHER MAIN TRAVELED ROADS

As travel penetrated the wilderness, the pioneer gradually widened the old trails to make room for his packhorse caravan, or he cleared an improvised road in order to shorten the distance between the point of departure and the place of settlement. Trade by the packhorse was commerce in its infancy. By necessity the single-file road gave way to the broader way over which traveled teams of horses and oxen.

The first constructed broad highway that influenced trade and travel in western Virginia was built by General Edward Braddock in 1755. The British general constructed this road from Fort Cumberland to the Monongahela Valley for the purpose of conveying his supply wagons and cannon to the place of battle. Although Braddock's military effort failed disastrously, his road remained a thoroughfare of great importance after the war had concluded. From Virginia, Maryland, and Pennsylvania, people from the seaboard followed Braddock's Road to the Ohio. Previous to that date the Ohio Company had broadened the trail up the Potomac to Wills Creek.

Three years after Braddock's expedition General John Forbes (1758) led his army from Philadelphia via York, Bedford, and Somerset to Fort Duquesne. This was another military highway, and when the British took possession of the Ohio Valley in 1763 an outpouring of immigrants trudged their way over Forbes' Road to reach the West. It was thirty years later (1793) that General Anthony Wayne greatly improved this much-traveled way when he conducted his American army to the Ohio on its expedition to Fallen Timbers, where he finally broke the power of the Indians east of the Mississippi River. After Wayne's victory multitudes crowded the two military roads to reach the Ohio, where they fanned out along all the adjacent valleys, including those of the Kanawha, the Guyandot, and the Big Sandy.

In the meantime other connections between east and west were taking form. The Midland Trail, connecting the headwaters of James River with the Greenbrier, afforded an outlet from eastern Virginia to the mysterious West. At Fort Union this way joined the military road built by General Andrew Lewis in 1774, which led to the mouth of the Gauley and along the Elk and formed a junction with the Ohio at Point Pleasant. Ambitious settlers, wishing to reach the region drained by the western rivers, built other paths that crossed the mountains in the spaces between the main-traveled roads that have just been mentioned. A good example of these was the Smith-and-Parsons trail, which connected the valley of the South Branch with the headwaters of the Cheat.

Though travel was slow and arduous, the East and the West never lost their connection, but maintained a meager commerce from the beginning. While establishing their homes the people brought with them only the bare necessities. It soon developed, however, that during the autumn season herds of cattle and droves of hogs were driven to market to points on the Ohio or to the South Branch Valley.

Early in the nineteenth century commercial interests demanded the building of better roads across the mountains. As a result of this interest the National Road was completed from Washington to Wheeling in 1818. Soon followed the James River and Kanawha Turnpike, which reached the Ohio in 1832. Between these important roads other highways soon developed. Travel over the Northwestern Turnpike, between Winchester and Parkersburg, began in 1838, and the Staunton-Parkersburg road reached the mouth of the Little Kanawha about 1852.

Now that western Virginia was spanned by four main highways, a lively commerce developed. Furs, wool, cattle, and hogs constituted the chief articles of trade. But the time soon came for developments of a greater industry based on lumber, coal, oil, and gas. These products could not reach a full flow of production until the construction of railroads.

RAILROAD CONSTRUCTION

The Baltimore and Ohio is the oldest railroad in West Virginia. It reached Wheeling in 1852, thus connecting the Ohio River with Baltimore, Maryland. Branch lines soon radiated out from the main road to the rich deposits of coal and the forest of virgin timber. In 1872 the Chesapeake and Ohio crossed southern West Virginia to the point where the city of Huntington now stands. The Norfolk and Western, the Virginian, the Ohio Valley, and several other railroads competed to gain their share of transporting the products of West Virginia to the markets of the country.

Commerce and Industry

AGRICULTURE

Agriculture has always been one of the chief industries in West Virginia. The mild climate, abundant rainfall, and fertile soil produce vegetables, fruit, and grain in great quantities. Many, if not all, of the early settlers depended on the soil for their livelihood, and that dependence has continued to increase as the population grows. With the development of scientific methods for restoring fertility to the soil and for cultivating and harvesting crops the quantity of products increases.

In every county in the state corn is grown, but it thrives best in the Eastern Panhandle and along the river valleys that are easily cultivated. Farmers in West Virginia, however, do not attempt to compete with western growers in the commercial production of corn; it is grown largely as feed for cattle and hogs. The yield per acre has constantly mounted until it has reached about forty-four bushels, and the annual crop approximates 25,000,000 bushels.

Wheat thrives in the same sections as corn, but is not grown as generally. Its total yield amounts to about one-tenth of that of the favorite cereal. Oats, barley, and rye are planted over wide areas but grow best in the upland regions. Potatoes and buckwheat are grown for commercial purposes on the flat elevations along the mountains and especially on the fertile plateaus. The Buckwheat Festival held annually at Kingwood attracts a wide gathering and is the culmination of the grain season in Preston County.

In Jefferson, Berkeley, and Hampshire counties growers produce extensive yields of apples and peaches that are shipped to many sections of the world. The winesap, delicious, York Imperial, and Grimes Golden decorate the long rows of trees with finely flavored red, pink, and yellow fruit. The commercial apple yield in West Virginia now exceeds 5,000,000 bushels, while the peaches amount to somewhat more than 1,000,000 bushels. Pears, grapes, and strawberries are grown in significant quantities. The Apple Blossom Festival at Winchester and the Strawberry Festival at Buckhannon emphasize the enthusiastic interest now manifested in fruitgrowing in those sections.

LUMBER AND OTHER FOREST PRODUCTS

Reference has been made to the heavy stands of virgin timber once common in West Virginia. This source of wealth could not be tapped until the railroads penetrated the forests so that the lumber could be shipped to the great centers of population. The deep evergreen forests of spruce, fir, and hemlock stood on the mountain tops and along the highland spurs leading out from them, while the deciduous, or hardwood, forests ranged from the valleys high up the hollows and mountain sides.

Sawmills followed the railroads, and then lumbermen set to work cutting the age-old, huge trees to the ground. Railroads even penetrated the forests for the sole purpose of transferring the logs to the mills. At one time more than two score band mills were running in West Virginia, and at the climax of their operation in 1909 they sawed about one and one-half billion feet of lumber. Since then forest products have been on a constant decline. Because pine and hemlock are light and soft yet strong and durable, this wood was widely used in building houses and making furniture. Builders converted hardwoods such as oak, chestnut and walnut into floors, frames, and furniture. The most useful of these woods is the oak. Out of tough woods like hickory, ash, and locust were made handles, spokes, staves, and posts. Tucker, Randolph, Pocahontas, and Nicholas counties led in the production of lumber.

About nine-tenths of the paper in the United States is made from a substance known as wood pulp. For many years the chief woods used to manufacture this preparation were pine, spruce, and hemlock. For this reason pulp mills were constructed near the soft wood forests and continued to operate there until the forests became exhausted. Leaders in this industry built mills at Piedmont, Davis, Parsons, Elkins, and Richwood, where many tons of pulp were produced daily.

The bark of the oak and the hemlock was used for the tanning of leather. Rather than ship the bark to distant points, tanneries were built near the West Virginia forests. During the late spring and early summer the lumbermen peeled the bark from the oak and hemlock logs. The bark was then shipped to the nearby tanneries and ground into a dust from which was made an extract used in the tanning process. When the forests disappeared, most of the tanneries closed; but those now remaining secure their extracts from South America, where it is made from the quebracho tree.

Lath was a by-product of the lumber industry. That part of the lumber that was not merchantable was transferred to the lath mill, which converted it into thin, narrow strips of wood used for nailing on walls and ceilings in preparation for plastering. This utilizing of small strips avoided a great deal of waste in the lumber industry. But the recent manufacture of various kinds of wall board has largely destroyed the demand for lath.

COAL PRODUCTION

Coal is the greatest source of power and the most valuable product of West Virginia. About 100,000 men are employed in mining coal in the state, and the annual production amounts to approximately 150,000,000 tons. West Virginia leads all the other states in the supply of this great source of power and wealth. Thirty-seven of the fifty-five counties regularly produce coal, and in times of excessive demand five more counties may draw on their reserves. McDowell leads all the other counties in production with an annual output in excess of 26,000,000 tons. Logan stands as a strong second with about 22,000,000 tons. From these high averages the amount declines to about 20,000 tons produced in Pocahontas County. Production by county may vary from year to year.

The regions of West Virginia in which most coal is mined comprise the extreme southern section and the Monongahela Valley, more than half being produced south of the Kanawha River. Here are found the famous "smokeless" coal and other highly volatile grades that may be successfully used in the production of coke and gas. The oldest fields are those located in the Northern Panhandle, along the upper Potomac, and in Marion and Harrison counties. The science of manufacturing gas from coal is still in its infancy, but the making of coke has been in process from about the time coal mines were opened here. The coke ovens on the upper Potomac at Thomas and Douglas and those on Deckers Creek, Monongalia County, and in Kanawha and Logan counties still exude their black smoke in the process of reducing coal to coke. This state now produces about a quarter-million tons of coke each year.

While at some places shaft-mining is done, most of the coal is reached from the horizontal outcropping along the hillsides. In many places there is a drop from the outcrop to the valley where railroad cars receive the flow of coal from the mouth of the mine. Owing to the ease of mining and preparation for transportation in this section, other regions find it hard to compete either in production or in price with the West Virginia operators. Improved safety devices for miners have been installed, and plants for the grading and washing of the product have become necessary.

The shipment of coal produces the greatest revenue for the railroads in West Virginia. Long lines of cars filled with the black fuel for mills in Pittsburgh, Cleveland, Philadelphia, and Boston move down the Monongahela Valley on the Baltimore and Ohio and the Pennsylvania railroads daily. Coal barges, fastened end to end, pulled by steamboats, run the river from Fairmont to Pittsburgh, floating thousands of tons to the "Steel City."

In the southern part of the state the Virginian Railroad reaches the mines in McDowell and other border counties. From the points of mining to Norfolk and other places on the seashore there is a slight declination most of the way in the drainage of the land. This condition reduces the cost of transportation and causes the railroad to devote itself to the business of carrying coal. The Norfolk and Western also operates to a great extent in southern West Virginia and transports enormous quantities of coal from that region to the Atlantic coast. The New York Central enters West Virginia at Point Pleasant and reaches the coal and manufacturing region at Charleston and the surrounding country. This railroad serves as a channel over which the products of the state reach the Great Lakes.

Among the outlets for the products of West Virginia to the markets of the world perhaps none has a greater utility than the Chesapeake and Ohio Railroad, which spans the south-central section of the state. This railroad tapped our natural resources at an early period. It transported the lumber out of the Greenbrier Valley and the New-Kanawha Valley, and when the development of coal mining started it pushed its branches up the valleys of the streams flowing into these rivers to reach the veins of coal exposed along the rugged banks.

Since 1940 strip mining has created considerable use of trucks for coal transportation. This situation has been encouraged by the development of motor power by means of the gasoline engine, the building of hard-surfaced roads, and the ease of mining by the use of huge shovels. Strip mining can be carried on only where the coal lies near the surface, and since the veins are in horizontal layers considerable quantities have been removed by this method.

Extensive experiments are now being carried on in the gasification of coal. The results of this work have not yet been published.

NATURAL GAS

Natural gas has been used in West Virginia for more than a century. Its utility was accidentally discovered in 1815 when salt wells were being sunk near Malden, Kanawha County. For a number of years it was used as a fuel for reducing brine to salt, which had a ready sale in western Virginia. Presently gas came to be used for heating and lighting homes and for cooking, and then for heating furnaces in factories. Because of the sharp demand for this fuel, which had now become a great and inexpensive convenience, a search was set on foot for other wells. This effort met with immediate success, and natural gas poured in unmeasured quantities from the subterranean regions of the state. Pipe lines soon conducted this fuel from the wells to the towns and cities. Here it was used not only for domestic purposes but also in glass, pottery and tile factories, where its cheapness and its capacity for producing a high temperature made it highly advantageous.

For many years the gas-producing region lay in the Ohio Valley, but within recent time flowing wells have been drilled as far east as Canaan Valley, near the crest of the Allegheny Mountains. In 1949 there were 13,800 live gas wells in West Virginia which produced 181,380,000,000 cubic feet, a decrease of eighteen per cent from the previous year. Although this state had shared its supply of natural gas with its neighbors, within the last decade pipe lines have been laid from the Texas fields into this region. One of the most important of these lines is the "big inch," which crosses the northern part of the state. Another one joins the Charleston district at Cornwell Station near Clendenin. So the time has come when West Virginia scarcely produces enough natural gas for its own use. The chief cause of the increased demand for this fuel at present is the great number of people who are converting their coal furnaces into automatic gas furnaces.

OIL PRODUCTION

From the time of its political formation, West Virginia has been an oil-producing state. Near the oil fields, which are along the Ohio and Kanawha rivers, refineries have been constructed that convert the crude oil into gasoline. According to the latest estimate, there are 15,000 oil wells in West Virginia that produce 2,830,000 barrels annually. This amount is an increase of 5.4 per cent over the previous reckoning; but it should be noted that in 1900 the total production was 16,000,000 barrels. The state has perhaps not used due diligence in the conservation of this natural product. The use of oil and gasoline for power, fuel, and lubrication expands from year to year, and civilization becomes more dependent on these products. The wise conserving of supplies adds strength to the country.

GLASS AND POTTERY

West Virginia contains rich deposits of sand and clay from which glass and pottery are manufactured. The sand mines at Berkeley Springs have an unexcelled purity. From this product glass may be made by means of the hot flames produced by natural gas. From the extreme northern part of the state at Chester and Newell down the Ohio Valley to Huntington, the glass factories are located. Morgantown, Grafton, Fairmont, and Clarksburg claim factories of importance.

In some of these factories expensive and artistically decorated tableware is made. This kind of work requires highly skilled craftsmen. In other places bottles, jars, and marbles are turned out by the thousands through the use of machinery. Some of the factories specialize in plate glass, used for windows and doors and in automobiles. Flat stained glass, for church windows and other expensive decorative purposes, is also made here. The famous Fostoria factory is located at Moundsville, Marshall County.

The making of pottery requires a special kind of clay and a hot gas fire. West Virginia contains quantities of both gas and the proper quality of clay. Our chief pottery factories are located in Hancock and Jackson counties. Marion, Taylor, and Harrison also have important factories. In the Northern Panhandle chinaware ranging from the most refined quality to the low-priced grades is made. These products decorate the shelves of the stores all through the East. Glazed porcelain used in kitchens and bathrooms, electric light bulbs, and glazed cooking vessels are made in these factories. Brick and building and drainage tile are products of the Grafton, Clarksburg, and Weston regions.

CHEMICALS

The Great Kanawha Valley has become one of the chief chemical-producing centers of this country. In this region are centered the natural elements needed in that industry. Here may be found in almost unlimited quantities bituminous coal, natural gas, oil wells, deposits of salt brines, and large waterfalls from which hydroelectric power is generated. These resources, combined and set into motion, have made Belle, Nitro, Charleston, and South Charleston a chemical workshop of the United States. During World War II a synthetic-rubber factory was built at Institute within the Charleston area. This factory, one of the largest of its kind, only extends the importance of the Kanawha Valley in the total pattern of American industrial life.

To facilitate travel and commerce in West Virginia, a web of hard-surfaced roads spreads over every county in the state. Excellent airports are now established at Charleston, Morgantown, Elkins, and several other cities. Factories, other than those named, run in a hundred other towns and hamlets. In consideration of their location, climate, soil, rivers, and other natural advantages, West Virginians are perhaps the most self-dependent people of the world.

CHAPTER 2

Historical Background

Introduction

To gain an understanding of the constitution and government of West Virginia, we must review briefly the political development of the region out of which this state was eventually formed. Starting with the granting of the first charter of Virginia in 1606, we shall trace the various changes in colonial and state organization down to the present time. Politically and otherwise the two Virginias had a common genesis, and the emergence of West Virginia as a separate state did not take place until long after a "republican form of government" had been guaranteed to each state in the Union by the national Constitution. The first part of our historical sketch must therefore deal with the whole Virginia territory.

Our political history falls into three divisions. The first is the *colonial period*, from 1607 to 1776. For these one hundred and sixty-nine years Virginians were British subjects, and English law was established and developed in Virginia.

With the Declaration of Independence Virginia ceased to be a British colony and became an independent state. From 1776 to 1863 eastern and western Virginia were under the same state government. This period we shall call the *middle period*. During this time all acts of state government originated in the capital, first Williamsburg and later Richmond. It was a period of rapid development. Through acts of the state legislature counties were created and named, towns were chartered, roads were built, and commerce was promoted; and a lively growth of population took place in western Virginia.

The *third period*, from 1863 to the present, covers West Virginia's existence as an independent state. On this period chief attention will be centered below. But first let us turn to a review of the earliest government of Virginia.

The First Charter

In answer to an application made by a group of his "loving and well disposed subjects – consisting of certain knights, gentlemen, merchants, and other adventurers,[1] of our city of London and elsewhere," King James I granted a charter to the Virginia Company in April, 1606.[2] The king had divided the Virginia Company into two branches, the London Company and the Plymouth Company; only the former interests us here. The charter issued a permit and a code of laws for the establishment of a "plantation and habitation " at any place that was thought fit and convenient on the coast of Virginia between the "four and thirty and one and forty degrees" north latitude. From the point at which the first plantation was established, the boundary of the colony was to front one hundred miles on the sea and to extend "directly into the main land by the space of one hundred like English miles." [3]

The grant of power to the company was conferred by the king on two councils, one of which was to sit in London, the other in the colony. The superior council in London, consisting of thirteen members chosen by the king, appointed the colonial council, which possessed a supervising power over the colony. The colonial council was empowered to pass regulations, elect and remove its presiding officer, remove its own members for cause, fill vacancies in the council, and try all legal cases arising in the colony, except those affecting life or limb.[4] A jury of twelve men was to hear all capital cases.[5] The Crown issued the regulations of government, and any

[1] An adventurer was one who ventured his money – i.e., an investor.
[2] W. W. Hening, *Statutes at Large* (New York, 1819), I, 58.
[3] *Ibid.*, I, 59.
[4] L. G. Tyler, *England in America* (New York, 1904), pp. 37 f.
[5] The law of the colony established the death penalty for nine different offences, including rebellion, mutiny, conspiracy, and murder.

order passed by the colonial or superior council was void if it conflicted with them. Thus the company and colonists were deprived of all rights except those granted by the king of England. It is to be noted also that the sole agency of government in the colony, the council, had executive, judicial, and legislative powers. All the property of the company was to be held in joint possession for five years after settlement.

The Colony of Virginia

At dawn on May 6, 1607, Sir Christopher Newport, commander, accompanied by one hundred and three colonists, dropped anchor at the mouth of the James River. The seaworn voyagers were almost overcome with joy when they beheld the tall trees, the fragrant soil, and the fair meadows of Virginia.[6] On the evening of that eventful day the seal that bound the commission and the code of instructions for the colony was broken, and the names of the appointed officers were made known. Seven men had been chosen as councilors, viz. Edward Maria Wingfield, Bartholomew Gosnold, Christopher Newport, John Smith, John Ratcliffe, John Martin, and George Kendall. The other councilmen elected Wingfield president. The provisions of the code of instructions, which constituted the laws for the colony, appeared to be agreeable to all concerned. In fact, the laws issued by the king for his loyal subjects in America were less severe than those exacted on the people in England. The superior council in London had also sent a list of instructions, chiefly concerning the spot to be chosen for the plantation. The advice was good, but little heed was paid to it.[7]

The misadventure that from the first dogged the little colony may be illustrated in part by the fortunes of the council. Within a few days Gosnold sickened and died. Then Kendall was accused of planning desertion; he was tried, condemned, and shot. In the council thus reduced, a combination formed by Smith, Ratcliffe, and Martin assumed a controlling influence. They deposed Wingfield from the presidency, held him in custody, and placed Ratcliffe in his stead. They then dispatched Smith, the most daring member of the council, together with a company of stalwarts, on an exploring expedition.

During Smith's absence, which was prolonged by his capture by

[6] Edward Channing, *History of the United States* (New York, 1905), I, 164.
[7] Oliver P. Chitwood, *Justice in Colonial Virginia* (Baltimore, 1905), p. 11.

Indians, president Ratcliffe, perhaps feeling a need of advisers, admitted one Gabriel Archer into the council. Smith and Archer were neither personal nor political friends, and when the Indians released their captive from the wigwam, Archer carried war into the council of Virginia. Two of Smith's aides had been killed during the expedition, and upon his return he was held responsible for their loss. The council immediately ordered his arrest, gave him a speedy trial, found him guilty, and sentenced him to be executed the next day. But on the very day of the trial Sir Christopher Newport arrived in port from England, carrying orders from the superior council that clothed him with sole authority over the colony. He ordered the release of Wingfield, set Smith free, and restored him to his place on the council; and before his return to England soon afterward, he elevated Smith to the presidency of the council.

Meanwhile the colony was endangered by more serious threats than political maneuvering on the part of the council. The people were struggling for life, both political and economic. They had no hand in the government, and it took weeks or months to communicate with London. What was more immediately serious, they did not have enough food. It has been pointed out earlier that the land was owned by the company. The settlers were forbidden the privilege of owning the fields they cleared and cultivated. The earnings of all were collected in a common storehouse from which each person drew supplies. The system acted as a blight on the lives of the persevering, the frugal, and the wise. The most industrious were forced to live on a parity with the indolent and the corrupt. The natural difficulties of getting a new settlement under way were aggravated by the ambitions of the council, the laziness of some of the settlers, and especially by disease that ravaged the colony and carried off many of its members.

At this stage of affairs death or sickness removed all the members of the council except Smith himself. Vigorous and self-reliant, he made no attempt to fill the vacancies on the council; instead he chose to rule the affairs of the disconsolate colony single-handed. To rescue the starving, he compelled the Indians to give the colonists corn; all hands were ordered to hard and fruitful labor; undue dissipation was strictly forbidden; and every person was denied the privilege of squandering his belongings. His orders were promptly and sternly executed. In the emergency the council form of government had failed and had been superseded by a dictatorship.

The Second Charter

Despite Smith's energy, the colony was on the verge of complete failure as a result of disease, Indian attacks, the greed of the parent company, and poor general management. In 1609 at the request of the Virginia Company the king set aside the old order and granted a new charter which enlarged the domain of the company, abolished the London council, and vested the government in the hands of the stockholders, who had power to appoint their own officers, make laws for the colony, and admit new members.[8] The stockholders promptly appointed Lord Delaware sole and absolute ruler over the colony. Delaware himself spent only nine months in Virginia; except for that period the colony was ruled until his death in 1618 by deputy governors, who were armed with a code of martial law provided by the new council chosen by the stockholders.

Of the deputy governors perhaps Thomas Dale was outstanding for his severity. He tortured, shot, burned, and hanged offenders. Swearing he punished by death; profanity by whipping, tongue piercing, or death; stealing, idleness, and killing of another's stock, by the lash, the knife, the pillory, and the gallows.[9] But it must be remembered not only that all this was in accord with the law he had come to enforce, but also that that law was no more severe than the English law. In the mother country as in the colony, the whipping-post, the branding-iron, the dungeon, and the gallows were used daily to punish offenders.

Nor did the inflicting of physical punishment alone distinguish Governor Dale. Much more to his credit was the establishment of new units of government in the colony. Charles City Hundred and Charles City he set apart from the rest of the colony. These were the first divisions of local government established in America. Dale perceived that the common store and the results of joint labor had failed. The settlers had been clothed and fed from the storehouse owned by the company, and all they grew from the soil became common property. To correct the economic evils that resulted, Dale gave to each person three acres of land, abolished the common store, ordered every able-bodied man to depend on his own labor,

---

[8] A third charter, superseding the second in 1612, brought no essential change; its chief purpose seems to have been to include in the colony's domain the Bermuda Islands, from which had come very exaggerated reports of their beauty and fertility.

[9] Channing, *History of the United States*, I, 183.

and emancipated the people bound to serfdom. Dale's laws served as a relief, yet all workmen paid heavy taxes. Two and a half barrels of corn per acre were exacted from each farmer, and an ample portion of other crops went to the tax collector.

Sandys and Yeardley

When Lord Delaware died in 1618, a brighter day dawned for the colony under the liberal influence of Sir Edwin Sandys, who had become the manager of the Virginia Company. In the conflict that was developing in England between royal supremacy and the exponents of greater political power for the common people, Sir Edwin espoused the side of popular rights. The colony of Virginia became his political laboratory where he could demonstrate the validity of his ideas. He wanted progress in the colony, and he believed that it would come about if the colonists were endowed with more privilege and power. On April 19, 1619, a new governor, George Yeardley, arrived in Jamestown to put into operation the instructions drafted by Sir Edwin.

Governor Yeardley soon announced a gift of land ranging from fifty to one hundred acres to each settler. The first colonists who had survived the hard years were now honored by the ownership of large plantations. To persons who brought more colonists to Virginia the governor assigned extensive estates, and with these freer grants there came wider political privileges to the settlers. From this humble beginning the plantation system in Virginia made its development. Through the influence of the more liberal policy the settlers gained release from an abject servitude to the governor, and were freed from excessive taxation and oversevere impositions.

Most important of all, the people were given a share in the making of their own laws. By 1619 eleven plantations existed in the colony. Two burgesses were to be "respectively chosen by the inhabitants" of each plantation, to meet in legislative assembly with the governor and council. The orders of election were duly carried out, and on July 30, 1619, the new assembly, consisting of the governor, six councilors, and twenty burgesses,[10] convened in the humble wooden church at Jamestown.

The importance of that historical event can scarcely be overestimated. It was the beginning in America of government authorized in part at least by the will of the governed. Sir Edwin Sandys's

[10] On the number see p. 61, note 5, below.

penetrating intelligence had perceived that government must come up from the people instead of being handed down to the people — that problems must find their solution in the minds and hearts of the people associated with the problems. As far as was allowable, he entrusted the political life of the colonists to their own keeping, a privilege that all self-respecting people dearly cherish. The seed of popular government was being separated from the parent stalk in England and was starting growth in a new soil. It is no wonder that Sir Edwin Sandys has been called the first American statesman.

Annulment of the Charter

Eventually discord arose among the members of the London Company. Sir Thomas Wroth, an adventurer, objected to the salaries paid to the company's officials. The council's manner of passing measures aroused criticism. Profits from the tobacco trade developed by the company had become a matter of interest to the Crown. Sandys and his followers disavowed the criticisms and accusations; but the opportunity for dissolving the charter had come. The royal authority would not be denied. By a writ of *quo warranto* [11] Chief Justice James Ley of the King's Bench on June 16, 1624, ordered the charter of the company voided. Thus the power of the Crown supplanted the power of the company, and Virginia passed from a proprietary status to that of a royal colony.

---

[11] The name of a writ issued by the government to recover an office.

CHAPTER 3

Virginia as a Royal Colony

The Reorganized Government

When the third charter was annulled and Virginia became a crown colony, a new government had to be organized. On June 24, 1624, King James appointed a commission of sixteen members who constituted the provisional government. After investigating the affairs of the company, the commission recommended that a governor and council be appointed by royal decree to take charge in Virginia. On August 26, 1624, the king appointed Sir Francis Wyatt governor and named twelve councilors to assist him. The supreme laws for the colony were to be issued from the Crown and transmitted to Jamestown. No provision was made for continuing the popular assembly so happily arranged by Sir Edwin Sandys. King James died the next year and his plan of government came to an end.

When Charles I succeeded James in the following year, he dismissed the royal commission appointed by his father and placed in its stead a committee chosen from his own privy council.[1] This

[1] The privy council was a group of the king's friends appointed by him as advisers in matters pertaining to the government.

committee, residing in London, had supervisory care over Virginia. The governor and council, living in the colony, were left undisturbed. Finally King Charles instructed the governor to call another meeting of the burgesses, whose sessions had now been suspended for four years. It was at length decided in London that an assembly composed of a governor, a council, and burgesses would come closer to satisfying both the colonists in Virginia and the king than any other organization. Soon set in operation, it determined the form of colonial control in Virginia for a period of about one hundred and fifty years.

This political organization was a combination of the royal and popular ideas of administration, originating in the thought of the wisest statesmen of England. The governor and the council, appointed by the king, were responsible to him. On the other hand the burgesses, elected by the freemen in the colony, came to be subject to the will of the voters. The British plan of king, lords, and commons now had a counterpart in America. Save for various interruptions, this political structure continued and the colony prospered until the Revolutionary War.

While disturbing political events followed fast in England, and king and parliament were in serious disagreement, Virginia was left largely to her own resources. In the colony population grew and settlement spread. Ships carrying immigrants embarked to Jamestown each year. Hence more land was occupied and industry went forward at a lively pace. Year by year fields of tobacco widened, new gardens were planted, fences took form around more and more acres of corn, and hogs, cattle and horses entered the harbor on ships from England. Though the settler lived a hard life, he was now privileged to provide his own food, build his own home, and manufacture clothing for himself and his family. He had good reason to hope that the independence and prosperity in search of which he had left England would soon be his in full measure.

The Land System

Already it has been related how the first division of land was made in the colony. Soon after this division a statute was enacted requiring that the land of "every private planter" be surveyed and the boundaries of the same recorded by the surveyor, who received ten pounds of tobacco for every hundred acres in each enclosure. Disputes concerning boundaries had to be referred to the surveyor for settlement. However, the law reserved the right of appeal to the governor and council.[2]

The colony retained possession of all land not privately owned. Anyone desiring to purchase a farm from the public domain made application to the governor and council. With the application there had to be filed a statement of the exact location and boundaries of the plot and a map drawn by an authorized surveyor. The title, bearing the seal of the colony[3] affixed to a parchment page and styled a patent, was issued by the governor and engrossed by his secretary, who was an expert penman.

Persons who imported servants into the colony often claimed patents for the good services they had rendered. By agreement with the governor and council a planter was allowed fifty acres for each person he imported. This system was fashioned for the purpose of increasing population and thus developing strength against the Indians on the frontier and augmenting trade in the colony. Those who claimed land in this manner had to prove the validity of their right by presenting to the governor and council a certificate of ownership from the county court, with a plat of the survey of the land, or else take up the matter of securing a title directly with the colonial government.[4] It was not unusual in Virginia for enterprising persons to pay in this manner for large estates – sometimes several thousand acres. They sometimes sent their agents to Europe for the purpose of collecting a shipload of immigrants and transporting them as indentured servants to plantations in Virginia.

Land was also granted to ex-soldiers in payment for services rendered in the French and Indian Wars and, later, in the Revolution. Regularly the quantity given to each soldier amounted to four hundred acres. This regulation developed home building on the frontier where land was plentiful and settlers were few. It was the ex-soldiers, tried and trusty, who made the most successful frontiersmen, and on the Spartan courage of this group the commonwealth of West Virginia eventually took form.

It often happened that persons crossed beyond the frontier, and there built homes on land to which they had no title. Sometimes, tomahawk in hand, they blazed the trees around a certain boundary that some newcomer desired to own. If the settler built a house and occupied it in undisputed possession for one year, he could present

[2] Hening, *Statutes at Large*, I, 125.

[3] The seal of the London Company was used before 1624.

[4] Hening, *Statutes at Large*, I, 274.

proof of such possession to the governor, who then issued him a legal title. The amount of land secured in this manner by an individual was generally four hundred acres; sometimes it amounted to as much as a thousand acres. Eventually this practice resulted in an entanglement of overlapping boundary lines and land shingled with titles in the west. To remedy this trouble the governor in 1779 appointed four commissioners to adjust disputed land claims in western Virginia.[5] The commissioners rendered good service, but many of their cases finally had to be brought before a judge and jury for settlement.

With the grant of land in Virginia the state exacted a quitrent, an annual tax paid by the conditional owner for the use of the farm. At one time the rent was two shillings per hundred acres, and could be paid in tobacco valued at three pence per pound. However, from year to year the amount of the quitrent varied.[6]

Another feature of the granting of land in Virginia was the issuing of titles for large plantations. Sometimes the king granted the titles, sometimes the governor. In 1664 King Charles II gave to Lord Colepeper all that boundary of land lying between the Potomac and Rappahannock rivers. Eventually Lord Thomas Fairfax inherited this extensive estate. The lord of the estate made surveys, issued titles, and collected quitrents. A person who bought a farm of Fairfax was charged an annual quitrent of twenty shillings of silver for every hundred acres. After the death of Lord Fairfax (1782) the legislature of Virginia disallowed the rental and gave clear titles to the landholders.[7]

In 1679 the general assembly granted to Laurence Smith a boundary of land on the headwaters of the Rappahannock River, extending five miles along the river and four miles inland. For this favor Smith promised to furnish fifty armed men ready to defend the frontier "on beat of drumm." [8] Another great landholder was William Byrd, who secured a wide acreage at the falls of the James River, and who possessed a title to his plantation much like the one granted to Laurence Smith.

The number of settlers on a single plantation did not exceed two hundred and fifty families. Together with two commissioners and six other men living on the plantation, the owner had authority to make laws to govern the settlement. These laws were to be as bind-

---

[5] *Ibid.*, X, 43.
[6] *Ibid.*, I, 316.
[7] *Ibid.*, XI, 160.
[8] *Ibid.*, II, 452.

ing as the laws of a county. The settlers had only the rights and privileges granted by the owner and the assembly of the plantation. The proprietor of the plantation was thus not only its owner but also its chief legislator.

Plantations usually bordered on a navigable river on which the planter had his private port. The port was very necessary, for there barrels of tobacco, bundles of staves, and bales of cotton were loaded on shipboard and sent to the West Indies and Europe. In return the ship brought back farming implements, domestic stock, articles for the home, and such other necessities to life and industry as could be used on a Virginia plantation.

As early as 1656, a transfer of land by a deed from one citizen to another is recorded in Virginia. It is remarkable how similar the deeds of that early age are to those made at the present.

Social Classes

FREEMEN

Further light on the daily life of colonial Virginia may be gained by a brief examination of the classes of people and their associations. The leading group were the freemen or freeholders,[9] people of quite varied degrees of culture and of wealth. Upon arriving at Point Comfort, the place of entry to the colony, each immigrant took the oath of allegiance administered by the commander of the fort. If the person entered as a freeman he had the liberty to purchase land, engage in trade, vote, and hold office. As early as 1646 the law required all freemen to vote or pay a penalty of one hundred pounds of tobacco. Perhaps the colony did not profit much from such fines, but at any rate the freemen guided the colonial destiny. They owned the farms and fields; to them belonged the slaves and other personal property; they were the leaders in industry, holders of office, and captains of the militia.

But one should not think that it was a small group that guided the destinies of the rank and file of the population. In 1671 there were in Virginia about 40,000 people; 32,000 of these were freemen, 6,000 white servants, and 2,000 Negro slaves.[10] Because of the gain realized from slave labor, the slaves thereafter increased until they out-

[9] "Every person who hath an estate real for his own life, or the life of another, or any estate of any greater dignity, shall be accounted a freeholder." Hening, *Statutes at Large*, III, 240.

[10] Henry Howe, *Historical Collections of Virginia* (Charleston, S. C., 1852), p. 134.

numbered the white population of the state, but the political power in the colony remained in the hands of the voting freemen.

INDENTURED SERVANTS

The indentured servants were white people imported under conditions of bondage into the colony. During the seventeenth century, there had grown up in England a class of vagabonds, men, women, and children, to whom was extended little mercy. For idleness or begging they were branded with hot irons, flogged, imprisoned, and even put to death. If they were found wandering in the city or in the rural region of the country, officers placed them under arrest, returned them to the parish in which they last resided, or ordered them to be banished. In the cities there lived many unkempt children who were not under the stricture of the vagrancy law, and who roamed about without parental care and without proper food. The English government, having found the maintenance in idleness of these prisoners, beggars, and abandoned urchins to be a burden, released them to the agents of Virginia, who promptly transported them to America. To pay their fare across the ocean these unfortunate people bound themselves to work several years for the captain of the ship in which they sailed. Upon entering port, the captain, not having any means of setting them to work, parceled out his human cargo to the landowners and householders. Thus he received payment for importing servants, who were released from one master only to be owned by another.

As to indentured servants the colony laid down definite laws. If these servants had attained the age of twenty or more years they could be bound for a period not to exceed four years; if they were between twelve and twenty their service could not exceed five years; and if less than twelve, seven years. Even though the quality of mercy was strained, the immigrants had better treatment in America than in England, for in Virginia, though work was hard, they had food, shelter, clothing, and above all the promise of freedom. Upon the expiration of their term of servitude the apprentices became free. Often they rivaled, and sometimes even surpassed, their former masters in virtue, wisdom, and progress.

The Indians

It has been estimated that when the first white settlement was established, about 8,000 Indians, in forty-three tribes, lived between the sea and the Blue Ridge.[11] The tribes dwelling between the Blue Ridge and the Ohio River probably numbered considerably fewer. It is known that only a few places in West Virginia were occupied by the Indians throughout the year.

Trouble between the white people and the natives began soon after the settlement of Jamestown and continued from time to time until the Indians had been driven west of the Ohio River. Therefore, laws were made and enforced for the protection of the white people, to the injury of the red natives. As early as 1631 the colonists refused to trade with the Indians,[12] and in the same year a law stipulated that "no person or persons shall dare to speake or parlie with any Indians either in the woods or in any plantation, if he can possibly avoid it by any means, but as soon as he can, to bring them to the commander, or give the commander notice thereof upon penalty of a monthes service for any free man offending and twenty stripes to any servant." [13] If the colonial court found a person guilty of selling arms and ammunition to the natives, he forfeited all his property and was imprisoned for life.[14]

The laws passed by the assembly when war was in progress with the Indians were sometimes ill considered. In 1676, for example, the assembly provided that Indians captured in war must be held in slavery. Earlier it had been illegal to sell Indians as slaves or servants except under the same conditions by which white people were bound to their master. As the white people grew more numerous, they drove the natives back beyond the frontier, but the Indians contested the ownership of every valley, hill, and river. As late as 1755 the colonial government paid ten pounds in money to anyone who took an Indian's scalp, and three years later the amount was increased to thirty pounds.

Nevertheless, the government of the colony gave some recognition to the Indian's right to his lands. The law prohibited white people from trespassing or intruding on the lands of the natives, and forbade Indians to sell their farms without the approval of the county court. This law protected Indians and restrained avaricious land buyers. Later, however, when the frontier had moved west of the mountains, little or no attention was given to the claims of the natives. By this time the state laid claim to all land not occupied by

---

11 Howe, *Historical Collections of Virginia,* p. 136.
12 Hening, *Statutes at Large,* I, 173.
13 *Ibid.*, p. 140.
14 *Ibid.*, p. 219.

the frontiersmen, and by its authority patents were issued without regard to the rights of the Indians.

The Negro Slave

It early became known that slave labor could be utilized to the profit of plantation owners in Virginia, and the importation of Negroes from Africa therefore became a lively industry in the colony. Slaves cultivated the fields, harvested crops, and did the rest of the drudgery. Since the plantation system scarcely extended into western Virginia, slaves were few and slavery never gained popularity in that region.

The slave was reckoned as personal property. The master could buy and sell man, woman, and child at will, often at public auction. A slave could not leave his master's plantation without a permit.[15] He could be set free, but freedom was usually granted only upon the rendering of some valiant service. If he wished to free a slave, the master made an application to the governor and council, and if the appeal met with favor the state issued a license granting such freedom.

The law required white people to keep arms and ammunition on hand, but Negroes were forbidden to own or possess arms.[16] Later an extension of this law forbade Negroes to arm themselves with a "club, staffe, gun, sword or any other weapon of defense or offence." Rules of this kind, it was claimed, kept down insurrection and local strife.

During the warm season of the year slaves planted, cultivated, and harvested corn, cotton, and tobacco. Their days of labor were long and sometimes severe. Some masters, however, treated their slaves with kindness, and gave them protection; they did not employ cruel methods of punishment nor require excessive toil. During the winter new fields were cleared, staves rived, and casks made in preparation for the following season. It was an expensive business to own slaves, and the owner therefore had to keep them employed all through the year or fail in his plantation enterprise.

The Cultivation of Tobacco

From the fertile soil of Virginia, planters grew crops of tobacco which increased in quantity from year to year. At first the crop

---

[15] *Ibid.*, II, 481.
[16] *Ibid.*, I, 226.

grown in the colony had a noxious bitter taste which made it far inferior to the kind shipped from Spain. It was soon discovered, however, that the method employed in curing the leaves caused the offensive flavor. After cutting the crop workmen stacked the green leaves in heaps which, on account of dampness, soon molded and so became unfavorable for market. But John Rolph, a thoughtful planter, soon discovered an improved method of caring for the harvest, and when Thomas Lambert found that leaves suspended from a line cured with a flavor equal or superior to that of the Spanish brand, the markets of Europe opened to the crop grown in Virginia.

In 1628 the colony formed an agreement, binding for seven years, to sell its entire tobacco crop to the king. The agreed price amounted to three shillings and sixpence per pound in Virginia or four shillings in London. This amount was a sharp reduction below the rate of twelve shillings a pound paid for Spanish tobacco. At the Spanish price a horse could be bought for sixteen pounds of tobacco sold in the market.[17] Demands increased and production developed. A great boom was launched in clearing fields and planting new crops in Virginia.

To prevent monopoly and to provide an equitable distribution of the lucrative business, the assembly limited production to three thousand plants for a single person, or two thousand plants for each member of a family.[18] The unusually abundant supply threatened a reduction in price, and therefore persons were not allowed to trade or exchange goods for tobacco at less than sixpence per pound. Later the law fixed twelvepence as the minimum price per pound. The colony had trouble to keep the rate up, for planters and laborers attracted from England by the new and profitable industry came in increasing numbers. They took up more land, and cleared and planted new fields on a wide scale.

As the interest in growing tobacco increased because of good markets and high prices, additional laws restricted trade in this new product. A public inspector was appointed annually by the county court at a salary of thirty pounds. No tobacco could be shipped until approved by him, and all that did not pass his examination was burnt at the warehouse. The weight of each cask or container had to be officially indicated by the inspector. The county court ordered tobacco warehouses to be built in every county; and at the market where the tobacco was delivered, bought, and sold, the in-

---

[17] Channing, *History of the United States*, I, 188.

[18] Hening, *Statutes at Large*, I, 134.

spector gave the planter paper money in exchange for his crop. It is not hard to imagine the slaves filling the hogsheads and rolling the big casks to a warehouse where they were weighed, stamped, and placed on board a waiting ship that lifted anchor and set sail for London.

Now the bartering in tobacco became so general that tobacco was exchanged as currency. The scarcity of gold and silver prevented wide use of metals in Virginia. Taxes, clerk fees, minister's dues, fines, bonds, wages were paid in tobacco. For instance, marriage fees amounted to two hundred pounds to the governor, fifty pounds to the county clerk, forty pounds to the recorder, and two hundred pounds to the minister. On many occasions in old Virginia a good tobacco crop preceded the marriage ceremony.[19] A footsoldier received fifteen pounds daily for his service, a drummer eighteen pounds, and a horseman twenty pounds. A juryman who failed to appear in court had to pay a fine of four hundred pounds of tobacco for his disobedience.

The Corn Laws

When the colonists first came from England, one of their most serious problems was maintaining an adequate food supply. After exhausting the scant provisions brought from England, the settlers at first procured corn by trade and by force from the Indians, but this effort failed to fill the demand, and hunger and even starvation stalked through the colony.

In this emergency the governor and assembly took active steps to promote the growing of corn on their own lands. Every man was required to "plant and tend sufficient of corn for his family." When this law failed to call the lazy to the fields, a more severe one was enacted, requiring "that two acres of corn near thereabout be planted for every head that worketh in the ground, and the same to be sufficiently tended," weeded, and protected from birds, cattle, and any other danger. An acre of wheat might be substituted for two acres of corn. Even in the face of these requirements, some people went without their daily bread. To feed the hungry each planter above eighteen years of age placed annually a bushel of corn in the public granary.[20] From this supply the poor drew their rations. Commissioners, appointed in each parish, administered the law and punished those who disobeyed it.

---

[19] Hening, *Statutes at Large*, II, 55.
[20] *Ibid.*, I, 125.

The price of corn threatened to increase on account of its scarcity. The governor and assembly ruled in 1623 that there could be no regulation of prices, but circumstances eventually forced a revision of this law. From time to time statutes were enacted to stabilize the price and to regulate or prohibit exportation. The assembly passed the last law of this nature about the time that land cultivation began in earnest in the Shenandoah Valley. Farmers who came into that region soon discovered that enough Indian corn could be grown in "the valley" to furnish an ample supply for all the people in Virginia. From this time onward no need prevailed for a legal regulation to govern the growing and selling of corn. The supply was always ample and the market open. West of the Alleghenies the fertile valleys produced corn, wheat, and vegetables in quantities sufficient for the needs of the pioneer and his family.

The Colonial Militia

INTRODUCTION

Self-protection was the first duty of the colonist. War with the Indians broke out soon after the date of the first settlement and continued, save for various periods of truce, one hundred and eighty-seven years. It was not until 1794 that General Anthony Wayne, with the help of Virginia frontiersmen, finally won the crowning victory at Fallen Timbers. Nor was it only the Indians who threatened the peace of the colony. The Spanish, whose relations with England were not always peaceful, gave the settlers of the south and west uneasy concern from time to time. Likewise the French in the north and west behaved in a manner unfriendly to the English, and finally waged with them a bitter war for the possession of the Ohio Valley. In view of these facts an army ready for instant use had to be kept in training during the entire colonial period. The Virginians learned to prepare themselves for the line of battle and passed on from generation to generation their manners and customs in warfare. In the French and Indian War the courage and skill of the Virginia militia excelled even that of the British regulars.

OFFICERS

The governor himself was the commander-in-chief of the militia. Necessity obliged him, therefore, to be well versed in military tactics and experience. All other officers and the regulars answered to his call and could be ordered to any place in the colony to repel an invasion or march against an impending foe.

For each county the governor appointed a colonel or county-lieutenant. To him was entrusted the training of the regiment, which consisted of all the white men between the ages of sixteen and sixty residing in a county. The colonel drilled the regiment in peace and commanded it in war. Annually he made a survey of the number of men, women, and children residing in his county and the amount of arms, ammunition, and food they possessed. From this survey he knew the strength of his army and the supplies on which it could depend.

Within a regiment were several companies, each commanded by a captain. The captains were appointed by the governor but were subject to the orders of the colonel. The lesser officers in the company consisted of lieutenant, ensign, and sergeant. Usually a company enlisted fifty regulars, one captain, one lieutenant, one ensign, three sergeants, and one drummer.[21] However, this number did not remain constant, and no special attempt was made to keep it so.

CLASSES OF SOLDIERS

The militia came to be divided into two main classes, troopers and footsoldiers. The trooper mounted a horse while the footsoldier carried his own burden.

Each soldier furnished his own equipment, specified by the law. Each trooper had a horse, saddle, and bridle, holsters, breastplate, gun, and sword, together with two pounds of powder and eight pounds of shot. The footsoldier supplied himself with a musket, sword, "and other furniture fit for a soldier," including the same quantity of powder and shot that the trooper carried. Even persons exempt from military service had guns, powder, and shot ready for instant use. Although the regular militia enlisted only white soldiers, the Indians, Negroes, and mulattoes served as drummers and trumpeters or marched with the army to do servile labor. Wheelwrights, smiths, and carpenters aided in keeping the army in motion.

Certain precautions had to be taken to prevent surprise attack. For instance, persons going to and from the parish church carried their guns as a matter of safety. Protection was the first line of defense, and danger was so constant that to discard arms invited disaster. The law recognized protection so preeminently that a person who owed a debt could not have his gun and ammunition sold

21 Hening, *Statutes at Large*, VII, 114.

to pay his creditor, though all the rest of his property could be taken away from him.

In the counties along the coast a militiaman from each regiment attended to "keeping a constant lookout to seaward, by night and by day, and diligently observing the courses and motions of all such ships or vessels as they, or either of them, shall discover upon the coast."[22] On the frontier rangers kept watch and if danger threatened they gave immediate notice to the captain. That the frontier might be more securely protected the governor and the assembly ordered (1756) that a chain of forts, twenty miles apart, be built, beginning at the home of Henry Enoch on the Great Cacapon River, Hampshire County, and extending to the South Fork of Mayo River, Halifax County, a distance of about four hundred miles. Thus a plan was made to fortify the frontier against an invasion from the west. Soldiers from the militia garrisoned all the forts. Four hundred soldiers remained on watch at Fort Cumberland after the defeat of General Braddock on the Monongahela, July 9, 1755.

TRAINING

The time set apart for military training was known as muster day. At a convenient place in the county, on a level field, the colonel at least once a year called his regiment together to drill. The captain drilled his company four times annually, or once every three months. When it is recalled that the names of all those qualified for military service, with ages ranging from sixteen to sixty, were listed on the muster roll, it is not hard to imagine the pioneer father closely followed by his sons in single file on their way to answer the summons to rendezvous on the field of muster. During the colonial period counties were large and distances between settlements long. When General Andrew Lewis summoned the militia of Augusta County to meet at Fort Union, some of the soldiers walked more than two hundred miles in obedience to his call.

The regimental muster excited uncommon interest; it was like circus day in the county. The curious gathered from all directions. Old people beyond military age, children, women, servants, and slaves came to see the excitement. Hour after hour soldiers marched through formations commanded by the harsh voice of the colonel. With fixed bayonets they charged unseen foes, and rushed double quick into imaginary battles. In this manner they carried on preparation for real war, and sometimes it was very real.

---

[22] Hening, *Statutes at Large*, II, 115.

As military duties grew in extent so did the severity of punishment for disobedience. A court-martial was held the day after every muster, and soldiers found guilty of offense bore the liability not only of being fined and ducked in cold water, but also of being tied "neck and heels for any time not exceeding five minutes." To be court-martialed left a shame hard to live down.

Thus the colony of Virginia organized its power for defense. But many instances of conflict arose in which the militia had no chance to take part. On frequent occasions workmen in the field were ambushed and shot, their homes robbed and burned, and women and children driven away to an Indian village to be adapted to the customs of the wild tribes. At other times the stealthy red men permitted themselves to be outwitted by their white antagonists, cut down, and scalped before they had a chance to attack. So every frontiersman became a soldier; he was a minuteman, primed and ready to go at the call of his captain or at the signal of danger from any source. It was the Augusta militiamen who beat Cornstalk at Point Pleasant, took the British post at Kaskaskia, fought with Washington at Yorktown, and completed the conquest of the Northwest under General Wayne at Fallen Timbers.

CHAPTER 4

Colonial Government under the Crown

The Governor

METHOD OF SELECTION

Different methods were used in the selection of the chief executive officer of colonial Virginia. At first (1607) he was chosen at meetings of the council of the London Company held in London and was designated president of the council. In 1609 the new charter changed his title from president to governor, but he was appointed by the same authority as before. After 1624, when the colony came under the power of the Crown, the governor of colonial Virginia was appointed by the king of England.[1]

After the governor became an appointee of the king it was his duty to administer the will of his sovereign. To accomplish this purpose, it seems that the governor would have had to reside in the colony, but he did not always do so. The four governors who presided over the colony from 1704 to 1768 all lived in England; the

[1] Percy Scott Flippin, *The Royal Government in Virginia* (New York, 1919), p. 61.

king sent lieutenant-governors across to take charge of affairs in Virginia. Important matters of colonial interest were referred to the governor resident in England, but the lieutenant was the responsible party in America.

DUTIES

Although appointed by the king, the governor took an oath of office formulated by Parliament. In turn he administered oaths to the members of the colonial council and to all the other important officers in the colony. His duties were outlined in a list of instructions emanating from his sovereign. As the colony grew in population and commerce the instructions increased proportionately and the duties of the governor became more numerous. The royal orders constituted a colonial code of laws, governing salaries, Indian affairs, the building of forts and workhouses, marriages, trade, and the care of the poor.

Twice a year the governor submitted to the home government a full report concerning the colonial affairs. This report contained a statement of the ships that had arrived and departed, the number of persons who had come into the colony, lists of goods imported and exported, the journals of the assembly, a full financial statement, etc. The governor had to answer for all that happened in the colony.

With the advice of the council the chief executive fixed all fees and salaries and duly made provision for the collection and payment of the same. From all the public lands that belonged to the colony the governor and council conducted the sale of farms and plantations and collected the rents and fees on the sales. The land patents, written on parchment, bore the signature and official seal of the chief executive.

The governor had duties spiritual as well as political, for he possessed supervisory power over the church. The ministers were ordained by the Bishop of London, but the governor presented them to their vestries and saw that they received their pay and protection. Sitting as a general court, the governor and council heard all complaints against the clergy and adjusted matters according to their best judgment. Any resident of the colony desiring to enter the ministry appealed to the chief executive for a recommendation for ordination, which in due time came to the attention of the bishop.

Considerable military power was placed in the hands of the governor. He served as commander-in-chief of the militia and appointed all the important military officers. British troops sent to the colony were placed under the orders of the colonial commander-in-chief, who also commanded ships of the British navy anchored in Virginia waters. Ships prepared and sent out by the colony sailed under the orders of the governor. Governor Spotswood led the first exploring party into the Shenandoah Valley in 1716, and Governor Dunmore commanded the northern wing of the army that invaded the Ohio Valley against the Indians in 1774.

The governor could call, prorogue, and dissolve the assembly. He suggested bills to be passed; he signed or vetoed acts passed by the assembly; he sat in meetings with the council when it acted as a general court; he licensed lawyers to practice their profession; he had the power to pardon persons convicted of any crimes except treason and murder; he could remit fines and forfeitures not exceeding ten pounds, but could not grant exemption from customs duties; and he issued warrants for the disbursements of funds. The colonial governor possessed royal authority in his domain, and royal authority he used. Nineteen governors served in Virginia from 1624 to 1776. Some were successful, others failed; however, the colony grew in numbers and in wealth.

SALARY

The salary of the governor changed from time to time. In the beginning his income was derived from the cultivation of his land, revenue from land grants, taxes on exported tobacco, and fines. In 1659 the assembly ordered that Governor Berkeley be allowed, in addition to his regular income, "seven hundred pounds sterling out of the imposition of two shillings per hogshead and fifty thousand pounds of tobacco out of the levy."[2] After 1704 the governor-in-chief, who resided in England, was paid twelve hundred pounds annually, and the lieutenant governor, living in the colony, eight hundred pounds.[3]

Originally the pay of the governor came out of funds derived from duties levied in Virginia and deposited in the treasury of England. During the war between King Charles I and Parliament England had more important business on hand than paying the governor of the little colony of Virginia, and his salary lapsed. In March, 1642, the assembly passed an act authorizing that his pay be drawn out of the regular income of the colony. Although this law was in-

---

[2] Hening, *Statutes at Large*, I, 546.

[3] Flippin, *The Royal Government in Virginia*, p. 76.

tended to be only temporary it became permament. Never again did the governor of Virginia receive his salary out of the treasury of England. Money for this purpose was collected from a levy of two shillings per hogshead on exported tobacco, from gifts of tobacco, from fees for commissions issued by the governor, and from a charge of one pound in sterling for affixing the seal to any legal form or title. It is estimated that the annual income of Governor Dunmore reached perhaps $20,000 in the value of our currency.

A spacious mansion was prepared for the colonial executive. It was supplied with expensive furniture, tapestries, and other costly adornments. The grounds consisted of well-kept lawns, walks, gardens, and terraces. An artificial canal flowed by the garden. It was a rare place for royal entertainment and pleasant diversion, and the king's representative in Virginia delighted in pastime of that sort.

The Council

Second in importance to the governor stood the council. This body was as old as the colony itself. We have seen that at the time of the first settlement a resident council of seven members was appointed by the London Company to supervise the affairs of the colony. From time to time the number of the councilors changed. In 1630 there were only two, by 1641 the number had increased to eighteen, and later it was reduced to thirteen. Finally twelve became the regular membership of this important body.

SELECTION AND TENURE

After 1624 the council for the colony was appointed by the king, but the governor recommended to the king persons for such appointment. They were required to be residents of the colony; usually they were leaders and men of proved ability. Membership on this advisory board carried great honor.

The term of office was for life or during good behavior. If a member desired to retire, as few did, he made application to the governor, who passed on his request to the king. Sometimes the king approved such a change without a request, which meant dismissal. The governor had authority to suspend a councilor, who in turn had the right to appeal his case to the king. The council as a body could suspend one of its own members, without right of appeal. If a councilor left the colony without the consent of the governor, his office was declared vacant; if he failed to be present at a meeting, he made himself liable to a fine. The councilor, although an important citizen in the colony, by no means had his own way about affairs.

PLACE OF MEETING

In matters pertaining to their executive and judicial duties the council and governor often met at the home of one of the councilors, or at any other place the governor chose. These distinguished men, being residents of the colony, plantation owners, and persons of influence, were a source of wide and varied information to the governor, who came from old England. He could well afford to seek pleasant agreement and friendly association with them. It is not hard to imagine the king's councilor, in the fashion of the times, pulling up in his carriage drawn by four horses at the gateway of a Virginia palatial home, dismounting, powdered wig, frock coat, and silk stockings all in evidence, and entering to find most cordial reception, leaving horses and carriage to the care of attendant slaves. An executive meeting had been called and important business was on hand. It might be to plan an expedition against murderous Indians, hear a petition, or review the reports on the revenue of the colony. It is thought that after the beginning of the eighteenth century, even for executive sessions, the council met at the capitol in a special room set aside for its use.

In all matters dealing with legislation the governor and council met at the state house. The members enjoyed freedom of debate and sometimes their opinions went a long way toward bringing matters to a settlement. Until about 1663 the governor, council, and burgesses met together, but after that time the two legislative houses convened separately. The reasons for their separation have not been ascertained.

SALARY

At first the councilor served without pay, his position being one of labor and honor. The records fail to give the date on which payment was first instituted, but it is known that in 1656 he received an annual stipend of 20,000 pounds of tobacco. Twenty years later the records reveal that the annual salary was three hundred and fifty pounds in English sterling; by 1740 the amount had reached six hundred pounds; and just before the Revolution it mounted to twelve hundred pounds.

The council did not have authority to regulate the salaries of its own members; the lords of the treasury in England fixed the amount. The lords specified that salaries be met from an export duty of two shillings per hogshead levied on tobacco shipped from Virginia. Checks for the proper amounts were issued from the office of the governor.

LEGISLATIVE POWER

In the beginning the sole function of the council was to act as an advisory board to the governor. But when the colony became a royal possession and the king selected the council, this appointive body was given more than advisory power. No bill could become a law until it had the council's endorsement. The council could approve, reject, or amend bills, but it possessed no power to originate legislation. Of course the council enjoyed the privilege of debate on all matters coming before it.

JUDICIAL POWER

In addition to its advisory and legislative powers, the council had a judicial function which it shared with the governor. The general court, made up of the council with the governor as presiding officer, constituted the highest judicial tribunal in the colony. Previous to 1661 the people knew it as the quarter court because the meetings were held four times a year, but in that year the name was changed to the general court, and eventually there were only two sessions a year, in April and October. At first meetings were held from place to place, usually in the home of a planter, but later they were regularly held at the state house. In addition, the governor and one councilor (or two councilors, in case the governor was detained at the capitol) annually visited each county court for the purpose of hearing all cases appealed from the lower court to the general tribunal. Cases of any value relating to members of the county court and vestrymen could be brought at first instance in the general court. The jurisdiction of the county court, by original process or by appeal, embraced all cases, ecclesiastical, criminal, or civil, providing the sum involved equaled or exceeded the minimum set by the statute, which was changed from time to time.

SPECIAL PRIVILEGES AND POWERS

The office of councilor carried with it certain privileges and honors in the colony. Members were exempt from taxation, a favor the colony could ill afford, since most of the councilors had extensive property holdings. Again, they were not required to report for military training on muster day, though some of them held office in the militia. A member of the council was not obliged to answer a summons to court if it were served during a meeting of the group to which he belonged. Perhaps this rule contained some element of justice but how could the councilman justify his privilege of sitting as a member of the court that settled cases in which he had a direct interest? Matters of this kind eventually made the office unpopular with the people. By right it should have been unpopular to the extent of repeal of the law that legalized such an extravagant condition.

Besides his position on the advisory board to the governor, the councilman often filled other offices of honor, trust, and profit, among them that of secretary, auditor, receiver-general, collector of revenue, commissioner of the militia, and member of the naval staff. He had an excellent opportunity to engage in land speculation, an advantage which he did not often deny himself. From all indications the council maintained a monopoly on offices and favors in colonial Virginia.

It should be noted also that the governor and council constituted a church court before which ministers and vestrymen brought their complaints. In this respect the council supervised affairs of church as well as those of state. The senior member of the council even filled the place of the governor when the chief executive was absent. Considering the special duties assigned to a councilor, together with his legislative, ecclesiastical, and judicial service, it may be properly concluded that he was not an idle person. He had work, much important work, to do.

The House of Burgesses

ORIGIN

We have seen that in 1619, largely through the influence of Sir Edwin Sandys, instructions were forwarded from London to Jamestown that henceforth the settlers would share in the making of their laws. Already the colony had been divided into eleven plantations; and according to the new instructions, two representatives, or burgesses,[4] were to be chosen by the freemen from each plantation to assist the governor and council in the affairs of the settlement.

Pursuant to this plan, the first popular legislative assembly in

[4] So styled because they were elected by the "borough" or plantation.

America met in the church at Jamestown on July 30, 1619. The assembly consisted of Governor Yeardley, six councilors, and twenty burgesses, "two of the most fit and able bodied men" from each plantation.[5] The meeting was opened with a prayer offered by the Rev. Richard Buck. Without objection, the burgesses took the Oath of Supremacy [6] and proceeded to judge the qualification of their own members by declaring that the two from Captain Martin's plantation could not qualify to remain in the assembly.

METHOD OF ELECTION

It has already been said that only freemen could vote. A freeman or freeholder was a resident who owned fifty acres of unsettled land, or twenty-five acres on which a house stood, or a house and a lot in town. The governor issued writs for elections. The writs were delivered to the secretary of the colony, who in turn forwarded them to the sheriffs of the respective counties. Within three days after receiving the papers the sheriff presented copies to all the ministers, who read them in the presence of their congregations every Sunday until the election had been held. The announcements contained the date and place of election.

On the day of voting, every white freeholder in the county reported at the appointed spot, usually the place where the county court held its sessions. The manner of balloting was viva voce or by show of hands. This method lasted many years before the adoption of the written and secret ballot.

Any freeman who did not vote was liable to a fine of two hundred pounds of tobacco, and one voting illegally might have to pay five hundred pounds of tobacco.[7] In case of a tie the sheriff had authority to cast the deciding ballot.

QUALIFICATIONS

A burgess, like a voter, had to be a white male freeholder at least twenty-one years of age. Free Negroes, mulattoes, and Indians could neither vote nor qualify for office. The burgess had to be a resident of the borough or county he represented. Generally he was a thrifty landowner who had made progress by industry and frugality.

---

[5] Twenty-two burgesses were elected but two were disqualified because they came from Captain John Martin's plantation, which was free from control by the colony except to help defend it against an enemy.

[6] An oath acknowledging the King of England as the only supreme head on earth of the Church of England.

[7] The amounts of the fines varied from time to time.

THE SPEAKER

Sometime before 1700 the burgesses found it more satisfactory to convene apart from the governor and the council. The exact reason for the separation is not definitely known. However, the time ultimately came when they perfected their own organization and assumed all the responsibility of a legislative assembly.

The speaker, chosen by his colleagues, presided at the meetings. The choice had to be approved by the governor, but this approval was automatic. In fact no law made the speaker responsible to or dependent on any other officer. This condition was deeply significant, since the governor was chosen by the king in England while the speaker was elected by the representatives of the people of Virginia.[8] It is thought that the home government really desired that the burgesses be controlled by the royal governor, but the members would not have it that way. They proceeded to select their other officers, sergeant-at-arms and doorkeepers.

In the beginning the burgesses held their meetings annually or oftener if called to convene by the chief executive. Certain records set forth that after 1659 most sessions were held only biennially, but the times of meetings seem not to have been regularly specified. Eventually the sessions convened at least once each year and continued to do so until the declaring of independence.

COMPENSATION AND PRIVILEGES

For many years the only compensation granted to the burgesses (an amount sufficient to defray current expenses) came from the plantations which they represented. It is known that salaries were first granted in 1661, when the assembly authorized that one hundred and fifty pounds of tobacco per day be paid each member for the time the session lasted. At the close of the colonial period the speaker's annual salary amounted to six hundred and twenty-five pounds current money. The salary of the clerk had been fixed at one hundred and twenty-five pounds for each session, and councilmen received ten shillings per day during the same time. All members received the full amount of their traveling expenses.

The burgess enjoyed certain privileges and immunities. He was

---

[8] During the period of the Commonwealth in England, four governors of Virginia – Bennett, Digges, Matthews, and Berkeley – were appointed by the assembly of Virginia and not by Parliament or Cromwell.

immune from arrest during the session and for a week before and after it. This rule protected him from being coerced or hindered in the performance of his appointed duties.

LEGISLATIVE POWERS

Bills passed by the burgesses had to be approved by the council and governor; they were then sent to London for final endorsement. Generally legislation became effective when the bill had been passed by the assembly and signed by the governor, even though a chance remained for royal annulment.

For a time it became the custom to include in bills a "suspending clause," which delayed putting the law into effect until word came from London that it had been approved by the home government. Bills with the "suspending clause" noticeably decreased after 1764, the year in which Parliament undertook to regulate colonial trade, and they were completely abolished in 1773.

Generally, but not always, the king approved the acts of the assembly. When he rejected a bill, he sent a notice of the action to the governor who issued a proclamation making the unwelcome news known throughout the colony. The proclamation was read in the presence of the assembly, to the congregations of all the churches, to the militia on muster day, and to the county courts. In this manner the news reached the most remote parts of the colony, as newspapers were generally unknown.

Since the burgesses were chosen by the people and the people paid the taxes, the feeling grew that the burgesses should have much to do with the public funds. Gradually this branch of the assembly acquired the power to make appropriations of money. This power increased until the burgesses completely controlled the colony's purse. It was a tremendous weapon in their hands. The royal governor could veto bills, but he would not stop the payment of his own salary or forbid payments to the militia or to the council. The burgesses had become the paymaster of the colony. Since they made appropriations they also levied, regulated, and collected taxes.

One should not conclude that the burgesses were entirely free from the influence of the governor. His appointive power could go a long way toward controlling the sentiment of a burgess. He made assignments to positions of honor, trust, and profit. Sheriffs, justices of the peace, and military officers were appointees of the governor, who did not neglect to ask favors in return for his benevolence.

Such favors could especially be shown at elections. In this way the governor could exert considerable influence in determining the composition of the house of burgesses.

EXECUTIVE POWER

In times of stress the house of burgesses became frequently an important deliberative body. During the French and Indian Wars it specified in detail the purposes for which funds and supplies were to be used. It created a committee of distribution that attended to the assignments of food, clothing, guns, ammunition, and pay for the soldiers. Moreover, it dictated the course of military action and brought influence to bear on the governor in his appointment of officers in the colonial militia.

From 1699 to 1766 the speaker of the house also served as treasurer of the colony. His office, therefore, took on the title of speaker-treasurer. From year to year his power grew so great that in time the governor could be ignored. But his power had been given by the house and by the house it could be taken away. When speaker-treasurer John Robinson used his prerogative in an autocratic fashion to sway the election of burgesses and heap upon himself personal favors, the house revolted under the leadership of Patrick Henry and reduced Robinson's authority. Thus the arbitrary power possessed by the governor in the early age of colonial Virginia had during its last years become the arbitrary power of the burgesses.

The Judicial System

THE GENERAL COURT

The operations of the governor and council as the highest judicial authority in the colony have already been described. Under this arrangement the council, as a legislative body, could assist in passing laws, and later convene as a judicial tribunal to render final judgment on these laws. Some members of the council had additional judicial power by virtue of appointment to the county court. Too much power was thus concentrated in the hands of a few.

This defect in organization was remedied somewhat as time passed by the gradual development of a system of lower courts that assumed an increasing proportion of the judicial authority. Eventually the legislative, executive, and judicial departments of the government were to be sharply separated.

THE ATTORNEY GENERAL

There was no attorney general in Virginia before 1643. Previous to that time the governor and assembly received instructions from England on legal questions of moment. However, seeing the need of a chief legal adviser in the colony, the king appointed an attorney general to represent him in matters of legal procedure. In 1700 the power of appointment was transferred to the governor, who held it until near the close of the colonial era; then the Crown took it over again, but left to the governor the privilege of recommendation.

The chief duty of the attorney general was to advise the governor and assembly on matters of legal procedure and to interpret the instructions sent to the colony from London. He prosecuted persons accused of criminal offenses in the general court and the court of oyer and terminer. He also decided suits between the masters of ships and the collectors of revenue at the port of entry. He prepared proclamations for the governor and advised with the burgesses on the legality of bills proposed to the assembly. At the close of the colonial period the attorney general was receiving a salary of two hundred pounds sterling annually.

COURTS OF OYER AND TERMINER

In 1692 the assembly created a court of oyer and terminer to indict and try slaves accused of committing capital offenses. In all the other courts there had been too much delay, it was thought, in such cases. Judges for this court were appointed by the governor. The court convened twice a year, in June and December.

When a crime committed by a slave demanded speedy prosecution, the sheriff of the county sent notice to the governor informing him of the crime and the arrest of the offender. In turn the governor issued a commission of oyer and terminer to any person in the county whom he considered qualified to judge the case. It then became the duty of the appointee (judge) to see that the offender was duly indicted and arraigned at the courthouse before the judge, who tried the accused and, if he was found guilty, sentenced him, "without the solemnity of a jury."

Later the assembly enlarged the duties of the courts of oyer and terminer to include the trial of all persons accused of treason, felony, piracy, robbery, murder, and other capital offenses committed on the high seas, rivers, and bays. For such trials the governor issued commissions of oyer and terminer to judges of the admiralty or any other persons he saw fit to choose. Thus the executive possessed considerable influence in directing the judicial power.

COURTS OF ADMIRALTY

Commercial interests manifested themselves from the beginning in the colony of Virginia and developed as population and wealth grew. Disputes and litigation involving the right of property and the fulfillment of contract inevitably occurred, and it became necessary for the colonial government to provide for an equitable settlement of such matters.

In 1659 a new law constituted the governor and council a court of admiralty to try cases defined in the statute. The business of the court was the adjustment of disputes between merchants and mariners, and all other cases concerning the loading and unloading of ships, freight, labor, and "all other business whatsoever among sea-affairs done on the water." The already powerful judicial powers of the governor and council were thus extended to cover affairs on the bays and the high seas.

In a manner the courts of admiralty had authority over the collection of taxes on imported and exported goods which demanded prompt attention. The governor appointed collectors stationed at the ports of entry. Each collector filed regular statements of the moneys he received with the auditor of the colony, another office filled by a member of the colonial council. In turn the auditor made an annual summary report to the governor and the assembly. Since the burgesses made the appropriations, it was they who bore the responsibility for the distribution of the funds collected on imported and exported goods.

Surveying the political organization of colonial Virginia in its entirety, one is impressed with the completeness of the structure. The burgesses, selected by the votes of the freemen, held a strong rein on the colony by controlling its finances. The people paid taxes (their own money) into the treasury, and it was altogether logical that their representatives should have the privilege of spending the funds for the general welfare. On the other hand, the British government, represented by the governor, remained the owner and protector of the colony. The governor's power was far-reaching. He appointed officers; he administered laws; he acted in a judicial capacity. His righthand helper consisted of his council, which acted in concert with him. Regardless of various defects of administration, the government of colonial Virginia contained elements of good organization.

Local Government

THE COUNTY

It is not definitely known when the first counties were organized in Virginia, but it is a matter of record that in 1634 the assembly established eight shires in the colony, to be governed like the shires in England.[9] Previous to this date plantations had been the only political divisions in the colony and from those units the first burgesses were elected in 1619. The eight original shires covered all the occupied land in Virginia and extended even beyond the line of settlement. The purpose of the new arrangement was to bring to the inhabitants a more perfect government centered in local areas.

As population increased it moved westward up the valleys of the Potomac, James, and Rappahannock rivers, and later crossed the Blue Ridge to the Shenandoah. The organization of local government naturally followed the settlements, for the frontiersman and his forest-locked family needed an assurance of security and protection even exceeding that of their own indomitable courage. The persons living beyond the fringe of settlement not only struggled against the stubborn wilderness but also had to combat a hostile race that had for centuries had undisputed possession of the West. So the local units of government, first known as plantations, then as shires, and at last as counties, organized in the beginning along the coast, moved westward with the frontier to the piedmont, and finally crossed the mountains to the basins of the western rivers.

Shires and plantations came to be known as counties by act of the assembly in 1642. The assembly established the boundaries of each county and provided for the choosing of its officers, which consisted of a lieutenant whose duty was of a military nature, a sheriff, a county court, justices of the peace, a coroner, and others whose official obligations will be explained presently.

THE MONTHLY COURT

The colonists in Virginia did not delay long in organizing their local government. It proved to be just as natural for them to transplant the institutions of government from England to America as it

---

[9] The names of the eight original shires were James City, Henrico, Charles City, Elizabeth City, Warwick River, Charles River, Accomack, and Warrosquyoake.

was to transplant their language. Even before the creation of shires in the colony, provision had been made by the assembly (1623) for a court to be held once a month "in the corporations of Charles City and in Elizabeth City." The monthly court therefore antedates both the shire and the county.

The members of the monthly court were appointed by the governor and council without a definite term of office. This provision followed a long-standing English precedent whereby the judiciary was appointed by the chief executive and held office for life or during good behavior. This principle, imported from England and long established in the colonies, eventually came to be embodied in the Constitution of the United States.

The monthly court heard controversies and suits with respect to matters not exceeding in value one hundred pounds of tobacco, and brought to trial persons accused of petty offenses. There was due allowance for the taking of appeals from these decisions to the governor and council, but if one appealed his case and the higher court sustained his conviction he had to suffer double the sentence originally imposed. This regulation evidently discouraged persons from pursuing litigation. One example will illustrate the strength of the law. By legal requirement the head of every family had to have in his possession a certain amount of lead and powder. If his supplies were inspected and found to be less than the law required, he was liable to be sentenced by the monthly court to be fined, whipped, or imprisoned. If he appealed, the dose might be doubled. Perhaps not very many offenders ventured to run the risk. More specifically the duty imposed upon the monthly court required it "to determine all controversies between partie and partie as exceed not the value of five pounds sterling. And further, that they take into their care the conservation of the peace, the quiet government, and safety of the people." [10]

Each member of a monthly court held the title of commissioner. The number in the different counties varied from five to eight. This early colonial judicial assembly was the forerunner of the county court which has played such an important part in the local history of West Virginia.

THE COUNTY COURT

In 1642, when the political divisions of the state were renamed counties, the assembly created the county court to take the place of

[10] Hening, *Statutes at Large*, I, 186.

the monthly court. The county court met six times a year instead of monthly. The members continued to be appointed by the governor and to be called commissioners.

The county court heard all causes at common law or chancery, excepting those cases requiring the death penalty upon conviction, which came before the governor and council, and those involving a value of less than twenty-five shillings current money or two hundred pounds of tobacco, which were tried before a member of the county court sitting individually and known as a magistrate or justice of the peace.

The county court had many duties to perform. In addition to hearing cases in court it built and maintained a courthouse and jail (the colony had no general prison) and such equipment as stocks, pillory, whipping post, and ducking stool for the punishment of crime. It was not unusual for a culprit to be sentenced to sit with hands and feet fastened in the stocks or stand with neck yoked and hands tied in the pillory, there to bear the jibes and insults of persons passing by. An offender might be lashed at the whipping post or soused into a pool of cold water for breaking the Sabbath, this to the great delight of a curious crowd, or he might be sentenced to stand tiptoe in the pillory for stealing a neighbor's corn.

The county court had duties other than judicial. It probated wills and recorded births, deaths, and marriages; it made official settlement of estates, allowed rewards, established ferries, fixed the rate of taxation and established tavern fees, built roads, and licensed ordinary keepers. The Virginia county court performed many important services, and the old record books written by the clerks assigned to the courts yield invaluable information to the modern historian.

THE JUSTICE OF THE PEACE

We have seen that the commissioners acting separately as judicial officers were called justices of the peace. Before 1700 the number of justices for each county was not always the same. At first as few as five were sometimes assigned to a small new county, but later the number increased to not fewer than eight and not more than twenty. Still later the number was fixed at eight. When it is considered that one county in early Virginia extended over an area larger than twenty counties today and that its population was widely scattered, it becomes clear why several justices of the peace were needed. At times every settler, however remote from the center of population, needed a legal authorization or approval of the deed to his land or a contract with his neighbor. A great many of the early colonists, though courageous and in many respects wise, were illiterate. They stood in need of the justice of the peace to administer oaths, certify affidavits, take the acknowledgments of deeds and other writings, form contracts, and try persons accused of petty violations.

In addition to these important duties the justice of the peace issued writs of mandamus, summoned witnesses, issued warrants, and acted as a court of record. If the occasion warranted his help he served as the coroner. Poor and orphaned children he bound out to some home where they could be sheltered and taught. In view of his extensive duties, the "squire," as he was often called, was exempt by law from military service.

All the justices of the peace in one county, meeting together, composed the county court. When a new county was created, the governor appointed the ablest and most judicious persons of the county to fill the positions both as justices of the peace and commissioners of the county court.

THE SHERIFF

The first record concerning the office of sheriff dates from 1656, when an act of the assembly required that the county court of every county submit the names of three or more persons to the governor and council, who then chose the one "most meet and fit for the place" of sheriff. A revision of the statute in 1661 provided that one of the members of the county court should serve as sheriff. The term of office was a single year; and the commissioners recommended one another for the office until all had served their county as sheriff. A second revision in 1705 required the county court to submit the names of three of their own members to the governor, who in turn appointed the sheriff from the limited list. This law increased the term to two years. Since the court was answerable for laying and collecting the taxes, and since an important duty of the sheriff was the collection of this revenue, it was thought wise to have this close relationship between sheriff and court. Many people paid their taxes in tobacco, a report of which the sheriff certified to the county court.

In addition to collecting taxes the sheriff exacted payment of quitrents and other county and state levies. He served summonses and warrants, arrested persons accused of crime and runaway slaves and servants, and carried out sentences of the court.

As compensation for his duties he received fees. For putting a

person in the pillory he was paid twenty pounds of tobacco; for ducking a disobedient violator he got the same fee; for serving a warrant for a justice of the peace, ten pounds of tobacco; for impaneling a grand jury, fifty pounds; and for lashing a sentenced servant or slave, twenty pounds. By no means did these fees establish a maximum, for on many occasions he received larger amounts. Perhaps his most responsible duty was the execution of a death sentence. For hanging a convicted criminal the sheriff received two hundred and fifty pounds of tobacco.

THE CONSTABLE

The office of constable had been in use for many years in England before it was adopted in Virginia. When the assembly divided the counties into districts it became necessary to have a conservator of the peace in each of the local units of government, and the constable took up that assignment. Constables were at first appointed by the assembly, later by the county court. The term of office was one year. The constable served the justice of the peace as an executive officer, much as the sheriff served the county court. His duties were manifold. When it was required by law that each settler plant at least two acres of corn, the constable inspected the work of the planter and reported violations. He served warrants, orders, and decrees issued by the county court; he collected fines levied on small offenders; he arrested violators of the revenue laws and searched for smuggled goods; he viewed tobacco fields and destroyed the leaves of inferior quality; he enforced the game laws, arrested runaway sailors, servants, and slaves; he summoned witnesses and coroner's juries, put felons into the stocks, and ducked "mischievous witches." For his services the constable collected small fees, ranging in value from two pounds of tobacco for serving a summons to fifty pounds for calling a coroner's jury.

THE CORONER

Each county had from one to four coroners. The county court recommended candidates, usually its own members, to the governor, who made the appointments.

The duty of the coroner was to hold inquests over bodies of persons who had met with violent death and through his jury to try to ascertain the cause of such accident. When the sheriff was incapacitated, the coroner served in his stead. The duties of this officer in Virginia the colony largely copied from the same office in England, which had included the administration of the estates of persons meeting death by violence, executing warrants, and serving summonses and other processes.

The Church and Civil Government

The established church exercised an enormous power in civil government in colonial Virginia. An old law required "that there shall be in every plantation, where the people use to meete for the worship of God, a house or rooms sequestred for that purpose, and not to be for any temporal use whatsoever." All persons were required to attend church on Sundays. Of course the church in Virginia was uniform in doctrine and discipline with the established church in England.

THE PARISH

The county court divided each county into parishes (in some cases a single parish covered an entire county). In each parish there was a church edifice, glebe,[11] and cemetery.

In order to support the church every tithable person in the parish paid a tax. The sum collected was devoted to building and maintaining the church edifice, paying the minister, and defraying any other necessary expenses. The parish register, kept by the minister and the church warden, contained a record of the births, marriages, and deaths occurring within the parish. The records were annually certified to the clerk of the county court and there made a matter of record.

THE VESTRY

In each parish the freemen chose twelve vestrymen to supervise the affairs of the church. The law specified that the vestry be composed of "twelve of the most able men of each parish." The vestry laid levies and assessments for building and maintaining the church and purchasing a glebe for the minister. At one time the annual church levy amounted to fifteen pounds of tobacco for each tithable.

The minister and the vestry in each parish annually selected from the vestry two or more church wardens. The warden collected

---

[11] The glebe was an enclosure of land on which the church and parsonage stood and which was extensive enough for the cultivation of crops by the minister and his slaves.

the levy, made disbursements of the funds, and reported violations of the Christian faith, such as swearing, profanity, and Sabbath breaking.

To keep the church clean and in good repair the vestry selected a sexton. When the time came for the regular religious worship, the sexton had attended to sweeping, heating, dusting the sanctuary, and even ringing the church bell.

THE MINISTER

The most important person in the church unit was the minister. On him very largely depended the Christian influence in the parish. Although church attendance was required by law, and the layman at times expressed his devotion by carrying his rifle with him to the Sunday service, a chance prevailed that the sermon, if not inspiring, would fall on sleeping ears. But the people generally exercised a devoted interest in their church and manifested a pride in their minister.

In the early days, most of the ministers in Virginia were natives of England who had been ordained before coming to the colony. A colonist who desired to be a minister had to go to England to be ordained. In either case, on arrival in Virginia the minister presented testimonials of his ordination to the governor, who stood at the head of the church in the colony. When a new assignment had to be made in a parish, the vestry presented its recommendation to the governor, who in turn appointed the minister.

In 1766 the assembly passed a law stating that "every minister preferred, or to be preferred or received into any parish within this domain, shall have and receive an annual salary of sixteen thousand pounds of tobacco and cash, with an allowance of four per cent, for shrinkage, to be levied, assessed, collected and paid in tobacco." In Frederick County tobacco was valued at three farthings a pound, a farthing being worth about half a cent. Thus the salary of the minister was fixed by the assembly but actually raised by a levy laid by the vestry.

Conclusion

Such, in brief outline, was the government of colonial Virginia. It applied not only in the east, where the original colony had been settled, but as far to the west as settlements had been established. Before the Revolution the frontier did not go beyond the Blue Ridge, except at isolated points far apart, but after the Revolution, as we shall see below, it was to extend to the Ohio Valley. The government that was ultimately established in the western territory was an extension of the system that had earlier been established in the colony in the region east of the Blue Ridge. Thus the system of government that we have just reviewed is the foundation of the political institutions of West Virginia today.

CHAPTER 5

From Colonial Government to Independence

Introduction

The political ingenuity of Virginia's statesmen was severely tested when a new government had to be formed to take the place of the old colonial organization which had been in operation more than a hundred and fifty years. Fortunately for our subsequent history, they were not found wanting. Perhaps the recorded history of all nations does not afford another unit of government blessed with such extraordinary political talent as did honor to Virginia at the time of the outbreak of the American Revolution. There were George Washington, John Marshall, Patrick Henry, George Mason, Thomas Jefferson, James Madison, Edmund Pendleton, George Wythe, Edmund Randolph, and many others, experts in the science of government, who would have been a prize and a pride in any empire or republic, however populous and extensive. The oldest of the American colonies proved to the world that it could take care of itself. Its men of genius were not indifferent to the clouds of conflict with the mother country that had been for years intermittently appearing on the political horizon each time more evident than before. They had seen the storm coming and were not to be taken unawares. Even before the Declaration of Independence, plans for self-government had been carried a long way toward completion. So when the time came to make the final decision a new order was ready to supplant the old.

The Virginia Convention of 1775

When it became evident that some definite steps had to be taken to reorganize the government of Virginia, a convention of delegates, elected by the counties and towns, met at Richmond in March, 1775, and again in July of the same year. The inevitability of military conflict was already evident to the leaders, and the primary purpose of the convention was to plan the defense of the colony. To secure this defense the Virginians had to take into their own hands the conduct of all affairs, civil as well as military.

PLANS FOR DEFENSE

The convention appointed the officers of two regiments that had already been organized. Provisions were duly made for additional enlistments, filling vacancies, training and paying soldiers, and supplying food, clothing, and medicine. It is worthy of note that every enlisted soldier took an oath to be "faithful and true to the colony and dominion of Virginia," with no mention whatever of any allegiance to England. Certain divisions of the militia enlisted as minutemen; these were strictly trained for emergency and expert service, and were organized into separate battalions under the command of an adjutant general.

To facilitate and expedite the raising of an army, the convention divided the colony into sixteen military districts, one of which consisted of the counties of Berkeley, Frederick, Dunmore,[1] Hampshire, and the District of West Augusta. Each district, with a single exception,[2] had one battalion consisting of five hundred enlisted men ranging in age from sixteen to fifty years. In turn each county, district, and borough was designated a military unit for the purpose of enlisting and training soldiers, and a committee of deputies supervised the management of those affairs in each district. Virginia did not go

---

[1] Later changed to Shenandoah County.

[2] The district consisting of Accomac and Northampton counties had to enlist a battalion of six hundred and eighty men.

about preparing in a half-hearted manner; its organization was complete from top to bottom.

THE COMMITTEE OF SAFETY

To carry out its orders the convention created a committee of safety whose jurisdiction extended throughout the colony. The committee consisted of eleven members named by the convention. Edmund Pendleton was made chairman. The organization functioned continuously.

The committee of safety exercised jurisdiction over the military affairs of the colony. It commissioned officers, made payments of money authorized by the convention, directed the army, called minutemen and other detachments of soldiers into services, requested aid from other colonies, issued orders to officers, and kept in touch with the county, town, and borough committees. From a military standpoint the success or failure of the colonial cause rested in the hands of this committee. Posterity may look back with pride and wonder on the wisdom displayed by those statesmen in organizing their power and in apportioning their responsibilities for this important work. It made few mistakes in selecting for the various places the men who could best fill them. The Virginians never lagged in their efforts to win independence, and the people of West Augusta abundantly deserved their share of the honor.

OTHER ACTION

Military matters were not the only concern of the committee of safety. It made other changes in the colony as fast as safety permitted. Trade and commerce it next took out of the hands of the royal government, and consequently discontinued the laws and regulations in operation under the English crown. The courts of admiralty, composed of the governor and council, were replaced by courts under the control of the popular assembly. Trials in the courts were decided by juries from whose decisions appeals could be made only to the committee of safety, the court of last resort.

Next the convention turned its attention to forming a new organization of local government. It authorized the freeholders of each county to convene at a common meeting place and choose from their number twenty-one persons to serve as a governing body until the next election. From the twenty-one freeholders the committee of safety selected five persons to act as a judiciary in all cases in the county, except those pertaining to maritime business. This court of five members held its regular sessions at the county courthouse and considered matters of business in the order in which they were presented. The clerk and the sheriff were to be present at court and faithfully perform their duties on all occasions and in all circumstances. In short, under the new state government authority was taken from the old county court and completely transferred to the new committee of five; the sheriff and clerk retained their former positions, but beyond question their allegiance was changed.

The Virginia convention of 1775, then, revised the laws of the colony, solely on authority conferred upon it by its own electorate. But this electorate did not by any means include all the freeholders of Virginia. Many men of influence, and many more of no particular influence, maintained an allegiance to the English government and an unswerving loyalty to Governor Dunmore. The authority delegated to the members of the convention was sufficient to warrant action, however, for it had been proclaimed in their recent Declaration of Rights "that all power is vested in, and consequently derived from, the people; that magistrates are their trustees and servants, and at all times amenable to them." [3]

Before the convention adjourned it made ample provision for its own perpetuation; its duties would not terminate with the closing of the session. Therefore, an annual election of delegates was called for the first Monday in May, 1776, and a new session was to convene soon thereafter.

Political affairs in Virginia had now reached a condition of irrepressible turmoil. Two governments were functioning, each only in part. The one had support from the king of England, residing three thousand miles away from the scene of activity, and from a loyal minority in the colony. The other was sustained by a militant majority of the colonists, endowed by nature with keen intelligence and far-seeing political insight, whose pride as citizens they thought had been humbled by unjust laws imposed from London. This group strove for self-government and revolted against repression from any quarter whatsoever.

Conditions could not continue thus. Those people who called themselves patriots could see themselves living only in a state of bondage as long as they endured the rule of England. In answer to their peaceful protests, asking for liberty, the mother country gave them tyranny; they petitioned as freemen and were made servants; they appealed for their burden to be made lighter and were assigned

[3] Hening, *Statutes at Large*, IX, 109.

heavier yokes to bear. They objected to being made to live in a way inferior to that of other Englishmen. The only way to break the ties of bondage was to appeal to arms, and appeal to arms they did!

The Second Convention

The annual election authorized by the first convention was held on scheduled time. The second convention assembled at Williamsburg on May 6, 1776. The provisional government in Virginia had now become aggressive, if not bold, for it dared to meet in the capital city near the very palace of the royal governor. The political temper of the people was clearly reflected in the actions of their delegates.

The first important business taken up was the formulation of a Declaration of Rights embodying the political ideals for which the people contended. For years these principles had been cherished in the hearts of Virginians and now the time had come for them to be written on the statute books. Among these cardinal principles their declaration proclaimed that by nature all men are equally free and independent; that all political power is vested in and derived from the people; that government is instituted for the common benefit, protection, and security of all the people; and that no man, or set of men, is entitled to exclusive privileges. In all, sixteen separate articles set forth Virginia's objections to the system of government that had been in operation in the colony and to the policy of the English governors. Many of its indictments appeared later, similarly expressed, in the Declaration of Independence. When the celebrated George Mason wrote in this document, and when the convention approved, the statement "that no government separate from, or independent of, the government of Virginia, ought to be erected or established within the limits thereof," the hour for final separation from England had struck. The declaration was unanimously adopted on June 12, 1776, and met a happy response from the people.

No longer did the representatives of the people plead for a revision of repressive laws or announce warnings. Already news had reached Williamsburg that the battles of Lexington and Concord had been fought, and a flame of indignation against English authority in America spread through the colonies. Virginia was by no means the last to be aroused, for the spirit of independence soon spread from the sea to the Ohio River. Not satisfied with proclaiming a declaration of rights, the convention proceeded to form a constitution for a state entirely independent of Great Britain.

The First Constitution of Virginia

INTRODUCTION

The original constitution of Virginia was "agreed to and resolved upon" and unanimously adopted June 29, 1776. The constitutional convention, meeting at Williamsburg, consisted of the same assembly of delegates that had confirmed the Declaration of Rights. By this adoption their ties to the people of England had been totally dissolved and a new government for Virginia created. Again the delegates turned to their veteran statesman, George Mason, for help in that trying time, and he rose in his full stature to the occasion by proposing the plan of government that the assembly adopted.

South Carolina and New Hampshire preceded Virginia in forming constitutions, but they expected these to last only until a reconciliation could be effected with the mother country. The Virginians did not seek a compromise; their action meant final separation. Therefore, among the states in America, Virginia has the honor of adopting the first constitution "framed with a view of permanent separation from Great Britain." [4]

Although the new document contained forward-looking principles generally adequate for the period in which it was written, it included some provisions that eventually proved to be deep disappointments. Let us briefly discuss the most outstanding one, the law relating to suffrage.

The constitution contained the statement, "The right of suffrage in the election of members of both Houses shall remain as exercised at present." These words emphasized the fact that one had to be a resident freeholder in order to be a qualified voter. For many years prominent Virginia statesmen clung to this unpardonable doctrine, which finally acted as a wedge helping to force apart the eastern and western divisions of the state. According to this law one without property was bereft of any political power or of a voice in the welfare of his own government. He could, and at times duty required that he should, enlist in the army, endure privations, and suffer the wounds of battle to help win freedom, only to find that freedom was denied to its defender. As a pastor a man without property could preach in terms of pity and veneration to a multitude; as a physician he could heal the sick; as a teacher he could train the illiterate; but unless he owned land all his services merited nothing politically.

[4] Henry Howe, *Historical Collections of Virginia*, p. 113.

Finally the patriots living in western Virginia challenged this erroneous doctrine. They became champions of the principle of universal suffrage and did not cease their efforts until they realized their objective some seventy years later. The fight was won, however, at the cost of the division of the state and the founding of a new commonwealth built on the principle that a government established on the rights of men is superior to a government based on the ownership of property.

THE LEGISLATIVE POWER

The new constitution vested the legislative power in a general assembly which consisted of a house of delegates and a senate. It is worthy of comment that the present constitution of West Virginia, drafted in 1872, retained the same titles for the two chambers of its legislative assembly. A study of the old document shows principles of government which have had potent influences on constitution making in the younger commonwealth.

The House of Delegates. Representation in the Virginia assembly rested on population with the county as the basic unit. The house of delegates consisted of two representatives elected from each county. A delegate had to be a resident and a freeholder of the county from which he was elected. If authorization could be secured through an act of the legislature, a city or borough could elect one delegate. The District of West Augusta maintained the same status as a county, having two delegates.

This system of representation borrowed largely from the one inaugurated in 1619. The provision for two representatives from each political unit and for the possession of property as the qualification for voting and for holding office had a familiar ring. The chief differences between the old order and the new were that plantations had been transformed into counties, and that supreme rule had been transferred from the king of England to the American people.

The center of legislative power had been established in the house of delegates. All the members came directly from the people as the representatives of the people. Believing firmly that the just powers of government are derived from the opinion of the popular majority, the makers of the constitution delegated the power of initiating laws solely to the representatives of those whom the laws would govern. The supreme law set forth that all bills must originate in the house of delegates and when there approved must be transferred in turn to the senate to be amended, confirmed, or rejected. Bills for raising revenue could not even be amended in the senate, but had to be passed or disapproved without change as they came from the house of delegates. These sweeping powers in legislation gave the delegates a wide margin of advantage over the upper house. The principle, written by George Mason into the new government, that all political power is vested in the people or their representatives had begun to be understood in Virginia.

The Senate. The first senate of Virginia consisted of twenty-four members, thirteen of whom constituted a quorum. The counties of the state had been divided into twenty-four senatorial districts, with one senator representing each district. To rotate the members so that all the terms would not expire at the same time, the districts were equally divided by lot into four classes. At the expiration of the first year after election, the six members from the first district retired from office and a new election filled the vacancies. This rotation continued in order until an election had been held for the entire number, one-fourth being elected each year for a four-year term.

Senators held office by virtue of the votes of the qualified freeholders residing in the respective districts. A candidate for the office had to attain the age of twenty-five years and be a freeholder residing in the district that elected him. As to the number of times he could be rechosen the constitution placed no limitation.

Each house had authority to choose its own chairman, secretary, sergeant, and any other officers necessary to carry on the business of the sessions. It adopted its own rules of procedure and issued writs of election to fill vacancies in its membership. The senate possessed equal power and authority with the house of delegates except in the instances previously pointed out.

THE GOVERNOR

The governor was selected by a method different from that used for electing the assembly. The chief executive was elected annually by a joint ballot of the house and the senate. Nothing forbade his being elected from the membership of either branch of the assembly. He could continue in office for three successive terms, but before he could be a candidate for a fourth term four years had to elapse. "An adequate, but moderate salary, shall be settled on him during his continuance in office." So read the constitution.

According to the laws of the state, he exercised, with the advice of the council, the executive power of the government. The law specifically set forth that the governor could not adhere to any law, statute, or custom promulgated under the authority of England. This principle may seem extraconstitutional as a part of the supreme law of the land, but it must be remembered that the power of England in Virginia did not cease with the adoption of the constitution but continued active for several years after that time. Hence the warning against any British influence as two governments strove to function at the same time.

With the advice of the council of state, the governor could grant reprieves and pardons, except in cases that had been prosecuted by the house of delegates. A further hampering provision in the constitution stated that the governor could not call the assembly into extraordinary session except with permission from the council of state or the house of delegates. To express the independent power of the assembly, as set apart from that of the governor, either house had the privilege to adjourn at its own pleasure, and in no way could it be prorogued, adjourned, or dissolved by executive authority.

The constitution tersely expressed in the following terms the power extended to the governor: "He shall, with the advice of a council of state, exercise the executive powers of government according to the laws of this commonwealth." By a legislative grant of power he occasionally sent soldiers to protect the western frontier, dispatched assistance to other states, superintended, with the help of his council, the public jails, appointed justices of the peace, etc. As time went on, the power of the executive increased in proportion to the increase in the number of settlers.

When the constitution came into force in Virginia, the people feared and mistrusted the executive authority. The colonial governor, as the agent of the king, had engendered hatred by having to announce and enforce royal decrees sent from England. The governor, therefore, had to endure the criticism and the attack made against the intolerable regal rule, and he eventually was driven from the shores of the colony so that the inhabitants might be free from this dreaded tyranny. Let it be remembered that the royal governor served by the will of the king and therefore was responsible to the king and not to the people of Virginia.

In view of the foregoing facts the governor occupied a position that had to be guarded carefully against liberal interpretations of power. He was restricted in authority and restrained in action by constitutional provisions. As far as the people in Virginia were concerned, no governor would soon possess again dictatorial power over them, for before his election preparation had been made to keep his wings safely clipped. As the years passed, apprehensions about executive power gradually faded, and the governor's authority, like aging wine, grew in agreeable flavor.

THE COUNCIL OF STATE

The council of state was modeled upon the governor's council under the colonial regime, whose function has already been described. It was composed of eight members elected by joint ballot of the two houses of the assembly. The council could be chosen from the membership of the assembly or from the people at large. The house of delegates possessed a decided advantage in the election of the council, since its votes exceeded those in the senate by more than half. No doubt, therefore, the council felt a preponderant obligation to the more numerous branch of the assembly.

The term of office was eight years, with one fourth of the members retiring every two years. Annually the members chose a president, who also served as lieutenant-governor of the state, and a secretary, who kept on file a careful record of all the proceedings.

The duties of the council were both advisory and administrative. Its chief function was to consult with the governor and advise him on public matters. For instance, with the advice of the council, the governor appointed officers of the militia.[5] On all important affairs pertaining to his administration, he no doubt generally appealed to the council of state for its opinion.

THE STATE JUDICIARY

The constitution made ample provision for an adequate judiciary, consisting of the general court, the high court of chancery, judges in admiralty, the attorney general, the county courts, and the justices of the peace.

Five judges, appointed by joint action of both houses of the assembly, composed the general court. Their term lasted for life or good behavior. Two sessions were held annually, one in March and the other in October, each continuing twenty-four days (Sundays excepted) unless the business coming before the court could be finished in less time. The governor, with the advice of his council of state, filled all vacancies by appointment.

The jurisdiction of the court "shall be general over all persons,

[5] Military officers serving only in a county could be recommended by the county court and appointed by the governor.

and in all causes, matters, or things at common law, whether brought before them by original process, by appeal from any inferior court, *habeas corpus*, *certiorari*, writ of error, *supersedeas*, *mandamus*, or by any other legal way or means." Thus the general court at the top of the judicial system in the state had wide jurisdiction.

In order to conduct its business in good order, the five justices appointed a clerk, "one or more assistant clerks, a crier and a tipstaff,[6] who shall hold their offices respectively during good behavior, and be entitled to such fees or salaries as shall be established by law; and the sheriff, or so many of the under sheriffs, as shall be thought necessary, of the county where such court may be held, shall attend the said court during their sessions."

Three judges, elected by joint ballot of both houses of the assembly, formed the high court of chancery. Their term continued during good behavior. The court had jurisdiction over all persons and all cases in chancery. It convened twice a year, at which times it granted injunctions, attachments, writs, and other processes.

The members of the court of admiralty received their appointments in the same manner as those just mentioned. Its three judges had jurisdiction of cases involving the capture and confiscation of goods and vessels on the sea. By decree of the court, cargoes and even merchant ships could be sold. The chief purpose of this court was to bring punishment to bear on persons conducting illegal trade.

It was the duty of the attorney general to represent the state when any of its interests became involved in court. He was elected by the same method as the judges. Public affairs need protection in legal matters just as private affairs do, and the attorney general served as the lawyer for the state when its officers needed legal service.

COUNTY GOVERNMENT

The justice of the peace was the local officer of first instance, and, as we have seen, his duties were manifold. Under the new constitution he was appointed by the governor, with the advice of the council of state. If the number of justices in any county had to be increased, the county court made recommendations to the governor, who filled the places by appointment.

The county court consisted, as before, of the justices of the peace meeting together in monthly sessions. Sheriffs and coroners were nominated by the county court and approved by the governor and

[6] An officer appointed to wait on the court and serve its process.

the council. Constables were appointed by the justices of the peace.

The duties of the county officers were not changed by the new constitution, and the incumbents were permitted to remain in office if they took an oath to support, maintain, and defend the constitution and government of the state of Virginia. In general they accepted the oath. Thus the change from rule by the crown to independence did not make as much difference in local administration as is sometimes surmised. Later the legislature from time to time created new offices or assigned new duties to old officers.

ADOPTION OF THE NEW CONSTITUTION

On June 29, 1776, the delegates, in convention assembled, adopted the new constitution of Virginia. To set the new government in motion the convention elected Patrick Henry governor and selected the eight members of the council of state. The other state officers, selected thereafter by joint ballot of both houses, were chosen by the convention on the same day that it ratified the constitution. Henceforth the new government went forward.

The First Assembly

The first regular assembly of the state met on October 7, 1776. Edmund Pendleton became speaker of the house and Archibald Carey president of the senate. One of the first matters of business was the appointment of Thomas Jefferson, Edmund Pendleton, George Wythe, George Mason, and Thomas Ludwell Lee as members of a committee to study the laws of the state and to present their suggested revision to the assembly for enactment. Since the states were in the midst of the Revolutionary War, all efforts of the people and their legislature turned to the winning of victory, and this revision of the laws and the formation of a code was kept in abeyance until the most important work had been concluded.

This is not the place to rehearse the events of the Revolution. Instead, we shall proceed to constitutional developments in Virginia after the war.

CHAPTER 6

Disaffection in the West

Introduction

When the Revolutionary War was over and strife with the Indians had ceased, nothing any longer excluded settlers from the extensive territory west of the mountains. Adventurers could now take active possession of the territory they had won, and Virginia likewise would fully occupy and administer her whole domain, the west as well as the east. Western Virginia had been explored and colonized before the war for independence began, and after their release from military service many of the veterans, true to Anglo-Saxon instinct, went pioneering beyond the mountains and established homes along the currents of the Monongahela, Kanawha, and Greenbrier rivers. To this same region came families from Maryland, Pennsylvania, New York, and all the New England states.[1] Thus western Virginia became a land of convergent states. This condition explains, in part, the dissatisfaction that eventually arose among those people against the laws made and administered at Richmond. Discord between the two regions did not happen by accident; it was inevitable.

---

1 From Virginia and Maryland the settlers came west by way of Braddock's Road, Seneca Trail, McCulloch's Path. From farther north they followed Forbes' Road, and to the south they used familiar Indian trails.

The Formation of New Counties

We have seen that in 1634 Virginia was divided into eight shires to be governed like the shires in England. One of these, originally called Charles River but in 1642 renamed York County, included all of western Virginia, though its western boundary had not yet been defined. As population spread westward slowly, few changes in county boundaries needed to be made until the formation in 1734 of Orange County, which included, together with other territory, all the land in present West Virginia. At that early date settlements established in the Shenandoah Valley came to be incorporated in Orange County, but they were few in number, and west of the Alleghenies there were as yet no white people.

Movement into the virgin valley after the formation of Orange County underwent a remarkable increase which continued from year to year. In 1738 the legislature recognized the growth of population in the west by creating two new counties, Frederick and Augusta, out of that part of Orange County lying west of the Blue Ridge. The legislature expressed the sentiment behind this action in the statement, "Whereas great numbers of people have settled themselves of late upon the rivers Sherrando, Cohongoruton,[2] and Opeckon, and the branches thereof, on the north-west side of the Blue ridge of mountains, whereby the strength of this colony, and its security upon the frontiers, and his majesty's revenue of quit-rents, are like to be much increased and augmented: for giving encouragement to such as shall think fit to settle there" the new counties are established.[3] Frederick and Augusta encompassed all the territory now occupied by West Virginia.

Of the present counties of West Virginia, Hampshire is generally known as the oldest. It was formed in 1754 from the parts of Frederick and Augusta lying west of the Cacapon Mountain and extending north to the Potomac. In 1772 Berkeley was formed from Frederick.

As population from the Shenandoah Valley continued to pour into the region of the South Branch and the upper reaches of the Monongahela, the Greenbrier, and the Kanawha, it became necessary to divide Augusta into smaller counties so that the settlers could have centers of local government nearer their homes. The first division occurred in 1769, when the legislature cut Botetourt County

2 The old names of the Shenandoah and Potomac rivers.

3 Hening, *Statutes at Large*, V, 79.

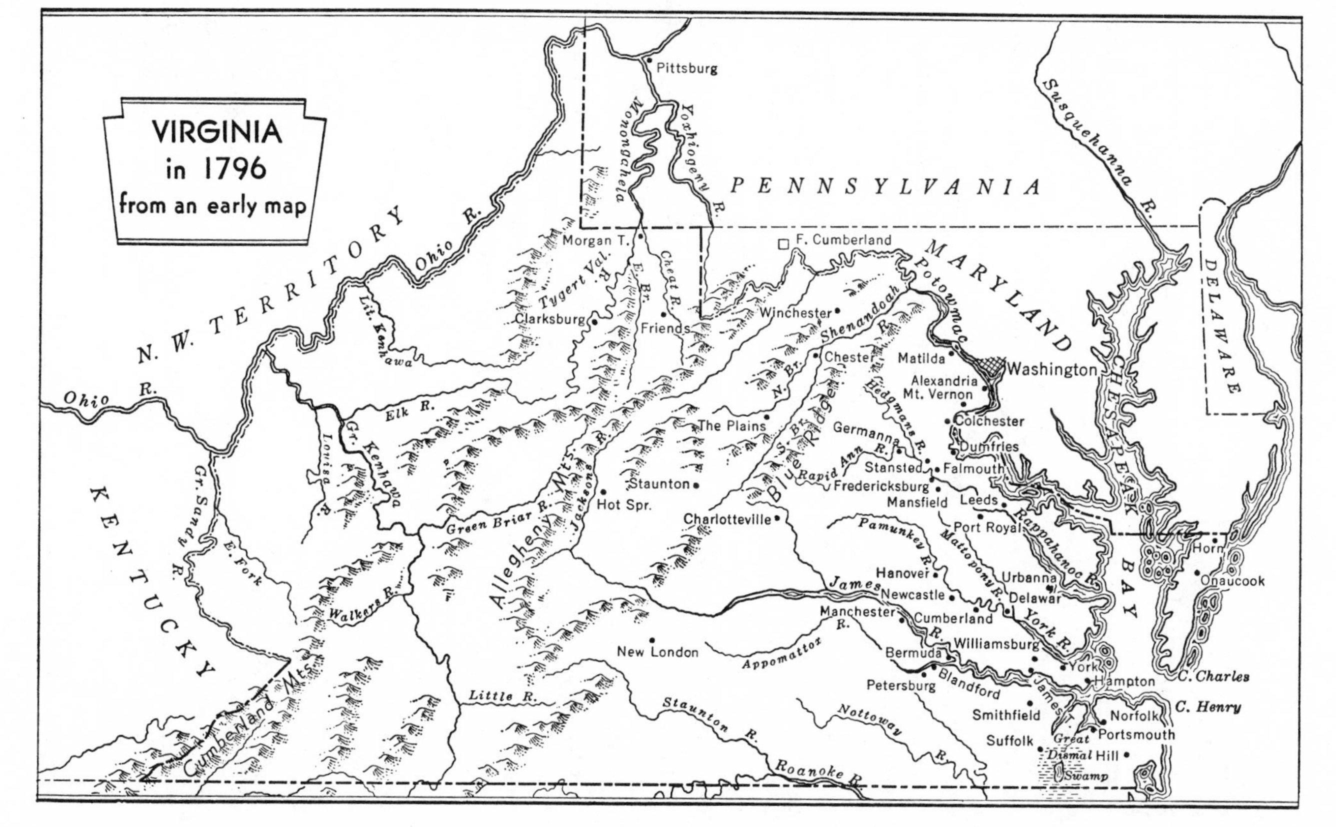

VIRGINIA
in 1796
from an early map
N. W. TERRITORY
KENTUCKY
PENNSYLVANIA
MARYLAND
DELAWARE
CHESAPEAK
BAY
Pittsburg
Monongahela
Yoxhiogeny R.
Ohio R.
Susquehanna R.
Morgan T.
F. Cumberland
Tygert Val. R.
E. Br.
Cheat R.
Clarksburg
Friends
Winchester
Lit. Kenhawa
Shenandoah R.
Potowmac
N. Br.
Chester
Matilda
Washington
Alexandria
Mt. Vernon
Colchester
Dumfries
Elk R.
Gr. Kenhawa
Louisa R.
The Plains
Germanna
Hedgmans R.
Stansted
Falmouth
Rapid Ann R.
Fredericksburg
Mansfield
Leeds
Blue Ridge
S. Br.
Staunton
Hot Spr.
Jacksons R.
Allegheny Mts.
Charlotteville
Green Briar R.
Port Royal
Rappahanoc R.
Pamunkey R.
Mattopony R.
Gr. Sandy R.
E. Fork
Hanover
Urbanna
Horn
Onaucook
James R.
Newcastle
Delawar
Walkers R.
Manchester
Cumberland
York R.
Williamsburg
New London
Appomattox R.
Bermuda
York
Hampton
C. Charles
Cumberland Mts.
Petersburg
Blandford
James T.
Little R.
Staunton R.
Nottoway R.
Smithfield
Norfolk
C. Henry
Portsmouth
Suffolk
Great Dismal Swamp
Hill
Roanoke R.

off from Augusta. It included that territory of present West Virginia lying south of the New River. Fincastle became the county seat. When Greenbrier was formed in 1777 it took from Botetourt all the territory that county possessed which is now included in West Virginia.

The year 1776 stands out as an important date for the formation of counties in western Virginia. That part of Augusta County lying west of the Alleghenies, which had long been called West Augusta, was recognized by the assembly as a separate unit and named the District of West Augusta. The boundary between Augusta and the District of West Augusta began at a point vaguely described in the statute as "a convenient point" between the headwaters of the Potomac, Cheat, and Greenbrier rivers, and ran on irregular bearings first on the highland dividing the Cheat, Greenbrier, and Tygart Valley rivers to the Monongahela, and thence up that river and the West Fort to Bingamon Creek, following that stream across to Middle Island Creek and thence down it to the Ohio. "All that territory lying to the northward of the aforesaid boundary, and to the westward of the state of Pennsylvania and Maryland, shall be deemed, and is hereby declared, to be within the district of West Augusta."

In the same year West Augusta was divided into three counties, namely Ohio, Youghiogheny, and Monongalia. When the Mason-Dixon line was extended to its western limit, it was found that the greater part of Youghiogheny lay within the boundary of Pennsylvania, and in 1785 the rest of the county was added to Ohio County. Thus Youghiogheny ceased to exist. It is sometimes referred to as the "lost county." Another county created in 1776 was Montgomery, containing the territory south and west of the Kanawha and New rivers.

It is unnecessary to describe in further detail the formation of county government in western Virginia. Enough has been said to illustrate how, as population in the west grew, counties were subdivided in order to bring the advantages of local government closer to the settlers. By the year in which American independence came, the territory of West Virginia had been explored, settled, and organized in county government. In 1776 there were nine counties: Ohio, Youghiogheny, Monongalia, Frederick, Augusta, Botetourt, Berkeley, Hampshire, and Montgomery.

The government established in these new counties was exactly the same as that in the older ones to the east. Let us now see if it proved satisfactory in the new and vigorous territory.

The Dissenting West

The political, social, and economic institutions that the people of eastern Virginia had been developing for more than a hundred and fifty years were adapted to their own peculiar manner of living. Their society was largely molded by the plantation owner and based on his ideals of daily life. Almost never did the plantation owner forsake his homestead to move to the west; he continued in possession of his land, slaves, and institutions that had been handed down from his fathers.

In the new west circumstances were very different. Many of the people coming into the Trans-Allegheny region had migrated from the states north of Virginia, and they brought with them manners, customs, and laws that had been used for years in the communities from which they came. The natives of Virginia who had changed their residence from the east to the west did not belong to the property-holding class. They were a courageous, aggressive, intelligent people of the yeoman class who had made the change of location with the hope of improving their chances for a happier life.

Beyond the mountain wall there existed an agreeable climate, natural possibilities for the development of new industry, and a materially different environment, as if it were a far country where society, institutions, and industry had to be built anew. The old rules under which the east lived could not be effectively applied to the new conditions in the west. A new, progressive policy had to be formed, with broader social, industrial, and political dimensions, to meet the needs of a wise and energetic people who occupied an undeveloped region.

In the disharmony that developed between east and west, perhaps the chief issue related to suffrage and representation. The west rejected the ownership of land as a qualification for voting, insisting that every free, white, male citizen who had attained the age of twenty-one should be a legal voter. The west also protested vigorously against inequalities of representation in the state assembly, feeling strongly that representation should be proportional to voting population, not to a ratio between population and property, which the east advocated. The latter method meant that slaves would be counted, since they were property. The west vehemently protested, arguing that since Negroes were not citizens, representation should be based only on white population.

Commercial conditions also caused discontent. When the National Road had been completed to the Ohio River (1818), convenient transportation connected the markets of western Virginia with Baltimore rather than with Richmond and Norfolk. This exclusion caused deep disappointment in the Virginia seaboard area, for the merchants there saw a lucrative trade from the Ohio Valley diverted from Virginia to the advantage of Maryland and Pennsylvania. When the Baltimore and Ohio Railroad Company applied to the Virginia legislature for a right of way through the northern part of the state, again the tidewater plantation owners interposed with objection. The building of the railroad would be a benefit to isolated western Virginia, but the east, trying to maintain its predominance, claimed that the enterprise would be of no economic benefit.

The fourth cause of difference had both a social and an economic basis. In the east slavery was popular; in the west it was very unpopular. While manual labor and personal industry were held respectable, even obligatory, by the people who had crossed the mountains, the "upper caste" in the cis-Appalachian lowlands continued to gain a livelihood through slave labor. The slaves and the non-property-owning white men did the drudgery while the masters and the property-owners devoted themselves to politics. This controversy grew. It became so heated that the men of the east sometimes referred to the people of the west as "peasants," while the westerners hurled back across the mountains such unfriendly epithets as "you eastern bourbons."

A fifth cause of division concerned the distribution of public funds for educational and institutional purposes. The west claimed that it had never been given educational privileges in proportion to the amount of taxes paid. There was a great deal of justification for this complaint, for an undue portion of the school funds had been devoted to eastern institutions. The same complaint was made with respect to funds for public improvements such as roads, bridges, canals, courthouses, etc.

A sixth cause of difference related to elections. The western reformers insisted that the governor, judges, and county officers should be elected by popular vote. Under the law, they were appointive. The west demanded also that the governor's council be abolished and that the sessions of the legislature be limited to a definite number of days. Strife over these problems ultimately became so sharp that in 1828 the question of calling a constitutional convention was submitted by the legislature to a popular vote. It carried by about 5,000 majority.

The Constitutional Convention of 1829–30

The convention of 1829–1830 was another assemblage of notable talent. Although most of the illustrious men who had made the convention of 1776 famous had passed on, others quite capable had arisen to take their places. The membership included two ex-Presidents of the United States, James Madison and James Monroe; the Chief Justice of the United States Supreme Court, John Marshall; Edmund Pendleton; and Philip N. Nicholas. To this group of popular statesmen may be added others quite as able: Benjamin W. Leigh of Chesterfield County, Abel P. Upshur of Washington County, Philip Doddridge and Alexander Campbell of Brooke County, Charles Morgan of Monongalia County, and many others of extraordinary ability.

Each of the twenty-four senatorial districts elected four delegates who met at Richmond, October 5, 1829. As a result of the sharp divisions of opinions on political principles and the presence of able spokesmen for both sides, a series of powerful debates followed.

SUFFRAGE AND REPRESENTATION

"The greatest grievance proposed to be remedied," said Philip Doddridge in the convention, "is the inequality in the representation, and this especially in the House of Delegates; the next, in point of magnitude and general concern, is the freehold restriction on the electoral franchise." These two questions were interrelated, the one depending on the other. Solving the one would go a long way toward solving the other. The east, as we have seen, insisted on property as a qualification for suffrage and wanted representation to be based on a ratio involving both population and taxation; the west demanded that the suffrage be extended to every white male of twenty-one or over and that representation be based on population alone. The possession of property was the point of difference.

The point of view of the east was expressed by Benjamin W. Leigh of Chesterfield County: "I insist that to insure wisdom in the Government, and a strict observance of justice, and a spirit of patriotism in the administration of public affairs, we ought to vest the right of suffrage (the fountain in our system of political power) in that class of men, who, holding the property of the State, are the most interested in the administration of justice; in that class of men, who own interests of the commonwealth. And this is the class of freeholders." From the west Alexander Campbell of Brooke County retorted: "I, sir, insist that the people are capable of self-government, and that they ought to enjoy it; that the power shall not reside in A or B, but in the whole community; and that no free white male citizen should be excluded, except those who have excluded themselves by the immorality of their own character."

Sentiment on these questions was not entirely divided by the mountain range. Early in the convention Chief Justice Marshall took up the issue in support of the people of the west, and perhaps no one presented their cause better than he did. In his plea Marshall said, "Your memorialists feel the difficulty of undertaking calmly to repel charges and insinuation involving in infamy themselves, and so large a portion of their fellow citizens. To be deprived of their rightful equality, and to hear as an apology that they are too ignorant and vicious to enjoy it, is no ordinary trial of patience. Yet they will suppress the indignant emotions these sweeping denunciations are well calculated to excite. The freeholders themselves know them to be unfounded: Why, else, are arms placed in the hands of a body of disaffected citizens, so ignorant, so depraved, and so numerous. In the hour of danger they have drawn no invidious distinctions between the sons of Virginia. The muster rolls have undergone no scrutiny, no comparison with the land books, with a view to expunge those who have been struck from the ranks of freemen. If the landless citizens have been ignominiously driven from the polls, in time of peace, they have at least been generously summoned, in war, to the battlefield. Nor have they disobeyed the summons, or, less profusely than others, poured out their blood in defense of that country which is asked to disown them. Will it be said they owe allegiance to the Government that gives them protection? Be it so: and if they acknowledge the obligation; if privileges are really extended to them in defense of which they may reasonably be required to shed their blood, have they not motives, irresistible motives, of attachment to the community? Have they not an interest, a deep interest, in perpetuating the blessings they enjoy, and a right consequently, to guard those blessings, not from foreign aggression merely, but from domestic encroachment?"

With respect to the conflict over representation, ex-President Monroe suggested a compromise: "Let one of the branches of the Legislature be placed upon the basis of white population alone, and the other branch on the compound basis of population and taxation. Will you give the basis of white population only to the House of Delegates or to the Senate? I think it will be safer, for both sections

. . . if you will give it to the House of Delegates, and for the compound basis to prevail in the Senate." This suggestion satisfied neither side. In the view of the west, a principle was involved which could admit of no compromise.

In the end no real principle of representation was adopted; instead, the convention accepted a temporary basis for agreement which reconciled but did not satisfy. This arrangement, suggested by William F. Gordon of Albemarle County, divided the state into four districts and allotted somewhat arbitrarily to each a definite number of assemblymen. The district west of the Alleghenies contained twenty-six counties and was to have thirty-one delegates in the state assembly; the district lying between the Alleghenies and the Blue Ridge, fourteen counties and twenty-five delegates; the one east of the Blue Ridge and reaching down to tidewater, twenty-nine counties and forty-two delegates; and the district occupying the territory from tidewater to the sea, thirty-six counties and four towns, thirty-six delegates.

Delegate Gordon provided for thirty-two senatorial districts in the state, each electing one senator. As well as the boundaries of these districts can now be ascertained, only eight senators were to be elected from that part of the state now occupied by West Virginia, and only six of these from the region west of the Alleghenies. In the state senate the voice of western Virginia would be smothered.

According to arrangement, adopted in the convention, the general assembly, after 1841, and at intervals thereafter of not less than ten years, would make a reapportionment of senators and delegates, provided two-thirds of the members concurred. The number of senators was never to exceed thirty-six and the membership in the house of delegates was not to be above one hundred and fifty. All assemblymen had to be freeholders. But as a matter of interest let us note that "all persons holding lucrative offices and ministers of the Gospel and priests of every denomination, shall be incapable of being elected members of either House of Assembly." This statement contains a strange doctrine that disqualified many enterprising and able citizens. It was specified that meetings of the assembly were to be held at least once annually; no other limitation was placed on the length of the session, which could therefore legally continue three hundred and sixty-five days if the politicians so ordained.

With respect to suffrage, the constitution stated: "Every white male citizen of the Commonwealth, resident therein, aged twenty-one years and upwards, being qualified to exercise the Right of Suffrage according to the former Constitution and laws; and every such citizen being possessed, or whose tenants for years, at will or at sufferance, is possessed of an estate of freehold in land of the value of twenty-five dollars" has the privilege to vote. This requirement disfranchised about 35,000 white men of legal age in Virginia. For the moment the east had defeated the west.

OTHER POINTS AT ISSUE

The western reformers pleaded that the governor and the judiciary, both elected by the assembly and therefore dependent upon it, be freed from the domination of the legislature by being made subject to popular election. With respect to the status of the governor, Philip Doddridge of Brooke County stated: "What is the executive power in Virginia? It is nothing more or less than an emanation of the legislative power. He is appointed every year, and is responsible only to those to whom he is looking for appointment." Doddridge wanted him made directly responsible to the people instead; and he urged that this principle be strengthened by the abolition of the executive council, on which the governor relied heavily for advice. Similarly it was urged that the judiciary be made independent of the legislature so that its decisions would be founded on law and justice, not biased by endeavors to assuage the irritation of some dissatisfied assemblyman.

The constitution as finally adopted made only slight concessions to this point of view. The governor's term was extended to three years, but he was still to be elected by joint ballot of the assembly. The council was reduced to three members, also elected by the assembly for three years. No material changes were made in the judiciary, including the county court. The assembly continued to choose the judges, while the sheriffs, coroners, and members of the county courts received their commissions from the governor's hand. Thus the legislature, still based on an unfair principle of representation, retained undue power in the executive and judicial spheres.

ADOPTION OF THE CONSTITUTION

When the new constitution was submitted to the qualified electorate, it was ratified by a vote of 26,055 to 15,566. But every county lying west of the Alleghenies that later became a part of West Virginia voted solidly against it, which made it more evident than ever before that in the west a strong unity of political sentiment existed against the way the business of the state had been conducted at Richmond. Local newspapers in the west sent out calls, asking for another convention to be assembled in the west to treat with the "eastern nabobs" for a division of Virginia. The new constitution was denounced as unfit for a free people and unwholesome for a civil society. From time to time echoes of "separation" and "division" resounded across the Alleghenies in a voice loud enough to be heard to the farthest limits of the eastern shore. The constitution had been adopted, but many points at issue remained unsolved.

From 1830 to 1850

Although the new constitution was a disappointment to the Trans-Allegheny people, they did not falter. As more immigrants moved into the west, improved conveniences awaited them. Trade and travel were invigorated by the building of turnpikes over which passed covered wagons and riders on horseback. Slowly the path of empire made its way westward. Neither mountain nor constitution could impede its progress. By 1827 a stage line was established between Charleston and Lewisburg, making one trip a week. Later this road continued to the coastal region of Virginia. It became perhaps the greatest bid for trade between the Ohio Valley and the seaboard since the completion of the National Road to Wheeling in 1818. The improvement of the military road made by General Andrew Lewis on his memorable march from Fort Union to Point Pleasant, where he defeated the Indians in 1774, afforded another important highway connecting the east with the Ohio. Farther north, the Staunton and Parkersburg Pike, which formed a direct connection between the Shenandoah Valley and the Ohio, was completed in 1856. The Northwestern Turnpike provided an improved highway between Winchester and Parkersburg; by 1848 it was macadamized from Grafton to Parkersburg. From these main highways other roads radiated to the most remote settlements.

An increase of western population was a natural consequence of the improved connecting highways. From 1830 to 1850 this increase amounted to more than 6,000 persons annually, besides many thousands more who passed through western Virginia on their way to the prairie region, the great plains, and the new cotton kingdom of Alabama, Mississippi, Louisiana and Texas. With the growth of population came the development of industry. The Baltimore and Ohio Railroad pushed westward and reached Wheeling in 1852. This project was only the start of railroad building in West Virginia. The extensive evergreen forests began to fall before the woodman's ax. Enterprising men explored coal fields and stimulated industry by building steel mills, coke ovens, and factories of many kinds. The old methods of forging implements, weaving cloth, making clothing, and building homes were breaking down to be replaced by the new.

All this growth of industry in the west required a more united political organization. By 1830 only twenty-three counties had been formed in western Virginia. In the next twenty years nineteen more came into existence. In the constitutional convention of 1830 it had been predicted that, should the present rate of migration continue, the west would soon exceed the east in white population. This prophecy was coming true and when it did come to pass, the militant west would demand equality instead of pleading for it. During the twenty years following the constitutional convention western Virginia had grown powerful; it had come of age and would soon ask for freedom. The east could scarcely continue to keep the discordant west under control.

There never was a people better prepared to establish a state and promote its welfare than those intrepid souls who had entered western Virginia. They were of excellent lineage, wise, courageous, frugal, and persevering. Many were descended from those who had fought in the Revolutionary War; others possessed the stamina to cross the ocean from England, Scotland, and Ireland to find a haven in the hills of West Augusta; they were the offspring of the heroes who fought with Bruce at Bannockburn, with Cromwell at Marston Moor, and with Wolfe at Quebec. Their representatives in the state assembly prosecuted their quarrel with the east. In every session the same old questions came forth to annoy the antagonists who had fought in vain to suppress them.

In the meantime western Virginia in fact suffered under the constitution. The legislature refused to permit the further extension of railroads into the west. No new institutions were created, no public buildings constructed, the highways already built were badly neglected, and natural supplies of coal, oil, and gas remained undeveloped. The region suffered as if it were not a part of the state. No United States Senator came from the west; only one governor had resided in that region; [4] and legislation both national and local neglected the western section. One cannot wonder that a cry for division came from beyond the mountains.

[4] Joseph Johnson of Harrison County was elected governor in 1851.

The slave-holding leaders in the east grimly held on to their waning power as long as they could, but at last, seeing the handwriting on the wall, agreed to another constitutional convention. They designed, however, to hold the controlling power in the meeting. In 1850 the state assembly passed a bill providing for a constitutional convention, with the definite stipulation that the number of delegates was to be established on the mixed basis and not on the white basis. If the white population had been the basis for representation, the west would have had a majority of thirteen in the convention, but with both whites and Negroes counted, the east had a majority of seventeen. Though the westerners stood out against a convention with delegates elected on this basis, the bill was passed by popular vote of the whole state.

CHAPTER 7

The Constitution of 1851

The Reform Convention of 1850–51

Many important changes had taken place west of the mountains during the twenty years since the last constitutional convention, and the eastern politicians were not altogether blind to what was happening. Industrialists projected railroads across the Alleghenies toward Wheeling and Parkersburg, thus opening great resources of coal and timber to the markets at Baltimore, Philadelphia, and New York. Within a few years the whistles of steam locomotives would arouse from their age-old slumbers the prairies of Ohio, Indiana, and Illinois, making western Virginia the door through which the industrial east brought its raw products from the agricultural west. And progress did not stop there. Plantation owners and lines of slaves, single file, came out of the old eastern seaboard region bound for the lower Mississippi via the National Road with its western terminal on the Ohio at Wheeling. Three other great highways were reaching out through western Virginia to the Ohio River, crossing the state west of the Blue Ridge.[1] Over these new avenues of trade and travel the wealth of the old east poured night and day into the Ohio Valley just as surely as the current of that river flowed toward the

[1] The three highways were the Winchester-Parkersburg, Staunton-Parkersburg and the James River-Kanawha turnpikes.

"Father of Waters." Over the new highways farmers came to buy cheap lands on which to build homesteads and artisans arrived to build new factories. A multitude of alien immigrants chose western Virginia as the most suitable place for their homes. While eastern Virginia grew weaker, the west increased in strength. Even by 1840 the white population west of the Alleghenies approached an equality in numbers with that of the slave-holding region of the state; ten years later, the west outstripped the east by approximately 2,000 white people and far surpassed it in the assessed valuation of wealth.

The newspapers printed in the new towns along the Ohio tirelessly inquired, "Why should our white population of 271,000 be represented by ten senators and fifty-six delegates while the 269,000 white people in the east have nineteen senators and seventy-eight delegates?" Charges not only of unequal representation but of fraud in elections, unfair appropriations, and a hundred other accusations were hurled back and forth across the Alleghenies. Talk of separation was not uncommon.

It was under these conditions that the constitutional convention met, one hundred and thirty-five delegates strong, in Richmond on October 14, 1850. It was the year for the taking of the census of the United States, and information gathered in the census would be of vital importance in the convention's work. The session was therefore adjourned until January 6, 1851, the earliest date at which the new information could be made available.

It is not necessary here to discuss the debates carried on in the meeting. Inevitably, sharp dispute arose at once. The issues had not changed since 1830, though at least one of them, the question of the abolition of slavery, had assumed new proportions. The war of words continued as before, but this time the west was in a better position to enforce its demands. The new constitution was approved by the convention on August 1, 1851, and accepted by the people by a vote of 75,748 to 11,063 on the fourth Thursday of the following October.

Let us now examine the provisions of the new document.

The Qualification of Voters

The old law requiring the ownership of property for the privilege of voting was replaced by the statement: "Every white male citizen of the commonwealth, of the age of twenty-one years, who has been a resident of the state for two years, and of the county, city or town where he offers to vote for twelve months next preceding an election — and no other person — shall be qualified to vote for members of the general assembly and for all officers elective by the people." Each county was to keep a register of the names of its qualified voters. After declaring that persons enlisted in the military, naval, and marine service could not claim residence in the state by reason of being stationed therein, and that paupers, persons of unsound mind, and anyone convicted of infamous offense could not vote, the constitution made this strange provision: "In all elections votes shall be given openly, or viva voce, and not by ballot; but dumb persons entitled to suffrage may vote by ballot." The extension of the voting privilege to all white male citizens is what the west had striven to attain for two score years. Its adoption was in line with the action of other states. By 1850 all the original states had revised their constitutional law in such ways as to increase the number of voters.

The Legislative Department

THE HOUSE OF DELEGATES

The constitution provided that the house of delegates should be composed of one hundred and fifty-two members, apportioned according to the census of 1850. Of this number the counties later incorporated in the state of West Virginia would elect only forty-seven. The term of office was two years.

Any person was eligible to the house of delegates who had attained, at the time of his election, the age of twenty-one years, and who was a resident, qualified to vote, of the district from which he was elected — except a person holding a state, county or city office for which a salary was paid, a salaried officer of a banking corporation, an attorney for the commonwealth, or a minister or priest of any religious denomination.

THE SENATE

The state senate was to consist of fifty members, one from each district, elected for a term of four years. To be qualified a senator must have attained the age of twenty-five years, be a resident of his district, and a legal voter. The exceptions mentioned above for the house of delegates applied to the senate as well.

Only eleven of the senators could be elected from that part of the state which later became West Virginia. The number of representatives allotted to the eastern part of the state was still out of proportion to that of the west and was not satisfactory to the westerners, but an agreement had been reached in the convention that in 1865 there should be a reapportionment of membership in the legislature. If this reapportionment was still not satisfactory, then the governor was to submit the question of apportionment to the voters for a final decision. This was the nearest western Virginia ever came to having the membership of the state assembly based on the number of white people living in the commonwealth.

Slavery

The general assembly could not emancipate any slave, but if a slave should be given his freedom by his master, he was required to leave the state within one year thereafter, otherwise he would again be reduced to servitude. The legislature, however, retained its power to limit the authority of the owners to emancipate their slaves. That is, supervision over free Negroes and slaves remained in the hands of the assembly. Every slave aged twelve or over was taxed on an appraisal value of three hundred dollars.

General Provisions

Lotteries were forbidden, and the sale of tickets or chances for lotteries constituted a violation of law. Lotteries had had wide use in the raising of funds to build churches, schools, and roads. A boundary of land usually constituted the prize for which eager people bought chances.

Definite rules determined the manner of forming new counties, one of which stated that a county exceeding fifty miles in length could be divided at the discretion of the state assembly.

The assembly was to confer on the courts the power to grant divorces, change the names of persons, and direct the sale of estates belonging to infants or to persons under legal disability. Unlike the national Constitution, the constitution of 1851 provided that bills and resolutions could originate in either house of the legislature. The state senate therefore had power to originate bills for raising revenue.

The Executive Department

THE GOVERNOR

According to the new constitution, the electorate of the state were to choose the governor by direct vote. His term was four years, and he was ineligible to succeed himself. In these laws one may see that the constitution of Virginia had begun to take on some of the colorings originated in the west for the people had become conscious of their own power and willed to use it.

To be eligible for governor one was required to be a native-born citizen of the United States, to have been a citizen of Virginia for five years, and to have attained the age of thirty years. The mother state of presidents of the United States did not take any chances on the qualifications of its governor. He was allowed an annual salary of $5,000, and was required to reside at the seat of government.

The constitution imposed many duties on the governor. He was to execute the laws, report to the assembly from time to time on the condition of the state, recommend bills to it, convene it in special session when he deemed it proper to do so, command the military and naval forces of the state, conduct matters of business with other states, remit fines and penalties under rules prescribed by law, commute capital punishment, grant reprieves and pardons, etc. The new constitution abolished the governor's council, against which much criticism had been directed.

THE LIEUTENANT-GOVERNOR

The qualifications and manner of electing the lieutenant-governor were the same as for the governor. In case of vacancy in the governorship all the duties of the office devolved upon the lieutenant-governor, who then became the acting chief executive. Officially the lieutenant-governor presided over the senate; for this service he received compensation equal to that paid to the speaker of the house. His role in the state government was strikingly similar to that of the vice president in the national government.

OTHER OFFICERS

A secretary of state, a treasurer, and an auditor of public accounts were to be elected by a joint vote of the two houses of the assembly; thus the state held on to the traditional custom of allowing the assembly to choose state officers who served two years only. The secretary of state was to keep a record of the official acts of the governor, while the powers and duties of the treasurer and auditor were continued as before, or as thereafter prescribed by law. The demand for reform had not been so much for a modification of executive power as for extension of suffrage and a change in the method of election.

The Board of Public Works

The constitution created a board of public works, consisting of three commissioners. The state was divided into three districts of nearly equal populations, and the voters in each district elected one member of the board for a term of six years. The law fixed the compensation of the members. These officers exercised extensive jurisdiction. They appointed all officials employed on the public work of the state and all persons representing the interests of Virginia — those concerned with internal improvements such as roads, bridges, canals, with the geological survey, and with borrowing money on the credit of the state. The business of public improvements was thus placed under their direct supervision, and this business was considerable, for the building of canals, railroads, and highways had become matters of major interest in Virginia.

Since the board had power to borrow money, it possessed authority to guarantee the payment of state debts. It raised money by placing tolls on roads and bridges, by foreclosing mortgages, and by other means. Annually the board of public works made a report of its transactions to the legislature. These reports contain information of great value to the modern research student and historian.

The Judicial Department

THE SUPREME COURT OF APPEALS

The highest court was styled the supreme court of appeals. It consisted of five judges, one elected from each of the five judicial divisions of the state. The judges were elected by the qualified voters for a term of twelve years. At the time of election a judge had to be at least thirty-five years of age, and during his continuance in office he was obliged to reside in his own division.

The supreme court had appellate jurisdiction only, except in cases of habeas corpus, mandamus, and prohibition. It had no jurisdiction in civil causes in which the amount involved, exclusive of costs, was less than five hundred dollars, except in cases concerning the title or boundary of land; the probate of a will; the appointment of a personal representative, guardian, committee, or curator; a mill, road, ferry, way, or landing; or the right of a corporation or county to levy tolls or taxes. The power of the court, therefore, was wide and comprehensive; its jurisdiction included matters of public interest which could scarcely be decided in any other court than the one having supreme jurisdiction.

DISTRICT COURTS

The five judicial sections of the state were subdivided into ten districts, in each of which the constitution required that a court be held at least once a year. The people elected no district judges as such: the judge of the supreme court of appeals residing in the section in which the district was located and the judges of the circuit courts within the district officiated at the district sessions. It appears here that the organization of the judiciary wisely prevented the election of too many officers. In general the judges of the district court heard appeals from the lower tribunals. However, it had original jurisdiction in cases of mandamus, habeas corpus, and prohibition.

CIRCUIT COURTS

The state had twenty-one judicial circuits, in each of which the voters elected a judge who held office for a term of eight years. At the time of his election he had to be at least thirty years of age, and during his continuance in office a resident of the circuit in which he served. The voters of each county, also, elected a circuit clerk for a term of six years.

The constitution required the circuit judge to hold court at least twice a year in each county in his circuit. The authority of the court extended to cases of general consequence: a major part of them amounted to appeals from the lower tribunals.

COUNTY COURTS

In each county there was a county court which held its sessions monthly. The justices of the peace, elected by the voters meeting in common council, constituted the county court. Each county contained a number of districts, as nearly equal as possible in territory and population. The voters in each district chose four justices of the peace, commissioned by the governor, for a term of four years. At their first meeting the justices selected one of their number as the presiding officer of the court. For their services they received a per diem compensation but were forbidden to accept any fees. This arrangement was a continuation of the old system of local judiciary that had existed many years.

The court acted as custodian for the courthouse, the clerk's office, and the jail. It had jurisdiction to hear and determine all cases at law or in chancery within the county, except criminal cases the punishment whereof might have been death or imprisonment in the penitentiary, and except civil cases wherein the property or money involved exceeded twenty dollars. The power and jurisdiction of justices of the peace were prescribed by law.

Other County Officers

The voters in each county elected a clerk of the county court, a surveyor, an attorney for the commonwealth, a sheriff, and at least one commissioner of revenue. The clerk and surveyor served for six years, the attorney for four years, the sheriff and commissioner for two years. One constable was elected in each district [2] and at least one overseer of the poor, with an additional number if the county court so directed.

Any person who had served as sheriff for two successive terms was ineligible to the same office for the next term, or to any other political office within one year succeeding the expiration of his term.

Conclusion

The constitution that became operative in 1852 was truly a reform constitution. The old idea of political power controlled by a few distinguished citizens had given way to a bestowal of power upon the electorate. No longer did the assembly choose the governor and judges; no longer did the governor appoint the members of the county courts. The three departments of the government were thus made independent of one another and responsible to the voters themselves. Above all, the voting privilege that had been enjoyed solely by the propertied class was now extended to all white male citizens of twenty-one years or over. Surely the government of Virginia was becoming a government of the people.

---

[2] In the fourth district of Greenbrier County the county court ordered the election of two constables.

CHAPTER 8

The Thirty-Fifth State

The Question of Secession

INTRODUCTION

By the time the constitution of 1851 was ratified and placed in operation, war clouds had begun to gather on the country's horizon. As time went on, the sky grew darker. The peril that menaced the whole country portended a division of Virginia. It has been related that many of the people who established homes along the tributaries of the Ohio had migrated from the states north of the Potomac. Along with other convictions, they had brought with them a hatred of slavery. Therefore, when the policy of extending slavery into the territories of the United States showed the ugly promise of dividing the Union into two hostile camps, it was not hard to predict which camp western Virginia would join. When the day of decision came, the government of the Old Dominion turned from the Union, while the western region of the state held loyally to it. The east and west had had many differences; this was to be the crucial one.

MEETING OF THE GENERAL ASSEMBLY

On January 7, 1861, the assembly met in extraordinary session at the call of Governor John Letcher. A special session foretold special and urgent business. Though the governor in his call had mentioned other matters for consideration, everyone knew that secession was the burning issue, and discussion of it began at once. Following very heated discussion of the course Virginia should follow in the national crisis, the assembly finally ordered an election of delegates to a convention which would determine whether Virginia should adhere to the Union or secede.

THE RICHMOND CONVENTION

The election was held on February 4, only three weeks after the call was issued. The electorate had only a short time to make its decision on such an important question. The campaign, though short, was vigorous and in some instances bitter. The candidates declared themselves for the Union or for secession, and on that principle all the votes were cast. The air was charged with feelings, and differences were sharply drawn.

The convention assembled at Richmond on February 13, 1861. There were one hundred fifty-two delegates, forty-seven from the counties later included in West Virginia. At first nonsecession sentiment prevailed strongly in the convention, but the rising pressure of external events as North and South prepared for armed conflict favored the secessionist members. While the session went on, President Lincoln was inaugurated, Fort Sumter was attacked, and the flag of the Union was torn from its place over the dome of the Richmond capitol. On April 17, amid wild harangues and confusion, the convention by a vote of eighty-eight to fifty-five passed the ordinance of secession and declared the tie of Virginia to the Union dissolved.

The convention had not been endowed with power to make the final decision, and provision was made for submitting the issue to the people for approval on May 23, the date for the regular election of members of the legislature. In the meantime, however, the convention ratified a league of union with the Confederacy, and preparations for war with the Union went forward.

War had already begun and Virginia was in a tumult before the day appointed for the election. Under the circumstances a reliable popular vote could scarcely be taken. According to a proclamation issued by Governor Letcher, the total vote of Virginia was 137,911 for secession, 23,607 against. At all events, the western counties voted strongly against it. The western members in the convention had voted thirty-two to eleven against secession (four cast no vote);

and according to the *Daily National Intelligencer* the popular majority in the western counties was 13,378 against secession.

The Clarksburg Meeting

When the convention passed the secession ordinance, the loyal western delegates hastened back across the Alleghenies to take the lead in crushing disunion sentiment in their home region. Among these leaders were Waitman T. Willey of Morgantown, John S. Carlile of Clarksburg, and Chester D. Hubbard of Wheeling. Upon arriving home they gathered the loyal people together in local assemblies to declare their fealty to the Union. Public gatherings were held in many places, such as Pruntytown, Morgantown, Parkersburg, and Wheeling.

The most important of these meetings, for subsequent events, was the one held at Clarksburg on April 22, largely through the influence of John S. Carlile. About one thousand Unionists attended. The meeting expressed its thoroughgoing support of President Lincoln and his policies. It vehemently condemned the action of the secessionists in the Richmond convention and supported a movement to form a provisional government to replace the one which had severed its connection with the union. To this end it adopted a declaration apprising the people of the political crisis in the state and recommending that each county of northwestern Virginia elect at least five loyal and patriotic delegates to an assembly at Wheeling on May 13, whose purpose would be to form a definite policy of action. The assembly then adjourned.

Express riders hastened from village to village and from county to county to inform the people of the results of the Clarksburg meeting and to urge the electorate to choose its wisest and most courageous men to go to the Wheeling Convention. On that April night in 1861 there were a hundred patriots moving in haste in western Virginia, as active and as worthy as Paul Revere had been more than four score years before in Massachusetts.

The First Wheeling Convention

The delegates whose election was authorized by the Clarksburg meeting assembled in Washington Hall, Wheeling, on May 13, 1861, and after various preliminaries began work under Dr. John M. Moss of Wood County as permanent chairman. The four hundred delegates represented twenty-six different counties, ranging in numbers from one from Roane to sixty-four from Wood. The chairman appointed a committee on state and federal relations, consisting of one delegate from each county represented, to which were to be referred all resolutions on which action would be taken by the convention.

A summary of the committee's report at the close of the session will indicate the temper and the accomplishment of the convention. The report declared that the action of the Richmond convention in attempting to repeal the ratification of the Constitution was itself unconstitutional, null, and void, and that the agreement to join the Confederacy was a violation of law. It implored the people to vote against secession in the May 23 election, and requested the voters of western Virginia to elect their members of Congress and their state and local officers at that time as they had done before. It continued that in event the ordinance of secession was ratified the electorate should, on June 4, 1861, choose delegates to another convention "to devise such measures and take such action as the safety and welfare of the people they represent may demand, each county to appoint a number of representatives to said convention equal to double the number to which it will be entitled in the next House of Delegates." It further provided that these assemblymen-elect chosen on May 23 who concurred in the views of "this convention" be entitled to seats in the next convention, which was to be held on June 11, 1861. Other resolutions asserted a hope for the settlement of the disturbance without war, declared a close adherence to the Union, and extended authority to a central committee of eight members to reconvene the convention when it was expedient to do so. The central committee had authority also to prepare and circulate an address to the people, setting forth the principles embodied in the resolutions.

But the most important section was one reflecting the deep and ultimate objective of the representatives of the people of western Virginia. Earlier in the session, delegate Carlile had offered a resolution to instruct the committee on state and federal relations to report an ordinance declaring the connection dissolved between the loyal counties of the west and the rest of the state, and to propose a constitution and form of government for the new state, to be known as New Virginia, all of which should be effective from the time it was approved by the national Congress. Severe criticism was leveled at Carlile for his haste and precipitate judgment, and the resolution failed of adoption. But the views expressed by many delegates in the discussion were such that the final report of the committee included the following significant statement: "Inasmuch as it is a conceded political axiom that government is founded on the consent of the governed and instituted for their good, and it cannot be denied that the course pursued by the ruling power of the State is utterly subversive and destructive of our interests, we believe we may rightfully and successfully appeal to the proper authorities of Virginia to permit us peaceably and lawfully to separate from the residue of the State and form ourselves into a government to give effect to the wishes, views and interests of our constituents." In this statement is found the backlog of the political fire burning in western Virginia.

The report was adopted with only two dissenting votes. This triumph was received with effusive cheers from the convention floor, and after a round of speech-making adjournment was voted amid great enthusiasm. The members, however, were not yet discharged from their duties; they would hold office till the meeting of the next convention.

The Work of the Committee

Upon adjournment affairs were left in the hands of the central committee. It vigorously urged the voters to ballot against secession on May 23. As we have seen, western Virginia voted strongly against secession on that day, but the statewide vote favored it. The committee then forcefully appealed to the loyal people of the state to be diligent in the choice of the delegates to be elected on June 4. It was also in constant communication with county organizations, gathering and consolidating power, vehemently driving onward in its effort to create a new state. The idea had taken hold and day by day it gathered momentum. Belated attempts of Governor Letcher to appease the west were ignored.

For a time the Unionists were hampered when the government at Richmond ordered a censorship on the United States mail. Letters, newspapers and other documents were destroyed. At some places postmasters refused to deliver the mail; at other places it was burnt upon arrival. This trouble continued until the postal authorities at Washington suspended mail service in Virginia, and directed mails in western Virginia to be sent to Wheeling in order that Union men might not be deprived of postal services.

While these important happenings occurred, General George B. McClellan moved the right wing of his army across the Ohio into western Virginia at Parkersburg and the left wing at Wheeling, in all 20,000 troops, thus carrying the conflict of arms to the soil of the discontented west. On June 3, 1861, the first land battle of the war occurred at Philippi.

It is no part of our present purpose to review the events of the war. Instead, we shall turn again to the events incident to the making of a new state.

The Second Wheeling Convention

MEMBERSHIP AND ORGANIZATION

At the election held on June 4, 1861, seventy-seven delegates were chosen from thirty-four loyal counties of western Virginia. Notice of the election had been adequate to allow the voters to make wise decisions and to permit the delegates to become acquainted with the sentiments of the electorate. In addition to the elected delegates there were present the loyal members of the state assembly, who brought the total membership of the convention to one hundred.[1] The members were empowered "to devise such measures and take such action as the safety and welfare of the people they represent may demand." Actually, the destiny of the people of western Virginia was in their hands, and they proved worthy of that responsibility. It should be noted that all the members swore their fidelity to the Constitution and laws of the United States, which act in itself was a repudiation of the ordinance of secession.

At two o'clock, June 11, 1861, the convention assembled in Washington Hall,[2] Wheeling. The session was opened with a prayer offered by the Reverend Gordon Battelle, presiding elder of the Methodist Episcopal Church of the Wheeling District. Francis H. Pierpont of Fairmont called the meeting to order, and on his motion Dr. Dennis B. Dorsey of Morgantown was installed as temporary chairman. Gibson L. Cranmer of Ohio County was chosen temporary secretary. After the appointment of committees on credentials, on rules, and on permanent organization, the meeting adjourned until the following day.

Upon receiving the report of the committee on permanent organization, the assembly made Arthur I. Boreman of Wood County per-

---

1 Three were later stricken from the list – one failed to appear, one refused to take the oath of office, and one resigned.

2 After the first two days the meetings were held in the United States courtroom in the customs house.

manent chairman, Gibson L. Cranmer secretary, and Thomas Hornbrook sergeant-at-arms. On motion of John S. Carlile, a committee on business, consisting of thirteen able men, was appointed. All matters relating to state and federal affairs had to be referred to this committee before final action could be taken by the convention.

Basing its claim on the provision in the Virginia Bill of Rights that the people have an unqualified right peaceably to assemble and to change and amend their form of government when it may become necessary, the Wheeling convention unanimously adopted an ordinance declaring their intention to resist all oppression and to maintain forever the rights and liberties of the people under the Constitution of the United States. This resolution had wide implications and was diametrically opposed to what had been done at Richmond.

REORGANIZATION OF THE STATE GOVERNMENT

On the fourth day delegate Carlile moved that the state government of Virginia be reorganized. He asserted that the regularly elected state officers, by joining with the secession movement, had definitely vacated their offices in the state, and that Virginia was therefore without a legal government. The assembly adopted his motion without a dissenting vote. Unity prevailed in the convention; business moved smoothly toward a definite objective.

The motion for reorganization was passed in the name of the people of Virginia. It contained five important divisions. The first one provided that a governor, lieutenant-governor, and attorney general be appointed by the convention for a period of six months or until their successors could be elected. The general assembly would arrange as soon as possible for a regular election of officers to succeed those appointed. The second resolution provided for a council of five members to be named by the convention. The function of this body would be to advise with the governor on matters of administration. Third, a declaration was made to the effect that the loyal delegates and senators chosen at the election held on May 23 constituted the true assembly of Virginia, which was called to convene in session at Wheeling on July 1 and to organize according to the law of the state. Fourth, all state and local officers were required to take an oath to support the Constitution of the United States and uphold the government of Virginia as restored by the convention then in session. The fifth provision, a continuation of the fourth, stated that any officer of the state refusing to take the oath would immediately be set aside and the office declared vacant. Following this act the governor would fill the vacancy by appointment.

The ordinances set up a temporary government of Virginia, loyal to the Union and designed to protect the safety and welfare of the people. There were thus at this time two governments in Virginia, the one functioning at Wheeling and the other at Richmond. They tried to attain opposite objectives. Each refused to recognize the other; each exercised the power of a state over a regional following.

NEW OFFICERS OF VIRGINIA

The day after approving the ordinance the convention elected a governor in the person of Francis Harrison Pierpont, of Marion County, a leading delegate in the convention. They chose Daniel Polsey of Mason County lieutenant-governor, and elected five councilmen, namely, Peter G. Van Winkle of Wood, William A. Harrison of Harrison, William Lazier of Monongalia, Daniel Lamb of Ohio, and James W. Paxton of Ohio. James S. Wheat of Ohio County was the choice for attorney general. These were the officers of the reorganized government of Virginia.

A declaration of the people of Virginia had been presented and signed by every delegate present. It soundly denounced the secession movement as having usurped powers to the manifest injury of the people, and further stated that the action would inevitably subject them to a military despotism, require the people to wage war against the government of the United States, and "transfer the allegiance of the people to an illegal confederacy." There were other indictments quite as severe. The declaration closed by imposing upon the reorganized government of Virginia a solemn obligation to declare the actions of the Richmond convention illegal, null, and void; and announced that the officers adhering to secession had all vacated their posts.

After the election of officers the governor was conducted to the convention hall and the oath of office was administered by Andrew Wilson, a justice of the peace of Ohio County. Governor Pierpont delivered a brief address in which he stated "that to the loyal people of a State belongs the law-making power of that State." This doctrine was compatible with the spirit of western Virginia.

FINISHING THE WORK

Chairman Boreman remarked that thirty-four counties had sent delegates to Wheeling and that as a result of their work they now needed to return home to assist in putting the reorganized government into action. The last business before departing for home was to issue an address to the people, denouncing the action of the Richmond convention as illegal for the reason that the legislature did not have authority to call a convention without being authorized to do so by the people. It further stated that when officers elected by the people forsake their offices, the temporary power delegated to them reverts to the people. Therefore, it was the duty of the people to choose representatives and commission them to organize a new government. The people had been told how their government came to be abandoned and destroyed. Now they were called upon to sustain the new organization made by their representatives, which would supplant the officers who had forsaken their posts.

The ordinance of reorganization called for a meeting of the legislature on July 1, 1861. Most of the members of the legislature had been elected on May 23, some senators were holding over from the election two years before, and some vacancies had been filled as they had occurred. It was the duty of the legislature to elect the auditor, treasurer, and secretary of the commonwealth. Thus having discharged its duty for the time the convention adjourned on June 25, to assemble again on August 6. In the meantime it would stand in readiness to be called in special session if the governor deemed such action necessary.

The Reorganized Government at Work

When the convention adjourned it left a heavy responsibility on the newly elected governor. But he was equal to the occasion. He and his council of wise men took up their task and valiantly worked both day and night. His treasury was depleted, war ravaged the land, and the power of the state was hopelessly divided. On the other hand the new government had an army in the field; it was supported by the federal government; all the loyal states held themselves in readiness to help; and taxes could be collected to sustain expenses.

That part of the legislature of Virginia adhering to the Union did not assemble at Wheeling until July 2, 1861. The senate convened in Linsly Institute, while the house held its sessions in the federal courtroom in the United States custom house. In the meantime Governor Pierpont had been in communication with President Lincoln and certain departments in Washington. He submitted to the legislature the results of his negotiations, stating that a large armed force of Union soldiers had been sent to free western Virginia from the Confederacy. The Confederate army, under Colonel George Porterfield, had been driven out of Grafton, routed at Rich Mountain, and completely dispersed at Corrick's Ford, where General Garnett was killed.

The legislature proceeded to complete the state organization by filling vacancies in important offices. Lucian A. Hagan of Preston County was elected secretary of the commonwealth; Samuel Crane of Randolph, auditor; and Campbell Tarr of Brooke, treasurer. In the election of May 23, three members of the national House of Representatives had been elected from western Virginia, all loyal to the Union; they hastened across the mountains, submitted their credentials, and were admitted to full membership in the Congress of the United States. William G. Brown of Preston County, Jacob B. Blair of Wood, and Kellian V. Whaley of Mason constituted this loyal triumvirate. But in view of the fact that R. M. T. Hunter and James Mason, the senators of Virginia, had vacated their offices by going with the Confederacy, the reorganized government of Virginia was without representation in the Senate of the United States. It was therefore incumbent upon the legislature to fill the vacancies in order to round out the state organization. On July 9, Waitman T. Willey of Monongalia County and John S. Carlile of Harrison were elected to the United States Senate. They reported to Washington and were admitted by a vote of thirty-five to five as the senators representing the state of Virginia.

Thus the reorganized government was recognized by the government of the United States and set in active and vigorous operation. The precision, regularity, and initiative with which the western leaders worked is an admirable exemplification of statesmanship. For many years they had been denied honorable consideration in the government of their own state. Now they had taken possession of that government.

The Reassembling of the Convention

According to previous provisions the convention reassembled on August 6, 1861. During its recess, plans for the division of the state had matured. After the opening exercises, delegate James G. West of Wetzel County presented a resolution calling for a committee, composed of one person from each county, to consider and report a plan for the formation of a new state. The resolution was adopted and a committee of thirty-one was appointed. On August 10 the committee submitted its report.

The report set forth a plan for dividing the state. The plan included the name of New Virginia for the proposed state, and recommended that the constitution of Virginia be modified by the convention to suit circumstances and then be adopted as the supreme law of the new commonwealth. It was proposed that New Virginia include the northern half of the original state, taking in that region lying north of a line running from a point on the Potomac just south of Washington to the top of the Allegheny Mountains, thence southwest to Tennessee.

The ordinance provoked a lively debate. Those opposed to separation asked how Virginia could be received back into the Union if divided, and what would become of the reorganized government if the new state were formed. Peter G. Van Winkle moved to change the proposed name from New Virginia to Allegheny. His motion was accepted. After the settlement of this point a long debate ensued concerning the proper method to follow in order to achieve the ultimate objective, a new state.

On September 19 it was voted, on motion of delegate Hooton of Preston County, that a committee composed of six members be appointed to form and submit a plan on division that would be agreeable to both sides.[3] On the following morning chairman Farnsworth of this committee submitted his report, which he presented in the form of an ordinance.

The ordinance proposed that a new state, to be known as Kanawha, be formed out of a part of the territory of Virginia. It was to be composed of thirty-nine counties, with the privilege extended to seven others, Greenbrier, Pocahontas, Hardy, Hampshire, Morgan, Berkeley, and Jefferson, to decide by popular vote whether to join the new commonwealth. The ordinance further provided for a popular vote on October 24, to decide on the matter of separation, and at the same time, if it carried, to choose delegates to a convention to frame a constitution for the state. It is thought that the ordinance was drawn by the skilled hands of Lamb and Van Winkle, two of the ablest of the delegates. This plan leaned definitely in favor of those desiring division, but it would be submitted for a final decision to the proper authority – the popular will. The ordinance, after a short spirited debate, was adopted by a vote of fifty to twenty-eight.

Other resolutions were offered, pertaining to the loyalty of the re-

[3] The committee was composed of Farnsworth, Carlile, Paxton, Van Winkle, Ruffner, and Lamb.

organized government to the Union, the obedience to civil authorities, and the establishment of order. Provision was made for collecting revenue, for electing representatives in Congress, and for raising at least one company of volunteers in each county to assist in suppressing the rebellion. Then the convention, having finished its work, adjourned *sine die* unless called together by its president or by the governor of the state on or before the first day of January, 1862.

On the third Thursday in October the election was held. It proved a surprise to those who opposed separation. Sentiment had been carefully spread and the fertile ground made ready to receive it. In all, 18,408 votes were cast for division, and only 781 against it. The delegates to the constitutional convention were also chosen in this election. Thus the movement for a new state had taken definite form.

The Constitutional Convention

ORGANIZATION

On November 26 the constitutional convention convened at Wheeling. Fifty-two delegates reported, representing in all forty-two counties. The place of meeting was the room in the federal building set apart for the holding of the sessions of the United States District Court. Chapman J. Stuart of Doddridge County called the meeting to order. John Hall of Mason was chosen temporary chairman and Gibson L. Cranmer temporary secretary. The assembly made the temporary chairman the permanent presiding officer and elected Ellery R. Hall of Taylor County permanent secretary. After the members had taken the oath of loyalty, pledging their faith to the reorganized government of Virginia, the convention assumed its work of making a constitution.

On the second day Peter G. Van Winkle, chairman of the committee on the distribution of work, reported a plan of procedure by naming eight committees. Later a ninth, on state boundaries, was added. The names of the committees and their chairmen were as follows: fundamental and general provisions, Van Winkle; county organization, Pomeroy; legislative department, Lamb; executive department, Caldwell; judiciary department, Willey; taxation and finance, Paxton; education, Battelle; schedule, Hall of Marion; and boundaries, Stuart of Doddridge.

A NEW NAME

After a brief discussion on the explosive subject of slavery, the convention took up the matter of the name of the proposed state. Already three names had been mentioned, New Virginia, Allegheny, and Kanawha. The ordinance for division which had been approved by popular vote had used the name Kanawha, and some members believed that the convention had no authority to make a change. But the convention, after challenging argument, finally decided by a vote of thirty to fourteen to name the new state West Virginia.[4] And this name endured all later tests.

ESTABLISHMENT OF BOUNDARY LINES

Next a determined effort was made to incorporate new counties within the boundaries on the south and on the east. The change proposed by Brown of Kanawha would have added the Shenandoah Valley to the new state. According to the August convention there could be annexed to the thirty-nine original counties the counties of Greenbrier, Pocahontas, Hampshire, Hardy, Morgan, Berkeley, Jefferson, and any other one contiguous to the boundary lines, if the people in one or all of them so voted. In all this region, except the Potomac Valley, public sentiment positively resented the separation of the people of Virginia; consequently, it appeared that Brown's motion might stop the whole movement to form West Virginia. But the leaders in the affair possessed too much wisdom to be so easily misled. Already some of the counties named were within the Confederate lines and therefore in no position to vote themselves out of Virginia. After several days of spirited debate a decision was reached to incorporate the counties that are today within the boundaries of West Virginia on the south and east, thus voting down the proposition presented by delegate Brown. Jefferson, Berkeley, and Frederick counties had the privilege to vote on the proposition of leaving the fold of Virginia, and the first two subsequently chose to ally themselves with the new state.

SLAVERY

A serious debate was provoked on the subject of slavery, which had hindered progress, increased taxes, and stifled political power of

[4] Before the vote was taken the names of Kanawha, Augusta, Allegheny, and Western Virginia were proposed but each was defeated in the final action.

the white people in western Virginia. Gordon Battelle, who possessed strong sentiments against the institution of slavery, introduced a provision that would have prevented slaves from being brought into the state for permanent residence. He added a second proposition that slave children born after July 4, 1865, would be free. The same ghost that had haunted Congress now roamed the convention hall. It had led to the disruption of the state, caused the revolt at Richmond, and was driving Virginia asunder. Nothing was said about abolition, but the propositions under discussion came pretty close to it. The convention almost unanimously accepted the first motion. No decision was made on the second one.

FORFEITED LANDS

Some unpatented lands still remained in the possession of the commonwealth. The committee on education, of which Gordon Battelle served as chairman, proposed that the public lands be sold and the proceeds be devoted to public education. This motion failed, but it was provided that all lands forfeited to the state since 1831 would be released and exonerated from forfeiture and payment of delinquent taxes, unless the tax exceeded twenty dollars and the tract did not amount to more than one thousand acres. All other lands so forfeited or sold could be redeemed within five years. This arrangement came as a hard blow to Battelle's plan to finance the schools, but a general school fund was created from the sale of unappropriated lands, from property claimed from Virginia for educational purposes, appropriations made by the legislature, etc.

COMPLETING THE WORK

The constitutional convention had been in session eighty-five days. Heavy and difficult problems had tested the statesmanship of the men who had refused to follow the ordinance of secession and who had promoted the new state movement. They had held courageously and faithfully to their ideals and now were about to conclude their work.

On February 18, 1862, the convention, having completed the writing of the new constitution, adjourned to meet again if the chairman deemed it urgent to do so. The new constitution was to be submitted for ratification to the electorate on April 4.

In the meantime the people had a chance to study and discuss the new order on which they were soon to vote. The work finished by the constitution makers had a popular appeal, for on election day the new form of government was confirmed by a vote of 18,682 to 514. The vote showed the unity of sentiment prevailing in the counties that had severed their connections with the Old Dominion.

Forming the New State

THE LEGISLATURE RECONVENED

Governor Pierpont at once called the state legislature of the reorganized government of Virginia to meet in special session on May 6, 1862. It was necessary to clear the way for the new state by conforming to the regulation in the national Constitution: "No new state shall be formed or erected within the jurisdiction of any other state; nor any state be formed by the junction of two or more states, or parts of states, without the consent of the legislatures of the states concerned as well as of the Congress" (Article IV, Section 3). The duty of the legislature was clear, and the members did not have much room for debate. On May 13, the general assembly gave its formal consent to the formation of the new state.

CONGRESSIONAL ACTION

A draft of the new constitution and a certified copy of the decision of the legislature were hurried off to Washington and placed in the care of Senator Willey. Later, on May 29, Willey presented to the Senate the memorial drafted by the legislature favoring the admission of West Virginia into the Union. He carefully reviewed events, conclusively defended the legality of the case, and explained that the reasons for separation embodied physical, geographical, social, economic, and political differences.

The case was then referred to the committee on territories, over which Senator Wade of Ohio presided. Senator John S. Carlile had been assigned to membership on this committee, and as a matter of courtesy was empowered to draft the bill for the admission of the new state. He presented his report on June 23, 1862. But here Carlile betrayed his trust. Instead of leaving the boundary lines of the proposed state as they had been fixed by the constitutional convention, he attempted to include the counties of the Shenandoah Valley in the new commonwealth. The Valley was proslavery and John S. Carlile knew it. The Valley was within the lines of the Confederacy, and he knew that, too. And in his draft of the bill he included a clause to emancipate all the slaves living in the state. An attempt to free the slaves in a proslave region of the new state might have defeated the whole movement. The motives behind Senator Carlile's action remain a mystery, but from that time his prestige in West Virginia receded.

When the strange move became publicly known, friends of the state movement implored Senator Wade to intercede and clarify the matter. Senator Willey had remained inactive, letting his colleague take the lead. But the time had come to act. Friends hastened to Washington and aroused Willey from his lethargy, beseeching him to be on his guard and to rescue their cause. On June 26 the chairman of the committees on territories reported to the Senate the bill for admission. But the bill sustained severe attacks because the constitution did not provide for the positive exclusion of slavery. If admitted under the original form of its constitution, West Virginia would have been only another slave state, and with that provision the bill could not pass Congress. If the constitutional convention had approved the measure submitted by Gordon Battelle the trouble now being encountered in the United States Senate would have been avoided. However, by the help of senators Wade, Sumner, Willey, and others, the Carlile bill was amended so that the boundaries of the state conformed to the original arrangement. Wade's amendment for the gradual emancipation of the slaves was also added.[5] In that form the bill for the admission of West Virginia into the Union passed the Senate by a majority of twenty-three to seventeen.

Then the House of Representatives took up the measure for confirmation. Though action in the House was postponed by adjournment until December, Brown and Blair, representing the reorganized government of Virginia in the House, and Willey, in the Senate, persisted in their work for confirmation. Finally, on December 10, the House approved the bill by a vote of ninety-six to fifty-five. It was then submitted to President Lincoln.

PRESIDENT LINCOLN SIGNS THE BILL

When the bill reached the hand of President Lincoln, he showed his usual care and wisdom. While deliberating on the matter he

---

[5] The amendment stated: "The children of slaves born within the limits of this State after the fourth day of July, eighteen hundred and sixty-three, shall be free; and . . . all slaves within the said State who shall, at the time aforesaid, be under the age of ten years, shall be free when they arrive at the age of twenty-one years; and all slaves over ten and under twenty-one years shall be free when they arrive at the age of twenty-five years; and no slave shall be permitted to come into the State for permanent residence therein."

sought the opinions of the members of his council at a cabinet meeting. He inquired, is it lawful? Is it expedient? Is it necessary? Having weighed on the balances of wise judgment the opinions expressed by his cabinet and having drawn from the resources of his own wisdom, President Lincoln signed the bill December 31, 1862, declaring, "We can scarcely dispense with the aid of West Virginia in this struggle." The President's endorsement of this measure guaranteed statehood to West Virginia.

FINAL ADOPTION

Since Congress had changed the new state constitution by adding the Wade amendment, it was necessary to secure again the approval of the convention and the people. The former met at Wheeling and on February 12, 1863, promptly approved the constitution as amended. It was then submitted to the people, the sovereign authority, for final adoption. March 26 was set aside as the day on which the vote would be taken. The verdict of the people was conclusive, there being 23,321 in favor and only 472 against.

After the result of the vote had been despatched to President Lincoln, the convention called for an election to be held the fourth Thursday in May to choose the regular officers for the new state. The officers included a governor, a legislature, judges, and county officials.

PRESIDENT LINCOLN'S PROCLAMATION

The constitution having been completed and approved by the sovereign authority, the President on April 20, 1863, issued a proclamation to the effect that upon the expiration of sixty days, West Virginia would become a member of the Union on an equal basis with the other thirty-four states.

After the proclamation was issued, a state convention assembled at Parkersburg on May 9 to select candidates to fill the state offices. Harmony existed in the convention, and the nominations were made without opposition.[6] Later in the month (fourth Thursday) the election was held. On June 20, 1863, in keeping with President Lincoln's proclamation, Governor Boreman was inaugurated and West Virginia began its life as a state. In the meantime (May 23)

[6] The nominations were as follows: Arthur I. Boreman, governor; Campbell Tarr, treasurer; Samuel Crane, auditor; Edgar J. Bayers, secretary of state; A. B. Caldwell, attorney general; Ralph L. Berkshire, James H. Brown, and William A. Harrison, supreme court judges.

Francis H. Pierpont had been elected by the people as governor of the reorganized government of Virginia. When Governor Boreman began his administration at Wheeling, the center of the reorganized government of Virginia was transferred to Alexandria, within the Federal lines, where it remained during the rest of the war.

The New State

The new state had a population in 1863 of 376,888 and an area of 24,282 square miles. It had a wise and courageous citizenry possessed of ideals that were worth striving for. It had rich and extensive deposits of natural resources yet to be explored, a temperate climate, and fertile soil. All in all West Virginia possessed the necessary qualities to make a state truly great.

This is an appropriate place to mention Virginia's later proposal for reunion. When the war finally ended and Virginia took time to ponder the dismemberment of the state, it deeply regretted what had taken place. The Old Dominion expressed a desire to reunite the territory of the states and appealed to West Virginia to concur in the adoption of suitable measures to restore the bond of unity. The assembly of Virginia appointed three commissioners to communicate with the legislature at Wheeling on this matter. But events had taken place that could not be recalled; and the people of the new state were satisfied. The legislature of West Virginia answered the appeal by passing on January 6, 1867, a joint resolution "most emphatically" declining to consider reunion.[7]

---

[7] *Acts of the Legislature of West Virginia,* Fifth Session, 1867, p. 177.

CHAPTER 9

The Constitution of 1863

It will be profitable now to survey in some detail the constitution of the new state. We have seen that it was the end product of a long period of conflict between the east and the west which had finally reached a climax of intensity so acute that separation was the only solution. The Civil War presented the opportunity. Let us now see how the new constitution embodied the principles that the western people had so long striven to attain.

The State

The constitution left no question as to the relationship between the state and the Union. It explicitly recognized the Constitution of the United States as the supreme law of the land. Treaties made by the United States and laws enacted by the Congress were declared superior to the law of the state, municipal ordinances, and all other enactments whatsoever. The makers of the constitution made this provision the introductory declaration of the whole document. They could not have done better; it was a relationship that needed to be recognized.

Forty-four counties, once in the state of Virginia, now constituted West Virginia.[1] Pendleton, Hardy, Hampshire, and Morgan were

[1] The state boundary line reaches to the low water mark on the northwestern shore of the Ohio River.

to be permitted to join the commonwealth if they endorsed the constitution, as they later did. Berkeley, Jefferson, and Frederick were offered the same option. The first two later voted to join West Virginia; Frederick County remained a part of Virginia.

The first article further stipulated that the powers of government were retained in the hands of the people; that the legislative, executive, and judicial powers were to remain separate; and that no person could be invested with or exercise authority over more than one of these departments at the same time.

With respect to citizenship the constitution declared that citizens of the state should be citizens of the United States. However, persons enlisted in the naval, marine, or military services of the country could not be classified as citizens of the state by reason of being stationed in the state. This regulation prevented any authority from affecting the political welfare of the people by shifting the armed forces from place to place. Only resident citizens could be counted as population, and on their number representation had to be based. The long-fought struggle to determine the true basis for representation had now been settled.

The Bill of Rights

The men who made the constitution for West Virginia adopted the Virginia Bill of Rights as a part of their own law. This document guarantees to the people the enjoyment of certain rights that cannot be curtailed by the legislative authorities. It is here that we find the guarantee of freedom of speech and the press, protection from excessive bail and penalty, and the forbidding of unreasonable search and seizure. These guarantees may be maintained only in so far as the citizen exercises his liberties within proper and decent bounds. It was emphatically stated that anyone who attempted to justify armed invasion or organized insurrection by speaking, writing, or printing would upon conviction be subject to punishment. No doubt the fathers expected occasion to invoke this regulation, since a state of rebellion existed at the very time of drafting and adopting the constitution. The Bill of Rights further guaranteed the protection of the citizen in the possession of his property, and assured him of due compensation if it should be taken for public use. And no one could be deprived of life, liberty, or property without due process of law. Judgment in trials of crime or misdemeanor was to be rendered by juries convened in the county in which the offense had been committed, unless prudence dictated another place for the trial. All trials were to be publicly held, the interested parties had to be given due and ample notice, both parties must have counsel, and the appearance of witnesses could be obtained by compulsory process if necessity required.

In no way could a citizen's religious principles affect his civil capacity. The constitution forbade the legislature to require any religious test, to favor any denomination, or to lay a tax for the support of any church. Religious worship was left altogether free and enjoyed protection by the authority of the state.

Treason was defined as levying war against the state, or giving aid and comfort to its enemies. No one could be convicted of treason unless on his own confession in open court or on the testimony of at least two witnesses. The severity of punishment depended on the nature of the act committed.

Elections and Officers

We have seen that the qualification of voters had long been one of the most bitterly disputed issues in the conflict between east and west. The new constitution dealt decisively with the matter. The constitution stated, "The white male citizens of the State shall be entitled to vote at all elections held within the election districts in which they respectively reside."[2] Paupers, persons of unsound mind, minors, and those under conviction for crime were disqualified. Previous residence of one year in the state and of thirty days in the county was required of voters. The influence of the war may be seen in the provision that any person who since June 1, 1861, had given voluntary aid to the rebellion against the United States could not be a citizen of the state unless he had subsequently volunteered into the military or naval service of the United States and had been honorably discharged therefrom.

The mode of voting was to be by ballot. On election day, the fourth Thursday of October, all voters had the privilege of taking leave from work or engagement in order to attend the election. Only persons entitled to vote could hold office, and before assuming the duties of office those elected were required to take an oath to support the state and the Union.

Officers began their duties on the first day of January next succeeding the date of election. Vacancies had to be filled in a manner

[2] *Code of West Virginia*, 1870, p. 22.

prescribed by laws. Powers, duties, and rate of compensation the legislature established and it could alter them, but salaries could be neither increased nor diminished during the term of office. Office-holders were liable to impeachment for irregularities in office; the house of delegates was to prosecute cases of impeachment while the senate sat as a court and rendered the verdict.

Dueling was positively outlawed. Any person participating in a duel directly or indirectly, as principal, second, or accomplice in any manner, forfeited his privilege of holding any office under the authority of the state. It was not long before the legislature increased the penalty.

The manner of conducting elections had to have legislative endorsement; the system would therefore be uniform. Provision could be made by the legislature for the registration of voters, but the constitution did not make registration compulsory. Fraud and disorder on election day were not punishable by constitutional regulation, but the penalty for such offenses was to be established by legislative enactment.

The Legislature

The legislative power of the state was vested in a senate and a house of delegates. Originally the lawmaking body consisted of eighteen senators and forty-seven delegates. The numbers could be increased by act of the legislature, but not diminished. The term of office was fixed at two years for senators and one for delegates; consequently elections were held annually. The state contained nine senatorial districts as nearly equal in white population as could be arranged, and each district elected two senators. The number of districts could be increased after each census but could not be diminished. The delegate districts were also determined on an equality of white population. In some cases two or more sparsely populated counties formed one district. Each district elected one delegate.

To qualify as a legislator it was required that a man must have been a resident within his district for at least one year preceding the election, that he must hold no other governmental office of profit, either state or national; and that if he had been entrusted with public funds, he must make a full settlement of the same before being eligible for membership in the legislature.

Sessions of the legislature convened annually, opening on the third Tuesday in January. The governor was at liberty to call special sessions when he deemed such action expedient. An arrangement of this sort is a rule in American state government; but even without this precedent it would doubtless have been given a place in a constitution written during the crises of war, when special meetings were likely to be necessary. Wheeling was declared to be the seat of government of the state, but the governor could convene the legislature at another place if safety so demanded.

Each house chose its own officers and judged the election of its own members. Sessions could not continue longer than forty-five days without the concurrence of three-fourths of the members elected. Votes were taken by yeas and nays and kept in the journal of the proceedings of the house so voting. The constitution guaranteed safe conduct for the members traveling to and from the sessions. Compensation, not exceeding three dollars a day for members and five dollars a day for the presiding officers, with the addition of ten cents for every mile traveled to and from the capital, had a constitutional status. Bills of any kind, even those for raising revenue, could originate in either house.

The Executive

The chief executive power of the state was vested in a governor elected by the qualified voters. This provision incorporated a reform long sought by the people in western Virginia. The term of office of the governor was two years, and he was eligible for reelection.[3] The constitution limited his salary to two thousand dollars a year, and the legislature had no power to change it.

As the chief executive of the state, the governor enforced the execution of the laws, administered the duties of commander-in-chief of the militia, and filled vacancies in offices by appointment during the recess of the legislature. Other powers delegated to the governor were to remit fines and penalties, to grant reprieves and pardons, to inform the legislature concerning the condition of the state, and to recommend the passage of such laws as he deemed expedient and proper. In case of a vacancy in the governorship the office would devolve upon the president of the senate; in the event of the latter's inability to act, the speaker of the house would succeed to the office.

The secretary of state, the treasurer, and the auditor were chosen by the same method and for the same term as the governor. The

[3] Governors Boreman and Jacob are the only chief executives of West Virginia ever to have been reelected to that office, the former having been chosen governor in 1863, 1864, and 1866, the latter in 1870 and 1872.

legislature prescribed the duties of these officials. All military officers above the rank of colonel were nominated by the governor and approved by the senate.

The Judicial Department

The constitution provided for three types of courts: the supreme court of appeals, the circuit courts, and inferior courts.

THE SUPREME COURT OF APPEALS

The supreme court of appeals consisted of three justices who were regularly elected by the voters and held office for a term of twelve years.

The compensation of a justice was fixed at two thousand dollars a year; this amount could not be changed except by an amendment to the constitution. Dismissal of the judges could be brought about only by a concurrent vote of a majority of all the members elected to each branch of the legislature. By constitutional regulation the court convened at the seat of government of the state.

Cases could be brought before the supreme court of appeals in two ways; by original suit in cases of habeas corpus, mandamus, and prohibition, or by appeal from a lower state court.[4] The appellate jurisdiction applied only to civil cases involving at least two hundred dollars, exclusive of costs, in controversies concerning the title of land, wills, taxes, and tolls; any case in which the constitutionality of a law was in question; criminal cases of felony or misdemeanor; and such other civil and criminal cases as the law prescribed. So the court had a broad field of jurisdiction and soon became a very busy tribunal.

The supreme court of appeals appointed its own officers, but their duties, compensation, and tenure in office were prescribed by law. The attorney general was elected by popular vote, but his duties were prescribed by acts of the legislature. He could be removed in the same manner as the judges of the supreme court of appeals.

[4] Anyone who feels himself unjustly detained by an officer may procure a writ compelling the jailer to present the person before a judge who shows the reason why the person is placed in the custody of the law. This process is a writ of habeas corpus.

A writ of mandamus is issued by a court, in the name of the state, directed to a person, corporation or inferior court, requiring the performance of some particular action.

A writ of prohibition is issued by a superior court commanding an inferior court to cease from the prosecution of some case.

THE CIRCUIT COURTS

The constitution stipulated that the state was to be divided into eleven judicial circuits, one judge being assigned to each circuit. The legislature had the power to rearrange at its pleasure the lines bounding the circuits, thus increasing or diminishing their number. The judges of the circuit courts were elected by popular vote for six-year terms. Several counties composed each circuit, and a court convened in every county at least four times annually. This provision made the judge a busy official, with all the duties of a circuit rider. One regulation provided that the circuit court should have supervision and control over all proceedings before the justice of the peace and other inferior courts. It also had general jurisdiction of matters at law where the amount in controversy exceeded twenty dollars, of all cases of equity, crimes, and misdemeanors, and of "such other jurisdiction, whether supervisory, original or appellate, or concurrent, as may be prescribed by law." A case appealed from an inferior court came directly to the circuit court for a hearing.

The voters of each county elected a clerk of the circuit court, whose term of office was four years. The duties and compensation of the clerk were fixed by acts of the legislature.

The County

The officers of the county consisted of sheriff, prosecuting attorney, surveyor of lands, recorder, and one or more assessors. The duties of the county officers were not specified in the constitution but were authorized by the legislature. The sheriff's term of office was four years, and he was denied the privilege of being elected for two terms in succession; the other county officers served for terms of two years.

The sheriff had numerous duties. He collected taxes and fines, served summonses, sold land for the payment of delinquent taxes, collected license taxes, made arrests, kept the jail, and executed persons condemned to death by the circuit court. The prosecuting attorney served as counsel for the state where its interests were involved. Whenever a court ordered a survey of lands, the surveyor made the proper measurements and filed a plot of them with the records of the court. The recorder of the county kept a statement of its financial accounts, issued licenses, registered births and deaths, kept a record of deeds, liens, wills, etc., and docketed judgments.

Berkeley County had one assessor for each township; the rest had only one or two for each county. Annually, on the first day of April, the assessor ascertained all the persons and property subject to taxation in his district, and made an estimate of the worth of the property both real and personal. His numerous duties were regulated by the legislature, which specified the rules for taxation and the exemption of certain property from tax.

The Township

Each county was divided into not fewer than three or more than ten townships as nearly equal in white population as could be conveniently arranged. The population of a township had to exceed four hundred. An assemblage of the voters in township meetings transacted all the business relating to their local affairs. Annually they held an election at which they chose a supervisor, a clerk for the township, and a surveyor of roads for each precinct in the township. Every four years the voters elected justices of the peace – one in each township having a population of less than twelve hundred white people, two in more populous townships. They elected an equal number of constables, whose term of office was two years.

At all township meetings the supervisor presided and the clerk acted as the recording officer. The constitution provided that the supervisors chosen in the townships of each county should constitute a county board known as the supervisors of the county. This board met at least four times each year at the court house and elected from its number a presiding officer. The township clerk kept a journal of the proceedings. The county board had charge of establishing and regulating roads, public buildings, ferries, bridges, and mills; granting licenses; laying, collecting, and disbursing county levies; appointing the places of holding elections. It was the judge of the election of all township and county officers.

The township meeting in which all the voters assembled for the transaction of public business had no parallel in the government of Virginia; it was borrowed from New England. It was to receive adverse criticism and, as we shall see, was presently abandoned. The actual structure of county and township administration was not very different from the county and district setup of the Virginia order. The great change was that responsibility for the government was now placed squarely on the voter, since nearly all officers had been made elective.

Taxation and Finance

The constitution declared that all property should be taxed according to its value, "but property used for educational, literary, scientific, religious or charitable purposes, and public property, may, by law, be exempted from taxation."[5] Each white male inhabitant who had attained the age of twenty-one years paid a poll tax of one dollar annually.

By constitutional requirement the legislature levied an annual tax sufficient to defray the yearly expenses of the state. If the payment of taxes fell short of the estimate, the deficiency was made up in the following year by levying a tax adequate to satisfy the shortage. A debt could not be incurred except to meet a deficit, redeem previous liability, suppress insurrection, repel invasion, or defend the state in time of war.[6] No county, town, corporation, or person could be granted credit by the state; nor could the state assume responsibility for the debt of any of those agencies, unless the debt was incurred in defense of the state in time of war or insurrection. These regulations safeguarded the people against a person or corporation inclined to demand special favors at public expense.

A matter destined to assume large proportions later was the new state's responsibility for a share of the public debt of Virginia. The constitution stated that an equitable proportion of the public debt of Virginia incurred prior to January 1, 1861, would be assumed by West Virginia. The amount of the state's share of this sum was to be ascertained by the legislature, and a sinking fund was to be created by taxation to liquidate within thirty-four years the principal and the accruing interest of West Virginia's part of the debt. However, the debt amounted to a great deal more than the original estimate, and it took a much longer time than thirty-four years to pay it.

Forfeited and Unappropriated Lands

Upon the formation of the new state no change was made in the titles of lands granted under the government of Virginia. However, warrants issued for land by the Virginia land office had now to be set aside, and the circuit court of the county wherein the unappropriated land lay issued a title to the same upon receiving the proper application. An estate forfeited on account of a failure to pay taxes

[5] *Code of West Virginia*, 1870, p. 35.
[6] *Ibid.*

was disposed of in a manner prescribed by the legislature. But any land returned delinquent before 1831 on which the unpaid taxes did not exceed twenty dollars, or to which the title was not properly entered on the record books of the county, was released and exonerated from a forfeiture if the tract did not contain more than one thousand acres. If the land had been forfeited for delinquent taxes since 1831, or if the estate exceeded one thousand acres and had been returned delinquent previous to that date, it could be redeemed by the original owner upon the payment of the taxes and any damages within five years after the adoption of the constitution. All lands not so redeemed or exonerated were considered forfeited to the state and were to be sold. If the sale price exceeded the amount of taxes, damages, etc., against the land, the surplus was given to the original owner.

Education

Public education had been for many years a subject of sore contention between the two sections of Virginia. Western Virginia wanted to extend the benefits of a public school education to all its citizens, but the legislature had been unwilling to authorize a program of such wide application. The new constitution gave the west the opportunity to carry out its principles. The regulations relating to the public school system of the state were drafted by a committee of which Gordon Battelle, a graduate of Allegheny College and a wise and able educator, was chairman.

To provide the necessary funds for education, the constitution directed that all money accumulated from the sale of forfeited lands, all grants made to the state for educational purposes, the proceeds from the estates of persons who died without leaving a will or an heir, funds left by Virginia that the state had a right to claim for educational purposes, and appropriations made from time to time by the legislature, should be set apart and be known as the school fund. The whole amount was to be invested in interest-bearing securities of the United States or of the state, and the accrued interest annually applied to the support of public schools. In addition, the fund was to be augmented by fines collected by the state and a general tax on persons and property. The legislature prescribed that a certain portion of the amount required for educational training should be raised by local taxation in each township for its own schools.

The legislature was required by the constitution to establish an "efficient system of free schools." Each county elected its own superintendent of schools, and each township elected the necessary officers to administer its schools. At its discretion the legislature was empowered to provide for a state superintendent of schools and also for a state board of instruction. The legislature was also to make suitable provision for the blind and deaf-mute and for other persons needing public care.

Thus the constitution contained broad provisions for the establishment of a system of schools, but it left much to the discretion of the legislature and much to the units of local government.

Miscellaneous

Lotteries and other games of chance were forbidden. The circuit courts were given authority to change the names of persons, grant divorces, and make sales of estates belonging to infants. The legislature could make laws to prohibit the sale of intoxicants.

By general law provision was made for the securing of property for religious use so that it could be devoted without hindrance to the purposes of the church, but no charter of incorporation could be granted to any religious denomination. There was a recognized separation of political and religious affairs. It was specified, however, that associations organized to promote the general welfare and for other purposes useful to the public could be incorporated, except banks of circulation and internal improvement companies. The same power that granted corporate privileges could modify or withdraw them if the law were disobeyed or the rules violated.

The part of the constitution that related to slavery is of special significance. The way in which it took form has been described in the preceding chapter. It set forth that the children of slaves born within the state after July 4, 1863, were to be free; slave children less than ten years of age on the date mentioned were to become free when they attained the age of twenty-one years; and all slaves over ten years and less than twenty-one were to be free when they became twenty-five. Slaves were forbidden to come into the state and take up a permanent residence here. President Lincoln's emancipation proclamation, issued January 1, 1863, did not affect slavery in West Virginia, for it applied only to slavery in the states in rebellion against the Union. The status of slaves in West Virginia remained unchanged until December 18, 1865, when the thirteenth amendment to the national constitution was ratified. This amendment abolished slavery in all parts of the United States.

All suits at law in the counties of the new state pending in the courts of Virginia at the time of the formation of the constitution of West Virginia were to be tried in the circuit courts of the counties having jurisdiction in the cases, or in the supreme court of appeals if the case came within the jurisdiction of that court. Records, books, papers, seals, and appurtenances belonging to the circuit courts and county courts in the counties now within West Virginia remained in the care of the circuit courts of the new state. Matters of business were taken up by West Virginia where the authority of Virginia ceased. Of course all business now had to be conducted in the name of the State of West Virginia.

Amendments

The constitution could be amended by a convention approved by a majority vote of both houses of the legislature, confirmed by a majority of the popular vote. The members of a constitutional convention could not be elected until at least one month after the decision of the voters had been declared and published. All the acts and ordinances of such a convention had to be validated by a vote of the people, and in no manner whatsoever could they be retroactive.

Either branch of the legislature could propose an amendment to the constitution, and if agreed to by a majority of both branches, it was then entered on the journal. Following this action the amendment was printed in each county having a newspaper, at least three months before the next general election. If a majority of the voters favored the change it was submitted again to the legislature at the next session and if approved again by a majority of both houses the legislature placed the proposed amendment a second time before the people for ratification or rejection. Upon ratification by a majority of the qualified voters the amendment became a part of the constitution of the state.

In view of the rigorous restrictions surrounding the adoption of amendments, there was little likelihood that any glaring mistake would find a place in the articles of the supreme law of the state. It is to be noted, however, that at all stages of action only a majority vote for adoption was required, while in some other states a two-thirds or even three-fourths majority vote had to be cast to bring about such changes.

Conclusion

In some respects the new constitution was an emphatic departure from the one under which the people of the state had lived. The township system, imported from New England, was one striking innovation. The plan for gradual emancipation of slaves embodied a reform for which western Virginia had long fought. So did the provision for wider suffrage and the replacement of appointment by popular election for most offices, which broadened the people's responsibility for their government and made the officers of government directly responsible to the people.

The new system of education, when fully administered, would reach every hamlet and home in the state. The people wanted that arrangement. The drafters of the law faithfully believed that a brilliant mind could be native of a cabin as well as of a castle and that educational advantages should be in reach of poor and rich alike. The soundness of this doctrine could be proved by the lives of the very men who achieved leadership in the formation of the state and the writing of the constitution.

In its main features the constitution of West Virginia followed the organization of the governments of the other states in the Union. The executive department was centered in the office of the governor; two elective houses composed the legislature; and the courts consisted of a well-planned, elective judiciary. The county government had been organized in such a manner that it would function without serious conflict or cross purposes. The new constitution reflected clearly the wisdom and ability of the statesmen of West Virginia.

CHAPTER 10

The New Government at Work

The First Year

THE INAUGURATION OF GOVERNOR BOREMAN

Arthur Ingram Boreman, the first governor of West Virginia, was inaugurated at Wheeling on June 20, 1863. A news reporter who witnessed the occasion wrote of it, "The ceremonies included a civil and a military procession. When the procession arrived in front of the Linsly Institute, the temporary Capitol of the new State, and mingled itself with the vast assemblage that filled every available space, Senator C. D. Hubbard called the multitude to order." [1] Governor Boreman delivered his inaugural address, after which he took the oath of office. West Virginia had now taken its place with the other states, making the thirty-fifth member of the Union.

In his address Governor Boreman made reference to the unfairness and inequality of legislation that had emanated from Richmond which, he said, appeared on every page of the statute books. He charged that the west had always been treated as a territory in a

[1] The *Wheeling Intelligencer* (Wheeling, W. Va.), June 21, 1863.

state of pupilage, though heavy taxes had been annually collected from it. The east and the west, he added, had always been two separate peoples between which there had only been a slight relationship, either social or commercial. In concluding he proclaimed, "And now, today after many long and weary years of insult and injustice, culminating on the part of the East in an attempt to destroy the Government, we have the proud satisfaction of proclaiming to those around us that we are a separate State in the Union." [2]

THE FIRST LEGISLATURE

The legislature which had been chosen in the statewide election held on the fourth Thursday in May, 1863, convened in Linsly Institute on the same day on which the governor was inaugurated. The senate had only twenty members, who elected John M. Phelps of Mason County president. The fifty-one delegates chose Spicer Patrick of Kanawha County as speaker of the house. Of the whole number of legislators forty-eight were natives of Virginia, three had been born in Maryland, and all of the rest had migrated from north of the Mason-Dixon line.[3]

Having completed its organization, the legislature set to work to put the state in order. On August 4 it elected Waitman T. Willey of Monongalia County and Peter G. Van Winkle of Wood County to represent West Virginia in the United States Senate. Both senators had rendered helpful service in the formation of their state and now were rewarded by being the first persons to represent West Virginia in the upper branch of the Congress of the United States. Jacob Blair of Wood County, William G. Brown of Preston, and Kellian V. Whaley of Mason were chosen by popular vote as the first West Virginia members of the national House of Representatives.

In the May election Ralph Berkshire of Monongalia County, William A. Harrison of Harrison, and James H. Brown of Kanawha had been elected members of the supreme court of appeals. At the same time the voters had filled all the offices in the counties within the lines of the Union army. With the inauguration of the governor, the organizing of the legislature, the qualifying of the judges of the courts, the filling of all county offices, and the election of representatives in the national Congress, West Virginia was ready to speed ahead.

---

[2] The *Wheeling Intelligencer*, June 21, 1863.

[3] Fast and Maxwell, *History and Government of West Virginia* (Morgantown, 1901), pp. 144 f.

Because the armies surged back and forth across the borderland, local government in parts of the state remained unsteady while the war lasted. Some of the counties along the Virginia and Kentucky boundaries found themselves within the lines of the Confederacy; consequently they could not take an active part in the government until restored to their normal status. Eventually the national government made West Virginia a military department and placed General B. F. Kelly in charge of it. He did a great deal to maintain order, but strife continued until after Appomattox. In the meantime the legislature passed laws disqualifying persons affiliated with the Confederacy from voting or holding office.

BERKELEY AND JEFFERSON COUNTIES

Berkeley County was not included in West Virginia when the state was formed. However, on January 31, 1863, the assembly of the reorganized government of Virginia gave the voters of the county leave to hold an election for the purpose of determining whether Berkeley would join West Virginia or remain a part of Virginia. The vote resulted in a strong majority favoring West Virginia, and Governor Pierpont certified to Governor Boreman the result of the election. Consequently the legislature of West Virginia, on August 5, 1863, passed an act entitled "An Act admitting the county of Berkeley into, and making the same a part of, this State." [4] Thus Berkeley County became a part of the state of West Virginia.

The county was made a part of the tenth senatorial district and of the tenth judicial circuit. Governor Boreman issued a proclamation directing an election of county officers, but all officers acting in the county at the time of the passage of this act continued to exercise the power of their respective offices, under the authority of West Virginia, until their successors were duly elected. The governor appointed a board composed of one person in each magisterial district in the county to divide the same into townships.

On May 28 of the same year Jefferson County voted to join West Virginia, but the act for admission was not passed by the legislature until November 2, 1863. Following annexation the county was made a part of the second congressional district, of the tenth senatorial district, and of the tenth judicial circuit of the state.[5]

Certain dissatisfied persons charged that if the two votes had not been taken at a time when a great many qualified voters were in the

---

[4] *Acts of the Legislature of West Virginia*, First Session, 1863, p. 33.
[5] *Ibid.*, p. 104.

armies of the Confederacy and were thus deprived of the suffrage privilege, the result would have been different and the two counties would have remained in Virginia; they therefore asserted that the act of annexation was irregular and unconstitutional. When the soldiers returned home in 1865, a movement was begun to ignore the acts of annexation and hold elections as if the counties were still a part of Virginia. Governor Boreman issued a warning to the discontented people and then ordered Major General Emory, with troops at his command, to keep order in the Eastern Panhandle. The crisis passed without military incident.

But Virginia now entered its objections to losing the two counties, and its legislature repealed the laws by which consent had been given for annexations. About the same time Congress passed an act approving the annexation of the two counties to West Virginia. This act was intended to supersede the power of the Virginia legislature. Resistance did not end here. Virginia brought suit against West Virginia, requesting the United States Supreme Court to declare the acts whereby the counties were transferred from the one state to the other to be illegal, null, and void. The court delayed rendering a decision until 1871, when it declared that the procedure of annexation had been legal. This decision by the supreme judicial tribunal of the country closed the matter.

EARLY LEGISLATION

West Virginia came into the Union during the darkest days of the war. To the task of organizing and administering its own civil government was added the heavy responsibility of defending itself against invasion and aiding the Union in waging the war.

One of the first acts of the legislature was to authorize the city of Wheeling to raise money by loans for the defense of the city against invasion. Public property could be mortgaged and a special annual tax levied on real estate to meet the obligations of any debt incurred for defensive purposes.[6] The law gave the governor power to procure all the arms and munitions necessary for the defense of the state, and to distribute this equipment to the loyal citizens of the various counties. By order of the governor bands of minutemen were organized in the counties. These organizations included men who were not ordinarily subject to military service but who could materially aid in defensive action.[7]

---

[6] *Acts of the Legislature of West Virginia*, First Session, 1863, p. 5.

[7] *Ibid.*, p. 5.

With severity the legislature set about curbing influences that would encourage insurrection. Any person found guilty of speaking, writing, or printing in a manner to support organized rebellion could be fined an amount not to exceed one thousand dollars and imprisoned for one year.[8] The board of supervisors in each county was given the privilege of laying a special tax for the purpose of relieving the distress of the families of soldiers living or deceased.[9] The family of the soldier in West Virginia was not to be deprived of the necessary comforts of life. Food and shelter could be procured at public expense.

Despite the war emergency, a very great part of the legislation had to do with ordinary civil matters. Acts were passed concerning the jurisdiction and powers of the courts, the levying and collecting of taxes, the powers and duties of officers, and the regulation of elections. The counties were grouped in three congressional districts;[10] a board of public works was formed and its duties, rights, and powers were defined; corporations were created by legislation and empowered to navigate the rivers of the state;[11] and companies were organized to build turnpikes across the public domain.

On December 10, 1863, the legislature inaugurated the public school system.[12] Legislative acts provided for the creation of a board of education in each township, the determining of qualifications of teachers, and the building of schoolhouses. The boards of education were directed to "establish a sufficient number of free schools for the education and instruction of every individual resident within their district, between the ages of six and twenty-one years, who may apply for admission and instruction, either in person or by parent, guardian, or next friend."[13] A superintendent of schools for each county was to be elected by the voters, and the state system of education was to be headed by a state superintendent elected by a joint vote of the two branches of the legislature. Duties, compensation, and terms of office of these officials were established by the law.

The first legislature of the state dealt severely with the soldiers who had joined the Confederacy. They were declared to be enemies of the commonwealth, and their property was forfeited. All whose loyalty to the state was questioned had to take an oath to support

---

[8] *Ibid.*, p. 15.
[9] *Ibid.*, p. 223.
[10] *Ibid.*, p. 38.
[11] *Ibid.*, p. 65.
[12] *Ibid.*, p. 245.
[13] *Ibid.*, p. 247.

the Constitution of the United States and the constitution of West Virginia.[14]

From 1864 to 1868

THE SECOND ELECTION (1864)

During the first year of the new administration armed strife provoked political and social cleavages, and feelings of hatred ran high. The state officials performed their duties under difficulties and were constantly faced by emergencies. But they did their work so well that when the second election was held on the fourth Thursday in October, 1864, there was little disposition to make changes. G. D. Hall succeeded J. Edgar Boyer as secretary of state and J. M. McWhorter became auditor in the place of Samuel Crane; the other officers of state were reelected.

By this time the battle of Gettysburg was history and the star of the Confederacy was receding. General Grant had begun his hammering campaign at the gates of Richmond, Atlanta had fallen before Sherman's march, and General Sheridan had taken possession of the Shenandoah Valley. Thousands of West Virginia soldiers marched with the armies in the last struggles of the war and consequently did not vote in the election of 1864.

THE RETURN OF PEACE

Order came speedily after Appomattox, but West Virginia was a border state where division had created hatreds that only time could mollify. The soldiers returning from the armies of the South found themselves disqualified from voting or holding office; their property could be confiscated; by reason of having taken part in the rebellion they now stood as aliens in the land in which they had been born and reared. Restoration of citizenship was to come in time, but meanwhile the animosities engendered by the war rankled.

On December 18, 1865, the thirteenth amendment to the national Constitution put an end to slavery in all parts of the Union. However, the freed slaves could not vote, hold office, or serve as witnesses in court. Having no civil or political privileges recognized by law, they found themselves and their property in a position to a great extent defenseless, and in many instances they were robbed by

---

[14] *Ibid.*, p. 131. Actually, the sale of property belonging to Confederate soldiers occurred only on rare occasions. The loyal people had no disposition to take the property of their neighbors even if they were in rebellion.

unscrupulous persons. In time the fourteenth amendment to the national Constitution gave the freed people the status of citizens. The Negro citizens of West Virginia voted for the first time in the election of 1870.

ELECTION LAWS

By authority of an act passed by the legislature on November 13, 1863, the assessor of each county made a list of the qualified voters in each township of his county; any person whose name did not appear on the assessor's list could not vote. To qualify as a voter one must have attained the age of twenty-one years and must have been a resident in the state for at least a year and in the county for thirty days. On a separate record the assessor kept the names of all persons enlisted in the military service of the United States who, upon enlistment, had qualified themselves to vote. For this service he received three cents for each name placed on the records. The law assured legal protection against plural voting, counterfeit ballots, bribery, betting, and other corrupt practices.

"The white male citizens of the State shall be entitled to vote at all elections within the election district in which they respectively reside." [15] Since this regulation was a part of the constitution, a law passed by the legislature could not legally change it. Nevertheless the election laws included the statement that "every person present and offering to vote shall, in time of war, insurrection, or public danger, if required by any voter of the township, take before the supervisor or one of the inspectors, an oath that he will support the constitution of the United States and the constitution of the State." [16] Persons disqualified by the law often refused to reveal the part they had taken in the war, thus hoping to improve their chance for registration. But someone familiar with local conditions usually knew the facts and had no reluctance in revealing them. So, the strife went on, though the war had ended, and violence frequently broke out at places of voting.

In 1867 the election laws underwent an extensive change. A county board of registration, consisting of three members appointed by the governor, was created in each county. In turn this board appointed one registrar for each township, who listed the qualified voters. The chief purpose of the change was to bring more stringent restrictions to bear on the persons who had assisted the Confederacy.

---

[15] *Acts of the Legislature of West Virginia*, 1863, p. 278.

[16] *Ibid.*, p. 119.

If the township registrar doubted the loyalty of any applicant, he did not register him until the would-be voter had subscribed to a severe oath declaring that he had rendered no aid to the rebellion against the United States. The rigorous application of this law resulted in strife, hatred, and in some instances bloodshed. So far the political weather had not cleared in West Virginia.

OTHER EARLY LEGISLATION

The period from 1863 to 1870 marked the beginning of industrial development in the state, and the types of industry that were promoted may be known from the nature of early legislation. The majority of the charters issued to corporations by the legislature went to oil companies; were granted to turnpike and bridge companies, railroad and navigation companies, and lumber companies. The eastern financial and industrial magnates who furnished funds for these new developments had their gaze fixed on the virgin forests, the coal, oil, gas, and other natural resources in the West Virginia hills. The time had come to open the way to these undeveloped riches.

At every meeting of the legislature charters were issued to new towns and changes were made in those of old ones. Changing county boundaries, fixing dates for holding courts, and establishing the duties of officers required devoted care and attention on the part of the governor and the legislature.

The Stevenson Administration

THE ELECTION OF 1868

The administration of the laws regulating the qualification of voters, the confiscation of property, and the liberal treatment of the Negro race at length turned a great many people against the Boreman administration. In the election of 1868 the Republicans nominated William E. Stevenson of Wood County for governor, and the Democrats named Johnson N. Camden of the same county. Stevenson was a native of Pennsylvania and had served in the legislature of that state. Upon coming to West Virginia he had purchased a farm in Wood County. He took an active part in the election of 1860, and he made valuable contributions as a member of the constitutional convention of 1861. When West Virginia became a state, Stevenson was elected a member of the senate, and he was later elevated to the presidency of that assembly. Camden was an aggressive industrialist. He had seen the possibilities of development in the oil industry and had become a leader in that field. His development of oil refineries stood out as a pioneer achievement that was destined to expand to great dimensions. Both men were able and capable statesmen. In the election Stevenson was successful, and carried into office with him the other candidates of his party.

Before the time for the inauguration of Governor Stevenson, the legislature elected Governor Boreman to the United States Senate as successor to Senator Van Winkle. Upon the resignation of Boreman as governor, the president of the senate, D. D. T. Farnsworth of Upshur County, succeeded to the chief executiveship, serving in that capacity only six days, February 26 to March 4, 1869.

THE POLICY OF GOVERNOR STEVENSON

From the beginning the new governor gave evidence of a liberal view of the voting restrictions on the people who had taken part in the rebellion. In his opinion, test oaths, confiscation of property, and other disabilities had never been intended to be perpetual. The repressive legislation had been passed at a time of stress and danger; now that the threat to public safety had ended, why continue it? Governor Stevenson recommended the repeal of the war laws. The legislature approved his recommendations, and the test oaths passed out of existence.

A change in the constitution was necessary to extend the privilege of voting to the disqualified soldiers, and the governor urged that such an amendment be made. The measure was taken up in the legislature by an able member of that assembly, W. H. H. Flick of Pendleton County. The amendment provided that all male citizens of the state be entitled to vote except minors, paupers, and others possessing inabilities, no reference being made to race or color. The amendment was accepted by the legislature, submitted to a vote of the people, and in due time (1871) ratified. This amendment ended discrimination against race, creed, or party on election day in West Virginia.

The enfranchisement of the southern soldiers and the unwise administration of the reconstruction laws had alienated a great deal of political influence from the governor and his party. Governor Stevenson's wish to re-establish good order, harmonious public endeavor, and an equality of political privileges in the state was carried out, but it worked to the undoing of his own party, for in the election of 1870 he was defeated for re-election, and John J. Jacob of Hampshire County was chosen as the first Democratic governor of the state. This change in party administration brought with it a desire to rewrite the constitution of West Virginia.

The New Constitution

POINTS AT ISSUE

The legislature of 1871 passed an act calling for a constitutional convention, and the act was approved by popular vote on August 24, 1871.[17] An election for delegates to the constitutional convention was then called.

These steps were the signal for vigorous controversy. Those opposed to revision of the constitution warned the public that in the convention the judicial department of the government would be attacked and perhaps entirely changed, that the free school system stood in danger of being abolished, and that the provisions forbidding the legislature to pass laws favoring private profits gained by public help would be set aside. Those favoring revision charged that the township system did not suit West Virginia, that the secret ballot entailed too much expense, and that the basis of suffrage was too broad. The illiterate white people and the Negroes, they considered, now had a dangerous degree of political power without the ability or experience to use it wisely. The heavy majorities favoring the convention came from the counties along the Virginia border, where the recently enfranchised ex-Confederate population was heaviest; and the objections to the constitution were distinctly reminiscent of the political ideas of old Virginia.

THE CONSTITUTIONAL CONVENTION

On October 26, 1871, seventy-eight delegates were chosen to form a new constitution for the state. In general the delegates were men of maturity and experience. They took conservative attitudes and declined to adopt a policy of experimentation in constitution writing. The chairman of the convention was Samuel Price of Greenbrier County, a lawyer who had served in the Virginia constitutional convention of 1850 and had acted as lieutenant governor of Virginia during the period of secession. Price was sixty-seven years old at the time of the 1872 convention. Later (1876) he received an appointment to the United States Senate to complete the unexpired term of Senator Allen T. Caperton.

The convention met at Charleston, the new capital,[18] on January 16, 1872. At first the prewar sentiment of Virginia made itself

---

17 The popular vote was 30,220 for, 27,638 against.

18 The capital had been changed from Wheeling to Charleston by legislative act in 1870.

militantly evident, as if there were to be an effort to take the state back under the government from which it had so recently freed itself. But responsibility sobers a constitutional convention just as it does an individual, and the conservative element in the meeting was strong enough to take matters into its own hands. Moreover, the radical group had to keep in mind the fact that some of its favorite measures would probably never be accepted by the voters even if they were adopted in the convention.

CHANGES IN THE CONSTITUTION

The new constitution will be analyzed in detail in the next chapter; here only the more important changes will be summarized.

The qualification for voting was widened to include both white and colored citizens, so that there would be no conflict with the fifteenth amendment to the Constitution of the United States, which forbids race or color to interfere with one's privilege of voting. In the debate to strike the word "white" from the qualifying clause with respect to voting, strife and strong feeling loomed up. Those opposing the change doubted the capability of the Negroes to govern themselves, but the voting privilege in the new constitution did not recognize race or color.

It has been seen that the constitution of 1863 made provision for secret voting. The reactionary element in the convention vigorously opposed this article and urged a return to *viva voce* voting, but fear of public disfavor forced a compromise. The constitution gave the voter leave to cast his ballot open, sealed, or secret, a rule unlike that in any other state.

Various revisions of the executive, legislative, and judicial departments will be discussed later. The office of lieutenant governor was discontinued, and it was provided that the president of the senate and the speaker of the house should succeed in turn to the governorship if a vacancy should occur. Although amendments to the constitution calling for the reinstatement of the office of lieutenant governor have since been submitted to the people, on each occasion they have been emphatically turned down.

During the period just following the war, railroad building in West Virginia underwent new development and perhaps exercised some influence in legislation to the advantage of that enterprise. Liberal franchises to corporations, including railroad companies, were forbidden in the new constitution – one of the many restrictive regulations placed in that document. Added to the list of matters on which the legislature was forbidden to pass local or special laws were the selling of property belonging to a religious denomination or charitable institution, the changing of county seats, the establishing of ferries, the remitting of fines, the regulating of legal interest, and various others.

The township system had been severely attacked as an institution borrowed from New England and unbecoming to West Virginia. The sentiment in the convention for the old Virginia plan of local government soon overcame all opposition, and the justice of the peace and the county court received the sanction of the convention with applause. The county court was soundly denounced by John M. Hagans of Monongalia County as a corrupt institution and one in which it was impossible to attain justice, but it was strongly supported by A. F. Haymond of Marion. Reaction had set in; the old guard now possessed the political field and would have its way even if it had to disregard precedent and good judgment. Finally, the West Virginia township was cast out and the county court returned much as it had existed in Virginia long before 1863.

Long and sharp discussions took place with respect to reforms of the judiciary, but sentiment was so much in favor of the reactionary side that no danger threatened of the convention's breaking up before its work could be completed. In general the judiciary underwent a rather extensive change, but the changes were logical, and the new system, amended by legislation, has stood the test of time, although at the present the need of the justices of the peace is seriously questioned.[19]

When the constitution was completed it was submitted to the vote of the people and ratified. Since 1872 there has not been another constitutional convention in West Virginia. Although the work of the convention may have had its defects, in the main it has been acceptable to the people for whom it was made. Thirty amendments have been ratified; many more have been offered but have failed to be approved by the people. It is generally conceded that if the law is what the people want it to be, there is no court or legislature that has a right to change it. So long as the general public is satisfied with its present supreme law, it will remain in fact and in practice.

[19] In 1920 an amendment to the constitution that would have eliminated the office of justice of the peace was voted down.

CHAPTER 11

The Constitution of 1872

Thus far we have made an historical survey of the development of the government of West Virginia from the beginning until 1872. Now it is in order to make a study of the constitution as it exists today. The present chapter will summarize briefly the articles of the document; later chapters will examine them in more detail. The ultimate aim of our examination will be to understand how the political framework of our state functions in serving the people for whom it was made. To serve the people, to protect them in their honest possessions and their worthy endeavors, and to promote the beneficent interests of all, are the ultimate purposes of government. And the best government is the one that serves all the people best.

For many generations our constitutional law has grown. By reason of changes in our civil life, new restraints have been enacted and new privileges granted for the welfare of the people. As civil life grows more complex, so do the rules of law regulating it; and our civil life has become complex to a degree beyond even the imagination of the fathers. Changing conditions have outmoded some old laws and created a necessity for new ones. For example, the general assembly of Virginia in 1720 passed a law offering a reward to anyone who killed a wolf, an animal which was at that time terribly destructive to the sheep, hogs, and cattle imported at great expense from Europe. Today there is probably not a wild wolf at large in West Virginia, so that the law has no longer any application. On the other hand, in 1720 the lawmakers gave no thought to regulating the movement of traffic on public highways; but today much time is given to the making of laws to protect the safety of the people in the rush of highway travel.

The First Article

POWERS OF THE STATE

It will be remembered that after the Civil War West Virginia was solicited by Virginia to lay aside all differences and reunite with her under the same governor and the same flag. West Virginia's refusal at that time is reiterated in the first sentence of the constitution of 1872, which declares that "West Virginia is, and shall remain, one of the United States of America."

Although West Virginia acknowledged the Constitution of the United States as the supreme law of the land, it further understood that the national government possessed only the powers delegated to it by the consent of the people. On the other hand, certain powers were denied to the state by the same authority. The people are sovereign; they may give and they may take away. Making treaties, coining money, passing bills of attainder, granting titles of nobility are examples of the powers which cannot be exercised by a state. So the power of the state is limited. But all rights and privileges lying without the bounds of expressed restraints are reserved to the power of the state and may be exercised by its authority.

Exclusive jurisdiction in the regulation and administration of its own government, both civil and police, is retained by West Virginia, and it becomes the solemn duty of its several departments to protect and promote the interests of the people. The actual purpose, then, as of all civil government emanating from the people, is to protect them, foster their rights, and hearten them in providing comfort and promoting industry.

The constitution is to continue operative in time of war as well as in time of peace. Any departure from that principle becomes subversive of good government and tends toward despotism. The power of the constitution, therefore, remains constant and is intended to operate adversely to despotic rule.

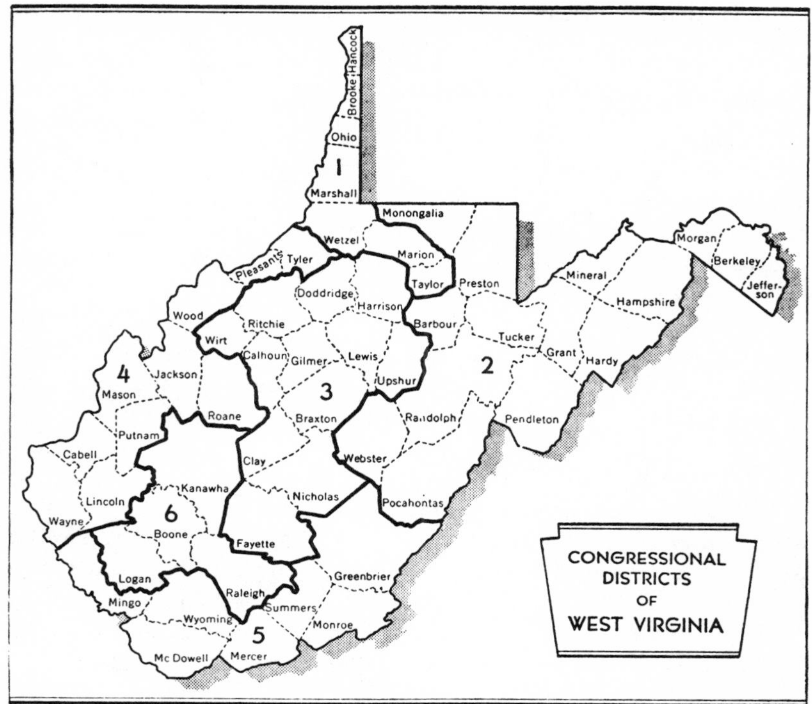

ELECTION DISTRICTS

The state must be divided into a certain number of districts, reasonably equal in population and composed of contiguous counties, for the purpose of electing representatives to the Congress of the United States.[1] The number of these districts is determined by rules prescribed by the national government. One representative is elected from each district. Like each of the other states, West Virginia chooses two United States senators.

BOUNDARIES AND JURISDICTION

The territory of West Virginia is declared to be formed out of territory once a part of the commonwealth of Virginia. It includes the "bed, banks and shores" of the Ohio and so much of the Big Sandy River as was formerly in Virginia; these form parts of the

[1] The state now contains six congressional districts. See the accompanying chart.

counties that lie contiguous to them. The power of the state of course extends to the farthest limits of its own territory.

WHO ARE CITIZENS

The powers of government reside in the citizens of the state. Any person born or naturalized in the United States, being subject to the jurisdiction thereof, and residing in West Virginia is accorded citizenship in the state. This regulation had to be in harmony with the Fourteenth Amendment of the national Constitution, which relates to the qualifications for citizenship.

The constitution declares that no distinction shall be made between resident aliens and citizens with respect to the acquisition, tenure, disposition, and descent of property; but the equal representation guaranteed to all citizens does not relate to aliens.

TREASON AGAINST THE STATE

Treason against the state is defined as consisting in levying war against it, or giving aid and comfort to its enemies. Persons may be convicted of this crime only on evidence rendered by at least two witnesses to the overt act or on confession made in open court. Punishment for treason may be a fine, imprisonment, or death, the degree of severity depending upon the character of the offense.

THE GREAT SEAL

It was necessary to adopt an official seal for the purpose of authenticating documents in the name of the state. Under the new constitution the seal originally devised in 1863 was continued. The design, wrought in a combination of attractive colors, is fashioned in the form of a disc, with two human figures and certain implements of industry, as the ax and the plow. The border bears the motto *Montani Semper Liberi* (Mountaineers Always Free), a sentiment genuinely applicable to the people of West Virginia. The whole is a symbol of unity and beauty, wisdom, industry, and fortitude. No change in the design has ever been made.[2]

---

[2] A state flag was first adopted by legislative act in 1905; later the original design was somewhat revised and the present emblem was adopted March 7, 1929. Its proportions are the same as those of the ensign of the United States. The general field is white, representing purity, and its border of blue signifies justice. On the center of the field is emblazoned the coat of arms of the state, the symbol of faith, authority, and unity. Above the coat of arms is a white ribbon bearing the words "State of West Virginia," and around its other three sides is a wreath of rhododendron with leaves of

The seal is kept in the office of the secretary of state and is affixed by him to all orders, commissions, and proclamations issued by the governor. Authentication by the seal gives documents full faith and credit in the courts and elsewhere. It is required by law that official documents shall be proved and attested by the seal of the office from which they are issued. The wording of this form is usually "given under my hand and seal." [8]

WRITS AND COMMISSIONS

The constitution requires that official documents issued under the authority of the state shall be in the name of the state of West Virginia. Under the name and by the authority of the state, commissions are issued to officers certifying that they are fully entitled to perform their duties as public servants upon taking the proper oath. Grants of property are issued under the authority of the state as an indication that the commonwealth will protect an owner in the possession of his property provided his title is legal. Writs (as mandamus, habeas corpus, and quo warranto) and injunctions are issued also in the name of the state. Indictments brought by a grand jury against persons accused of violating the law must conclude with the statement that the act is committed "against the peace and dignity of the State."

The Bill of Rights

The idea of equality for individuals has been handed down from as early as the thirteenth century in England, when man owned by man was still driven to the field and scourged to his dungeon, and when government by the people had not been written in the laws of nations. Autocratic knighthood had been invented to compel men to work, to pay, and to serve. But eventually those who served revolted against the royal forces and wrote their code of freedom in the statute books. When the Revolutionary War ended in America, the rule of kings had become anathema to the patriots who wrote a Bill of Rights into their national constitution. This list of laws was the citizen's code of protection against unreasonable or unjust treat-

---

glossy green and flowers of delicate pink – the natural attractive colors. The ensign of the state is attached with a golden cord to a staff, on the top of which is mounted the American eagle. It is displayed at suitable places on fitting occasions.

[8] When the seal of an individual is required on a contract or other document he may affix to it a written, printed, or engraved scroll. This insignia may be made by another and adopted by the person signing the paper.

ment by his government. Following the century-old custom in America of embodying in the constitution a list of principles to protect the citizen against the tyranny of an oppressive government, the constitutional convention of West Virginia formulated its Bill of Rights and placed it under the third article. Here are found the guarantees of freedom of speech and press, of peaceable assembly, and of religious worship; freedom from unreasonable search, seizure, and detention; rights of private property and of trial by due process; and various others. The individual items in the Bill of Rights will be discussed below, in the chapter on "The Citizen and His Constitutional Protection."

Elections and Officers

SUFFRAGE

There is nothing hard to understand in the constitutional provisions concerning the qualification of voters in West Virginia. They shall be at least twenty-one years of age, citizens of the state, residents of the state for one year and of the county in which they offer to vote for sixty days preceding that offer, and duly registered. A person of unsound mind, a pauper, or one who is under conviction for treason, felony, or bribery in an election cannot vote while such disability continues. Soldiers or sailors quartered in the state cannot claim the privilege of voting by reason of the fact that they are quartered in West Virginia on election day. The manner of voting shall be by ballot only, but the voter is left free to submit an open or sealed ticket which he has marked either secretly or openly.

In order that the voter shall be duly protected in the exercise of his privilege he is free from arrest upon *civil* process on election day, or until he has cast his ballot. One is not protected against arrest for a *criminal* charge, and if he violates the election laws on the day of voting he may be placed under arrest. The voter is not compelled on this day to attend court as a juror or a witness, work on the public roads, or render military service unless public danger demands. All in all, one qualified to vote has full legal protection in the exercise of his privilege, and it is usually his own fault if he does not take advantage of this favor.

QUALIFICATIONS FOR OFFICE

Every officer in West Virginia, whether state, county, or municipal, must be a citizen of the commonwealth. This is the first requirement. The second is that the governor and judges must have attained the age of thirty years, while the attorney-general and senators must be at least twenty-five at the beginning of their official service, and must have been citizens of the state at least five years preceding their election or appointment. For the other officers there is no age requirement, except that they must be of legal voting age.

Before entering upon their duties, all persons elected or appointed to office must take an oath pledging that they will support the Constitution of the United States and the constitution of West Virginia, and that they will discharge their duties to the best of their skill and judgment. No other pledge is required; no other should be given. Faithfully to obey the law and render service to the best of his ability are all that the demanding public should expect of an officer, and no less than that service should an officer expect to give.

After the officer has been elected according to law and the oath administered he is ready to begin his duties. The duration of his term is specified either in the constitution or by the legislature, and his powers, duties, and compensation are likewise provided. If his duties are not properly fulfilled any officer of the state is liable to removal by impeachment.

IMPEACHMENT OF OFFICIALS

The constitution states, "The House of Delegates shall have the sole power of impeachment. The Senate shall have the sole power to try impeachments." That is, the lower house of the legislature presents the charges on the basis of which the senate must conduct the trial. A member of the house of delegates first presents charges to the house against a civil officer of the state. If the charges are accepted they are referred to a special committee for investigation. If the committee considers the charges genuine it recommends to the delegates assembled that articles of impeachment shall be passed and transmitted to the senate.

When the senate sits as a court of impeachment, the president of the state supreme court of appeals presides, and a vote of two-thirds of the members elected is required for conviction. The decision is final; no appeal from it can be made. Even the pardoning power of the governor cannot be extended to the relief of the one so convicted, for he himself is liable to impeachment.

Following impeachment and conviction the punishment may not extend beyond removal from office and disqualification from holding any other office under the state. But if the person so convicted has by his offense committed a crime against the state, he stands liable to indictment, trial, and punishment in the courts according to the offense for which he has been declared guilty.

DISQUALIFICATION FOR DUELING

Although at one time dueling was considered an honorable way of settling a dispute or adjusting a personal insult, the constitution of West Virginia condemns the nefarious practice by disqualifying any citizen who directly or indirectly takes part in a duel from holding any office in the state. This provision was followed by acts of the legislature which provide severe punishment for dueling or even for sending or accepting a challenge.

REGULATION OF ELECTIONS

It would naturally come within the power of the legislature to enact laws regulating elections in the state, but the makers of the constitution did not fail to make specific provision on this important point. They emphasized its consequence by requiring the legislature to prescribe the manner of conducting and making returns of elections. Intimidation, disorder, and violence at elections must be forbidden by law and the guilty duly prosecuted. No doubt this provision was prompted, in part at least, by the strife that occurred in the choosing of officers after the Civil War. It has served well through the years, but on occasions it has been notoriously abused.

The original constitution stated that a citizen shall *not* be denied the privilege of voting because his name is not registered as a qualified voter. Again in this clause one may see an effort to widen the suffrage privilege to all citizens regardless of their wartime experience. But when this principle had fulfilled its purpose it was set aside by amendment. The amendment was proposed by a joint resolution of the legislature, passed on February 22, 1901, and adopted in November, 1902. The new clause in the constitution states, "The legislature shall enact proper laws for the registration of all qualified voters in this State."

The general election of state and county officers is held on the Tuesday next after the first Monday in November.[4] Municipal officers are chosen at times designated in the city charters. The legislature prescribes the manner of conducting elections and making

---

[4] As changed by Amendment in 1883. The day originally set was the second Tuesday in October.

returns of the same, and passes laws to prevent disorder or violence at the polls, to regulate the counting of votes, to ascertain and declare the results, and to punish fraud, corruption, or intimidation at elections.

Division of Powers

As a recognized principle of a republican form of government the constitution of West Virginia requires a separation of the powers of government into three distinct branches, the legislative, the executive, and the judicial; and the authorities of the state are forewarned that no one of these powers shall exercise the jurisdiction "properly belonging to either of the others." However, an exception is made in the fact that the justice of the peace is eligible to election to the legislature. It is hard to account for his exception, since a justice of the peace is as much a judicial officer as a judge of the circuit court. The harmlessness of this act rests with the infrequency of its use, not with the principle involved.

The Legislature

The constitution next takes up the election, terms of office, and duties of the legislators. The legislature is a bicameral body, divided into a senate and a house of delegates, both elected by the citizens. In these two bodies all the legislative power of the state is vested. Each body meets in a separate assembly and chooses its own officers.

The duty of the legislature is to make laws and transact other business for the good of all the people. The legislator assumes a great responsibility, one upon which only the wisest and most courageous should dare to enter, for to make laws operating with justice on all the people befits only those who excel in knowledge, equity, and discernment. A discussion of the duties and modes of procedure of the legislature will be taken up in detail in two later chapters of this book.

The Executive Department

The executive authority of West Virginia is not vested in one office but in several, including those of the governor, secretary of state, auditor, treasurer, attorney general, superintendent of free schools, and commissioner of agriculture. The term of all these officers is four years, beginning on the first Monday after the second Wednesday of January next after their election. They must reside at the seat of government and keep there the public records pertaining to their offices.

The constitution specifically states that "the chief executive power shall be vested in the Governor, who shall take care that the laws be faithfully executed." It further defines his special powers and duties. He is to issue his message to the legislature informing it of the condition of the state; he may call the legislature to convene in special session; he may appoint and remove officers; he has power to remit fines and forfeitures and to grant pardons; he is commander-in-chief of the military forces; and he must sign bills passed by the legislature before they become law.

Each of the other executive officers has special powers and duties independent of the governor. All are elected by the people and are responsible to the people. Their duties, other than those defined in the constitution, are granted and regulated by acts of the legislature. In a later chapter the duties of all the executive officers will be examined in detail.

The Judicial Department

The state needed a strong judiciary, and the work of organizing it was no small task. Beginning with the district as a judicial unit, there are the justices of the peace, then the county courts, the circuit courts, and finally the supreme court of appeals. The legislature has authority to create additional courts that may function in town and city government.

THE SUPREME COURT OF APPEALS

Provision was made for a supreme court of appeals consisting of four judges; the number was later changed by an amendment to five. In many particulars relating to this court the constitution sets up very definite requirements. In addition to its appellate functions, it is to have original jurisdiction in specified cases. The frequency of the sessions of the court, its officers, the filling of vacancies in it, and the extent of its jurisdiction come within the scope of constitutional regulation, but salaries are fixed by the legislature.

CIRCUIT COURTS

The state is divided into twenty-four circuits, in each of which the people elect a judge. Although the circuit court ranks above the justice of the peace, it stands near to the people and is accessible to their needs. A circuit may be composed of one county or of two or more, depending largely on the population. Originally there were only thirteen judicial circuits in West Virginia. The constitution defines the term, the jurisdiction, and to a certain degree the place of meeting of this court.

COUNTY COURTS

"There shall be in each county of the State a county court, composed of three commissioners." [5] The members are elected by the voters of the county; they hold at least four regular sessions in each year; [6] and they have the custody of all deeds and other papers presented for record in the counties. Although the constitution establishes the county court as part of the judicial organization of the state, in many respects its duties are not of a judicial nature. The details of this tribunal will be discussed presently.

COURTS OF LIMITED JURISDICTION

The constitution provides that courts of limited jurisdiction may be created by law. The purpose is to allow a county, an incorporated town, or a village the convenience of a special court for the purpose of taking care of local business. The only court of this nature mentioned in the constitution is that at Wheeling: "The municipal court of Wheeling shall continue in existence until otherwise provided by law." This privilege has now been extended to several other cities. Appeals in civil cases from the court at Wheeling go directly to the supreme court of appeals. Other municipal courts have the right of appeal to the circuit courts.

JUSTICES OF THE PEACE

Finally, there is provided the court of the justice of the peace representing the district government. Each county is divided into districts, "not less than three nor more than ten in number." In each district not exceeding twelve hundred population the qualified voters elect one justice; in more populous districts, two. The jurisdiction of this officer is countywide. In local government the justice's court is the court of first instance, where disposition is made of petty cases, and its services are brought close to the people for the purpose of preventing breaches of the peace and bringing immediate punishment to persons guilty of violating the law.

---

[5] Preston County has ten members.

[6] Provision may be made by law for holding special sessions.

In addition to his duties in conducting his court, the justice takes acknowledgments of deeds and other instruments of writing, administers oaths, and certifies depositions. The legislature may widen at its discretion the jurisdiction of the justice, but the power of the court may not extend to suits in which the damage or money sought to be recovered exceeds three hundred dollars.

Perhaps no other officer in this state has invited so much adverse criticism as the district "squire," largely because the law does not impose qualifications as to education and legal experience. The result is that many justices do not have proper knowledge and training to meet adequately their responsibilities. The office of justice of the peace in West Virginia was put on trial before the people in 1940, when they voted on an amendment to the constitution to eliminate this office. The electorate sustained the office by a big majority.[7]

County Organization

For the organization of county government the constitution specifies a definite plan. There are no lines distinctly separating the legislative, executive, and judicial powers within the county; there is no officer corresponding in authority to the governor of the state or the mayor of a city, no lawmaking body to compare with the state legislature. There are, however, officers whose duties unite in executive, judicial, and legislative matters. The lack of a responsible administrative head is perhaps the greatest defect in county government.

According to constitutional requirement the voters in each county elect a sheriff, a prosecuting attorney, not more than two assessors, and a surveyor of lands, who hold their offices for a term of four years. In addition to this number, and in the same manner, there are chosen a clerk of the county court, a clerk of the circuit court, and a county board of education. The county court appoints coroners, overseers of the poor, and supervisors of roads. The term and duties of each officer are prescribed by the constitution or by laws passed by the legislature. The government of the county is thus placed in the hands of officers who are held responsible for the conduct of the people's business and are subject to indictment for official misconduct or neglect of duty.

---

[7] If the amendment had carried the legislature would have been authorized to create a summary court in each county. This office would have absorbed all the duties of justice of the peace and a part of the work of the circuit court. The popular vote stood 133,256 for the amendment, 300,979 against.

Taxation and Finance

Revenue for the government is derived from taxation, and as the cost of maintaining the government increases so do taxes. In order to maintain an organized civil society there must be an expenditure of revenue, and therefore an income has to be assured. A safe and sound financial policy, adjusted to the needs of the people, is a cardinal virtue of government.

TAXATION

The article of the constitution relating to taxation was amended in the general election of 1932.[8] It now specifies that taxes shall be equal and uniform throughout the state, that property shall be taxed in proportion to its value, and that all values on property shall be ascertained as directed by law.

As a curb to an unreasonable increase in taxation, property is divided into four different classes and a maximum rate of levy is fixed on each by the constitution. In addition to the property taxes, revenue may be also derived from taxes on privileges, franchises, incomes, inheritances, and sales. During the recent increase in government expenditures there has been a relentless search for a source of public income to meet, at least in part, the unusual outlay of money. It is the business of good government to strike annually a balance of receipts with expenditures. An unreasonable deficit becomes as dangerous to the business of government as to any other business enterprise.

Certain exemptions are allowed. Property used for educational, literary, scientific, religious, and charitable purposes, cemeteries, and public property are nontaxable. Persons afflicted with physical infirmities may be exempt from paying the capitation tax collectible from all other male inhabitants of the state who have attained the age of twenty-one years.

CARE OF PUBLIC FUNDS

Money must not be drawn from the treasury of the state unless an appropriation is made by an act of the legislature in which the amount and purpose of the same are definitely specified. Conforming with the act of the legislature, the auditor issues a warrant of the amount so designated. This arrangement protects the money deposited in the treasury, accumulated from the people in the pay-

[8] The tax limitation amendment was adopted by a vote of 335,482 in its favor, to 13,931 against it.

ment of their taxes. All this money has been paid by the people, and for the people it must be spent. A complete statement of the receipts and expenditures of the public funds must be published annually.

CONTRACTING OF STATE DEBT

The constitution places a strict limitation on the legislature concerning the creating of public debt. No debt shall be contracted except to meet current deficits, to redeem liabilities already made, to suppress rebellion, to repel invasion, to defend the state in time of war. If a debt is ever created for any or all of these purposes, its payment is to be distributed equally over a period of twenty years or more.

Again, the taxing power of the state extends only to the raising of revenue for the payment of the annual estimated expense, the reduction of the public debt, and the support of the public schools. If a deficiency should exist in any year, the legislature at its next session must levy a tax to meet such deficiency and to defray the current expenses of running the government. The constitution places no limitations on "the current expenses of the government," so that the legislature has almost unqualified power to raise revenue. The ultimate means of doing so is by taxation.

Now, can the state assume a part or all of the public debt of a county or a town? Can it be a stockholder in a company? Can it extend credit to a person or a corporation? All of these questions the constitution answers in the negative. The constitution limits the credit of the state and all payments made by it in terms of the interest of all the people and not of any particular group of them.

LIMITATIONS ON LOCAL TAXATION

To protect the people from the possible extravagances of local government, county authorities, with a few exceptions, are forbidden to lay a levy to exceed ninety-five cents on the hundred dollars valuation of property unless the matter has been submitted to a vote of the people and approved by three-fifths of the votes cast. Counties, towns, and school districts, after the adoption of the constitution, are not to become indebted in an amount exceeding five per cent of the value of their taxable property. All debts incurred by a county or municipality must be authorized by at least three-fifths of the votes cast. The legislature possesses power to authorize the officers of towns and cities to collect taxes for their own uses, but all such taxes must be uniform within the corporate limits of the municipality.

When the limitations with respect to debt, taxation, and collections are considered it becomes evident that the legislature stands obedient to the constitution. Amounts are restricted, time is limited, purposes for which funds may be used are designated, and the manner by which appropriations may be made is fixed. All this care is taken in order to safeguard the money paid in taxes by the citizens so that values may be returned to them in proper proportion to the amount they give.

Corporations

A corporation is a body consisting of one or more persons, established by law for some definite purpose, and continued by a succession of members. The chief characteristic of the corporation is its continuity, which may extend from generation to generation. This characteristic gives the organization a chance for long-continued concentration on the purpose for which it was designated. The corporation uses the political organization of the state as its model for administration, always within legal limits, and secures protection from the state. For present purposes only the two classes of corporations are mentioned, public and private.

A municipality forms its organization in the following manner: by an act of the legislature a charter is granted to a town or city, conveying to it authority to form a civil government and transact business. Its purpose is to control populous centers of the state and thus assist in the administration of government. Incorporation promotes good order, the protection of life and property, and the general welfare of the citizens. Such town or city government is known as a public corporation.

The legislature also charters private corporations, that is, associations of persons authorized by law to transact business for private gain. Banks, railroads, and mercantile companies are examples of such organization.

With respect to all private corporations the constitution lays down controlling principles, or extends to the legislature the power of regulation. This control protects the citizen from being humbled or deceived through the power of a corporation. For instance, a railroad is declared to be a public highway, free to all persons as a facility for transportation, keeping its charges within reasonable maximum rates prescribed by law without favor or discrimination.

No corporation may be created by special law; all must be created by general laws, uniform as to classes, except, adds the constitution, that nothing in this section "shall prevent the Legislature from providing by special laws for the connection, by canals, of the waters of the Chesapeake with the Ohio river, by line of the James river, Greenbrier, New river, and Great Kanawha." The means of modern transportation have forever put to flight this old idea of building canals.

The stockholders of corporations and joint stock companies, except banks and banking institutions, are liable under the constitution for their corporate indebtedness to the amount of their stock subscribed, but not exceeding that amount. The legislature provides that stockholders in companies and corporations shall have the right to vote in the elections of the directors and managers, according to the number of shares held.

The legislature provides by law for the organization of state banks which may issue notes of circulation and serve as depositories and places of discount. The stockholders in state banks are personally responsible to the creditors for liabilities equal to their respective shares, if such liabilities accrue while these persons are stockholders.

State banks may or may not belong to the federal reserve financial system. If such a bank joins the system, the Federal Deposit Insurance Corporation insures deposits to the extent of $10,000. Consequently the state banks draw nearer in likeness to federal banks as time goes on. Of right this similarity should exist, for a unitary money system thrives best under regulatory laws that are not too dissimilar.

Education

For many years before the division of Virginia, the west pleaded for an equal share with the east in the schools of the state. But the plea was never fully answered. When West Virginians drafted their first constitution they declared that "the legislature shall provide, as soon as practicable, for the establishment of a thorough and efficient system of free schools." [9] Gordon Battelle, chairman of the committee on education in the constitutional convention, developed this principle and deserves to be remembered as the father of the public schools in West Virginia. The legislature was further empowered to arrange "for the organization of such institutions of learning as the best interests of general education in the State may demand." [10]

[9] *Code of West Virginia,* 1870, p. 37. [10] *Ibid.*

In 1872 the constitutional convention extended further the plan then in use. It provided for an administrator who would have supervision over all the public schools of the state, and empowered the legislature to provide for county superintendents and other necessary officers. It established a permanent and invested school fund. In 1902 an amendment to the constitution created an irreducible school fund of $1,000,000 and a general school fund for the support of the public schools of the state. This fund came from appropriations made by the legislature, from fines and forfeitures, and from general taxation on persons and property. Counties and districts were enabled to lay levies for the support of their schools. Concerning such levies an annual settlement had to be made with the county court.

White and colored persons were not to be taught in the same school.

Further, in order to forbid imposition or abuse of duty, any person connected with a state educational institution of any grade or name was forbidden any interest in the sale of books or articles to the schools, except that the law did not apply to any work written or any useful device invented by such person. The exceptions promoted authorship and invention.

Independent school districts could not be created in any county unless the residents in such district approved the measure by a majority vote. Under this provision a great many independent school districts came into existence in West Virginia, with the purpose of centering a local school system within the incorporation and thus utilizing the advantages afforded by the municipality. But the creation of the county unit system in 1932 did away with school districts.

The number of state normal schools [11] was limited to the number chartered at the time of the adopting of the constitution, and no appropriation was thereafter to be made to any such school, or branch thereof, excepting those already established.

The legislature was placed under constitutional obligation to encourage the intellectual training of the people. Moral, scientific, and intellectual improvement in the state became a duty, not a promise, of the state assembly. And wherever practicable the blind, the deaf-mute, and the insane were given the care in institutions of safety and learning that their best interest warranted.

---

[11] Now known as state colleges.

Land Titles

That a confusion in land titles existed in western Virginia before 1863 admits of no doubt. In the process of marking out farm boundaries, lines were crossed and recrossed. The titles to such lands had been acquired according to the laws of Virginia. When West Virginia became a state all rights and interests owned within its boundaries were declared to be valid and secure and "determined by the laws in force in Virginia prior to the formation of this State." Therefore, no changes in the titles of lands occurred by virtue of the formation of the new state.

In the early history of the state of Virginia, land was granted to an individual by a warrant issued by the governor. In turn the grantee presented his warrant to the surveyor of lands, who located by survey the amount of land set forth in the title.[12] This plan was followed largely for the purpose of rewarding soldiers for military service, and the lands so assigned had been unpatented. By the time West Virginia became a state the conflict of claims and overlapping of titles had become so troublesome that it was inadvisable to issue further land warrants. So the constitution forbade any further entry by warrant on land in the state.

FORFEITED LANDS

The state itself became an extensive land owner. A part of the public domain had been unappropriated to settlers, and other parcels of land came into the possession of the state through forfeitures on account of the owner's failure to pay his tax, and through escheats.[13] But it was not the policy of West Virginia to hold wide tracts of soil easily cultivated if such land could be honorably granted to the citizens of the commonwealth. The constitution, in keeping with this principle, gave encouragement to people to own farms and to reside in their own homes.

It was often the case that an individual asserted his claim to land for which the state had a title. The constitution provided that a tract of land held in the name of the state might be transferred to a person who "under color or claim of title" possessed the tract for ten years and paid the taxes on it for five years; or, lacking such a person, to anyone who had title or claim to the land and had paid the

---

[12] *Revised Code of Virginia, 1819* (Richmond, 1819), II, 404.

[13] Escheat means the reversion of land to the state by reason of the failure of the owner or his heirs to hold the land.

taxes on it for five successive years after 1865 or after the date of the grant if issued after 1865; or, again lacking such a person, to anyone who had claim to the land and had possessed it and paid the taxes on it for any five successive years after 1865. By these provisions forfeited, waste, unappropriated, and escheated lands were legally granted to citizens who otherwise would have been unable to buy farms.

The state had also become a claimant to lands to which no individual laid any claim or had any title whatsoever. This situation existed in 1872 and continues today. Every year farms and real estate in towns are forfeited to the state by the owner's failure to pay his taxes. Such titles remain in the name of the state until sale is made to the highest bidder by proceedings in the circuit court convening in the county wherein the land is located. If the sale price exceeds the amount of taxes, with interest at the rate of 12% a year, and the cost, the surplus is paid to the former owner.

LAND BOOKS

It is the obligation of every owner of real estate to have his land listed on books kept by the county clerk for that purpose, so that taxes may be levied on it. The acreage and the location of the same are entered in the statement of record in the county in which the property is located. By virtue of the fact that the individual owns land, he assumes the obligation to pay annually a tax levied on it. If for five successive years the owner of such property is not charged legal taxes on the same and recorded on the land books, the estate is forfeited and the title vested in the state of West Virginia. The original owner retains the right to redeem his land, but this right in no case extends beyond twenty years from the time of forfeiture.

Amendments

An amendment is the altering of a regulation which was originally a part of the constitution or the adding of a new principle to the supreme law of the land.

HOW AMENDMENTS ARE MADE

The perpetuity of the constitution is assured in its own structure. It may be revised in two ways. The first is by means of a convention called definitely for that purpose. First, the legislature must pass a law, setting aside a day, not less than three months distant, on which the voters cast their ballots for or against the calling of a constitutional convention. If a majority of the votes cast favor a convention, at least one month later another election chooses delegates to this constitutional convention. When the convention has assembled and finished its work of altering the constitution, all its acts must be submitted for ratification or rejection to the legal voters.

"Any amendment to the Constitution may be reposed in either house of the Legislature," and if, after being read on three days in each house, it is passed by a two-thirds majority of all the members elected, it must then be submitted to the voters, at the next general election, for ratification or rejection. Before the popular vote is cast the proposed amendment must be published in every county in the state having a newspaper, at least three months before the election. Through this arrangement the people have time to give consideration to the proposed change in their law. If a majority of the votes cast approve the amendment, it becomes a part of the constitution of the state from the time of ratification.

The constitution of West Virginia has been amended twenty-four times. Twenty of the amendments have been discussed in this chapter as if they were a part of the original law. The remaining four have grown out of entirely new conditions in the state and will be taken up separately. Three of them have to do with the power of the state exercised in the building of roads, and one (1946) is known as the Forestry Amendment.[14]

THE GOOD ROADS AMENDMENTS

With the advent of the automobile, revolutionary improvements in our highway system became an urgent necessity. The building and improvement of roads up to this time had been largely left to the counties, but it now became evident that the new highway program was entirely beyond the capacity of the county government. So the state assumed in a large measure the road-building program and the improvement of highways. Hence the amendment of 1920.

This amendment placed on the legislature the burden of making provision for a system of state roads and highways "connecting the various county seats of the state." In order to put this program into operation new sources of revenue had to be found and new officers and agencies had to be made available. The law stipulated that the legislature should authorize the issue and sale of bonds for which the state was surety, the total amount of which could not ex-

[14] For this amendment see below, p. 345.

ceed, at any time, fifty million dollars. To pay this indebtedness and the accruing interests, the legislature had to lay and collect an annual tax on the people of the state, sufficient to make complete payment within thirty years. Bonds were issued and sold to care for this expense. The new state road program, to connect all the county seats in the commonwealth with hard-surfaced highways, was energetically set under way.

After the lapse of a few years it became evident that the program exceeded the anticipations even of those who had planned it. In 1928 another good roads amendment was proposed to and accepted by the voters of West Virginia. This new arrangement authorized the increase of the bonded indebtedness of the state by thirty-five million dollars solely for the purpose of constructing, or assisting in constructing, the system of highways provided in the amendment adopted in 1920. Of course, the legislature, by an annual tax, provided for the payment of the interest and principal of this amount. Under laws rendering effective the good roads amendment, West Virginia has not only joined the county seats with a modern highway system but has also constructed a network of hard-surfaced roads that compares favorably with the best public thoroughfares in the country.

By the general election of 1948 another amendment authorized the expenditure of an additional fifty million dollars for the improvement of roads. At this writing the plans for improvement are in the process of formation. Considerable time must pass before the people realize the results of these expenditures. In the meantime, however, laws will have to be enacted and taxes collected to defray the expense.

CHAPTER 12

The Citizen and His Constitutional Protection

Our form of government is the handiwork of the citizens who live under it and whose lives are affected by it. The laws made under the constitution are enacted by delegates chosen by the citizens of the state and administered by officers elected for that purpose. "The powers of government," says the constitution, "reside in all the citizens of the State, and can be rightfully exercised only in accordance with their will and appointment."

Officers, elected or appointed, live and move and have their being under the same code of laws as any other citizen. The fact that they are officers does not give them special rights; rather, it imposes special duties. They are placed under severer restrictions than other people, for they are sworn to do their duty, obey the constitution, and faithfully execute the duties of their office to the best of their ability. The administrator of the government, therefore, cannot assume special and imperious rights under the law. The purpose of his office is to serve, not to enjoy special privileges.

It is worth repeating that our political organization is of the citizens, by the citizens, and for the citizens. As far as the law is concerned there is no class of overprivileged or underprivileged. A distinction is properly made, however, between two classes of people living in the state, the citizens and the aliens, and definite emphasis is placed on the freedom and power of the citizens.

How One May Become a Citizen

According to the Constitution of the United States "all persons born or naturalized in the United States, and subject to the jurisdiction thereof, are citizens of the United States and the State wherein they reside." This provision shows that there are two kinds of citizenships in our country; the one is of the state and the other of the nation. Concerning citizenship of the state, the principle set forth in the national Constitution and repeated in the constitution of West Virginia is that all persons who establish legal residence in this state, and who were either born or naturalized in the United States and are subject to the jurisdiction thereof, are citizens of this state. There are two conditions, therefore, under which one may become a citizen of the United States – by birth or by naturalization. All persons of whatever parentage, regardless of nationality or race are citizens by birth if born under the jurisdiction of this country, which includes American embassies abroad, and American ships of war and merchant vessels anchored in any harbor of the world or sailing the high seas. It includes also Alaska, Hawaii, and Puerto Rico, but not the Philippine Islands. On the other hand, children born in the homes of foreign ambassadors and ministers to the United States are not citizens by birth for the reason that embassies, though located in Washington, are not within the jurisdiction of our nation.

Children born of American parents on foreign soil are citizens of the United States. But if they continue to live in the land of their birth they are required to register at an American consulate, declaring their intention of remaining American citizens. This registration must be recorded when the persons arrive at the age of eighteen years, and three years later they must take an oath of allegiance to the United States. Thus it is possible to be a citizen of the United States and at the same time not to be a citizen of any state. Residents of the District of Columbia and persons of American parentage residing abroad are typical examples of this situation.

The other group of citizens consists of those who have been naturalized. Laws passed by Congress establish the requirements for naturalization, and when applicants have fulfilled these regulations they become citizens of the United States and of the state wherein they reside. The three steps in the process of naturalization are the declaration of intention, the filing of petition for citizenship, and the granting of naturalization. In West Virginia this procedure may be followed before a federal district court or a state circuit court.

Any alien of the white or African race who has become eighteen years of age and who is able to speak the English language may file his declaration of intention. Then after five years of continuous residence in this country and not less than two years or more than seven after filing his application of intention, he is ready to take the second step, which is the filing of his application for citizenship. This application must be signed by two citizens certifying that the statements it contains are altogether true. Time and place of arrival in the United States, length of continuous residence, age, character, and nationality are some of the points on which information must be given in this application. Before further action is taken, ninety days must elapse, during which time public notice of the filing of the petition is posted in the courthouse. Finally the judge sets apart a day for the third and final step, the granting of naturalization. The applicant appears before the judge and is asked a series of questions concerning the structure of our government and the duties of citizenship. If his answers are approved, he is granted full citizenship by the court. Let it be remembered that during the process of naturalization the applicant, under a sworn statement, must absolve himself from his ties with any foreign government or rule and solemnly declare his allegiance to the government of the United States.

There is nothing to prevent West Virginia from allowing aliens to vote and hold office, but these privileges are denied to all persons except citizens. The laws of West Virginia forbid aliens to hunt, fish, and possess firearms, but no distinction is made between resident aliens and citizens with respect to the acquisition, tenure, disposition, and inheritance of property. They also are taxed, protected in their privileges, and punished for law violations exactly as if they were citizens.

Treason

The citizen has constitutional protection; in return it is his solemn obligation to protect the constitution. To keep the supreme law whole and strong as an armor of defense, crimes are defined and punishment is provided for those who violate its principles.

At the head of the list of all crimes is treason. The definition of this old offense may be traced back to the early laws of England, although since that time the penalties for it have been made less severe. Treason is now defined as levying war against the state or, in the language of the ancients, adhering to its enemies or giving them aid and comfort.

The offense may be against the state or the nation. It may be committed within or without the jurisdiction of the government, by a citizen or by an alien. But planning treason is not enough for conviction. An overt act must be committed. John Brown was tried, convicted, and executed for committing treason, against the state of Virginia. The legality of the proceedings of this case, conducted by Virginia, has always been questioned because the crime was committed on soil in the possession of the government of the United States and not of the state of Virginia.

Conviction for other crimes may be based on evidence given by one witness, but the constitution requires that conviction for treason must rest on the testimony of at least two witnesses to the overt act, or on the confession of the accused in open court. Such confession is to be given voluntarily and not under duress or constraint.

The constitution states that "treason shall be punished according to the character of the acts committed, by the infliction of one, or more, of the penalties, of death, imprisonment or fine, as may be prescribed by law." The legislature has declared that whoever is guilty of treason against West Virginia shall be punished by death, or, at the discretion of the jury, by confinement in the penitentiary for not less than three nor more than ten years, and by the confiscation of the real and personal property of the convicted person.

The Bill of Rights

The law rests on the assumption that all men are by nature equally free and independent, and that they have certain inviolate natural rights: the enjoyment of life and liberty, the means of acquiring and possessing property, and the means of obtaining happiness and safety. Of these inherent rights they may not be deprived, nor may they enter into any agreement that will deprive their posterity of them. Men have organized government in order to unite the power of the people for their own protection, security, and happiness; but the ultimate political authority remains with the people, and the power of officers of government is derived from that authority. Hence officers of government are not masters of the people but their trustees and servants. That government is best that produces the greatest happiness and affords the firmest security against danger. If any government should prove inadequate to those ends, the people have power to alter it or to overthrow it and replace it with another that will better serve their interests.

The section of the constitution which contains guarantees of these inalienable rights is called the Bill of Rights. Its first three articles assert the principles which have just been summarized.

WRIT OF HABEAS CORPUS

"The privilege of the writ of habeas corpus shall not be suspended." This important provision permits a person who feels himself unjustly detained by an officer, or who is under arrest for an unknown cause, to secure a statement from the court that compels the jailer, sheriff, or policeman to present the person in court and show a valid reason for his detention. If such reason cannot be shown, the court will order the prisoner's release.

In days gone by, the writ of habeas corpus was a great safeguard to personal freedom. It is yet upheld as a cardinal instrument in good government for protection against promiscuous arrest and imprisonment.

BILL OF ATTAINDER

Another power forbidden to the legislature is to pass a bill of attainder. This principle goes back to early English law. A bill of attainder is an act passed by a legislature that declares a person an enemy to the state and imposes severe punishment, perhaps death, upon him. A conviction of this sort declares the accused guilty without giving him a chance for defense or allowing trial in open court. Such judicial procedure is contrary to the American system of government. Although it was once allowed in England, the great injustice of the bill of attainder caused it to be outlawed.

Since there is absolute prohibition by both state and national government against passing a bill of attainder, there are left only two ways by which one may be tried, found guilty, and sentenced to punishment. The first is by judgment rendered in open court, and the other is by impeachment and conviction.[1] Only officers can be

[1] This method includes both civil and military courts.

impeached; the other cases remain for the courts to decide. The constitution also provides that one accused of a crime not cognizable by a justice of the peace cannot be held for trial except on indictment by a grand jury.

EX POST FACTO LAW

In the third place, no ex post facto law may be passed. An ex post facto law has been defined by the United States Supreme Court as follows: "1st: Every law that makes an action done before the passing of the law, and which was innocent when done, criminal; and punishes such action. 2d: Every law that aggravates a crime, or makes it greater than it was when committed. 3d: Every law that changes the punishment, and inflicts a greater punishment than the law annexed to a crime when committed. 4th: Every law that alters the legal rules of evidence, and requires less, or different, testimony than the law required at the time of the commission of the offense, in order to convict the offender." [2] Thus not every retroactive law is an ex post facto law. Only retroactive laws relating to criminal cases can be ex post facto, and not even those when the new law is to the advantage of the accused.

OBLIGATIONS OF CONTRACT

The next prohibition written into the constitution to protect the citizen is that the legislature cannot pass a law impairing the obligation of a contract. A contract may be defined as an agreement made between two or more people and enforceable by law. This agreement usually binds the persons entering into it to fulfill certain obligations. If the contract is legal at the time it was made, no law subsequently passed by the legislature can change or invalidate it. Nor can it be impaired by the action of a county court or a city council. The obligation of contract is as binding on the state, the county, or the city as it is on a person. The only way by which an agreement of this kind can be legally modified is by the mutual consent of all parties to it.

It should be remembered, however, that charters granted under the laws of the state to corporations and municipalities are not held to be contracts in any sense of the law. They are grants of power by the government to form corporations, either municipal or private, securing to them the enjoyment of certain rights.

---

[2] *Calder vs. Bull*, 3 Dallas, 386.

EXCESSIVE BAIL AND PUNISHMENT

The legislature and the courts cannot impose excessive bail or unjust fines, or inflict cruel and unusual punishments. The object of the law is to require that punishment be in proper proportion to the gravity of the violation committed. Having enunciated the principle, the constitution leaves to the legislature a great deal of latitude in fixing the limitations of punishment in criminal cases, the amount of fines, the term of imprisonment, and the amount of bail. If the alleged violation is serious enough, bail may be denied altogether. For instance, it is stated "A justice may admit to bail a person who is charged with, but not convicted of, an offense not punishable with death. If the offense be confinement in the penitentiary, he shall not admit such person to bail in a sum less than five hundred dollars." [3] By this provision, if the accused is to be allowed bail the minimum is fixed by law, the maximum by the justice.

There was a time when persons could be punished by branding with a hot iron, piercing the tongue, cutting off the ears, or confinement in the darkness of a dungeon. Such methods this law sets aside. It is readily seen, however, that the terms "cruel and unusual" may be given a broad interpretation by the courts. A sentence might be considered just by one judge, unjust by another. But the divergencies of opinions also have their limitations, and sentence to punishment is so limited by law that the variation of judgment is not likely to constitute an abuse.

A further limitation is placed upon punishment for crime by the constitutional provision that no person can be transported out of the state or forced to leave the state for an offense committed within its boundaries.

WITNESS IN TRIAL

In a criminal case the accused cannot be compelled to be a witness against himself. The practice in American law, both state and national, is that the one who brings a charge against another must sustain it; otherwise the accused goes free. Therefore, the prosecutor, acting on behalf of the state, must make his own case, without help from forced admissions by the suspect. The accused is required to appear for trial, and by his own choice he may give evidence, even make open confession, but he cannot be compelled to answer questions if he believes the answers will be incriminating. Confession obtained by force is absolutely illegal.

[3] *Code of West Virginia*, 1932, pp. 1968, 6152.

TWICE IN JEOPARDY

A regulation sometimes misunderstood is that one accused of a crime cannot be "put twice in jeopardy of life or liberty for the same offense." This provision relates, of course, only to the law of the state. The citizen lives under two governments, state and national, and sometimes an offense is a violation against both state and national law. In that case the offender is subject to trial and, if convicted, to punishment by both governments.

UNREASONABLE SEARCH AND SEIZURE

During the Revolutionary War the English government issued writs of assistance that authorized soldiers and local officers to search at will the homes of the colonists and seize the goods found. This power was greatly abused and many innocent people had their homes invaded and their belongings taken. When the war was over, the American people wrote into their constitution their right to be secure against unreasonable search and seizure. This popular provision of law has been copied by the states in drafting their own constitutions, hence the constitutional law in West Virginia.

But there is a difference between unreasonable and reasonable search and seizure. If a complaint is made on oath that personal property has been stolen, embezzled, or obtained by false pretense, and that it is believed to be concealed in a particular house or other place, the justice before whom the complaint is made, if satisfied that there is reasonable cause for such belief, may issue a warrant authorizing an officer to search the place for the concealed property. The warrant issued to the sheriff, constable, or police must describe the place to be searched and the person or property to be seized. Any claim of unreasonableness arising from such action must be submitted to the court. But a search warrant is not required in all cases to authorize an officer to make search and seizure. If the officer has good reason to believe that a violation is being committed he does not have to wait for a complaint to be made to stop this violation.

FREEDOM OF SPEECH AND PRESS

The constitution declares that no law shall be passed that abridges the freedom of speech and of the press. But these rights are by no means unlimited. Protection is extended only to the utterance or publication of truth. Liberty to speak and to print does not allow one to speak or print libels or false defamations. Matter published with good motive and found true is justifiable under the law; but the utterance of falsehoods may entail prosecution and punishment of the author. It is legal, then, to tell the truth; it is illegal to speak or write falsely. The West Virginia legislature, by constitutional enablement, has also passed laws forbidding the sale of obscene books, papers, and pictures.

PRIVATE PROPERTY

Although the right to acquire and possess private property is guaranteed, there are times when this right must be waived. Private property is not allowed to stand in the way of public progress. If the citizens of the state reserve to themselves the power to possess property, they also acknowledge that there are times when they must surrender it to the common good.

The constitution reads, "Private property shall not be taken or damaged for public use, without just compensation." In this quotation there are two points of interest. The first is that private property may be taken for public use, and the second is that just compensation must be paid for it. This power of the state to acquire property is known as the right of eminent domain. The eminent power of the state is superior to that of the individual citizen when the general welfare requires its exercise. Often the reason for taking over property in this manner is to create and enlarge parks, construct public buildings, build highways, and so forth; but corporations may also acquire property by reason of this law when it is proved beyond a doubt that such use will promote the general welfare. Rights of way for railroads, canals, and electric lines are sometimes secured in this manner. A business of this kind is known as a *public utility*.

When property is taken from a private owner for public use, just compensation must be paid for it. If a mutual agreement as to the actual value cannot be reached by the parties directly concerned, either party may require the services of a jury of appraisers, composed of twelve men. This jury ascertains the compensation to be paid for the property. In case the owner should refuse to sell the real estate, it may be condemned by the court and transferred under compulsion. But compensation must be given just the same as if it were voluntarily sold.

DUE PROCESS OF LAW

The constitution states that "No person may be deprived of life liberty, or property, without due process of law, and the judgment of his peers." Volumes have been written, and many judicial decisions rendered, for the purpose of defining *due process*. Perhaps the best brief definition is Daniel Webster's cogent statement that it means "to hear before you condemn, proceed upon inquiry and render judgment after trial." This protection may be applied to limit arbitrary or unjust procedure by the courts and unfair administration of any kind by the government. Due process is considered the greatest constitutional safeguard reserved by the people. All in all it means that the accused must have a just trial.

One is tried before his peers or equals. In the United States citizens are considered equal in function. There are no classes; there is no provision in law for different ranks. Therefore, every citizen is a peer, or an equal, of another, and it is the citizens who constitute the juries of the courts.

POLITICAL FREEDOM

By the first constitution of West Virginia persons who had voluntarily given aid to the rebellion were denied citizenship in the state and consequently could neither vote nor hold office when the war was over. This condition grew out of the bitterness and division engendered by the war. After time and peace had begun to heal the wounds of war, hatred became less severe and harshness was mollified. Consequently by an amendment to the constitution, adopted April 27, 1871, the status of citizenship was restored to those from whom it had been taken, and the privilege of voting reinstated. This change in the law is known as the Flick amendment in honor of W. H. H. Flick, a member of the house of delegates from Pendleton County, who introduced it.[4]

The constitution of 1872 abolished all political and religious tests for voting. The constitution states that no political or religious test shall be required as a qualification to vote, serve as a juror, sue, plead, appeal, or pursue any profession or employment. This regulation is made broad enough to equalize the privileges of all citizens and reestablish to their full and unqualified rights the soldiers who had joined the Confederate army. With the passage of time those feelings of division that were once so violent have been completely forgotten.

---

[4] The Honorable W. H. H. Flick had been a member of the 41st Ohio Regiment of the Union Army.

MILITARY AND CIVIL POWERS

There is no question in our law as to whether the civil or the military power is superior. As our constitution is constructed the inferior military power is an arm to the superior civil power, used as an instrument for protection and to keep peace in the land. The home is declared to be free and protected, and in time of peace no soldier can be quartered in any home without the consent of the owner. Even in time of war regulations must be prescribed by law for the occupation of homes.

Persons enlisted in the army are subject to trial and punishment by military courts but such courts have no power whatsoever to summon anyone else to trial. The people are warned that a standing army is dangerous to liberty, a warning, of course, that no one heeds. No doubt those patriots who wrote the constitution retained vivid memories of the powers exercised by the armies during the war from 1861 to 1865, and especially of the military government placed over the southern states during the period of reconstruction. If the constitution were to be rewritten now, it would perhaps be less emphatic on this point.

TRIAL BY JURY

The right of trial by jury is an old principle of English law, and has been handed down to the American government with all its force intact. It is guaranteed to citizens on trial in the national courts, and it is followed, with various modifications, in all the courts.

As applied in West Virginia, in civil cases, if the amount in controversy exceeds twenty dollars, either party to the trial may demand a jury. In the court of the justice of the peace the jury may consist of only six members; otherwise it numbers twelve. This provision of law takes the power of rendering the verdict out of the hands of the judge or the justice, as the case may be, and submits the case to the judgment of the peers of the parties to the trial. The jurymen are placed under oath; their decision must be unanimous. All this is designed to insure a fair trial and an unbiased verdict.

Criminal cases must be tried before a jury of twelve in the state courts. The accused is entitled to a speedy and fair trial conducted in the county in which the offense was committed. The court has the power to remove the trial to another county on petition of the accused, if there exists a just reason for doing so.

In all cases the accused must be fully informed of the character of the charges against him. If he does not have counsel the court must furnish it by appointment. He must be given a reasonable time to prepare for trial, and must be permitted to confront directly the witnesses testifying against him. If necessary the court will compel the attendance of witnesses for either party in a trial. The object is to make the evidence complete and to render judgment on the true presentations of the circumstances involved.

Within recent years rather widespread complaint has been registered against that part of the constitution giving protection to persons accused of crime. Many people think that the law hampers the state in the prosecution of criminals and gives the guilty an unfair advantage. Of course the laws were made with the object of protecting innocent persons from highhanded officers, but now it is charged that thieves, bribetakers, and racketeers are taking shelter behind the protective features of the law. They deceive, falsify, and disguise through counsel which bends its paid efforts to make their false claims seem credible. A heavy responsibility rests with our judges and juries to separate the guilty from the innocent, so that laws devised for the protection of the innocent are not distorted into a screen for the misdeeds of the guilty.

RELIGIOUS FREEDOM

Religious freedom is a cardinal principle in American law. It is guaranteed in the nation and in the states. Worship is neither restrained nor promoted. Church affiliation is voluntary. A citizen cannot be forced against his will to frequent or support a place of worship, and he cannot be forbidden to attend his place of worship. He is protected in his opinions and beliefs, both in the church and out of it. And in their worship, all people are equally protected. They shall not be interrupted in their devotion, in person or in their goods, or otherwise suffer molestation for their convictions.

The legislature is forbidden to prescribe any religious test or confer an advantage on any sect or denomination. It cannot require a tax for the purpose of constructing a church building, for the payment of church salaries, or for any other religious support. All these things must be done within the organization of the church. The citizen is left entirely free to worship as he thinks best. There is no alliance in administration between the church and the state — between the organization of religion and the political organization.

But all this freedom has its limitation. The constitution does not mean that any person or group of persons can carry on immoral or indecent conduct in the name of a religious sect. One cannot unjustly take money or property from another under the guise of exercising his religious freedom; he cannot impose pain or punishment; he cannot take or occupy property against the will of the legal owner; in no way can he violate the civil law in the name of belief or worship. The law, therefore, protects the church against its use as a refuge for vicious persons who would hide their disorder; it is against those who would act under the mask of devotion to disrupt its innocence.

PUBLIC ASSEMBLY

The right of the people to public assembly is insured by the constitution. It is deemed that an assembly by the people is at times a public good and a political necessity. The opportunity is thus given to consult together on matters of local interest, to instruct representatives, and to mature plans for public improvements. The town meeting in New England is a public assembly that legislates. Its utility still exists. In other parts of the country a meeting of this nature serves to voice the sentiment of the people on matters of common concern.

In order to hold a public assembly a permit is sometimes required from the mayor or chief of police. This is not the violation of a right but a regulation in the interests of good order, for meetings of this sort must be conducted in a peaceable and orderly manner. The right of public assembly may even be suspended if it is thought to endanger the health, morals, or safety of the people. It is clear that the right of public assembly carries with it the duty to keep within the bounds of safety and good order.

ADMINISTRATION OF JUSTICE

The courts of the state are institutions of the people and are created to remedy injury, settle matters of dispute, and care for certain conditions which are not of a controversial nature but which require legal procedure. In all these matters it is the principle of our judiciary to render strict justice without help or hindrance. Every case must stand on its own merits.

It is provided that conviction shall not work corruption of blood or forfeiture of estate. At one time under English law a person convicted in court could be required to forfeit his estate to the Crown or to the lord of the manor. Moreover, his descendants might be forbidden to hold office or property – a condition known as "corruption of blood." Such situations cannot exist here. No court may declare a person incapable of receiving an inheritance or of transmitting property to another person, or render him incapable of retaining property in his own name; nor may punishment for a crime extend beyond the person who has committed it.

HEREDITARY HONORS

Just as it is forbidden to extend punishment from an individual to his heirs, so it is also forbidden to confer hereditary honors, privileges, or favors on any citizen. If one is to achieve distinction, he must earn and not inherit it.

THE FINAL ARTICLE

The last article of the Bill of Rights wisely reminds the people that free government may be preserved only by strict adherence to the principles of justice, moderation, temperance, frugality, and virtue. If at any time the administration of government departs from these principles, the blessings of liberty are endangered or withdrawn. Therefore it is essential that a frequent recurrence to fundamental principles be made to keep their importance fresh in the minds of the people.

RIGHTS AND DUTIES

A great deal has now been said about the rights reserved to the citizens and the powers created to protect those rights, but not much has been written about the duties and responsibilities which those rights entail. Through the power expressed in the constitution the citizen has reserved for his own contentment his right to life, liberty, property; his privilege to vote and hold office; his freedom of worship. But these conditions are not self-perpetuating. How is the citizen to maintain this protective power?

Invariably the felon, having willfully violated the law, will plead for its protection when his liberty is required of him. He will implore help under the government whose decency he has defiled; he will beg for protection in the temple that he has so unjustly tried to destroy.

Let it be solemnly remembered that rights and privileges walk hand in hand with duties. The government grants to the citizen the right to live and it is his sacred duty to protect that right in the lives of other people. One who voluntarily takes a life forfeits his own right to live. If he takes away liberty, in turn he sacrifices liberty;

if he secretly takes property, his property is taken as a punishment; if he despoils happiness, he suffers the loss of his own happiness. It is, therefore, the highborn duty of every citizen to protect his rights so that they may be fully enjoyed by all. Let it be said once more without equivocation that the right to be protected imposes the duty on one to protect. "A state worth having is a state worth serving." One who is given the privilege to vote accepts the duty to vote. Our government is so arranged that the citizen helps to make the laws and is therefore obligated to obey the laws. Rights and duties are inseparable. They are parts of the same physical body. It is very inconsistent, therefore, to claim rights without assuming duties.

CHAPTER 13

Elections

Suffrage

ELECTIONS AND THE MANNER OF VOTING

The constitution of West Virginia provides that a general election shall be held on the Tuesday next following the first Monday in November in each even year. Any election held on a day not fixed by law is declared to be null and void. Presently we shall see the extensive preparation necessary for conducting an election.

In all elections the manner of voting is by ballot. Ancient ways of expressing one's political sentiments, such as a show of hands or *viva voce*, long ago were set aside. In this state the voter has the wide privilege of casting his ballot secretly, openly, or sealed. For secret balloting a definite procedure is prescribed by law, and any violation of this rule may cause the vote to be declared invalid. Of course, the casting and counting of open and sealed ballots are likewise properly supervised.

ELECTION PRECINCTS

To facilitate the conducting of elections in West Virginia each magisterial district is divided into election precincts. The population in a district may warrant the establishment of more than one precinct, but however sparse the settlement is there must be at least one place of voting in each magisterial district.

To arrive at a standard for fixing the boundaries of the election unit, it is arranged that in urban centers a precinct shall contain not fewer than six hundred nor more than eight hundred registered voters, while in rural areas there may be not fewer than two hundred nor more than seven hundred persons registered. The county court may increase or diminish the number of voting precincts when a change of population warrants such action. In the general election of 1950 there were 2825 voting precincts in West Virginia.

WHO MAY VOTE

For many years after the formation of West Virginia proper administrative care was not applied to the regulation of voting, and cases arose in which persons were accused of fraudulent conduct on election day. In more recent times legal restraints carefully regulate the manner of voting.

In the first place, one's privilege to vote is strictly qualified. To be legally qualified to cast a ballot an individual must be a citizen of the state and a resident of the precinct in which he offers to vote; he is required to have been a resident of the state for at least one year and of the county for sixty days. And this is not all. He must have his name legally registered, with a statement of his party, age, and residence. Even though he can successfully meet all of these requirements, other conditions may deprive him of voting, such as being under conviction of treason, felony, or bribery in an election. Of course, minors and those of unsound intellect are forbidden to vote.

A person enlisted in the military, marine, or naval services of the United States cannot be considered a resident of a state by reason of being stationed in it. This principle is carried a step further. An employee of a corporation or of the state cannot claim his residence in a voting precinct on account of being employed in it. The qualified voter, therefore, must be registered only in the precinct in which he actually resides.

REGISTRATION OF VOTERS

On the first Monday in March next preceding a presidential election, and on the first Monday in May next preceding other general elections, the county court meets at the courthouse for the purpose of appointing persons to make an official list of the qualified voters in the county. For each voting precinct two registrars, one from each of the two leading parties, are chosen. If the county executive committee of either of the two leading political parties should recommend the selection of a qualified voter, residing in the precinct, as one of the registrars, it is the obligation of the county court to make the appointment as recommended.

A registrar is disqualified if he is not a legal voter in the precinct, if he has been convicted of felony, if he holds an elective or appointive office, if he is a candidate for office, or if he is in the employment of the state or the United States. In addition, it is required that a registrar be able to read and write the English language.

If no persons qualified to serve as registrars reside in the precinct, the chairmen of the political executive committees may recommend competent voters from another precinct in the county, whom the court appoints. If the vacancy should continue, by the refusal of the appointee to serve, the county court may make the selection. But if the court should not convene, its clerk may take the matter in hand and choose someone in order that the registration may be properly carried on. In all events we have ample provision for the periodical registration of all *bona fide* voters in West Virginia.

DUTIES OF THE REGISTRARS

Within five days after their appointment the clerk notifies the registrars of their selection and at the same time files with the chairman of the executive committee of each party a copy of this notice. It is then in order for the clerks to deliver to the registrars the books and blanks prepared for listing the names of the qualified voters.[1]

Upon receipt of the proper blanks the registrars proceed to make an authentic list of the names of the qualified voters residing in the voting precinct. To make their work complete they visit the homes or places of residence, for a personal interview with every voter. In the process of registration the name, place of residence, age, color, place of birth, and party allegiance of each voter are made matters of record. The true purpose of the law is to provide means by which every competent voter may cast his ballot and to deny that privilege to those who fall short of the legal regulations.

---

[1] In years of presidential elections the books and blanks must be delivered to the registrars on or before the second Monday in March; in years of other elections, on or before the second Monday in May.

To guard against fraudulent practice the power of the registrars extends a long way. They may require a person to make an affidavit as to his status and to answer under oath questions covering his eligibility. The forms of the questions are prescribed by law, and no other means may be employed.

It appears that the procedure thus described would be sufficiently safe, but lest the name of some qualified voter be omitted from the registration books, further care is taken. At some accessible place in the district the registrars meet for two days, the first Monday and Tuesday in April preceding a presidential election, the first Monday and Tuesday in June preceding other elections, to receive the names of qualified voters not earlier registered. Upon the completion of this work, the registrars draw up two lists of all the names they have recorded. This report they forward to the clerk of the county court, who keeps the records open to public inspection until five days prior to the election.

On the last Tuesday before the election (primary, general, or special) the county court convenes for the purpose of hearing any questions pertaining to the registration. At this time the court makes an official review of the report submitted by the registrars. Names that are deemed illegally registered may be cancelled; others may be added that are considered valid. A person whose name is stricken from the list has the privilege of carrying his case to the courts for final adjustment.

Of the two lists furnished by the registrars to the clerk of the county court, one is retained in his office, while the other one he delivers to the commissioners of the voting precinct. Likewise the ballot boxes and all other election supplies are given over by the clerk to the precinct commissioners. This, in brief, is the process used in West Virginia in preparation for conducting an election.

The constitution and the acts of the legislature extend to the qualified citizen the privilege of voting and duly protect him in exercising this power. Definite guards are set against any fraudulent use of this privilege, and punishment may be dealt out to anyone who attempts to abuse it. The power to vote is the power to govern; therefore, the civic standard of the voter establishes the civic standard of his government. Misconduct in office is not always principally the fault of the officers; it may be largely the mistake of those who put them into office. Corrupt government is usually the result of bad voting.

Rights and privileges carry with them responsibilities of equal gravity. It is easy to complain about a lack of rights but hard to assume full responsibility. With the privilege of voting goes the duty to vote. Protection in voting is rendered for the purpose that the citizen may mark his ballot without being intimidated, browbeaten, bought or biased. He should exercise this privilege as a free citizen.

Since voting is largely promoted through the work of political parties, let us now turn to party organization in West Virginia.

Political Parties

THE RISE OF POLITICAL PARTIES

It is uncertain when political parties were first organized in America. It is known, however, that they gained prominence during the colonial period and continued as political institutions under the English government until the time of American independence. From that time on, national political organizations have had a great deal to do with the civil government of the states as well as the nation.

In a government controlled by the will of the people, differences of opinion arise with respect to public administration and the making of laws. After a free discussion of questions of public importance, the people have an opportunity to make the final decisions, and the opinion of the people is seldom wrong. In such public discussions usually someone who is capable of leadership and who has formulated some definite political principles takes the initiative. Those who believe in his doctrine flock to his standard proclaiming his merits in speeches and in the press. In case the movement gathers sufficient momentum, organizations are eventually formed in district, county, state, and nation for the purpose of promoting public favor for the leader and his cause. The efficiency of the organization depends to a great extent upon its officers – president, secretary, treasurer, and committees. Through their efforts the machinery is set in motion to reach the minds of the electorate. Soon there exists an organized political party, with leaders, principles, banners, emblems, and officers who proclaim their cause to the sovereign people and plead for their unequivocal endorsement. In short, political parties are organized for the purpose of electing to office men who stand for certain popular principles.

But on such principles there is not likely to be unanimity of opinion. Another leader, discerning a threatening weakness in the program already launched and perhaps doubting the reliability of its leadership, comes forth with principles of his own on which he would have the safety and prosperity of the country based. He warns the people against the danger of adopting his opponent's program; he urges them to accept his own leadership and favor his platform. In turn organizations are formed; the press, the radio, and the public forum are utilized to reach the ear of the people. Thus we have competitive political parties in state and in nation, waging their campaigns in the American way to gain official control of the government. Back of these parties, of course, is the will of the voter, ultimately directing both the domestic and the foreign policy of his country.

POLITICAL PARTIES IN WEST VIRGINIA

Although the constitution of West Virginia does not mention political parties, it recognizes them by implication. Acts passed by the legislature acknowledge parties as operative units in our political and civil life. Their structure follows that of the governmental organization. The divisions of government such as ward, district, county, and state also serve as units for the organization of political parties. Competitive parties, then, placed in power by the choice of a majority of the voters, administer the government.

In view of the fact that political parties play such an important part in our civil life, the legislature of West Virginia has seen fit to define them. The law states that any affiliation of voters that cast at least one per cent of the votes for governor at the most recent general election and that represents a definite principle is a political party. If an organization posing as a party fails to meet this requirement, it is forbidden to participate in the primary election, but it may make its nominations by party conventions.

THE STATE EXECUTIVE COMMITTEE

A political party, like any other efficient organization, builds on a reliable plan and structure. A strong state organization is the chief bulwark of party strength; and whether the party meets failure or success in the election, the state officers in the main are held responsible. The state party organization largely functions through committees.

The state organization is headed by the state executive committee. At the May primary in the year of the presidential election the voters of each of the leading political parties in each senatorial district elect two men and two women to membership on the state executive committee. These sixty-four members, representing the sixteen senatorial districts, meet and appoint three additional members, bringing the total to sixty-seven in each party. It is a large committee to organize for effective work. This group chooses a state chairman, who may or may not be one of the elected members of the committee.

On the call of the chairman these politicians meet as a board of strategy to plan the political campaign. And a board of strategy it is! Each member tries to maintain control over the voters in his district. He knows the people and greets them by their first names; he will come to their help in time of need; he knows the details of the voter's life, where he lives, where he works, and above all his political sentiments. In this manner he tries to exercise control over the voters, but it is evident that where economic independence exists and education advances, there is less likelihood of political control. Political chicanery lives in the region where poverty thrives and people are forced to be dependent. Government by bounty contains many dangerous elements.

OTHER COMMITTEES

At the same election at which the state executive committee is chosen, each party elects one man and one woman in each magisterial district in the county to form the county executive committee. Moreover, in every city with a population of ten thousand or more, two persons (one man and one woman) are elected from each ward to form the urban executive committee.

There are also a congressional, a senatorial, and a judicial committee. For each of these two members (a man and a woman) are elected from each of the counties composing a congressional district, a senatorial district, or a judicial district, respectively. In general these three committees play rather a negligible part in the functioning of party work, though they may rise at times to fill a special need. The real party power comes from the state, county, and city executive committees, and the strength of the party is measured by their ability. However, a really active political party commands the services of all its workers.

The term of office of all committeemen is four years. Vacancies in the state committee are filled by the vote of the remaining members, but any other vacancy is filled by the county organization in which such vacancy occurs. Each committee, at the call of the outgoing chairman, organizes by electing a president, secretary, and treasurer, and is then ready to swing into action at the command of its chief, the state chairman.

The ultimate purpose of this whole procedure is to land candidates safely in office when the campaign closes. Headquarters established in each county and city serve as centers where literature is disseminated and where meetings are called to plan the work of the party. Here visitors are entertained, the program for public speaking is arranged, and rallies are planned at various community centers. Lithographs bedeck the windows, and the Star Spangled Banner waves as a token of patriotic loyalty. The momentum of the campaign increases until election day, after which half of the candidates rejoice at success, while the other half depart bag and baggage bound for the remote region of "salt river" for an indefinite period of political hibernation.

POWERS OF THE STATE COMMITTEEMEN

The state committee makes the rules by which its party is governed. It may also revoke or amend rules previously in use. The adoption of emblems, devices, and slogans for the party is at the discretion of this committee, and it may create subcommittees or make special appointments of individuals, delegating to them such power as seems expedient. Of course all this action must be conformable to the laws of the state; and any regulation adopted by the executive committee is subject to review by the courts of the commonwealth.

With its numerous duties the state executive committee must be very busy during the campaign year. It serves as a supervising power over the other committees, largely directing their actions. It observes the flaws in the strategy of its opponents and tries to take advantage of them to win votes. At the same time it advocates principles of public interest, for a party can scarcely wage a campaign by defensive methods alone. After the election is over, the committee becomes inactive until another campaign approaches. Then begins a recurrence of activity which lasts until the next election day. This election procedure in West Virginia does not differ essentially from that in any other state of the Union.

THE NATIONAL COMMITTEEMEN

To complete this account of political organization in the state we must mention the national committee, which directs the national campaign much as the state committee directs the state campaign.

Like the state committee, the national committee does not function continuously; between campaigns it places its power in the office of the national party chairman, who directs party policy.

Each state, territory, and district in the Union is entitled to select two members of the national committee. The states have adopted various methods for their selection. In West Virginia under the procedure required by law the state executive committee of each party elects one man and one woman to membership in the national committee.

The national committee derives its authority from legislation enacted by the national convention in session. No law restricts the convention, but of course it cannot act in any manner contrary to national or state statutes. If the rules adopted by either party should provide some other manner of electing committeemen, the state of West Virginia would scarcely oppose it. In other words, the state law is elastic enough to permit the following of the rules adopted by a national convention, provided they do not contravene other statutes.

The term of office is four years. Vacancies are filled by action of the state committee.

The Primary Election

There are two methods of nominating candidates for office in West Virginia, the direct primary and the party convention. For many years a third type, the caucus, was used, but this has now grown obsolete. The caucus may be defined as a meeting of party leaders for making nominations and prescribing policies. It was of general use in urban sections where difficulties were not encountered in attending meetings, often secret. Its only remnant may now be found in the legislature, where each party calls a legislative caucus for shaping policies to be followed during the session.

As population grew it became necessary to devise some system of representation for party meetings. From this necessity sprang the convention. Under this system party members meet in the district and the ward, and select delegates to the county and city conventions, which in turn elect delegates to a state convention. The state convention nominates delegates to a national assembly. Theoretically this procedure is a truly representative system, but in practice it degenerated; it became a boss-ridden institution, making a fertile field for the party boss accused of buying votes by wholesale. The monstrous machine eventually became corrupt. So the party convention had to give way to the direct primary.

The direct primary is the method of nominating candidates in an election held within the political party. Several persons aspiring to the same office become candidates for the nomination. On a day set apart for that purpose the members of the party go forth to an election and nominate their choices for the various offices which are to be filled at the general election. All parties make their nominations on the same day.

There are two types of the direct primary in use — the open and the closed. In West Virginia the closed method is in operation. Under this system the voter has recorded with registrars his party preference, and when he appears to vote and announces his name, his party ticket is handed to him by the election official. At the open primary the names of all candidates are printed on one ballot, and the voter has the privilege of making his party choice at the time of voting.

The chief objection leveled against the party primary is the great expense incurred in conducting it. But civilization is expensive. Not much sentiment exists in West Virginia for the repeal of the primary election law, nor does the standard complaint against the closed primary, that it violates the principles of the secret ballot, seem widespread.

TIME OF THE PRIMARY ELECTION

In the presidential election year the primary is held on the second Tuesday in May, while two years later it comes on the first Tuesday in August. The reason for the difference in dates is that in the presidential election year the delegates to the national convention are chosen at the primary election, and those conventions usually meet in June or July. Two years later nominations are made only for offices to be filled at the general election held in November. It should be understood, however, that both the May and August primaries select candidates for both state and local offices to be filled by the voters in November.

WHO MAY VOTE IN THE PRIMARY ELECTION

All persons qualified to vote in the next general election after the primary are entitled to participate in the primary election. In West Virginia the method of nominating candidates is legally controlled just as the general election is, but a municipality is not required to register its voters for local elections unless required to do so by its own charter. It should be understood, however, that there cannot be any "splitting of the ticket" in the closed primary election, as one may vote only for candidates of his own party.

NAMING DELEGATES TO THE NATIONAL CONVENTIONS

According to the apportionment of delegates to the national nominating conventions, West Virginia is entitled to sixteen, two for each member of the national House of Representatives and two for each United States Senator. Both of the leading political parties follow this plan. Qualified persons desiring to serve their party in this capacity voluntarily offer themselves as candidates, and a formal election takes place on the first Tuesday in May of the presidential election year. Alternate delegates, equal in number to those regularly elected, are also chosen, so that any vacancies that occur may be filled.

In West Virginia the voters have the privilege of expressing their choice of candidates for the presidency of the United States, by electing delegates who have declared what candidate they will support. The delegates may thus present themselves with or without instructions from the electorate. In the former case they are bound strictly by their instructions. If, as frequently happens, hope of nominating the designated choice vanishes, they may of course shift their support to another candidate.

THE NOMINATION OF CANDIDATES

A person aspiring to an office whose jurisdiction covers a single county or a part of a county files a certificate of declaration with the clerk of the circuit court. One aspiring to an office whose jurisdiction covers more than one county files the certificate with the secretary of state. For this purpose a legal form is specified,[2] which must

[2] I ________________, hereby certify that I am a candidate for the nomination for the office of ____________ to represent the ____________ party, and desire my name printed on the official ballot of said party to be voted at the primary election to be held on the ___ day of ________, 19___; that I am a legally qualified voter of the county of ____________, State of West Virginia; that my residence is number ___ of ____________ street in the city (or town) of ____________ in ____________ county in said State; that I am eligible to hold the said office; that I am a member of and affiliated with said political party; that I am a candidate for said office in good faith.

________________ Candidate

Signed and acknowledged before me this ___ day of ________, 19___.
Signature and official title of person before whom signed.

____

be properly signed and acknowledged before an officer qualified to administer an oath. The certificate of declaration must be filed at least thirty days before the primary, so that eleventh-hour candidates are forbidden entry.

After the candidates have complied with these several conditions, the secretary of state certifies their names to the clerks of the circuit court in the various counties. From the names so certified, together with those filed in the clerk's office, the ballot commissioners of each county prepare sample official ballots. After they have been published and examined, the legal ballots are printed for voting purposes, to the extent of one and one-half times the number of registered voters. Again, the ballot commissioners take a hand in the matter by designating one of the commissioners of election in each precinct to "attend at the office of the clerk of the circuit and county courts, at least three days before each primary election, to receive the ballots, ballot boxes, poll books, and all other supplies" for conducting the election. To avoid complications, the secretary of state even selects paper of a special color to be used in making the ballots for each party. After these and other details that need not be mentioned here have been attended to, another matter has to be taken up before the election goes into full swing. That is the provision of election officials.

ELECTION OFFICIALS

Matured plans for holding the election must be made before the day comes for voting, and the county court is responsible for the making of these plans. On the second Tuesday in the month preceding the election day, at a meeting of the court, three commissioners of election and two poll clerks are appointed.[3] These officers must be qualified voters of good standing, and not addicted to intoxication. In order that both parties may be fairly represented on the election board, not more than two of the commissioners and one of the clerks may be a member of the same political organization.

If there should be more than four hundred voters registered in the precinct, the court appoints two boards of three persons each. One is called the receiving board, the other the counting board. They have separate duties. The receiving board organizes the election officers and takes general charge of the election; the ballot boxes are turned over to the counting board, whose members count the votes

[3] If the county executive committee of either party requests the court to appoint a specific qualified individual to this board, the court complies.

as the process of voting continues. In smaller precincts one board fulfills both functions.

Before beginning his duties each election official subscribes to an oath that he will faithfully support the Constitution of the United States and the constitution of West Virginia, and that he will not disclose or communicate how any elector has voted. If no one else authorized to administer an oath is present, one of the commissioners performs this duty, and afterwards one of his colleagues administers the oath to him.

CONDUCTING THE ELECTION

Perhaps few people conceive the basic importance of a popular election. It selects a leader for two, four, eight, or even twelve years and places in his hands power of tremendous weight, which he may use to the advantage or to the detriment of the people's welfare. Election day is decision day, and the power to choose is at the command of the voter.

Upon entering the room the voter announces his name and the party to which he belongs. If qualified, he is handed a ballot of his party and immediately repairs to a booth to fill out his ticket. Upon leaving the booth, he again announces his name, presents his ballot to the receiving commissioner, and retires at least sixty feet away from the election room. This procedure is followed as voters come and go throughout the day. If a voter is illiterate or is otherwise uncertain how to mark his ballot, he solicits the assistance of one of the election clerks, who designates the choice according to the voter's will.

As the process continues from hour to hour, the counting commissioners take charge of the ballot boxes and enumerate the votes. By the time the polls are closed, the final results may be fully ascertained; but when the voting is heavy, or when only one board functions, the counting may continue late into the night.

As soon as the final results are known, the clerks and commissioners sign four certificates for each party represented. These certificates contain a statement of the total number of votes cast for each candidate. Three of these are sealed and returned, one to the clerk of the county court, one to the clerk of the circuit court, and one to the secretary of state.[4] The other one is posted on the door of the building where the election was held. The responsibility of

[4] The results of the votes cast for county and district officers are not required to be sent to the secretary of state.

counting, sealing, and certifying the results is equally shared by the counting and receiving boards.

One of the commissioners, as we have seen, received from the authorized persons the proper supplies for conducting the election. When the ballots have been counted, this same commissioner, within twelve hours after sealing the results, returns to the clerk of the county court the ballot boxes, registration lists, poll books, ballots, tally sheets, and certificates. To the circuit clerk he delivers one poll book, one tally sheet, and one certificate for each political party. Thus is concluded the conducting of the primary election, the cost of which, not to exceed five dollars a day for each election official, is paid out of the treasury of the county.

CANVASSING THE RESULTS

Again we turn to the county court as an agency in the procedure of the election — this time to confirm the final results. On the first Friday following the election the county court convenes at the courthouse for the purpose of approving the reports made by the election officials and making a declaration as to the final results of the balloting. At this session the court carefully considers the total results in the county and in each district. It keeps a record of the votes for each candidate and the total of those cast in each district. In this record the court places a certificate showing the number of votes for the parties and for each candidate. Thus a summary statement of the election is made a matter of record and kept open for public inspection.

Upon the completion of its work as a canvassing board, the court forwards to the secretary of state a statement of its conclusions regarding candidates having more than county status, and to the office of the circuit clerk its report for other candidates. In turn the secretary of state, having accumulated all the totals, notifies the circuit clerk, by a certificate signed and sealed, of the candidates nominated in each political party for offices having more than county wide authority. The clerk's office issues certificates for county and lesser candidates. This procedure constitutes authorization for the printing of the names of the successful candidates on the official ballot for the general election. And with this action the work of the primary election is declared closed.

Any irregularities permitted in the election are subject to review by the county court and may be appealed to the state courts by application made by the dissatisfied party. Nominations may be set aside in this manner. Vacancies on the ticket may be filled by action of the committees belonging to the party in which the vacancy occurs.

CONCLUSION

The direct primary method of making nominations is perhaps the best that may be used in a government based on the people's will. It is not perfect; but in any event a government in which the people nominate and the people elect is surely a government by the people. Where the people are responsible for making and executing the laws of the land, the government reflects their level of political education. To have better government, a prime necessity rests on the people to elevate their own culture and refinement; they must be wiser in consideration, more honorable in disposition, and more courageous in daily living.

The General Election

Since the manner of conducting the general election follows in many respects the same procedure as that used in the primary, the following account will be largely confined to the points of difference between them.

PLACES OF VOTING

Preparations for the general election again devolve upon the county court. As the day approaches the court provides in each voting precinct a suitable place for holding the election, usually a schoolhouse located at a central and easily accessible point. It is accepted that the schoolhouse, being public property, may be used for holding an election as well as for keeping school.[5] The courthouse at the county seat and the town hall in other municipalities, being public property, are also used for this purpose. After selecting the place for holding the election, booths or compartments, furnished with proper shelves and pencils, are set up, into which voters may repair and secretly fill out their tickets. Curtains cover the entrance to the booths for the purpose of secluding the voter in complete privacy.

ELECTION OFFICIALS

Here again the services of the county court are employed. On the first Tuesday of the month preceding the general election, the

[5] In earlier days, elections were generally held in private homes.

county court appoints the election board. The organization of the board, the administration of oaths, and the certifying of affidavits are the same as for the primary. To be qualified to serve on the election board one must be a voter and a resident of the district in which he serves; he cannot be a candidate or have any wager on the result of the election; he must not be addicted to drunkenness; he cannot have under his employment or supervision ten or more voters of the precinct. These are rigid regulations for election officers, but not excessively rigid. Let us keep in mind that the general election is the most important political institution in our land. Millions of people have the privilege of taking part in it. The rules of the institution are made by officers to whom the people have delegated their power, and they should be closely adhered to.

ELECTION SUPPLIES

The greatest source of expense in conducting the election is the furnishing of supplies. Each of the more than 2500 precincts in West Virginia has to have registration books, ballots, ballot boxes, tally sheets, printed instructions, booths, etc. The total expense amounts to many thousands of dollars.

From the office of the clerk of the county court the election commissioners secure the poll books, ballot boxes, booths and so on. It is the duty of the circuit clerk, chairman of the board of ballot commissioners, to designate one of the commissioners of election in each precinct to appear at this office at least two days before the election. There he receives under seal the ballots that are to be used by the voters in his precinct, and he is required to give a bond for the safe keeping and guarding of these ballots. After completing this part of his mission the commissioner goes to the office of the county clerk and there secures the roll of the registered voters, two ballot boxes, two poll books, tally sheets, blanks for affidavits, and envelopes in which the final returns are to be made.

OPENING THE ELECTION

On election day the officers appear and are sworn to proceed legally; the commissioners, in the presence of their colleagues, break the seal of the packages containing the ballots and deliver them to the poll clerks; the commissioners carefully examine the ballot boxes to ascertain that no ballots are in them and then securely close them under lock. It is then in order for the commissioners to proclaim the election open. The day is "Tuesday next after the first Monday in November, in each even year," and the hour is six-thirty o'clock in the morning, eastern standard time.

As the voting continues through the day the counting board (where two boards are functioning) takes possession of the ballot box in which the first votes have been deposited, retires to a place of privacy in the election room, and proceeds to count and tabulate the votes. During the day some votes are being counted while others are being cast. This process is continued until the hour arrives for the commissioners to proclaim "in a loud and audible tone of voice" that the polls are closed. The hour for closing is six-thirty o'clock in the evening.

Wide privilege is given to the voter in marking his ballot. If he cannot read, or needs help for any other reason, one of the clerks goes to his aid; if he decides to vote for a person whose name is not on the ballot he may do so by writing the name in; the constitution gives him the choice of voting an open, sealed, or secret ballot; and his vote may not be rejected unless "it is impossible to determine the elector's choice of candidates."

DETERMINING THE RESULTS

When the polls are closed both boards join efforts to conclude the counting and the certifying of the totals, and to issue and sign certificates of the results of the voting. If only one board has been employed, counting is delayed until the voting has been concluded. Then the commissioners take from the boxes the ballots one by one and read the record of voting, which the clerks carefully tabulate. The board remains in session until the counting is completed, even if its work continues through the night. Certificates of the results are issued and the returns prepared for delivery to the county clerk. The duties of the election board are then over, and it dissolves not to meet again.

Within twelve hours after the completion of the work of the boards one of the commissioners must deliver the sealed ballots, a set of the poll books and tally sheets, one of the certificates, the registration book, and the ballot boxes to the clerk of the county court. One certificate of the results and one set of the poll books and tally sheets are delivered to the circuit clerk. The clerks thus become the custodians of this property, and the records are protected under their care.

On the first Monday after the election the county court convenes to review the results of the election as reported from each precinct.

If deemed expedient the court may require the presence of any election official in the county to give evidence in determining the official results of the voting. A careful record is kept of the proceedings of the court, and when the canvass is completed the ballots are again sealed, but if some dissatisfied candidate should demand it they may be opened and recounted.

The court officially declares the final results of the election and notifies each successful candidate by certificate. If there is no issue pending and no question involved in connection with the election, the ballots, poll book, tally sheet, and certificates are burned after a lapse of sixty days.

Thus is concluded an election with all its agitation and glamour. Usually lines have been rigidly drawn, hot words spoken, and unnecessary expense entailed. Before the voting perhaps most candidates boasted of the certainty of their election. After the canvass at least half of them experience disappointment. The electorate of this country all too slowly realizes the weighty importance of election day. Election day is of rare consequence. Let us be vigilant in keeping it.

Miscellaneous Regulations

THE ABSENT VOTER

The laws of West Virginia make it possible for a qualified voter to cast his ballot in a primary or general election if he should be necessarily detained out of the state on election day. The person so detained makes a formal application to the clerk of the circuit court for an absent voter's ballot. Ten days before the election the clerk mails a blank ballot to the applicant. In the presence of a person authorized by law to administer an oath the elector fills out his ticket and returns it to the clerk, having subscribed to an affidavit certifying its validity. This ballot is delivered to the election commissioners before the closing of the polls on election day and it is properly counted in the tabulation and the canvassing of the final results. The intent of the law is to allow every qualified elector to vote, and the stringent regulations protect him in his privilege.

PENALTIES FOR VIOLATIONS

The laws enabling a citizen to vote also protect him in exercising this privilege. If he meets the legal requirements, which are numerous indeed, his position is not to be abridged or denied. Neither is it to be abused. Any election official who corrupts his office by bribery, forgery, or false action in any other way, may be found guilty of a felony and punished by fine and imprisonment. It has been found expedient to place bounds of legal protection around the ballots. Votes count. During the entire conduct of the election the ballots are kept solely in the possession of the election officials except while the voter actually marks his ticket. The clerks are sworn not to reveal the way the elector has voted. It is forbidden to place distinguishing marks of any sort on the ballot; seals and locks must not be tampered with; bribery and betting are forbidden; and electioneering must not be carried on within the voting room or within sixty feet of it. No employer or other person may prevent a voter from freely exercising his suffrage at any election. Anyone found guilty of any of these violations may be fined not more than a thousand dollars or committed to jail for not more than one year.

EXPENDITURES AND ACCOUNTS

Campaigns involve the parties in considerable expense. In securing money to meet this expense and in disbursing it they are bound by certain regulations.

In the first place, contributions of money may be made by individuals but not by corporations. This supply is the main source of revenue of the political party. Entertainment of various sorts may be used as an inducement to people to give financial support to a party. The Lincoln Day dinner held by the Republicans and the Jackson Day dinner by the Democrats are typical examples of this method of financing a party.

The treasurer of the party must keep a record of receipts and expenditures and confirm it by a sworn statement. The same is true with respect to candidates or any financial agents in the interest of a party. Candidates in political divisions greater than the county file reports concerning receipts and expenditures with the secretary of state; candidates for county and district offices, with the clerk of the county court. Failure to file a report makes one liable to punishment by fine.

Now for what purposes are expenses incurred? Under present conditions campaigns are carried on at great expense; by all rules of right and justice, too great. This outlay of money is made for the payment of rentals, secretarial help, supplies, printing and distribution of printed matter, advertising, traveling, expenses of speakers, radio privileges, and a multitude of other causes. Expenditures grew to such excessive proportions that the law stepped in and put a limitation on them. But the law does not reach into all the ramifications of a political campaign. Let us examine some of the regulations.

The amount of expense is apportioned according to the importance of the office. For candidates for the United States Senate, and for state offices, the sum shall not exceed seventy-five dollars for each county in the state; for the United States House of Representatives, seventy-five dollars for each county in the district; for the state legislature, one hundred twenty-five dollars for each county in which the candidate is voted for; for county offices, two hundred dollars; for any other office, fifty dollars. These amounts apply to the primary election; the same sums are fixed for the general election. The law reaches far enough to forbid even a friend or agent of the candidate to contribute money or incur indebtedness that would exceed the maximum fixed by law. The purpose of the regulation is obviously to curb corruption.

FORBIDDEN PRACTICES

The election laws of West Virginia not only curb a candidate in his activities but also protect him from impositions. One is forbidden to solicit money from a candidate for office. It constitutes a legal violation for a religious, fraternal, or charitable organization to request financial aid from one who is aspiring to office. He cannot even be requested to buy tickets to an entertainment, or pay for space in a program or a book. He may, however, make donations of this sort voluntarily. And the law interposes as protector of the candidate against any threat of violence, force, or restraint, and the same protection applies to any qualified voter. Any person who knowingly publishes a false statement about an opponent makes himself liable to a heavy fine and even to imprisonment. Although it does not always succeed, the law attempts to insure fair play on both sides.

Contested Elections

In elections, as in all other contests, disputes sometimes arise concerning the final results. When the total vote is close, the losing candidate may request a recount of the ballots, and at times the original declaration of the results is reversed. Contested elections for county and district offices are referred to the county court for final judgment. During the contest witnesses may be summoned, poll books reviewed, and ballots recounted. When the evidence has been collected the court gives the matter due consideration and renders a verdict to the best of its skill and judgment. However, an appeal may be taken to the circuit court, and then to the state supreme court, whose verdict is final.

A contested election for a seat in the state legislature is referred to the house for which the person is a candidate. Again, the committee on elections gathers evidence from records and witnesses, and hears arguments. A majority vote of the house decides the issue. In case of a tie vote in the general election the house again renders the final decision as to which contestant shall occupy the office.

A contested election for the governorship of the state would be referred first to a joint committee consisting of two senators chosen by ballot by the senate, and three members of the house of delegates elected by the members of that assembly. The purpose of this committee would be to collect evidence in the case and submit it in a report to a joint session of the two houses. The president of the senate would preside. A majority vote of the assembly would determine the result of the election.

When the election of the other state officers and of the judges of the courts is contested a special court hears and decides the case. The court is composed of three members, one chosen by the contestant, one by the contestee, and the third by the governor of the state. The three persons so selected convene in regular session, hear and consider the evidence, and finally certify their report to the governor. An appeal may be made from this decision to the state supreme court, whose verdict is final.

Filling Vacancies

Vacancies in elective offices occasionally occur by resignation, by death, or by dismissal. Methods for filling such vacancies are provided by law.

If the governorship becomes vacant, the president of the state senate succeeds to the office. If the president of the senate cannot qualify, then the speaker of the house of delegates becomes governor. If in turn the speaker is disqualified, the governor is chosen by a majority vote of a joint session of the state legislature.

Vacancies in the United States Senate and in judgeships in the supreme court of appeals, circuit courts, and inferior courts are filled by appointments made by the governor. But to fill a vacancy in the West Virginia representation in the United States House of Representatives the governor calls a special election in the district in which the vacancy exists.

A vacancy in the clerkship of the circuit court is filled by an appointment made by the judge of the circuit court involved. If at any time the membership of the county court is incomplete the remaining members choose commissioners to fill the places left open. The county court also takes action to keep the offices of justice of the peace, sheriff, prosecuting attorney, assessor, and constable filled and functioning. If the number of vacancies in the county court itself should deprive the court of a majority, then the governor makes appointments necessary to create a quorum. When the membership of the county board of education is incomplete the remaining members themselves select persons to bring the number up to five, the legal membership.

Appointments are regularly for the unexpired term. The power to appoint carries a great deal of prestige but it has a time limitation. The method used for filling vacancies saves expense and avoids delay in our state and local government.

CHAPTER 14

The House of Delegates

Importance of the Legislature

From the beginning of popular government in Virginia to the present time, it has been considered a political right for the qualified voters to choose from their own number delegates to make laws for the people. The principle involved is that legislators, coming from the farm, the mine, the shop, the mill, belong to the rank and file of the citizenry, and know their joys and sorrows, their wants and needs, the feelings of their hearts and the thoughts of their minds. Having a true and intimate knowledge of the daily life of the people, the legislator works and votes to improve their condition. The legislature is composed of delegates of the people, elected by the people to govern for the people. And that is the basis of good government.

Under these circumstances it is unfortunate that the public sometimes fails to appreciate fully the real importance of the state legislature, and this lack of appreciation perhaps gains gravity as the power of the national government expands. Let it be remembered that the structure of our legal system rests on the rock foundation of legislative power. It is this power that formulates bills that become laws which citizens must obey. The legislature repeals laws no longer needed; it provides for protecting the home, life, and property of every citizen of the state; it appropriates money for making roads, maintaining schools, and constructing public buildings; it modifies the privilege of voting and of holding office; it protects the health of the people and maintains sanitary conditions; it licenses the doctor, the lawyer, the teacher, the grocer, and the automobile driver; it regulates the sale of drugs, alcohol, and tobacco; it makes laws for the registration of births and issues permits for burial. All in all, the acts of the legislature affect, directly or indirectly, the life of every resident every hour of the day. In consideration of these facts one is compelled to conclude that the legislator is a very important officer. He should be wise, just, courageous, and well informed, so that he may execute adequately the duties of his office.

Membership of the House of Delegates

BASIS OF REPRESENTATION

The constitution originally provided for delegate districts as units of representation. A single county might constitute a delegate district; but counties having a small population were attached to some contiguous county or counties to form such a district. This arrangement did not prove altogether satisfactory, and the districts were later abolished, leaving the county as the basic unit for representation. It is now required that every county shall have at least one representative.

The constitution wisely left the apportionment of delegates open to change after every census. The first house of delegates consisted of sixty-five members, or one delegate for about 6,000 population. Since then the membership has grown to one hundred, or one to about 20,000 population. Thirty-nine counties still have only one delegate each, but the more populous counties have more. Kanawha is represented by eleven, the largest number from any one county.

ELECTION

As has been stated earlier, delegates are chosen by direct vote of all qualified citizens. They are nominated in primary elections and elected at general elections.

Any person desiring to contest the election of a delegate must submit to him the objections in writing within thirty days after the election. Then the person whose election is being questioned has fourteen days to file his answer to the contestant. Each party may file affidavits supporting the truth of the charges. Other evidence having a bearing on the case may be taken in writing.

The petition of the person filing the contest is presented to the house in session within ten days after the date of its next meeting, for each house remains the sole judge of the election returns and qualifications of its own members. The matter is then referred to the committee on elections and privileges, which gathers and studies the evidence and finally makes its report to the house. Should the committee report the charges unwarranted, the matter ends there; but if it supports the charges, the affair is aired before all the members and a final vote is taken, definitely settling the case. No appeal can be made from this decision. Of course if the person laying claim to the office fails to validate his claim, he is set aside and the governor makes an appointment to fill the vacancy unless someone else who has been a candidate can prove that he has been legally elected. If the vote in the election was a tie, the members decide which candidate shall be seated.

It comes within the jurisdiction of the house to make the rules for its own proceedings. These rules will be discussed later. The house possesses full authority to preserve good conduct and by a two-thirds vote to expel a member for disorderly behavior.

QUALIFICATIONS

Extensive qualifications are not required for membership in the house of delegates. In fact they are almost as simple as the requirements for the voter. Each member must be a legal voter and a resident of the county from which he is elected. If at any time he should change his residence to another county, his office becomes vacant. There is no legal age specified for a delegate beyond the twenty-one years which he must attain in order to vote. However, no one who holds office under the United States, the state, or the county, or who is an official of a railroad company or a collector of public funds, can qualify for a seat in the state legislature. One who has been convicted for an infamous crime is also disqualified. The law through its qualifying regulations very properly intends that only persons of merit and excellence shall be chosen to take a part in the making of the laws.

Before exercising the authority of office members of both houses subscribe to an oath, or affirmation, that they will support the Constitution of the United States and the constitution of West Virginia, and that they will faithfully discharge the duties of their office to the best of their ability. They are also required to take an oath not to accept directly or indirectly anything of value for their vote or influence, given or withheld. This puts on restraints in double layers. If one should refuse to subscribe to the declaration or be convicted for the violation thereof, he would be disqualified not only from holding the office of senator but from holding any other office in West Virginia.

The constitution also stipulates that one who is a public official in the state or nation, or salaried by a railroad company, cannot qualify as a senator or delegate. It may seem strange that the political ambitions of a railroad official should be condemned by the constitution of the state. It should be remembered that when the supreme law was written (1872) railroad building was mounting to high tide in West Virginia, and the officials identified with the railroad corporations were suspected of seeking political position in order to sway legislation in their favor. To a certain extent, no doubt, this was true. The writers of the constitution, therefore, set to work to break the connection between politics and the railroad corporations. But times have changed. Today other industries have grown to exceed the extent of the railroads, yet the constitution does not debar their directors from holding office.

A sheriff, constable, or clerk of a court of record cannot qualify for a seat in the legislature. One who has collected money for state or local government is disqualified from holding a place in the assembly until he has made a final financial settlement of all accounts. And those persons who have been convicted of bribery, perjury, or any other infamous crime are not fit, so says the supreme law of the land, to serve as legislators. The principle followed here is that people who cannot obey laws should not make them. However, the doors leading to the legislative halls sometimes swing open wide enough for demagogues to pass through.

RESTRICTIONS AND PRIVILEGES

A member of either house of the legislature is forbidden, during the period for which he has been elected, to hold another office, either appointive or elective, which has been created, or of which the profits have been increased, during his term. Nor is he permitted an interest in any contract with the state or one of its counties authorized by a law passed during his term.

Legislators are thus limited in their activities, but they are also given special privileges. In the first place all members of the legislature are privileged from arrest in all cases except treason, felony, and breach of the peace, during a session and for ten days before and ten days after it. This privilege extends only to civil cases. A member of the state senate, like any other person, may be placed under arrest and detained for a criminal offense. This law is made only for the purpose of protecting a legislator from being intentionally or unduly detained from his official duties, but it does not give him unrestricted liberty.

Again, legislators may not be questioned for words spoken in debate or in motions, propositions, or reports, except in the house in which such matters originated. This immunity extends to words both spoken and written, in open session and in committee, but not to what goes on outside the capitol. Thus the legislator is given freedom of tongue and pen. He cannot be prosecuted by any court, state or federal, for what he has said or written in the session.

Members of both houses receive an annual salary of five hundred dollars, and are allowed traveling expenses of ten cents a mile going to and returning from the capital.

THE LEGISLATOR'S POLICY

It is clear that the people have entrusted the delegate with heavy duties and responsibilities. The question then arises, should he exercise only his own judgment in the disposition of his manifold public duties, or should he consult in matters of legislation with his constituency and act and vote in accordance with their sentiments? Should he be the leader of the people in his county, or should he be led by them? These questions have baffled many legislators. It is the opinion, however, of some of the best political thinkers that voters place their welfare in the hands of the public officer during the time for which he is elected, and that it is his privilege to exercise his best judgment in matters presented for a decision. He is entrusted with public business, he is sworn to be true to his duties, to be loyal to the state, and to dispose of his responsibilities according to the best of his ability. In fulfilling this mission he will find himself sometimes in disagreement with the people back home but never will he be untrustworthy. If he acts wisely, it is likely that he will be reelected time after time if he so desires; if unwisely, he stands a good chance of being recalled and ordered to the rear lines of duty.

TERM OF OFFICE

The term of office of a member of the house of delegates is two years, and there is no limitation, except the quirks in politics, as to the number of times he may be reelected. The legislature meets in regular session only once in every two years, and the session is limited to a maximum of sixty days.

Is the term too short? Probably not. The plan now in use has worked well for about four score years. Should a delegate prove to be incompetent, his term is already too long; if he succeeds in caring for the people's business, they can reelect him. The period may be too short for a new member to prove his full worth, but even one term usually gives the voters enough evidence to make a wise decision during the delegate's next candidacy.

PERSONNEL OF THE HOUSE OF DELEGATES

To turn the searchlight on the personnel of the house proves interesting. In a recent session there served ninety-two white men, one white woman, and one Negro man. The average age of the entire number was forty-five years. Some of them had given long and worthy public service; others were serving for the first time. Occasionally it happens that more than half of the membership serve only in one session; during a recent session sixty out of the ninety-four members served their first term. This condition brings into the legislative forum so many inexperienced persons as to invite adverse criticism. But wisdom is more vital than experience, and if the session contains enough men of wisdom and common sense it will succeed beyond any doubt.

As intended, the members come from all vocations in life, such as lawyers, merchants, farmers, teachers, ministers, and others. This varied condition makes the house of delegates truly a representative assembly of the industrial as well as the professional interests. Regardless of how the members might be chosen, they could scarcely be more typical agents of the people than they are at present.

THE QUALITY OF DEBATE

The quality of speeches made by the members of the house sometimes is criticized as being inferior to that of good statesmen. Although the legal profession has more than its proportionate share of the membership, apparently this does not improve the standard of the speeches. The power of straight thinking, united with the art of clear explanation and emphasized by strong courage, is needed at all times in legislative assemblies. However, it requires a great crisis in the life of a state, just as in the life of a person, to bring out the strongest qualities of its statesmen. Like a giant battleship in a long period of peace, those powers might lie dormant for many years. For this reason, no doubt, the rank of debate in the house has never again reached the high level it attained in 1863. Although the leadership is usually in the hands of experienced and capable men, perhaps the house of delegates has been considered too much a training field for politicians to permit a high standard of debate.

On the other hand, wise legislation does not necessarily involve logical argument, skilled debating, or eloquent oratory. Most bills are written by persons expert in that work; they originate in the brains of industrialists, workingmen, professional men, or politicians; they are worked over and reshaped in the legislative committee room. When they are finally submitted to be accepted or rejected in the general assembly, they may be still further amended, but the most important work in formulating laws is done in committee meetings. Again, the restriction of a session to sixty days makes impossible prolonged debate on most business.

Yet the voters will think well of the legislator who can think straight and who can set forth his thoughts clearly and in good language. This power in some is a natural gift; others may develop it by training.

Organization of the House of Delegates

PLACE OF MEETING

"Like a massive jewel in a setting of verdant beauty among the West Virginia hills, skirted by the swiftly flowing Great Kanawha, the new State Capitol rises in its architectural splendor — a fitting and enduring monument dedicated to all the people of this and coming generations who shall mold the destinies of West Virginia." Perhaps no state capitol in the Union excels in beauty and fineness the one standing on the banks of the Kanawha. If surroundings of beauty and stateliness have an influence in creating sublime thoughts and aspirations in the human mind, surely the members of the legislature of West Virginia should entertain only designs of the most noble excellence. There is nothing common in the structure of the capitol. Let the lawmakers profit by its example.

The house of delegates assembles in a room in the east wing of the main unit, on the second floor. The chamber is carpeted in a soft plush. Convenient desks of the finest finish, arranged in rows in crescent fashion, accommodate the members, and the marble walls express an impressive beauty. The speaker's voice is distinctly audible to the farthest recess of the chamber.

One of the modern conveniences installed in the assembly room is an electrically controlled device for voting. The old method of calling the roll and listening to the responses of *yeas* and *nays* took at least thirty minutes. The new way takes about thirty seconds. Attached to the desk of each member is an electric button, which when pressed by the finger immediately flashes a red or blue miniature light in a wall chart placed in the front of the chamber. Red indicates negative, blue affirmative. The attentive clerk keeps the record as the lights flash in rapid succession, and relays the result to the speaker, who announces the decision.

THE FIRST MEETING

Before transacting any formal business the house of delegates must effect an organization, so that its procedure may be guarded by its own chosen officers and under recognized rules of order. Usually the day before the session opens the delegates belonging to each political party assemble in separate rooms in the capitol. The meetings, known as caucuses, select persons whose names will be placed in nomination when the time comes for organizing. The officers to be elected are speaker, clerk, doorkeeper, and sergeant-at-arms.

At twelve o'clock noon on the second Tuesday in January of the odd years, the house meets. The clerk of the last session calls the roll and administers the oath of office to the members-elect. In case the legality of the election of any member is questioned, he stands aside until the matter has been definitely settled by the house. But when the oath has been administered the oldest delegate, in point of service, calls the members to order and presides until a speaker has been elected. This election is merely a confirmation of the action in the caucus on the previous day. When the nominations are called for, both parties present their candidates and usually the election is carried by a strictly party vote. Having been elected, the speaker takes the chair and presides while the other officers are chosen. The house of delegates now having organized, the speaker appoints a committee of three to convey word to the senate that the house is ready to begin its regular business. In turn the president of the senate selects a committee to join with the one from the house, and jointly they wait on the governor to inform him that the legislature has convened and is ready to hear his message.

THE SPEAKER

The origin of this office dates back to early English government. It was inherited by the states from the colonies, where it had been functioning for more than a hundred years. In Virginia the speaker of the house had become a powerful official before 1776, and the office continued in the state after independence. It was transmitted to West Virginia in the constitution of 1863.

On each day when the legislature is in session, precisely at the hour of meeting, the speaker takes the chair and calls the house to order, and the chaplain offers prayer. The members then proceed to take up the order of business, the speaker presiding. Before addressing the house a member must be recognized by the speaker; when two or more members simultaneously arise and call "Mr. Speaker," he must name the one entitled to the floor. In this manner he may promote legislation or he may defeat it. He may recognize one who favors a bill; he can fail to recognize another who opposes it. But the decisions of the speaker are expected to be impartial. If he chooses to do so, he may take part in debate by calling another member to preside during his discussion.

When a question of order arises in the house the speaker makes a ruling on the point. On the demand of ten members, there may be an appeal to the house from his decision, but only on rare occasions do the members resort to this extreme measure. In the house chamber, in the galleries, and in all other rooms assigned to the use of the members, the speaker has general control in keeping order, and may call on the sergeant-at-arms to enforce his word. To maintain proper conduct he may order the galleries and corridors cleared.

One of the most important powers of the speaker is that of appointment. He appoints the chaplain who opens each daily session with prayer. This lot usually falls on one of the ministers residing in Charleston. Through the direction of the house he chooses clerks for committees, stenographers, pages, and attachés. On the other hand he may remove any of these appointees.

In making these numerous minor appointments no considerable power is wielded, but there are other places to fill that have preeminent importance. In each regular session of the house of delegates the speaker names twenty-eight standing committees. (The same number exist in the senate.) [1] These committees have a great

[1] The Standing Committees are: Agriculture; Arts; Science; General Improvements; Banks and Corporations; Claims and Grievances; Counties,

deal to do with legislation. By virtue of his office the speaker acts as chairman of the committee on rules, which determines the rules and procedure governing legislation. In other words, it serves as the steering committee. It is also the duty of the presiding officer to designate the chairman and vice chairman of each committee and by his way of so doing he may stimulate the groups of members to action or smother them in inaction. In the process of legislation all bills introduced in the house are referred to the consideration of committees who will either approve or reject every measure entrusted to their care. Just here lies the most important power of the speaker. Through his choice of the personnel of the committees and his presiding over the group that determines rules and procedures, the speaker may exercise great influence over legislation. Of course the majority party always has more than half the members on each committee and also the chairmanship of each.

All acts passed by the house bear the signature of the speaker. Unless excused, he votes on measures calling for the yeas and nays. On the roll his name is called last; he is thus given an opportunity sometimes to tie the count by voting with the minority, in which case the question is lost. In addition to these duties he makes a daily examination of the journal before it is read and offers such corrections as he deems proper. In view of his many powers the speaker stands in a position to do great good or render lasting harm in the legislative program.

THE CLERK

The clerk has charge of the clerical business of the house. He calls the roll, reports the absentees, and notes the results when a vote is taken on a bill and on joint or concurrent resolutions. In brief, he acts as a general secretary to the house.

When the committees are chosen it is the clerk who notifies each member of his appointment. He judges and discriminates in referring to the various committees the business submitted to the house; he supervises the printing of the journal of the daily proceedings; he engrosses and enrolls bills; he attests writs, warrants, and subpoenas

---

Districts, and Municipal Corporations; Education; Elections and Privileges; Executive Offices and Library; Federal Relations; Forestry and Conservation; Forfeited, Delinquent and Unappropriated Lands; Game and Fish; Humane Institutions and Public Buildings; Insurance, Judiciary; Labor; Medicine and Sanitation; Military Affairs; Mines and Mining; Penitentiary; Printing and Contingent Expenses; Railroads; Redistricting; Rules; State Boundaries; Taxation Finance; and Temperance.

issued by the order of the house. The clerk keeps the accounts of the members with respect to salary and mileage, and issues payments to the officers, pages, and attachés. He attends to the payment of other expenses of the session, as for printing and supplies.

Nor does this exhaust the list of his duties. The private papers and records of the house are entrusted to his care and custody. Only through permission given by the house may he allow the official records to be examined or used for any purpose by persons whose names are not on the roll of members. To facilitate the execution of business he keeps all the records carefully catalogued.

Because of the heavy demands made on the time of the clerk he is allowed to choose assistants, whose appointments are authorized by law. To his office a much needed secretary and a stenographer are assigned, whose pay is fixed by the committee on rules. The clerk is a very necessary and closely occupied officer when the house of delegates is in session.

THE SERGEANT-AT-ARMS

The duties of the sergeant-at-arms come under the direction of the speaker. The sergeant must be present at all sessions for the purpose of keeping proper order. He executes orders passed by the house, distributes papers and documents to the desks of the members who need to be informed on the business of the day, and keeps watch, when the house is not in session, over the desks, books, and files of the delegates, since disturbance or disarrangement of these is forbidden. The speaker commands order in the halls, galleries, and rooms assigned to the house in the capitol, but when need arises the sergeant enforces the rules. Persons not entitled to the privilege of the floor of the house are excluded by a word or a wave of the hand of the sergeant, who also attends to seating visitors. He superintends the work of the janitors and cloakroom attendants. Under this duty is included proper ventilation, heating, and lighting of the house chamber, the committee rooms, and the halls.

THE DOORKEEPER

In some particulars the doorkeeper is an assistant to the sergeant-at-arms. He helps to see that all members are properly admitted to and other persons excluded from the general assembly room. In performing this work he attends the main door of the chamber and takes care that the other doors are properly attended by his assistants. He announces all messages sent to the house. His duties require regular attendance at all meetings, for the speaker refers special and general matters to his care.

THE RULES

The rules of the house are very complex, and the speaker must be an expert parliamentarian if he is to acquit himself with honor while presiding and rendering interpretations of parliamentary law.

One of the last steps in the process of organizing the house is the adoption of the rules. These are the same as those used in the last preceding session unless some change is made, which does not often happen. This long list of regulations sets forth the duties and rights of the speaker, the roles of the other officers, the privileges and restrictions of the members, and the procedure of the committees. It should not be overlooked that the members of the house propose and adopt the rules, and that the manner of applying the rules is left solely in the hands of the legislative assembly. The government of the house of delegates forms an interesting political unit, for all those who are governed make and enforce their own regulative laws. Here we have a miniature democracy in which the members elect their officers and retain in their own hands safe authority over the executive, legislative, and judicial power – in which, in short, the members exercise sovereign authority.

He would be a poor delegate indeed who failed to learn the rules of his own organization, for they enumerate his duties and privileges, state the order and decorum to be observed in making a motion, debating, putting a question, and voting, determine the order of business, and explain a hundred other things that a good legislator should know. If one has ever entertained the idea that the house of delegates is a place for a free lance or for a political boiler to blow off his excess steam, this idea needs immediate change. Rigid rules (laws) prevail in the government of the house just as in the government of the state.

COMMITTEES

In the house there are four different kinds of committees, namely, standing, select and special, conference, and committee of the whole. The speaker assigns to each committee a secretary who keeps records of the time and place of the meetings, attendance by members, names of persons appearing before it, and the vote of each member on all motions.

The standing committees are most important. There are twenty-eight of them, with membership varying from seven to twenty-five. Their role in the legislative procedure will be described below. Some of them are of vast importance, while others have little consequence. Those on rules, appropriations, and judiciary do perhaps half the business of the session. They have frequent long meetings in which important legislation is considered. On the other hand such committees as those on state boundaries, federal relations, and redistricting will have little or no work to do; they may not meet once during the entire session.

For each standing committee the speaker designates a chairman who is a member of the majority party. Meetings are held upon call issued by the chairman and announced from the floor of the house.[2] The committee hearings are open to the public, but only members may be present when the vote is taken. Usually the person who introduced the bill under consideration is given a chance to be heard when the committee deliberates on the proposed legislation.

Unless otherwise provided, the speaker appoints the select or special committees to fulfill special duties such as representing the state at the dedication of a monument or the inauguration of the President, or conferring with the governor on some important matter. When the committee has fulfilled its mission it is dissolved.

Conference committees are also appointed by the speaker. Their purpose is to confer with a like committee from the senate on matters of difference between the two houses. If their report should be signed by a majority of both committees, it is made an item of record and printed in the journal. In this manner, when it becomes expedient, the two houses coordinate their work and resolve questions arising between them, for both assemblies have to agree on every item in a bill before it can pass.

THE BUSINESS OF THE HOUSE

When a member desires to speak he rises, stands at his desk, and addresses the presiding officer thus: "Mr. Speaker." Upon being recognized, usually by name, he proceeds with his remarks, confining himself to the question under consideration. The rules will not permit him to indulge in personalities or to use disrespectful language. During a debate a member does not usually recognize a colleague by name but generally as "the delegate from ________ County."

The presiding officer may call to order one who is speaking. If

[2] He may have the speaker or the clerk make the announcement.

this action should be necessary, the one so called to order resumes his seat, but, if he desires to do so, he has an opportunity to explain his remarks. The matter may be appealed to the house if there is a demand for such action, or a reprimand pronounced by the speaker may be considered final. In case the house takes the matter of disorder into its own hands and renders a decision in favor of the member called to order, he may then proceed with his remarks, but if the decision is against him, he becomes liable to censure exacted by his colleagues. By a two-thirds vote he can be expelled. However, a member while speaking cannot be interrupted unless he violates the rules.

The rules put a limitation on the times one may speak in debate. Twice is the maximum on the same question unless special permission is given. By a majority vote of the members present, any limitation may be put on the time set apart for debate and on the frequency of speaking. Sometimes it becomes necessary to invoke this rule to close debate for the purpose of expediting business.

FLOOR LEADERS

Each political party represented in the house has its floor leader who pilots through the assembly important bills introduced by the members of his political faith. The greater responsibility, of course, rests on the leader of the majority, whose party is always expected to have a program of procedure for proposing measures and having them passed. If he fails to prosecute such a program, or if he allows the members of his party to become divided over proposed legislation, his watchful opponents will seize the advantage.

The minority leader is expected to keep careful watch over all matters of procedure. In case a member proposes a bill that is derogatory to public interest or for private benefit, he musters his forces to make an attack on it, and thus embarrasses the administration. By adroit leadership he may confuse, delay, and even defeat a bill. By holding the strength of his party together as a militant minority, he keeps the majority on its guard, and this political strategy makes a healthy tonic for a legislative program. In this brief explanation may be seen the advantages of representative government based on the freedom of political expression. By and by the majority party has to submit its work to the sovereign people, who may either accept or reject it. If it is rejected, the majority today may be the minority tomorrow.

THE LEGISLATIVE CAUCUS

Much of the business promoted in open session on the floor has been previously considered in the legislative caucus. The members belonging to each party hold meetings, called by the floor leader, for the purpose of mapping out their program and the strategy to be followed in carrying it to success. If the leader should deem it necessary a caucus may be held to consider a measure, or any other business worthy of attention. In this manner decisions are reached concerning party policy and an understanding is achieved between party members.

The caucus often decides which bills will be offered, what is to be the order of their introduction, who will introduce them, and who will take the lead in debate. The majority party has been placed in authority by the voters and is responsible to them for the success or failure of helpful legislation. Meanwhile the minority remains vigilant, watching for opportunities of advantage. A good parliamentarian is a handy man to have around, for he possesses one of the able qualities of a party leader.

The Making of Laws

WHERE BILLS ORIGINATE

The matter of making laws is more complicated than most people think. In the beginning a bill must be placed in written form, and this form is not always the work of the legislator. The bill may be written by a member himself, and without pretense or fiction, introduced as his own work containing his own sentiments. But it may be written by an expert draughtsman, employed by the legislature for that purpose, or by some lawyer seated in his office a hundred miles from Charleston. By no means all bills originate in the minds of the legislators.

During a recent session of the legislature the members of the house introduced four hundred and fifty-nine bills, of which only one hundred and twelve passed both houses. All those passed were approved by the governor. During the same session they offered ninety-three resolutions and adopted only forty of them. Since all of this work had to be finished within the time limit of sixty days, a burden of business was placed on the house of delegates, surely no place for a lazy person to take refuge.

REFERENCE OF BILLS TO COMMITTEES

Not later than the day preceding the day on which a bill is introduced, it must be filed with the clerk, who gives the document a number, reviews it, and makes corrections if they are needed. When the hour comes in the order of business for the introduction of bills, the clerk reads it by title and refers it to the appropriate committee. The main part of the document begins with the enacting clause, "Be it enacted by the Legislature of West Virginia."

Now in obedience to the call issued by the chairman, the members of the committee report at a designated place and time to consider the new legislation so recently referred to it. One or several meetings may be called, during which time the faults and merits of the bills are carefully weighed. The hearings are open to the public. Perhaps many persons, some having traveled long distances, appear to file objections or to urge the adoption of the proposed law. Possibly behind the scenes the governor, or some other person having political power, exerts a deciding influence.

The committee has broad discretion in rendering its decision. It may report a bill with the recommendation that it be passed or not passed; report it out without any recommendation; report it out with amendments; set it aside and substitute a new bill in its place; or take up the bill for consideration. Suppose a bill is reported out with the favorable recommendation of a majority of the committee. Then it is placed on the calendar for consideration on the next day and will be taken up on first reading unless the house directs otherwise. On the following day the bill appears in the order of business and is read in full by the clerk. This reading informs the members on the contents of the measure. If no objection is offered, or if offered and lost, the bill is ordered to its second reading.

SECOND READING

At this stage of development the measure must be printed, with the lines numbered and triple spaced. A printed copy is delivered to the desk of each member of the house so that he may have a chance to inform himself concerning every detail of the bill. After at least one day has elapsed, it is placed on the calendar again, this time for the second reading, and then considered at the proper time in the order of business. Again the clerk reads the bill line by line to the audience of members.

Perhaps this is the most critical stage in legislative action. The measure has now been read and studied by the members; it is now subjected to their discussion and arguments, and on the demand of any two members may be read section by section for the purpose of hearing amendments. Unless the house orders otherwise, when all amendments have been set aside or adopted, the speaker asks, "Shall the bill be engrossed and ordered to the third reading?" By a majority vote it is so ordered. The bill is then reprinted and becomes known as the engrossed bill.[3]

THIRD READING

At this stage the measure is placed in an open envelope on which the clerk writes its title, number, and the name of the person who introduced it. By title the clerk records the measure on the calendar for the third time. Again at least one day must pass before it comes up for consideration. When the proper hour comes it is read for the third time by the clerk. By this time the members of the house have read the bill, have heard it discussed in open session, and have voted twice on it, and they are not likely now to refuse their approval. If no objection is entered, the speaker puts the question, "As many as are in favor of the bill say, 'Aye.'" After the affirmative vote has been counted he says, "As many as are opposed say, 'No.'"

Just before the ballots are cast the clerk prepares the electrically controlled machine for voting. He then sounds the gong as a signal for the members to begin voting. After due time has been given, the speaker asks: "Have all members voted?" He then votes himself and directs the clerk to determine the result of the ballot. When this has been done the clerk hands the statement of the result to the speaker, who at once makes an announcement of the decision.

If the bill originated in the house it now goes to the senate, which puts it through the same course that has just been described, but if it originated in the senate and now has passed the house, it goes to the governor for his signature or veto.

THE GOVERNOR'S DECISION

A period not exceeding five days (Sunday excepted) is allowed to the governor for considering the bill. If he approves, he signs the measure and in ninety days, unless otherwise stated, it becomes a law. Should he disapprove, he returns the bill with a statement of his

---

[3] Engrossment means that it is to be copied in a distinct and legible manner for the final reading.

objections to the house in which it originated. If the governor takes no action within five days, the bill becomes a law just as if he had signed it. By a majority vote of the members of both houses a measure can be passed over the governor's veto. This provision allows the legislature final authority in lawmaking. If the adjournment of the legislature should prevent the return of a vetoed bill within the time limit, it must be filed, with the objections, in the office of the secretary of state within five days after the legislative session closed; otherwise it becomes a law. This provision prevents a pocket veto from occurring in West Virginia.[4] When the governor has signed a bill it becomes a law at the expiration of ninety days unless by a two-thirds vote of the members of both houses the time is extended or shortened.

Anyone who has studied the process of legislation in West Virginia must be impressed with the thoroughness of the procedure. After a bill is introduced it has to undergo the careful scrutiny of all the members of each house on three different occasions before being submitted to the governor, who has five days to study it. In view of these facts one finds it hard to understand why there is not a greater appreciation on the part of the citizenship of the justice, rectitude, and equity expressed in the laws of the state.

Closing the Session

As the time draws near for adjournment there always remains a great deal of business to be transacted in a short time. Sometimes the general appropriation bill has been delayed until the last days of the session, and if this measure were not passed the government could not continue to function. But the legislators rush to finish their work. Perhaps each member has an interest in having some bill passed at the eleventh hour. The chance of passing is largely determined by the order the bill has been given on the calendar. All cannot be first. If it ranks near the top of the list, it may be reached; if at the bottom, its prospects are very unfavorable.

On the last day of the session the rush of business reaches a climax, and when the hands of the clock near the hour of midnight, they may be turned back in an attempt to prevent the end of the day. In

[4] In the national government, as well as in some states, if the legislature adjourns before the time limit on a bill has expired and the President, or governor, takes no action before adjournment, the bill fails to become law. This is called the pocket veto.

this confusion and haste defective laws are likely to be passed and good proposals defeated. Matters should be expedited from the beginning so that disorder and obstruction may be avoided during the last days of the session.

Joint Meetings

There are three conditions that necessitate joint assembly of the two houses. The first is at the opening of the session to hear the address of the governor on the condition and need of the state. In this address he outlines in the presence of all the legislators the work that he deems most urgent and needful. The second reason for a joint session is to decide a contested election for governor. This condition has not occurred in the state since 1881, when a joint resolution passed declaring the election of Governor A. B. Fleming over General Nathan Goff. In the third place a joint session may be convened to hear the official returns of the election of state officers. These returns are opened and announced by the speaker on the first day of the session next following the election, in the presence of a majority of each house of the legislature, assembled in the hall of the house of delegates. Nothing may intervene to prevent meetings in joint session at any other time when the action is deemed expedient by both assemblies. Such procedure, however, seldom occurs.

Distribution of the Acts of the Legislature

During the session of the legislature a resolution in which both houses concur authorizes the printing and distribution of the new laws. It becomes necessary for all state and local officers to be informed concerning the statutes and to have them in their possession. The clerk of the house of delegates is authorized to edit and have published by the public printer a sufficient number of copies of the new laws for distribution among the members of the legislature, the judges of all courts, and the county officials. Complete volumes indexed and bound in buckram may be purchased by any citizen from the supervisor of printing in the state department of purchases. The citizen can therefore keep himself well informed concerning the laws of the state, a privilege that should not be neglected. In fact it is a duty for every citizen to know the rules as well as the rulers of his government.

CHAPTER 15

The Senate

The Bicameral System

The constitution of West Virginia declares, "The Legislative power shall be vested in a Senate and House of Delegates." It is a principle deeply imbedded in American civil government that the legislative power shall consist of two branches. This arrangement has a long history. It was used by the ancient nations and came down to us from England; it operated in the government of the colonies and eventually came to be incorporated in the Constitution of the United States. This bicameral, or two-council, system is a feature in the government of all the states in our Union save one, Nebraska, which since 1934 has had a one-house legislature. The success of the exception is not at all assured: it still remains in the experimental stage and the results are being watched with curious interest.

The chief purpose in having two branches in the legislature is to provide an additional safeguard against the making of unwise laws. Under this plan a bill, in order to become a law, must be introduced into both houses, read in each on three different occasions, openly discussed, and passed in identical form by a majority vote. There is consequently less probability of enacting defective laws than if a bill had the consideration of only one assembly. One deficient law is one too many.

Membership of the Senate

ELECTION AND QUALIFICATIONS

The constitution of 1872 stated that the senate was to be composed of twenty-four members, representing twelve districts, which numbers might be increased but not diminished by acts of the legislature. Under this provision the number has now been increased to sixteen districts and thirty-two members.[1]

Two senators are elected in each district by the qualified voters residing therein. Some districts are composed of several adjoining counties, for the boundary lines cannot cross the county borders. From time to time boundaries are changed. The constitution provides that a readjustment of senatorial districts shall be made as soon as possible after each decennial national census. The legislature made the latest adjustment in 1937, although the last previous census was taken in 1930. According to the present arrangement the third, twelfth, and sixteenth districts contain six contiguous counties each, while the populous eighth embraces only Kanawha County. The second district, composed of Marshall, Tyler, and Wetzel counties, is the least in population, having 74,950 inhabitants. The eighth district, with a population of 157,667, is more than twice the size of the second, but each elects two senators.

Senatorial representation is not based on population alone; more particularly it is regional. By a glance at the map on page 230 one may see that the district lines do not conform to any rule; if an equality of population in districts had been sought, a great many curves could have been ironed out of the irregular boundaries now existing.

Senators must have attained the age of twenty-five years at the beginning of their term of service and must have been citizens of the state for at least five years next preceding their election or appointment and of the district from which they are elected for one year. The term is four years.

FILLING VACANCIES

In case of death or resignation of a senator the governor fills the place by appointment upon recommendation of the executive committee from the senatorial district. This committee of the party

---

1 The last change was made by the legislature in 1937, when the districts were increased from fifteen to sixteen and the membership from thirty to thirty-two.

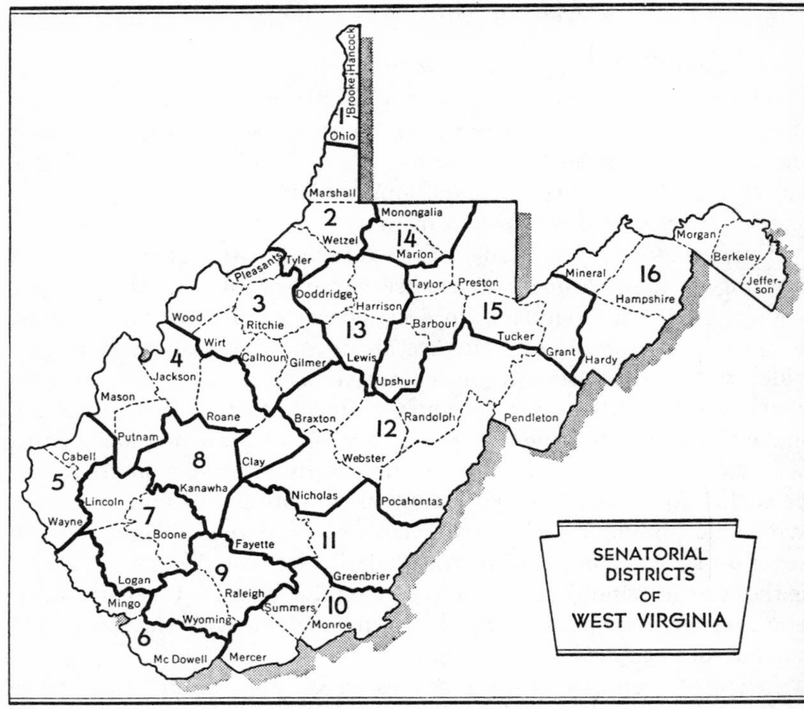

with which the recent incumbent was affiliated recommends to the governor the names of three legally qualified persons, and from this list the chief executive makes the appointment. If the unexpired portion of the term is less than two years and two months, the appointment is made for the rest of the term; if more, the newly appointed senator serves only until the next general election. It is fortunate that vacancies do not often occur, for a legislator should be directly responsible to the voters rather than to the chief executive.

Organization of the Senate

THE FIRST MEETING

The legislature regularly convenes on the second Monday in January of each odd year. All sessions, except those called by special order of the governor, meet for sixty days unless, by a vote of two-thirds of the members, the time is extended. It is always the purpose to complete the business on hand within the time limit. To extend the session, unless the circumstances were very unusual, might be looked upon by the sovereign people as an expression of inefficiency.

Just preceding the convening of the senate each party holds a caucus of its own members and decides on candidates for the senatorial offices. It is a foregone conclusion that the majority party will elect its list of candidates. The election thus amounts to a mere formality.

When the hour comes for the session to begin, the oldest member in point of service calls the meeting to order and presides until the president is elected by a majority vote of his colleagues. In addition to the presiding officer the senators elect a clerk, a sergeant-at-arms, and a doorkeeper. All assume their new duties immediately after the election.

Upon assuming his official position the president names the standing committees, designating the chairman of each, and appoints a president *pro tempore* who presides in the absence of the president. The organization having been thus completed the president appoints a committee of three members who join with the same number chosen by the speaker of the house, to go forthwith to the office of the governor to notify him that the legislature is organized and ready to take up its regular business.

THE PRESIDENT OF THE SENATE

To be chosen as the presiding officer of the senate is a distinct honor. He is usually a person who has had experience as a legislator and is noted for his ability and integrity. It would be a dangerous place to give to one who was narrow in his vision and revengeful in spirit. The responsibility should be borne only by one of unusual composure. Of course the president has to be a leader in the majority party, a requirement which sometimes precludes the honor's being given to the oldest member.

The president of the senate possesses uncommon power. In the first place, he enjoys extensive powers of appointment. He appoints the twenty-eight standing committees into whose hands are committed the bills to be reshaped for final consideration in open session of the assembly. The other committees he also names. By exercising this source of power the president has a great deal to do with the shaping of laws. Upon recommendation of the rules committee he also selects the pages and attachés.

In the second place, he possesses the power of recognition. To gain the floor a speaker must be recognized by the presiding officer. By recognizing one speaker rather than another he may delay legislation or he may speed it up. In this manner, too, he may take a powerful part in the legislative program.

In West Virginia the president of the senate stands next to the governor in official importance. If the governorship should become vacant he succeeds to the place. Although he has no additional power by virtue of this fact, yet it conveys prestige and distinction.

COMMITTEES

Most of the committees have a membership of not fewer than five nor more than nine. The Committee on Forestry and Conservation and the Committee on Public Buildings and Humane Institutions have not fewer than eleven nor more than fifteen each, the Committee on Roads and Navigation has seventeen, those on Judiciary and on Finance have eighteen each.[2]

In addition to the standing committees there are others that fill important functions. The select committees receive appointments for special purposes, such as to notify the governor that the senate has organized and is ready to take up its work, to attend the funeral of a deceased member, to represent the state at an important meeting, or to notify the house that the senate has completed its business and stands ready to adjourn. There are joint committees whose purpose is to meet the appointees from the house to work out amicable agreements on the provisions in bills, for proposed laws must be passed by both houses in identical wording before being presented to the governor. The committee of the whole is made up of the membership of the assembly. To form this committee the president calls to the chair another senator, who presides until the work under immediate consideration has been finished. This committee usually is called to consider revenue and appropriation bills. After a bill has been read amendments may be proposed and considered, and when the discussion has closed a vote can be taken on the amendments. The president then resumes the chair and hears the report of the

[2] The names of the standing committees are: Privileges and Elections; Judiciary; Finance; Education; Counties and Municipal Corporations; Roads and Navigation; Banks and Corporations; Public Buildings and Humane Institutions; Penitentiary; Railroads; Militia; Federal Relations; Insurance; Agriculture; Mines and Mining; Medicine and Sanitation; Labor; Claims and Grievances; Forfeit, Delinquent and Unappropriated Lands; Public Printing; Rules; Joint Rules; Joint Committee on Enrolled Bills; Public Library; Examine Clerk's Office; Temperance; Forestry and Conservation; and Redistricting.

action of the committee, after which a vote is taken by the senate in regular session.

To a great extent the work of a senator depends upon his committee appointments. During a recent session one senator served on sixteen different committees, including the most important ones, while another senator was appointed to only three minor committees. This illustrates the unequal distribution of the senatorial load, which calls for reform.

The chief work of the senate is not done in the open discussion of legislation but in committee meetings. After a bill is introduced it is referred to the desk of the clerk, who assigns it to the proper committee. In the sessions of these small groups of legislators the good bills are separated from the bad. The ones deemed unworthy – and many of them are – never reach the forum of general debate but die in committee. The bills that receive the favorable consideration of the committee are reported back to the assembly and submitted for second reading.

While considering a bill a committee may summon before it witnesses to give further information on the questions involved. Among them no doubt will be persons who are able to give expert advice. In this manner the committee gathers knowledge on which it bases a final decision.

THE RULES

At the beginning of each regular session, the senate adopts its own rules to govern its proceedings. Usually the rules that have been used in the past session are adopted with little or no revision. At the opening of the session one of the members who has had experience in the assembly makes a motion that the rules used in the previous session be adopted. The motion passes. This procedure is scarcely just to the new members, who have no knowledge concerning what had been done before, but it gives a distinct advantage to those who have served in other sessions. When the rules have been adopted, they are binding alike on young and old.

Space will not permit here a detailed discussion of the rules of the senate. It is sufficient to state that they prescribe the duties of the officers and the powers and privileges of the members, regulate roll calls and absences, designate the committees, the order of business, and the procedure to be followed in the passing of laws. The president of the senate interprets the rules; at times he does not find this altogether an easy matter.

Joint rules for both houses are also adopted. These regulations prescribe uniform procedure to be followed in conducting joint meetings, settling disagreements, exchanging messages between the houses, operating joint committees, and in many other situations. Business that needs to be transacted jointly is extensive, and necessity requires that it be done in a regular manner.

THE COMMITTEE ON RULES

Although it is unnecessary here to give a separate discussion of the functions of each committee in the senate, it is important that a brief insight be given into the powerful committee on rules. It stands first on the list, and the president acts as chairman *ex officio*. By degree of importance it should stand first, for with the five members of the committee is lodged the success or failure of the legislative program of the session.

At the beginning of the session, the president appoints to the committee four senators on whose judgment he depends and in whom implicit confidence can be placed. The committee is bipartisan; it meets daily behind closed doors, each member being pledged to absolute secrecy. No secretary is chosen and no records are kept of the proceedings. The meetings permit to each member complete freedom of expression. Its business is to arrange the calendar of bills that are to be taken up for final passage. Even a bill that has been approved by the appropriate committee and passed second reading has no chance of becoming a law unless it is given a place on the calendar. And its position in the order of consideration has much to do with its chances of passing. A bill far down on the list is rarely reached in the business of the day. The unfinished order of business of one day is never taken up on the next day where it was left off; the order of business begins anew each time the assembly is called to order.

THE ORDER OF BUSINESS

In the rules of the senate a regular order of business is prescribed, to insure consistency in the proceedings. Matters are taken up in the following order:

1. Reading of the journal (record of business of preceding day)
2. Disposal of communications from the house and from the governor
3. Reports of standing committees

4. Reports of select committees
5. Reception of bills, resolutions, motions, and petitions
6. Action on unfinished business
7. Third reading of senate and house bills
8. Second reading of senate and house bills
9. First reading of senate and house bills
10. Miscellaneous business

Usually business is passed without much delay until the time comes for consideration of bills on second reading, and then there must be more deliberation. The bills are presented in the order designated by the rules committee. The committee even has the power to omit bills from the calendar, which means their consignment to the scrap heap. As each measure is taken up it involves general debate by the members present.

FREEDOM OF DEBATE

The senatorial chamber is the arena for open discussion of proposed legislation. All members share equally the privilege of debate. In the senate of West Virginia, as in any other assembly, the leaders are few and the followers many. Those who have taken part in writing the bill under examination understand it best and are expected to open the debate. The deluge of words follows. Some speeches exhibit a fine sense of reasoning and consequently are of high order; others descend to frivolities.

When speaking, a member addresses the president, stands at his own desk, and after concluding takes his seat. A member may be called to order for words spoken in debate, but this action is not often taken. In order to broaden the freedom of debate and restrain those inclined to take up too much time, a rule forbids any member from speaking more than twice on the same subject without having special leave from his colleagues, and no one person may speak more than once until every member has had a chance to present his views.

There are different ways to limit debate. The length of time for each speech may be limited to five, eight, or twelve minutes. A motion may be passed fixing the time when discussion shall end, and when the hand of the clock reaches that hour the vote must be taken. Debate may also be closed at any time by the adoption of the motion to adjourn, which motion is not debatable. The passing of a motion to take up the previous question also closes the debate, by requiring that the main question under discussion be put to a vote.

PARTY SPIRIT

West Virginia stands at the crossroads of party influence in the Union. Sometimes one of the great political parties has a majority in the legislature; then the other holds sway. This condition is politically healthy. It is the ambition of each party to succeed in its legislative program, for the other, always stationed on the watchtower, takes advantage of any mistake.

Usually the majority party gives honorable consideration to the minority. Although the party in power keeps a majority of its members on the committees, it also places on the most important committees the leading members of the minority. Perhaps the condition that shows the greatest party animosity is the division of the state into senatorial districts. Each time this matter is taken up by the legislature the monster gerrymander is unleashed and makes a notable scramble of the counties of West Virginia. The map of the present districts shows conclusively what has been done in this respect.

DISCIPLINE

The senate is the judge of the election of its own members. That is to say, if there is an alleged violation of law in the election of a senator, the matter is brought before his colleagues in session for adjudication. The charges are presented, arguments are heard, and the defense is given a chance to file its answer or rebuttal. If, in the judgment of a majority of the members, the accused is found guilty, he is dismissed and his seat declared vacant. In case the accusation is filed before the session assembles, the one accused may be required to stand aside and forgo the taking of the oath of office until his case can be decided. If he is found innocent the oath is administered, but if guilty he is denied a place on the senate floor.

In case a complaint of breach of privilege is made against a member, by order of the president he may be taken into custody by the sergeant-at-arms. Or if a senator is so stupid as to indulge in disorderly behavior he may be rebuked by his colleagues for his conduct or expelled by a vote of two-thirds of the assembly. This is a severe weapon held against any member who might be inclined to debase senatorial dignity by unbecoming conduct.

The rules of the senate reach even beyond its own membership. It is clothed with power to preserve good order and protect the members from outside influences. Any person, not a member, may be imprisoned by order of the senate for disorderly behavior, for obstructing any of its officers in the discharge of his duties, for any assault, threat, or abusing words spoken in debate. The imprisonment, however, cannot extend longer than the duration of the session. The senate of West Virginia has therefore ample power to preserve good order and protect its members from insult and restraint.

Powers of the Senate

SHARE IN LAWMAKING

The senate is a coequal branch with the house in the enactment of laws. Bills and resolutions of any sort may originate in either house. In most legislatures bills for raising revenue must originate in the lower, and more numerous, branch of the general assembly. Such is not the case in West Virginia, where revenue bills may be originally introduced in either house.

The legislative process in the senate resembles in all essentials that in the house of delegates, described in the preceding chapter.

SPECIAL FUNCTIONS OF THE SENATE

The powers of the two branches of the legislature are not equal in all respects. Although the membership of the house is far more numerous than that of the upper branch, in some particulars it is inferior in power.

Approval of Appointments. The constitution provides that "by and with the advice and consent of the Senate" the governor shall make appointments of officers whose duties are established by the constitution or created by law. Confirmations take place in closed sessions. The senate meets in executive session. The chamber is cleared of all nonmembers except the clerk, his assistants, the sergeant-at-arms, and the doorkeeper, all of whom are sworn not to divulge anything that is said or done in the meeting. The information and remarks relating to the character of the nominees are matters to be kept from the critical public. The senate reports its action to the governor; it may be for or against the person nominated. If the nominee is approved, he takes the oath of office and thus has met the qualifications to begin his duties; if he is disapproved, the governor sends in another nomination. Although the matter of selecting appointive officers rests in the hands of the governor, the responsibility of filling the offices devolves equally on the senate. This is a responsibility that cannot be avoided by the upper branch of the legislature, and indeed there is no disposition to avoid it. As far as can be ascertained this power has not been abused by those to whom it has been entrusted. This constitutional provision is wise, for it places an additional check on the power of the governor.

If the senate is not in session at the time a vacancy occurs in an appointive office, the governor may fill the place until the meeting of the legislature. Such a recess appointment, as it is called, becomes at times urgently necessary. The business of the state cannot stop at the door of a vacated office. It must proceed, and the chief executive is held responsible for clearing the way.

Trial of Impeachment Cases. "Any officer of the State may be impeached for maladministration, corruption, incompetency, gross immorality, neglect of duty, or any high crime or misdemeanor." So reads the constitution of West Virginia. Let it be emphasized that "any officer of the State" comes within the range of impeachment. The house of delegates has the sole power to bring the impeachment charges, which have the same status against an officer of the state as an indictment brought by a grand jury against any other person. Many people erroneously suppose that impeachment removes one from office. It does not. Only trial and conviction bring about displacement.

After impeachment is brought by the house of delegates, the trial follows. The president of the supreme court of appeals presides. The senate hears the evidence and renders a verdict. The accused cannot be convicted unless two-thirds of the members elected concur in their vote to find him guilty. In case the accused is convicted, the punishment imposed may not extend beyond removal from office and disqualification from holding any office of honor or profit in the state. However, the guilty individual may be indicted and tried in a civil court of the commonwealth.

An officer of the state who has been impeached cannot escape trial by resigning. Even though he vacates his office, the trial is continued to a definite conclusion.

Impeachment is an extreme measure – the last resort. The honest business of the state and its good name stand above an encroachment made by any of its officers. The constitution is wise to provide that an officer may be removed to protect the state.

Special Sessions

It comes within the power of the governor to convene the legislature in special session when he deems the move expedient, as occasionally it is. In his proclamation the governor sets forth the business that demands immediate attention, and no other matters can be taken up during that session.

The sixty-day limitation does not apply to the extraordinary sessions. In fact no time limitation is set for them. The possibility exists, and the writers of the constitution foresaw it, that emergencies might demand the prolonged attention of the legislators; consequently they are not limited to a specific period.

Nothing forbids the governor to convene the senate in special session for the purpose of securing its counsel and approval in the making of appointments. Although, as we have seen above, it is within his power to make recess appointments when the senate is not in session.

Conclusion

As time goes on, perhaps more comes to be expected of the senate by the electorate than of the other branch of the legislature. Since the membership is comparatively small, responsibility can be centered in that body more effectively than if the number were greater. Special powers imposed by the constitution place on the senate burdens that do not have to be borne by the house, and increased power brings to its attention more matters for which it is answerable to the people. Again, the term of four years, twice as long as that for the house of delegates, charges the senate with a double portion of liability. Although the upper branch of our legislature accounts for much good at present, no doubt more will be expected in the future.

CHAPTER 16

The Executive Department

Introduction

An earlier chapter has told how the governorship was established in Virginia, the oldest executive office in the United States. Also, it may be added, it is older than the state assembly or the state courts. The office of chief executive was continued throughout the colonial period, was inherited by the state when royal Governor Dunmore was succeeded by state Governor Patrick Henry in 1776, and was passed on to West Virginia in 1863.

In some political societies the office of chief executive is elective, in others appointive, in others hereditary. After the Declaration of Independence, some of the states placed the power of choosing a governor in the hands of the qualified voters. In Virginia, however, a joint ballot of the legislature made the selection. The manner of electing the governor eventually became a matter of discord between the eastern and the western regions of the state, and, as we have seen, the reform constitution of 1851 finally placed the power to choose the governor in the hands of the electorate.

EXECUTIVE OFFICERS

Sometimes the executive department is looked upon as consisting only of the office of the governor. But that is too narrow a view of the matter, for the constitution declares that it shall consist of governor, secretary of state, superintendent of free schools, auditor, treasurer, commissioner of agriculture, and attorney general. These officers all serve for a term of four years, which commences on the first Monday after the second Wednesday in January next following the election. All are required to reside at Charleston during their term of office and to keep there the public records. They perform such duties as the laws prescribe.

In this group of executive officers the governor stands head and shoulders above the rest in importance. While the official duties of all of them will be discussed, first attention will be addressed to the chief executive.

EXECUTIVE AND ADMINISTRATIVE POWERS

Sometimes there is confusion or misunderstanding about the distinction between executive and administrative powers. Let us clarify this point. The executive officers are provided for in the constitution and have their duties chiefly outlined in that document. For this reason their official functions are elevated above the possibility of modification by the acts of the legislature or the decisions of the courts. In other words, they are responsible to the sovereign people, and to the people only, for the faithful execution of certain duties.

Administrative officers, on the other hand, generally fill places created by the acts of the legislature. Their duties are definitely outlined in the statutes of the state, and may be changed at the will of the lawmakers. Administrative officers consist, in large measure, of boards, commissions, and councils, such as the Board of Public Works, the Forest and Park Commission, and the Public Health Council. Some of these offices are regarded as permanent, others as temporary, but the offices and their duties are always subject to change by order of the legislature.

The Governor

CHARACTER OF THE GOVERNOR'S OFFICE

The governor is regarded as the first citizen of the state. His position is such that, if his duties are fully and wisely executed, he can render more good service to the state than any other person. In electing a governor the people have entrusted to his care a great deal of their political power, with the faith that it will be used to further their own good. The public focuses its gaze on his office. He is praised, and he is censured; he is applauded, and he is condemned; he is sought out, and he is evaded. The people ask much of their governor. He meets troops visiting in the capital, makes a thousand speeches, dedicates buildings and monuments, inspects the national guard, and annually crowns festival queens. But such official appearances do not constitute his chief business. He hears applications for positions; he makes many appointments; he reads volumes of reports from other officers, boards, and commissions; he hears appeals for mercy from friends of persons condemned by the courts; he makes recommendations; and he performs a thousand other public duties. We shall presently examine these duties in detail.

QUALIFICATIONS AND ELECTION

The eligibility requirements for the governor, set forth in the constitution, are higher than those specified for the members of either branch of the legislature. He must have attained the age of thirty years at the beginning of his term of office and must have been a citizen of the state at least five years preceding his election. The average age, at the time of their election, of the twenty-two governors who have served West Virginia is forty-eight years. Six of them have been born outside of the state, but the last eleven have been native sons.

Perhaps tests imposed by practical politics are more significant than any other requirements, for one who would have himself even considered for governor must possess the qualities of leadership, be prominent in his party, and have the ability to make a personal appeal to the voters. His place of residence often has an influential bearing on his political success. He could scarcely be a resident of the same county in which his predecessor lived or the county from which any of the other executive officers came. The electorate is jealous and watchful lest one section of the state gain a dominating influence over any other.

Candidates for governor are nominated by the statewide primary election. Usually each of the two great parties has several candidates for the nomination, and the campaign sometimes grows furious. But after the primary the choices simmer down to two candidates who lead the campaign until the general election day, the Tuesday after the first Monday in November. On that day the final choice is made by the electorate.

By some thoughtful people it is considered unfortunate that state officers are chosen at the same time as national leaders. They reason that state problems become completely overshadowed by national affairs and so receive less attention than they deserve. There is truth in this analysis, but the added expense involved in holding two separate elections is a substantial obstacle. And there is advantage in confining the tumult of campaigns to a single period.

The governor's annual salary is $12,500.[1] In addition to this amount, an annual maintenance of $9,000 is appropriated to cover his expenses. In 1925 the state built for its chief executive a mansion, at an approximate cost of $75,000, on the north bank of the Kanawha River, near the spacious office rooms maintained in the capitol. The people of West Virginia, then, make ample provision in salary, home, and other maintenance for their chief executive. The salaries of only a few governors in the United States exceed that paid to the governor of West Virginia. His public income is high enough to make the office attractive to a poor man and low enough to prevent anyone from seeking it for salary alone.

REMOVAL FROM OFFICE

The office of governor may become vacant by death, impeachment, or resignation. It is most fortunate for this state that a vacancy has never been caused by death or impeachment, and only on one occasion by resignation, when Governor Boreman resigned in 1869 to take up his office as United States Senator.

In order to protect the office and the people the governor may be relieved of his official duties on account of maladministration, corruption, incompetency, gross immorality, neglect of duty, or the commission of any high crime or misdemeanor. As already explained, the house of delegates has the sole power to bring charges of impeachment, and the senate alone may try the case. That is,

---

[1] Changed by statute March 8, 1937, from $8,000 to $10,000, and in 1951 from $10,000 to $12,500. The highest at present is $25,000 in three states.

the senate convenes as a court to hear the evidence and arguments and finally renders the decision. Conviction requires a two-thirds vote of the senators elected. The president of the supreme court of appeals presides over the senate when the governor is on trial. In case of conviction, punishment cannot extend further than removal from office and disqualification from holding any other office of honor or trust in the state. No fine or imprisonment can be imposed by the senate, but its action does not necessarily terminate the punishment of the offender. He may be indicted and tried in the ordinary courts if his offense should warrant such action.

Any other officer of the state may likewise be impeached. But West Virginia has been notably free from such impeachments. The only cases of the kind in the life of the state occurred in 1875 when the house of delegates brought articles of impeachment against the treasurer and the auditor. The treasurer was found guilty of malfeasance and corruption in the conduct of his office and was dismissed. The auditor was acquitted.

In some states the governor may be removed by the "recall" instead of by impeachment. This process is put in operation by a petition signed by a certain number or percentage of the voters. The issue is then submitted to a popular vote and if a majority supports it the governor's office is declared vacant. Sometimes the matter is submitted in the form of a new election in which the name of the governor and the names of other candidates for the office appear on the official ballot. The one receiving the greatest number of votes wins the election. By this method the governor may be recalled or he may be given a vote of confidence.

The "recall" is expensive, and it arouses a great deal of animosity. During the last few years much of its former popularity has vanished, and at the present time the author finds no disposition on the part of any state to incorporate the principle in its constitution. Apparently the idea has run its course in American state government.

SUCCESSION IN THE GOVERNORSHIP

West Virginia has no lieutenant governor. From time to time amendments to the constitution have been proposed calling for the creation of this office, but always it has been rejected by the voters.[2] In case of a vacancy in the governorship the president of the senate succeeds to the office until the next election or until such time as the

[2] When such an amendment was submitted in 1930, the vote was 48,781 in favor, 172,703 against.

governor's disability is removed. Upon the resignation of Governor Boreman in 1869, the president of the state senate, D. D. T. Farnsworth, became governor and served from February 26 to March 4, when Governor W. E. Stevenson took the oath of office.

If, for any reason, the president of the senate should be incapable of filling the office, the duty then devolves upon the speaker of the house of delegates. But if he too should fall short of meeting the requirements the legislature, acting in joint session, chooses the governor. The constitution requires, however, that if the vacancy occurs before the expiration of the first three years of the term, a new election shall be held for the purpose of filling this important office. Vacancies in all the other state executive offices are filled through appointments by the governor.

About four-fifths of the states have lieutenant governors. In most instances this officer presides over the senate.[3] His powers are not extensive but he may vote to break a tie. The chief purpose of the office is to provide a successor to the governor in times of emergency, and the West Virginia electorate considers that such an emergency has been satisfactorily provided for without the creation of an additional office.

POWERS OF THE GOVERNOR

The constitution states, "The chief executive power shall be vested in the Governor, who shall take care that the laws be faithfully executed." In a large measure this grant of authority is general. It is more specifically defined in the constitution and in the acts of the legislature. But the governor has general powers and duties that do not need legal definition or limitations.

It is incumbent on him as the highest officer in the state to represent the commonwealth in its business and other relations with the rest of the states. States do not live alone any more than people do. They are hedged and bounded by other political, social, and industrial commonwealths. A continuous interchange of business plays across the boundary lines. There are also matters of deep concern to be considered between the state and the national government. The governor is the agent of the state in state-federal relations. He is also, in a large measure, held responsible for the material success or failure of the people over whom he governs. In these matters a tendency exists to extend his power rather than to restrain it. Al-

[3] In Massachusetts the lieutenant governor does not preside at sessions of the senate.

ready he appoints boards, councils, and commissions in many fields of activity, and with the power to appoint often goes the power to control, for some of those officers help to form the policy of the administration.

Legislative Power. Though the theory of our political organization is that the chief executive does not have legislative authority, the governor nevertheless possesses extensive positive power in the making of laws. In the first place he has authority to call special sessions of the legislature, in which only the business recommended in his call may be taken up. Even to the regular sessions he presents in his message the urgent needs of the state and recommends that laws be passed to care for such conditions. And the legislature does well to consider his recommendations carefully, for he has special opportunities to observe public conditions and to come to an understanding of what is most needed. His office is kept open all the time, while the legislature is in session for a short period only once in two years unless called by special order.

In the second place, by virtue of his position, the governor is leader of his political party, and there exists a close relationship between lawmaking and party politics. It often happens that during his candidacy he has made certain pledges to bring about definite changes if elected, and upon taking the oath of office he has a covenant with the people to carry out his pledge. If his party has a majority in the legislature, there can scarcely be a hindrance to passing the laws that are promised. In his message, in conference with party leaders, and in contact with legislators, he will promote the passage of some bills and the defeat of others. From day to day the governor confers with legislative committees to keep informed on the program of business and to learn the sentiment of political leaders. It may be concluded, therefore, that a major part of the governor's work concerns promoting the enactment of laws.

The patronage of the governor is an influence that should not be overlooked. Members of the legislature and other political leaders recommend but the governor appoints. Paying political debts by placing friends in public office is a source of political power. A political leader is likely to suffer a distinct loss of power when he opposes the recommendations made by the governor. In matters of this kind help is mutual. Members of the governor's party and others, too, make an effort to gain his approval of their personal and legislative handiwork.

In the next place the governor has the power to veto. Every bill passed by the legislature must be presented to the chief executive for his approval or disapproval. He may sign a bill within five days (Sunday excepted); he may hold it longer than the time limit and permit it to become a law; or he may use the veto and return the bill with his objections to the house in which it originated. If the vetoed measure is reconsidered and passed by a majority of both houses it becomes a law as if it had been signed. If the legislature by adjournment prevents its return, the vetoed bill, with the governor's objections, must be filed in the office of the secretary of state within five days after the adjournment or it becomes a law.

In cases of this sort does the governor not have legislative power equal to that of half of the members elected to the legislature? It takes a majority of their votes to override his veto or pass a bill against which he has entered objection. To say that the governor does not have legislative power is far from the fact, for in his office exists the most potent lawmaking influence in the state.

Previously it has been shown how bills are crowded through the legislative hopper in rapid-fire succession during the last days of the session. In the same manner they are rushed without mercy to the hand of the governor. He has only five days to consider them, and when legislative activity is at its peak he may not even have time to read them, let alone deliberate on the principles involved. Usually these eleventh-hour bills are signed, and the chances of making vital mistakes are considerable. In fairness to the governor it would seem wise to extend the time limit on the signing of bills. Five times five days would not be too long.

In addition to his official veto power, the governor's political influence is such that sometimes even the threat of a veto prevents a bill from gaining headway in the legislature. Having considered with the proper legislative committee the merits of a pending bill and found it to be not to his liking, the governor often causes it to be killed in committee. Or he may suggest an amendment. It is not usually the disposition of the legislator who cares for his political record to run counter to the governor. The possibility exists of disregarding any threat of veto and forcing all parties concerned to use their ultimate power, but it is by no means easy to muster a majority in each house to defeat executive objections.

Ordinance Power. The legislature not infrequently delegates to the governor certain duties known as ordinance powers. In the enactment of laws the general principles involved may be set forth and the details left for the governor to arrange. For example, the governor may require the director of the budget to perform certain duties consistent with the law, and he fixes the director's annual salary, within the maximum limit of $6,000. These details are not formulated in regular legislation, yet they have the same force as laws. Again, the governor may authorize the State Road Commission to purchase toll bridges. These are only two examples of the wide application of the ordinance power in public affairs.

Executive Powers. Despite the far-reaching legislative powers possessed by the governor, his chief duties are executive. In the political organization of the state the other officers, elective and appointive, state and local, major and minor, have in the governor a central authority to whom appeal may be made. Without a governor the organized state could not function, for under his general supervision exists the power to provide for the common defense, to promote the general welfare, and to secure the blessings of liberty to the people.

The executive powers of the governor may be classified as general, appointive, pardoning, military, financial, supervisory, and power over federal-state relations. It is altogether possible that some of his official work would not even come within these titles, for demands on his services are so numerous and his activities are so diverse that it is difficult to give all of them a precise classification. An explanation of each of the seven divisions will help toward a clearer understanding of this office.

(1) The appointive power of the governor is great and ever growing greater. As the population increases and civil government grows more complex from year to year, more offices are created, new work is assumed, and unforeseen demands are made on the state. Although new offices must be created by acts of the legislature, they are seldom filled by elections; ordinarily they are filled by appointments made by the governor. He names members of commissions, boards, and councils at the opening of each administration. Most of these offices have technical and special functions; as examples may be named the Health Department, the Conservation Commission, and the Department of Mines. Such offices should stand outside the realm of politics; they should be filled by trained specialists. The responsibility for filling them suitably rests with the governor and this responsibility has come to be a heavy tax on his time and patience.

Unless otherwise provided by law, the governor's appointments have to be approved by the senate. This check on the power of the governor is no doubt wholesome. He does not always find an available person who is honest, qualified, and industrious. The part exercised by the senate divides the responsibility and on various occasions perhaps saves the public from paying unqualified officials.

The power to appoint carries with it the power to remove. The governor has constitutional authority to dismiss his appointees for incompetency, neglect of duty, immorality, or malfeasance in office. The legislature cannot change or modify this law. It is a wise one, for if the governor is held answerable for the conduct of affairs, his power to administer them should not be unduly curbed.

(2) By authority vested in the governor by the constitution he may remit fines and forfeitures; he may grant reprieves and pardons; he may commute capital punishment. The remitting of fines and forfeitures can be expected only when the governor is convinced that the decision of the court was too severe or unjust. A reprieve delays the application of a sentence until some necessary adjustment can be made in the case. A pardon may be absolute or conditional. An absolute pardon absolves the person sentenced from any further punishment and restores all his political rights as if he had never been convicted. The conditional pardon is granted under a pledge made by the person punished that in order to be relieved of the penalty he will fulfill some requirement, for example, to conduct himself henceforth in an exemplary manner. Commutation is the substituting of a milder penalty for the one imposed by the court.

In rendering decisions on these matters the governor surely is put to the hardest tests. He hears the pleading and supplications of husbands and wives, fathers and mothers, children and friends, to spare the life, end the imprisonment, or shorten the punishment of people sentenced by the courts. But his verdicts have to be based on wisdom and law. He does not dare to overrule the courts without a righteous reason; he must cooperate with them. Although a fitful ray of hope based on the trust that new evidence will be discovered always shines dimly in the life of the condemned, the governor is bound by an oath to discharge faithfully this duty of his office to the best of his skill and judgment.

(3) With respect to the power of the governor over the army, the constitution declares that he shall be the commander-in-chief of the military forces of the state, except when they are called into active services for their country. The purpose of this provision is to entrust to the care of the chief executive the duty of maintaining order after all other authorities have failed to do so. In the execution of

this law he may call out the national guard to suppress insurrection and repel invasion. This power is most likely to be used during times of disorder in industry, such as strikes and lockouts, and its use almost always brings upon the governor bitter accusations of injustice from one or both of the contending parties. Nevertheless, it is the sworn duty of the governor to preserve good order and protect the people from violence.

It is possible for a disturbance to grow in volume until the governor must declare martial law to restore good order. In taking this action he sets aside for a time the authority of the civil officers and orders the army to take charge. Everyone living then within the restricted area becomes subject to the orders of the military commander. The people go and come at his beck. If an uprising should grow so great that it is beyond the power of the governor to control, he may call upon the Secretary of War of the United States to use the national army to restore order. A condition of that sort is deplorable in any state at any time. Every means of adjustment should be exhausted before the army receives orders for action.

To obviate the calling of the military power the governor may request the action of the state police, which is under the direction of the superintendent of public safety. These men are well trained and carefully chosen. Their purpose is to enforce regulations for safety on the highways and at any other place. They are at the command of the governor when an occasion demands their services.

(4) In financial matters the power of the governor reaches far. By act of the legislature in 1909 the Board of Control, consisting of three members appointed by the governor, was created for the purpose of supervising the humane institutions maintained by the state and the financial affairs of the public educational institutions. By virtue of this law the governor has a direct means of keeping in touch with matters pertaining to the management of these interests.

In 1918 the "Budget Amendment" to the constitution was ratified. It required that the Board of Public Works, consisting of the governor, secretary of state, auditor, treasurer, superintendent of free schools, attorney general, and commissioner of agriculture, shall submit to the legislature a complete schedule of proposed expenditures and estimated revenue for each of the two succeeding fiscal years. As chairman of this board the governor wields a powerful influence in shaping its policies. Since he is responsible in a large measure for directing the expenditures and accumulating the revenues of the state, he has a deep interest in the passage of the appropriation and revenue bills that come before the legislature. The governor's power in public financial matters, therefore, is of first-rate importance.

(5) The general supervision of the state government rests in the hands of the chief executive. He makes numerous appointments; he is commander of the military power; he has first control in directing the financial policy; and he may pardon, suspend sentences, and remit fines of persons sentenced by the courts. The manner in which his public business is conducted depends on the man himself. One takes hold of matters in a vigorous way; he forms a policy for each department in the state and forces it to hew to the line. Another is less energetic in the use of his power; he assumes his constitutional authority and permits each high officer to follow his own views of administration. It may be concluded that the power of administration is at the command of the governor, who may control it if he chooses, or delegate his authority to other officers if he prefers.

(6) Federal-state relations largely depend on the good office of the governor. In times of war the President of the United States is dependent on the governors for cooperation in raising an army, keeping transportation lines open, and accumulating and distributing food. During the world wars the President made appeals to the governors for assistance in the enforcement of the draft laws by which the armed forces were increased to several millions of men. They promptly rendered this indispensable service without any serious blunders. And in the solicitation of loans to sustain the enormous expense of waging the wars, the governors of the states stood at the right hand of the President in selling war savings stamps, liberty bonds, and so forth.

During the depression years from 1929 to 1940 the national government called upon the governors for cooperation in the administration of relief to the poor and the unemployed. This policy was followed in rendering help to the people living on the western plains during the recent terrible drought years, to those living in the Ohio Valley injured by the flood of 1936, and to the inhabitants of New England after the devastating hurricane of 1938.

A sharp question has recently arisen between the governors of certain states and the national government concerning irrigation, flood control, and reforestation. Sometimes it is hard to tell where the authority of one begins and that of the other ends. Can the national government take charge of matters of this sort without the consent of the authorities of the states in which the projects are located? The question is one that has to be solved by mutual cooperation in promoting the public welfare.

It is fitting for the governor to keep the state in friendly relations with the other states. Questions concerning boundary lines, transportation, river pollution, property ownership, and many other matters have at times disturbed the amicable relations between state authorities. Questions of this sort, if taken to the courts, have to be tried in the United States Supreme Court. The extradition of persons who have escaped from the authorities of one state and gone into another takes place through the offices of the governors of the states concerned in the case. In these particulars the responsibility of the chief executive amounts to more than a trifle.

(7) There are certain powers possessed by the governor that defy exact classification. Every year he receives, on behalf of the state, many hundreds of guests visiting the capitol; he is a member of various boards and commissions; he signs documents and reviews reports; he hears applications for offices; he confers with party leaders; he attends various functions and makes speeches by the score; he hears the petitions of delegations. Adding all these activities to his other manifold duties, one must conclude that the governor is a very busy man.

THE CONFERENCE OF GOVERNORS

On May 13, 1908, President Theodore Roosevelt invited the governors of all the states to the White House to discuss the conservation of natural resources. Thirty-eight governors were able to attend the conference. It was the first time in the history of the country that the chief executives of the states had met in a common assembly, and the problems demanding their attention were of nationwide interest.

The governors, with a number of other well-informed men, discussed at length means for conserving the land, water, timber, and mineral resources of the country. The conference made a good beginning, and since that time the governors have met annually at an appointed place. The matters which they have taken under observation have widened to include state and federal cooperation in the transaction of business of common interest. Perhaps the outstanding achievement reached by this annual conference is the development of confidence, good will, and cooperation between the states.

In 1935 the Governors' Council formed connections with an organization known as the Council of State Governments, which established for the use of the governors a research bureau. Since then a series of bulletins relating to state governments has been issued. The bulletins contain detailed information concerning the governments of the states, names of governors, names of members of the legislatures, salaries, meetings, and other matters of interest. This work has met with a great deal of approval and there is every indication that it will be continued.

The Secretary of State

The executive department of the state consists not only of the governor, but of six other leading state officials. They are secretary of state, superintendent of free schools, auditor, treasurer, commissioner of agriculture, and attorney general, all of whom are elected by the qualified voters for a term of four years.[4] They reside in Charleston and have offices in the capitol. A brief review of the duties of each of these officers follows.

The secretary of state ranks next to the governor in official standing. His duties are fixed by statute. He is secretary to the Board of Public Works; under his jurisdiction is kept the state seal, which is affixed to official documents; he is charged with the duty of publishing the laws, and in his office the acts of the legislature and other state papers are filed; he receives the applications of candidates for office and certifies them to the county authorities before the ballots are printed; he officially publishes the results of elections; he grants charters to corporations. His duties are summarized thus: "He shall be the keeper of the seals of the State, keep a journal of the executive proceedings, arrange and preserve all records and papers belonging to the executive deartment. He is charged with the clerical duties of that department, and renders to the governor, in the dispatch of the executive business, such service as he may require."

The Superintendent of Schools

The free schools of West Virginia are under the direction of a state superintendent. He is the chief executive officer of the State Board of Education; he is charged with general supervision of the work of county superintendents and county boards of education.

[4] The secretary of state was made an elective officer by an amendment to the constitution ratified in 1901.

In his office blank forms are prepared for the making of reports necessary for carrying out in a uniform manner the details of the school system of the state. His office supplies forms and instructions for reports and it is to his office that these reports are in turn submitted.

The state superintendent of schools issues licenses (certificates) to teach in the schools of the state, and he may withdraw this privilege if a teacher should prove himself legally unworthy. He recommends legislation for the improvement of the standards of education; he calls conferences of school administrators; and upon the request of a citizen he gives interpretations of the school law. Just preceding the meeting of the legislature, he presents to the governor a report concerning the condition of the public schools. This report may include an expression of his views on needed legislation and other information that the governor may request.

The Auditor

In view of the extensive public business carried on by West Virginia, it is essential to provide for auditing the accounts of the state. In his office the auditor keeps a careful account of the various sources of public revenue and has records that he keeps with the state treasurer. He has statements of the names of officers and other persons paying money to the state and all those receiving money from the state. All amounts received are charged to the account of the treasurer. Statements of amounts appropriated by law are carefully kept, and at all times his records show the balance undrawn on each appropriation. By consulting the records kept by the auditor, an interested citizen may learn of the receipts and disbursements of the state.

The auditor audits, adjusts, and settles the accounts of all persons employed in the collection of revenue. In this particular he makes a final settlement of accounts with each of the fifty-five sheriffs of the state. If there occurs a default in payment by any sheriff, within sixty days after the date for settlement the auditor notifies the sureties on the official bond of such sheriff.

At the end of each quarter the auditor compares his books with those kept by the treasurer. The receipts and disbursements are duly ascertained and a balance is struck which shows the amount left in the treasury.

The fiscal year in the business of the state ends June 30. Within one week after that date the auditor's annual report is submitted to the governor. This report contains a summary of the amounts received and spent during the year; it shows the balance or the deficit in each fund and the total balance at the close of the year. It also contains an estimate of the revenue and expenditures for the current year. If, in the auditor's opinion, the future revenues are likely to prove inadequate, he must recommend plans for a sufficient increase. It may be concluded that the auditor is more than a bookkeeper for the state; he is a supervisor of its finances.

The Treasurer

Persons or corporations owing money to the state make payment to the official or the department having the account on which the amount is chargeable. In turn those who make collections of public revenue deposit with the state treasurer all amounts collected by them. This money makes up the general revenue of the state.

The public revenue can be used only for purposes directed by the legislature, except money received out of appropriations made by the Congress of the United States, endowment funds, and fees collected at state educational institutions. In these cases provision for expenditure has already been made by law. Corporations, counties, districts, and towns make their payments of collected taxes to the treasurer. It is understood that the treasurer collects and is entrusted with the revenues belonging to the state.

The sums received from taxes and other sources amount to millions of dollars each year. Not all of this money can be kept in Charleston; various amounts of it are deposited in banks located in other sections of the state, which are known as state depositories. These public funds are kept subject to demand by the treasurer.

The Commissioner of Agriculture

The Department of Agriculture, headed by the commissioner, has the public obligation of promoting interest in the land and its products. In carrying out his duties the commissioner works in cooperation with other state departments and also with county officers. Through them he organizes societies and associations for encouraging the improvement of agricultural interests, such as production, marketing, and distribution.

In cooperation with the United States Department of Agriculture, his trained agents inspect and grade farm produce at receiving and distributing points. In the same manner he collects information concerning soil, climate, health, natural resources, and mineral products of West Virginia. This information is printed and distributed for the use of people living on farms and of anyone else who requests it. The literature mailed from the commissioner's office includes statements concerning the resources of the counties and the adaptability of the soil to the production of vegetables and grains; the breeds of horses, cattle, and sheep best suited to the climate and land of West Virginia; the science of horticulture; and diseases injurious to animals and plants. The state department of agriculture serves as a source of scientific information to farmer, stockman, and horticulturist.

The legislature has created an agricultural advisory board, consisting of the governor, the commissioner of agriculture, and the director of the Agricultural Extension Division of West Virginia University. This board meets at least four times annually to consider the farming interests of the state. It examines the functions of each office in the state department of agriculture and prevents the overlapping of work.

The commissioner of agriculture makes a biennial report to the governor and the legislature, which includes an itemized statement of all receipts and disbursements of his office, the names of all persons employed, and the amount paid to each. The legislature makes appropriations for maintaining this department, which carries on work of interest and help in all the counties. Agriculture in West Virginia is treated further in Chapter 20 below.

The Attorney General

The attorney general is the lawyer for the state. In the conduct of their affairs the other officers depend on him for legal advice. So do the prosecuting attorneys of the counties. Upon request he will give written opinions and advice on questions of law to the heads of institutions, officers, boards, and commissions serving the state. In general he is the head of the law-enforcing agencies created by the acts of the legislature and the constitution.

He appears as counsel for all cases the state has pending in the supreme court of appeals, in any federal court, or in any other court in West Virginia. He defends actions for the state on behalf of its officers, for any reason, but if public action is taken against an officer the attorney general prosecutes him. Upon the request of public boards and commissions he serves as their attorney.

The attorney general may appoint three assistants to perform such duties as he assigns to them. Each one receives a salary fixed by statute. Next to his office stand the prosecuting attorneys of the counties and the attorneys appointed or elected by the incorporated towns. An expert knowledge of the law and its interpretation is a prime necessity in all of these offices. The public wants fair and honorable treatment and has a right to expect it from all persons transacting business with the people's government.

CHAPTER 17

The Judicial Department

In its plan of government the state has, in addition to a legislature and an executive, a judiciary, or system of courts. The legislature enacts the laws; the judiciary interprets them; the executive enforces them. Authority for the system of courts is derived from the constitution, which declares: "The judicial power of the States shall be vested in a supreme court of appeals, in circuit courts, and the judges thereof, in such inferior tribunals as are herein authorized, and in justices of the peace." All these classes of courts will be discussed below.

The Federal Courts and the State Courts

The relationship existing between the national and state governments is not always clearly understood. An explanation has already been made of how the legislative and executive powers of the state operate in harmony with the corresponding powers of the national government. The same is true with respect to the judiciaries.

Article III, Section 1, of the Constitution of the United States vests the judicial power of the United States "in one supreme court, and in such inferior Courts as the Congress may from time to time ordain and establish." The judicial power of federal courts extends to all cases arising under the Constitution of the United States, the laws of the United States, and treaties made and to be made; to cases affecting ambassadors, ministers, and consuls; to cases of admiralty and maritime jurisdiction; to controversies in which the United States is a party; and to cases between two or more states, or between citizens of different states.

In general, the federal or national courts deal with the construction, application, and interpretation of the Constitution of the United States and the laws enacted by the Congress of the United States, and to controversies between citizens of different states. All other cases, civil and criminal, are tried and determined in state courts.

Courts of the State under the First Constitution

The first constitution of West Virginia declared that "The judicial power of the State shall be vested in a supreme court of appeals and circuit courts, and such inferior tribunals as are herein authorized." The supreme court consisted of three judges, two of whom constituted a quorum. They were elected for a term of twelve years, and could be removed by a concurrent majority vote of all the members of each house of the legislature. The salary was fixed by the constitution at $2,000 a year, and hence could not be increased or diminished without a constitutional amendment.

The state was divided into nine circuits. The judge of each was elected for a term of six years at a salary of $1,800 a year, with an allowance of ten cents a mile for traveling expense. The legislature was given power to rearrange the circuits and at intervals of ten years to increase or diminish the number. This law proved to be unwise. Because of the growth of population and commerce, revisions were actually needed more frequently than once a decade. Four times annually sessions of the circuit court were held in every county.

Each county was divided into not fewer than three nor more than ten townships, in each of which a justice of the peace was elected for a term of four years. If the population of the township exceeded twelve hundred, two justices were chosen. Every township had as many constables as justices, elected every two years.

To reduce the work that might come before the circuit court, the legislature was empowered to establish courts of limited jurisdiction within any incorporated town or city. Appeals from these courts of limited jurisdiction could be made only to the circuit courts.

To act as lawyers for the people an attorney general for the state and a prosecuting attorney for each county were elected for four year terms. In all cases in which the county or the state was a party, the attorney for the public appeared in its behalf.

For each township a supervisor was elected. Acting jointly the supervisors constituted a board that took the place of the old Virginia county court. This feature of the new government was denounced as having been borrowed from New England. This objection in itself had no weight; but there was enough sentiment aroused to reestablish the county court in place of the township supervisors' board when the new constitution was formed.

Changes under the New Constitution

After serving the state for approximately ten years, the first constitution was supplanted by the second. The changes in the judicial system were not extensive.

The new constitution provided for four justices of the supreme court of appeals, to be elected for terms of twelve years. This arrangement continued until 1902, when by an amendment to the constitution the membership was increased to five. Salaries were now established by law, and could be changed from time to time by the legislature. The new constitution provided that sessions of the circuit court in each county must be held at least three times annually. The county court, an old institution which had had a long existence in Virginia, was restored as a part of the county government of West Virginia. The offices of attorney general for the state and of prosecuting attorney for each county continued under the new order.

The courts of West Virginia are thus of several different kinds. Although each court has a distinct function to perform, a definite relationship exists between them. If one of the courts were eliminated the others would have increased burdens to bear. The greatest number of cases come to the courts nearest to the people – the justices of the peace and the police courts of the towns and cities.

It is the general practice in West Virginia to elect judges, not to appoint them. Their terms range from four to twelve years, and their salaries are fixed by the legislature. Judges may be removed from office for incompetency, neglect of duty, or maladministration. The sessions of the courts and their jurisdiction are regulated by both constitutional and statutory law. The powers of the courts are limited; their powers are delegated by the sovereign people in whom all the authority of government resides. If any officer of the law, judge or otherwise, proves himself incapable of administering his duties to the best interests of the people, he may be removed, held liable for his misconduct, and replaced by another person. To gain a better knowledge of this branch of government, let us now turn our attention briefly to the judiciary as it is organized in West Virginia today.

The Justice of the Peace

HISTORY OF THE OFFICE

The courts of first instance in West Virginia are the justices of the peace, of whom there are now six hundred and nine. Through this local officer the services of government are brought near to the people. It was early recognized in colonial Virginia that "divers inconveniences attended the people on the frontier by reason of their great distance from the courthouse" – reason enough for the forming of a new county and the building of a new courthouse.

The justice of the peace followed the organization of county government in America. The office was one of common usage in England and was transplanted to Virginia with the early colonists. The "squire" usually possessed a great deal of common sense, some legal knowledge, and a rugged body. He preserved good order by exercising his power over criminals. The importance of the office is indicated by the fact that provision was made for it in the original state constitutions. The main object was to have in every community an arbiter authorized to settle controversies of a petty nature between neighbors. Frequent need arose for a rough and ready justice. The office of justice of the peace endured through the colonial period, was inherited by the states, and has come down to the present in possession of its original powers.

ELECTION AND TERM OF OFFICE

In old Virginia the governor appointed the justice of the peace. His power to do so was severely criticized by the people living west of the mountains. When this state was formed the justices came to be elected by the qualified voters in the magisterial districts. The term of office was four years. The county court filled vacancies by appointment.

Although the law requires the justice to be a resident and a qualified voter of the district in which he is elected, it does not impose upon him any qualifications as to learning and legal training. In filling this office in most cases the voters act wisely by selecting persons qualified in all respects to perform their official duties. Legal training of course could be put to excellent use but it is not everything. If some of the justices are poorly prepared and incompetent, the same statement can be truthfully made about the occupants of other offices.

No salary is provided for the justice of the peace. His official income is from fees charged for his services. For trying criminal cases the justice may collect a fee of three dollars. In civil actions his compensation varies from ten cents for swearing a witness to five dollars for holding an inquest.

The judicial proceedings of the justice's court are carefully kept in a book known as the docket, furnished at the expense of the county. These records furnish sources of interesting information concerning controversies which arise between neighbors and are brought to the court for settlement. The docket follows the office; when a new justice is elected he takes over the records from his predecessor.

The number of justices of the peace is determined by the population of each magisterial district. If the population does not exceed twelve hundred, one justice is elected; if it is more than twelve hundred, two are chosen. In some districts the population has decreased; consequently the number of justices may have been reduced from two to one. At the present some districts in West Virginia do not have a justice of the peace. In such instances it is likely that an election was duly made but the person elected failed to qualify. In that case business which ordinarily would come before that court is transferred to a justice residing in another district in the county. Responsible citizens should make every effort to insure that all departments of the government function continuously with a full complement of officers. When one officer fails to perform his public duties or fails to qualify for a public office to which he has been elected, another officer must perform the duties of his office. This has a tendency to centralize authority, and is not a healthy condition for the state or the republic.

JURISDICTION

Much of the business taken to the justices consists either of petty crimes or of trivial controversies arising between neighbors. Most of the civil suits could be settled in the court of common sense if it were not for envy, jealousy, and selfishness. But these are human frailties that disrupt social and business relations and are not always to be finally disposed of either in or out of court. Only occasionally should there be a need for an application of the law for settlement in court.

Although the justice receives his office by the will of the qualified voters of the magisterial district, his jurisdiction extends throughout the county. A case arising anywhere in the county may be brought before any justice of the county. But under ordinary circumstances matters of business referred to a local court are taken before the justice residing in the district in which the parties concerned reside. The cause of action brought to the court must have originated in the county or the defendant must reside therein. If a defendant is not a resident of the state, but can be served, or owns real property or has other effects within a county of West Virginia, he may be sued before a justice of that county.

The official duties of the justice of the peace may be clarified by classifying them in three divisions. In the first place, he takes the acknowledgment of deeds and other writings, and issues summonses, warrants, and subpoenas. Second, he tries civil actions for the recovery of money or property in compensation for an injury or wrong, where the amount involved does not exceed three hundred dollars exclusive of interest and cost. If the judgment rendered by the justice should exceed fifteen dollars, an appeal may be taken to the circuit court. Therefore the final authority of this court is exercised only in small cases. Third, he has jurisdiction over criminal offenses committed in the county or on a river or a creek adjoining it. These offenses include assault and battery, trespass on personal property, offenses against morality and decency, petit larceny, carrying concealed weapons, disturbing religious services and schools, breaking and entering, and so forth.

In the rural parts of West Virginia the justice of the peace usually holds his court at his home or in a schoolhouse or country store. In towns he has an office and rooms set apart for the convenience of persons having business in his court. At times curious bystanders take up no small part of the space, and sessions of this court serve as a source of community entertainment.

TRIAL BY JURY

If either party to a civil action brought before the justice of the peace demands it, he is entitled to a trial by a jury, if the amount involved exceeds twenty dollars. The jury must be composed of six competent men between the ages of twenty-one and sixty-five. The party demanding the jury deposits with the justice the sum of six dollars as payment for the jurymen. In criminal cases, if the penalty authorized by law is a fine of more than five dollars or imprisonment, the accused is entitled to a trial by twelve jurors. It is not unusual to resort to this method of trial in West Virginia. The persons rendering judgment are the citizens of equal rights and liberties with the parties interested in the case, and no doubt the decision rendered comes as near being a just verdict as could be reached in any other way. The decision of the jurymen must be unanimous.

POWERS DENIED TO THE JUSTICE

Certain matters of importance are held by the law to be beyond the jurisdiction of the justice of the peace. His realm of limited powers is fixed both by political boundary and by the magnitude of controversies. It has been seen that he does not have power over actions arising outside his county. The county and the waters bounding it form the geographical limitation to the jurisdiction of the justice. If the amount in controversy in a civil case should exceed three hundred dollars, exclusive of interest and costs, it cannot be brought in the justice's court. Other matters in which he does not have jurisdiction are false imprisonment, malicious prosecution, libel, slander, breach of marriage promise, seduction, or any action involving the title to real estate. These are matters referred to a higher court, usually the circuit court. It is the intention of our legal system to dispose of the small cases in the court of the justice of the peace. Small cases are far more numerous than large ones; therefore, the justice courts try the greater number of cases.

THE CONSTABLE

With each justice of the peace there is elected a constable. His term is four years. Vacancies in this office are filled by appointment made by the county court. The constable must be a citizen, a resident of the district he serves, and a qualified voter.

Here is another office that has been handed down to us from England. The original meaning of this word is *count of the stable.* In old England every parish was under the jurisdiction of its constable, who had to see that men had proper armor for the pursuit of criminals and for combat with enemies. He was a military officer concerned with making hue and cry after malefactors and with defensive warfare. But as time passed he was supplanted in military matters by the militia and became a police officer; as such he functions in American government. Our state police forms a modern constabulary.

The duties of the constable require him to be present at the court of the justice. He keeps good order and enforces the lawful commands of the court. It is his obligation to serve summonses, attachments, and warrants and to make arrests. He is a conservator of the peace and may place persons under arrest for committing violations of law in his presence. Under the direction of the justice the constable makes collections of accounts, for which he must render a statement to the justice. Again, he has custody of juries until they are duly discharged by the court, and he has charge of persons ordered by the justice to be delivered to prison, where they become wards of the sheriff. It is within the power of the justice of the peace, when he deems the action wise, to appoint a special constable to serve a summons, an attachment, or a warrant, and to take under his charge the delivery of persons to prison. As compensation he receives fees for his services. For example, for an arrest in case of felony his fee is one dollar and for serving a subpoena in a civil suit it is twenty-five cents.

THE NOTARY PUBLIC

In the conduct of business there is need to have at hand a person qualified to attest the genuineness of any deeds or writings in order to render them available as evidence of the facts stated therein. Of course this could be done by a justice of the peace, but sometimes the securing of his services would entail delay. Provision is therefore made for a notary public in order that ordinary business transactions may be expedited.

This officer, upon approval of his competency made by the county court, is appointed and commissioned by the governor for a term of ten years. The number has no limitation except the judgment of the governor, who may make as many appointments as he deems proper. The notary public administers oaths and takes depositions, affidavits, acknowledgments of deeds, and other writings. Further, he has authority by law to be a conservator of good order, and in this function his power equals that of a justice of the peace. The notary public keeps an official seal which he affixes to documents acknowledged before him and signed by him.

His duties also include the requirement of the acceptance of foreign and inland bills of exchange,[1] including checks and promissory notes. Bills of exchange are used extensively in the transaction of business at home and abroad.

THE COMMISSIONER

The commissioner has duties resembling those of the local notary public but exercised outside the state. As in the case of notaries, commissioners are appointed by the governor, and their number is left to his discretion. They serve for four years, unless they are sooner removed by the governor.

Commissioners are assigned to states, territories, and districts outside West Virginia but in the United States. There they administer oaths, take affidavits and depositions for use in West Virginia, and take acknowledgments of deeds and other papers that are to be admitted to record in this state.

The commissioner provides for his own use a seal which he affixes to the documents that he approves. A copy of the seal is kept in the office of the secretary of state. The use of this seal serves as a protection both to the officer and to the state.

The Municipal Court

Municipal courts are frequently referred to as corporation courts because they are located in incorporated towns and cities. Provision for the creation and regulation of municipal courts appears in the charter granted by the state to the municipality. The court may be conducted by the mayor, by a police judge, or by some other person designated in the charter.

In general, these courts have only the same criminal jurisdiction as that of a justice of the peace. They hear cases involving infractions of the law of the city and of the state, such as violations of parking regulations, speeding, drunkenness, vagrancy, gambling, and a thou-

[1] A bill of exchange is a written order issued from one person to another, directing the person to whom it is addressed to pay to a third person a sum of money specified in the order.

sand other offenses. The function of the municipal court is to keep good order in the town and maintain a high standard of daily conduct. Persons convicted by the mayor or the judge may be fined, imprisoned, or sentenced to work on the streets to pay their fines.

A great deal of progress has been achieved in the organization of municipal courts. In town it is possible, but not always practical, to secure the service of well-trained lawyers to serve as judges of the court. Steps are being taken to classify cases in definite divisions, as juvenile, criminal, civil, or domestic relations, and to place a capable judge over each division. In some places this division of functions has proved to be of great advantage.

The County Court

HISTORY

The county court is an institution of ancient date. In England, even before the Norman Conquest (1066), each shire had its "shire moot" which was a court for the shire or the county. And in each of these courts the king appointed an ealdorman as the chief man of the shire, the president of its court, and the leader of its soldiers. In this court also sat the bishop and the shire reeve or sheriff. In time the county court was transferred from England to Virginia and became a fixed feature in the government of the colony from which it was inherited by the state and passed on to West Virginia.

Although the functions of the county court have been changed from time to time it still fills an important place in local government. The changes have tended to reduce rather than to increase its authority. For a time, from 1863 to 1872, under the first constitution, the county court entirely disappeared from this state, its place being taken by a board of supervisors for each county. But when the new constitution of 1872 was formed and adopted, the county court was restored to all its former glory. Even though it has been shorn of much power, it is still a potent force in the county government.

MEMBERSHIP

Except as otherwise explained, in each county of West Virginia there is a county court composed of three commissioners elected for six years.[2] At the courthouse of the county the court holds four regular sessions annually. Each year the commissioners elect one of

---

[2] In Preston County each magisterial district elects a commissioner of the county court, making a total of eight members.

their number president. Not more than one member may be elected from the same district. The members must be citizens of the county and qualified voters.

JURISDICTION

It is the official duty of the county court to have the custody of deeds, wills, and other documents, to be made matters of record in the office of the county clerk. The court also has charge of matters of probate or proof of the validity of wills; the appointment of personal representatives who are the executors of wills and the administrators of the estates of persons who have died without a will; the appointment of guardians for children under twenty-one years of age; the selection of committees to take charge of incompetent persons and their property; and the appointment of curators, that is, persons to manage and control the property of deceased persons until an executor or administrator is appointed and has qualified. The county court makes settlement of the accounts of all its appointees and keeps a public record of these proceedings.

As an administrative duty the county court has supervision and control of the financial affairs of the county, and as a legislative function it fixes the rate of taxation to raise money to take care of the expenses of the county. The court lays the levy, collects the taxes, and disburses the money for the best interests of the public welfare. At one time it had charge of building and keeping in repair roads and bridges within the county, but by amendment to the constitution in 1920, and by statutes enacted by the legislature in 1933, this power came to be vested in the State Road Commission.

This court provides appropriate courthouses equipped with offices and other rooms suitable for conducting the business of the county. It buys and installs furniture and other office equipment at public expense, and provides secretarial help for the officers of the county.

The county court makes a general review of the results of elections and determines the result of contested elections for county and district offices. Vacancies in the office of justice of the peace, county commissioner, assessor, clerk of the county court, county surveyor, and prosecuting attorney are filled by appointments made by the court. And through this same authority registrars are appointed to enroll the voters, district boundary lines are determined, and monuments, tablets, and memorials may be provided. The business of the county court is worthy of the efforts of our best citizens.

THE CLERK OF THE COUNTY COURT

To keep the records of the proceedings of the court and to hold them open for public use, a clerk is elected by the voters for a term of six years. The clerk serves as a secretary to the court; he records deeds, wills, and other papers; he issues marriage licenses and hunting and fishing licenses; and, as agent of the state, he issues licenses to hotel keepers, druggists, restaurant owners, and certain other businesses.

Suitable filing cases and record books are furnished to the clerk for keeping the public documents and records. If the population of the county is extensive and its wealth great, it requires much care and attention by the clerk to keep his office in good and regular order. On some days scores of requests for information come to his office. The lawyer resorts to the county clerk's office to find land records; there too is kept the list of registered voters of the county.

THE PROSECUTING ATTORNEY

In each county of West Virginia the voters elect a prosecuting attorney for a term of four years. His office is usually kept in the courthouse and maintained at public expense. With the assent of the county court he may appoint an assistant (two in the more populous counties) to aid him in the discharge of his official duties.

It is the duty of the prosecuting attorney to attend to the criminal business of the state in the county in which he is elected. Upon receiving knowledge of any criminal act, he institutes and prosecutes all necessary and proper proceedings against the offender. It is also his duty to prosecute or defend civil suits in which the state or any department or board thereof is interested; and to advise, attend to, prosecute, or defend any suit in which the county or any county board of education is interested. He gives legal counsel to the county court, the board of education, and other public agencies.

Suit may be instituted by the prosecuting attorney against any person failing to pay a gasoline tax or an inheritance tax, or failing to return property for assessment. Anyone contributing to the delinquency of children, violating the food and health law, or violating any other law is liable to public prosecution by the prosecuting attorney. He is a member of the county health board, serving with the county health officer and the president of the county court. It is the duty of these officers to enforce all the rules and regulations issued by the state public health council. The prosecuting attorney gives his attention, therefore, to protecting persons in the exercise of their rights and civil duties, assisting public agencies, and enforcing the law against people who violate the statutes of the state.

THE CORONER

Far back (1194) in the history of the English government it may be found that the county court elected a coroner to act as a check on the sheriff. This office has lived down through the English and American governments to the present time, but the years have changed its duties.

Today in West Virginia the county court in each county is required to choose a coroner, not for a fixed number of years but to serve during the pleasure of the court. In some instances, however, this duty has been neglected, and where no appointment has been made, a justice of the peace in the county may act in the place of a coroner.

The coroner is appointed to serve the county. It is his duty upon learning of a death which there is reason to believe was not due to natural causes, to make inquiry for the purpose of determining the cause. He commands the constable to summon six suitable residents of the county to serve as the coroner's jury. The six persons appear at a place and time designated to hold an inquest in an effort to determine how the person came to his death. If the need should arise, the coroner summons witnesses who he has reason to believe know of the circumstances attending such death.

After making all needful inquiries and hearing the evidence, the jury, if satisfied, renders a decision known as an inquisition, naming by what means, person, weapon, or instrument the person was killed. The coroner makes a report to the circuit court; if it accuses of agency in the death a person still at large, the coroner issues a warrant for his immediate arrest.

Courts of Limited Jurisdiction

With the growth of population and commerce in West Virginia the duties of the courts grew and their dockets eventually became burdened. In some places towns grew to cities, and in nearly all sections business developed beyond the fondest expectations of the fathers. All this change brought a greater burden to bear on the courts. But provision was wisely made in the constitution to meet just such an emergency. In some of the most populous regions the circuits were reduced to include only one county. Moreover, the state constitution provided that "The legislature may establish courts of limited jurisdiction within any county, incorporated city, town, or village," [3] and to this provision resort has been made to relieve the courts of excessive business.

The courts of limited jurisdiction are established by acts of the legislature. They are located in the centers of population where it has been necessary to establish additional courts to deal with the great amount of legal business.

The names of these courts are determined by the act of the legislature creating them. In some counties the court is called the criminal court, in others the intermediate court, the court of common pleas, or the domestic relations and juvenile court. The number of sessions varies and the terms of the judges are not the same as for the circuit courts but all of the judges are elective.

In Wheeling this tribunal is known as the Intermediate Court of Ohio County. This court was originally created in the year 1893, but its title was changed and its powers were enlarged by an act of the legislature in 1925. The judge is elected for a term of six years, and holds three sessions of court annually in the City-County Building in Wheeling.

The jurisdiction of this court is concurrent with the circuit court in all criminal offenses committed in Ohio County. It has original jurisdiction in all civil cases at law, including motions for judgment where the amount in controversy exceeds fifty dollars and does not exceed five hundred dollars; of all unlawful detainer cases; and of appeals from the justice of the peace. Its concurrent jurisdiction with the circuit court also extends to the supervision and control of all proceedings before the justices of the peace, mayors, police judges, or police courts of the cities in Ohio County. The fact that this intermediate court has extensive concurrent jurisdiction with the circuit court shows that its services greatly reduce the burdens of the latter court.

In Clarksburg the court of limited jurisdiction is styled the Criminal Court of Harrison County. It was established in 1909. The judge is elected for four years, and three sessions of the court are held annually.

This court has concurrent jurisdiction with the circuit court in the trial of all felonies and misdemeanors committed in violation of the state law in Harrison County, over criminal cases appealed from

[3] Constitution of West Virginia, Art. VIII, Sec. 19.

the court of the justice of the peace and the municipal courts of the county, and over juvenile matters, including the custody of neglected children. In populous centers like Clarksburg this court has on hand much important business of far-reaching influence.

In the city of Charleston the Intermediate Court of Kanawha County, established in 1891, has jurisdiction over all criminal offenses in violation of state law committed in Kanawha County, except crimes committed by juveniles. Its civil jurisdiction extends to cases involving not more than five hundred dollars. The judge is elected for a term of eight years. Four sessions are held annually.

Kanawha County also has another court of limited jurisdiction known as the Court of Common Pleas of Kanawha County. This court has original jurisdiction within the county of Kanawha, concurrent with the circuit court in all civil causes, both at law and in equity, except where the amount in controversy exceeds five hundred thousand dollars. This court tries all appeal cases from justices of the peace and is the juvenile court of Kanawha County.

In Huntington the Criminal Court was created in 1893, and in 1917 its title was changed to Court of Common Pleas. The judge is elected for a term of eight years. This court has concurrent jurisdiction with the circuit court in the trial of all criminal cases, and hears cases appealed from the justices of the peace.

In this city there is also a Domestic Relations Court which was established in 1921. Four sessions are held annually to hear cases concerning domestic relations, and each week the court convenes to care for juveniles brought before the judge. In domestic relations it has to do with divorce, annulment, and alimony causes, separate maintenance, custody of children, and property division. In matters concerning juveniles it hears cases with respect to the care and disposition of delinquent, defective, neglected, or dependent children; adoption proceedings; cases concerning desertion and nonsupport of wives and children; and the enforcement of the general school law in Cabell County.

Other cities in which courts of limited jurisdiction have been established are Welch, Beckley, Fairmont, and Princeton. The powers and purposes of these courts are similar to those just described. The legislature has power to create additional courts of limited jurisdiction or to discontinue those that are already in operation.

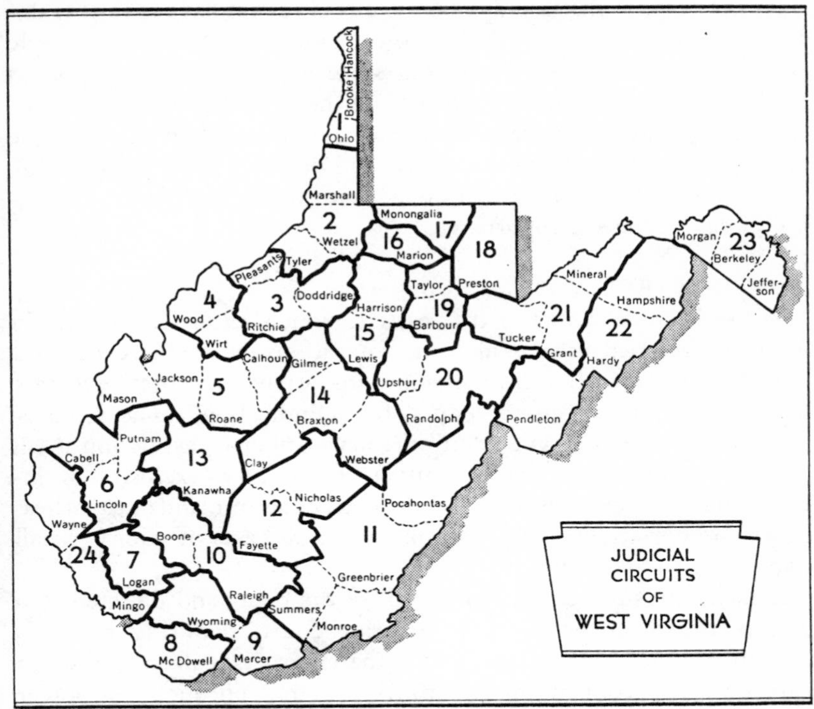

The Circuit Court

THE CIRCUIT JUDGES

The division of the judiciary standing next above the courts of limited jurisdiction is the circuit court. The counties of West Virginia are divided into twenty-four circuit districts over each of which presides a judge elected for a term of eight years.[4] The judge must reside in the district that he regularly serves although he may preside, if invited to do so, over any circuit court in the state. In case of a vacancy the governor fills the place by appointment until the next general election.

Each judge must have attained the age of thirty years at the beginning of his term of service, and must have been a citizen of the state for five years next preceding his election. The constitution

[4] In the first district, composed of Brooke, Hancock, and Ohio counties, two judges are elected.

does not require that a judge of the circuit court have special training in the law; this matter is left to the common sense of the people who elect him. The circuit courts are generally looked upon as final arbiters in matters brought before them. Under certain conditions cases may be appealed from the circuit court to the supreme court of appeals, but expense, delay, and doubt in securing a change in the judgment of the circuit court tends to discourage the appealing of cases of lesser importance.

JURISDICTION

It has been seen that petty matters, which exceed all others in number, are tried usually in courts of the justice of the peace and municipal courts. But cases of more importance are presented in a higher tribunal, the circuit court, for adjudication. The twenty-four circuit courts in West Virginia have original jurisdiction in all matters at law where the amount in controversy, exclusive of interest and costs, exceeds fifty dollars; in all cases of mandamus, habeas corpus, quo warranto, and prohibition; in all cases of equity; in all crimes and misdemeanors.

A mandamus is a command issued by the court and directed to a person, board, corporation, or inferior court, requiring the performance of a particular act, which the law specifically enjoins as a duty resulting from an office, trust, or station. Through this power the circuit court exercises superior authority over county, municipal, and district officers and over persons and corporations within its jurisdiction. The writ of habeas corpus is the most famous writ in the law; it is often known as the great writ of liberty. Its purpose is to remove illegal restraint upon personal liberty. One who feels himself unjustly arrested and detained may petition the court for a writ directing the person in whose custody he is detained to bring him into court and show a legal cause for detaining him, and if proper grounds be not shown, the judge orders the release of the person in custody. Quo warranto is a proceeding by which the state determines the legality of a claim which a party asserts to the use or exercise of an office or franchise; it may oust the holder from its enjoyment if the claim is not well founded or if the right to the privilege has been lost or forfeited. The court commands the sheriff to summon the defendant to appear before it and show by what authority he possesses the office or the franchise. Prohibition is an order issued by a superior court to an inferior court, commanding it to cease action in a case over which it does not have jurisdiction, or in which, though having such jurisdiction, it has exceeded its legitimate powers.

The circuit court has charge of cases, both civil and criminal, appealed to it from justices of the peace, police courts, and courts of limited jurisdiction. It has supervision and control of all proceedings before justices and other inferior courts by mandamus, prohibition, and certiorari.[5]

The regular terms of the circuit courts convene at the county courthouse in each county in the state three or four times a year. If he deems it necessary, the judge may call a special session of court at any time. But the judge is forbidden to preside over cases in which he is directly interested or where he is related by blood or marriage to either party of the suit. In these instances the law relieves the judge of conditions that might otherwise become embarrassing to him.

THE CIRCUIT CLERK

The clerk of the circuit court is elected in each county for a term of six years, and in case of a vacancy the judge makes an appointment to fill this office until the next election. It is the duty of the clerk to keep a permanent record, properly indexed, of the proceedings of the court, to preserve all papers filed in his office, issue summonses for jurors, administer oaths, and have custody of the records and seal of the court. He keeps a docket of the cases set for trial; draws juries; makes transcripts of records of the court; collects court costs; prepares and approves bonds given before him.

The clerk of the circuit court and two persons appointed by him (one from each of the two political parties who cast the largest number of votes in the last preceding general election) are ballot commissioners of the county. The ballot commissioners prepare the ballots and have them printed. Before an election they deliver the ballots to one or more of the commissioners of election of each precinct. Persons declaring themselves candidates for county and district offices file proper certificates with the circuit clerk. He supplies applications and ballots to absent voters, preserves such ballots when returned to him, and delivers them to the proper precinct election officers.

Annually the judge appoints two competent persons to make an

---

[5] Certiorari is a writ issued by a superior court to an inferior court requiring the submission to the superior court of the record in a particular case for the purpose of reviewing the judgment of the inferior court.

examination of the clerk's office. The examiners investigate the fee books and the records and papers of the office, and file with the judge a report of their investigation showing whether or not the clerk is faithfully discharging his duties.

THE GRAND JURY

The grand jury deals only with criminal charges. In order to be brought to trial in the circuit court for a criminal offense, one must be indicted by a grand jury. At each session of the circuit court a jury is summoned, unless it is dispensed with by order of the judge or there is in the county a criminal court that has jurisdiction over felony cases. At a special term the grand jury may or may not be summoned, the matter being left to the discretion of the judge.

In each county there are two jury commissioners belonging to opposite political parties, appointed by the judge for a term of four years. From a list of not fewer than one hundred and not more than two hundred names of bona fide citizens of good moral character in the county, the commissioners draw the names of sixteen persons who constitute the grand jury. In turn the circuit clerk issues a summons for each of these persons to appear at a stated time at the courthouse. Before entering upon their duties the jurymen are sworn to present "the truth, the whole truth, and nothing but the truth." Following the administering of the oath, the circuit judge issues instructions to the jurymen for the purpose of guiding them in their deliberations, after which they retire to the jury room to begin the hearing of witnesses.

In this room witnesses appear before the jury and submit evidence concerning the violations of law. With the help of the prosecuting attorney, they investigate all alleged offenses, including misdemeanors and felonies. If it be proved to the satisfaction of at least twelve of the jurymen that a violation has been committed, an indictment or a "true bill" is returned against the accused, who is then taken into custody and held for trial.

Let it be understood that no defense is made and no counsel heard before the grand jury. Its purpose is simply to determine whether or not the one accused of crime should be brought before the bar of justice to answer to the charge. If an indictment is found, the accused is taken into custody by the sheriff and either kept in jail or released under bond until the day of trial that will determine his guilt or innocence. But in case no indictment is found the person is not molested.

The judge of the court fixes the compensation of the jurors, which shall not be less than two dollars nor more than five dollars per day. Five cents for each mile to and from court is allowed to cover traveling expenses. The session of the grand jury is often concluded in one day, and pay will not be given for more than four days, except that in certain counties the time may be extended to ten days.[6]

THE PETIT JURY

From a jury list containing the names of not fewer than two hundred or more than one thousand citizens of the county, of sound judgment and good moral character, the petit jurors are drawn. At least thirty days before court convenes thirty names (or more at the discretion of the court) are blindly drawn from the jury list, and these persons summoned to appear as petit jurors or veniremen. If any person summoned as a juror neglects to appear without good cause, he must pay a fine not to exceed fifty dollars to be imposed by the court. As each case is called, twelve jurors are chosen from those summoned to form the trial jury. This procedure is known as impaneling the jury. The clerk of the circuit court swears the jury to render a true and impartial verdict according to the law and evidence. In all criminal and civil cases in which the amount involved exceeds twenty dollars, exclusive of interest and cost, the trial by jury shall not be denied.

Trial by jury is regarded as one of the firm foundation stones of our whole system of government. The object in a court trial is to discover the facts and arrive at a just and true verdict according to the law and the evidence. The petit jury determines these facts and the judge construes and applies the law.

Due inquiry is made to insure that those selected to serve as jurors have not discussed the case or formed an opinion on it. Counsel on either side has the opportunity to eliminate a certain number of jurors from the case without assigning any cause. Relatives of either party, or persons interested in the case, are forbidden to serve. Only male citizens between the ages of twenty-one and sixty-five are qualified to serve as petit jurors. The jury is complete only when twelve qualified men are placed under oath and assigned a place in the jury box.

These twelve men selected as a jury hear and see the witnesses give their evidence. They hear the pleadings of the counsel and the judge's instructions, or charge, covering their duties and the points

---

[6] Jurors may be paid for ten days service in Harrison, Kanawha, McDowell, Fayette, Cabell, Marshall, Marion, Mercer, Wood, Ohio, Mingo, Monongalia, Preston, and Summers counties.

of law involved in the case. The jury then retires to a private room to deliberate and reach a verdict, determining whether or not the accused is guilty of the alleged crime. This verdict must be unanimous. If all do not agree the result is a mistrial, or a "hung jury," and the case is continued until the next term of the court to be retried before a new jury. If the jury's verdict, in the opinion of the judge, has been rendered contrary to the law and the evidence, he may set the decision aside and order a new trial.

In criminal cases the trial is held in the county in which the alleged offense was committed, unless for good reason the place of trial is changed by order of the court.[7] The accused must be fully informed of the character of the accusation and is entitled to the assistance of counsel. Witnesses may be required to appear under a subpoena or a capias if necessary and testify in the presence of the accused.

In civil actions the petit jury determines whether or not the defendant is liable to the plaintiff on the cause of action stated in the plaintiff's declaration. If the jury finds the defendant is liable to the plaintiff, it also determines the amount of plaintiff's damages. In such case the jury returns this verdict: "We, the jury, find for the plaintiff, and assess his damages at $ ___ ." This verdict is signed by one juror selected by the jury as its foreman. Should the jury be of the opinion that the defendant is not liable to the plaintiff, it returns a verdict for the defendant.

The Supreme Court of Appeals

In the system of courts there must be one having final authority. Of course all courts have final authority in certain cases, but in matters of prime importance there must be a court of last resort. In West Virginia that is the supreme court of appeals. In the constitution, the power of this tribunal, like the authority of the other two divisions of the government, is limited. The constitution states what the court may and may not do.

Membership

The supreme court of appeals in West Virginia had its beginning in the constitution of 1863. It was then composed of only three

[7] This process is known as a change of venue.

judges, who held their office for a term of twelve years. The new constitution of 1872 provided that the supreme court should consist of four judges, any three of whom constituted a quorum for the transaction of business. In 1902 an amendment to the constitution increased the number of judges to five. Since then no change has been made with respect to the number of members.

The supreme court of appeals then is composed of five judges elected by the people for a term of twelve years, a longer term than that of any other elective office in the state. The court elects one of its members president, and each judge has a law clerk to assist him. The court appoints a clerk, a deputy clerk, an assistant clerk, a court crier, and a messenger. Two regular sessions are held annually at Charleston. The place of meeting is in the capitol building, where spacious rooms are set apart for the use of the court. The regular sessions commence on the second Wednesday in January and the first Wednesday in September. If it should deem the change expedient the court may hold its sessions at another place and at another time. Special sessions may be called at the will of the court. This court has no juries; its decisions are rendered by a majority of the five judges.

The only constitutional requirements for the judges are that they must have attained the age of thirty years, must be entitled to vote, and must have been citizens of the state for five years next preceding their election. It may appear somewhat strange that the constitution does not even set forth that a judge of this high tribunal must possess thorough legal training and experience. Would the people elect one who is not qualified? It is possible. Would one who lacks proper training be a candidate for the office? It might be. What then is lacking? The definite purpose of the wise men who drafted our constitution makes the requirements for officers very general. The rest is left to the common sense of the qualified voters in a government by the people. In case a vacancy occurs in the supreme court the governor appoints a judge who serves until the next general election.

It is very fitting that judges of the supreme court should be given a long tenure in office. This condition makes them secure in their office and serves as a protection against harmful influences. Although the judges may be removed by impeachment, it is to the honor of the court that there has never been such an impeachment in the history of West Virginia. Capable men have usually been chosen to serve as judges.

JURISDICTION

An examination of the jurisdiction of this court shows the purpose for which it was created. In a government in which there exists freedom to enjoy life, liberty, the pursuit of happiness, and the possession of property, there will be misunderstandings, controversies, and disputes between the citizens. There must therefore be a final arbiter to maintain peace in the land; there must be a power to which appeals may be made for final settlement. Otherwise the organization of the government would be incomplete. This final umpire in our system of government is the supreme court of appeals; five judges, sitting in judgment on matters of difference brought for final adjudication by the citizens of the state, and on questions involving the life or liberty of those convicted of crimes.

This court has both original and appellate jurisdiction in cases of habeas corpus, mandamus and prohibition. It has appellate jurisdiction in civil cases in which the matter in controversy, exclusive of costs, is of greater amount than one hundred dollars; in matters of boundaries of land, probation of wills, and the appointment and qualification of personal representatives, guardians, and committees; in affairs concerning mills, roads, ways, ferries, and landings; in the levying of tolls or taxes by a county or a corporation; and in cases of quo warranto and certiorari. It also hears appeals from the decisions of certain administrative officers and boards, notably the Workmen's Compensation Appeal Board and the Public Service Commission. It has appellate jurisdiction in criminal cases in which there has been a conviction for felony or a misdemeanor in the circuit court, and in cases relating to the public revenue. Clearly the power of the court touches many vital interests in the lives of the people.

The supreme court is as busy as it is responsible. Besides the cases in which it has original jurisdiction, appeals are taken to it from all of the twenty-four circuit courts. There is business on hand all the year except for a short vacation during the late summer.

During terms, the court is in session almost daily. Except in cases of original jurisdiction, all cases are heard on the records made in lower courts or tribunals. These records are usually printed and the points of law briefed and argued by counsel. At an appointed time the judges confer on the legal arguments and merits of the case. A decision is reached by a majority vote, after which the president prepares, or designates one of his colleagues to prepare, the opinion of the court in written form. The court then makes a careful review of the written opinion and may make changes in it. Finally the decision is publicly announced. If one or two judges disagree with the opinion of the majority of the court, he or they may file a dissenting opinion. By no means are all decisions unanimous, for judges, like anyone else, do not always see principles in the same light.

The decision of the supreme court of appeals is final in matters which do not involve federal questions. However, the Supreme Court of the United States, on proper application, may review decisions of the state supreme court in cases which involve the construction and application of the Constitution of the United States, or laws or treaties of the national government.

OFFICERS OF THE COURT

It is the duty of the clerk of the court to attend all sessions, care for the records and papers, and perform other duties prescribed by the court. All records and papers filed are kept in an office set apart for this purpose and are arranged in good order so that they will be accessible for reference. The crier is in attendance at all sessions. He maintains good order, keeps the halls clean, ventilates the rooms, and obeys the orders and directions of the court. The messenger is an attendant at the meetings and his services are at the command of the five judges.

The supreme court has the sole control and management of the splendid law library located in the state capitol. It appoints the librarian and his assistants, and makes rules and regulations governing the use of the library; it may purchase new books and incur such expenses as are necessary to keep the library in good condition.

In 1945 by legislative enactment the supreme court was given power to appoint a director of the administrative office of the supreme court of appeals. He has charge and supervision of all administrative matters relating to the offices of clerks of the circuit and intermediate courts, justices of the peace, and the personnel of these offices; the examination of the dockets of the various courts; the making of reports of the business transacted by the courts to the Judicial Council;[8] the preparation of a proper budget for the maintenance and operation of courts; and the purchase and distribution

[8] By act of the legislature in 1933 the Judicial Council was created, consisting of nine members appointed by the governor. The council proposes recommendations to the governor and the supreme court of appeals concerning the improvement of judicial procedure in the state courts, and hears the report of the director of the administrative office of the supreme court.

of supplies needed by the court. He also acts as secretary of the state Judicial Council and fulfills such other duties as may be assigned to him by the court.

Summary

The courts of West Virginia have performed and are performing a vital function in our government with honor and integrity. They are entitled to the respect and support of every citizen. In 1945 the legislature created as a part of the judicial department of the state the West Virginia State Bar, to which all practicing attorneys belong. The State Bar enforces the rules prescribed by the supreme court defining the practice of law, judicial ethics, and the code of ethics governing the professional conduct of attorneys-at-law.

CHAPTER 18

County and Municipal Government

It has been seen in a previous chapter how the county was created for the purpose of bringing the blessings of government near to the people, so that they might enjoy the full measure of benefits derived from our local political institutions. This condition is as true in West Virginia as in any other state of the Union. The people and their possessions around which the county boundary line has been drawn constitute a unit of government through which is woven a system of rules and regulations common to all the inhabitants living within the enclosure. But the development of modern industry has required the concentration of population in certain centers. And the tide of emigration, attracted by social advantages and the benefits of medical and sanitary science, is still in full flow from country to city, from farm to factory. In view of this fact two forms of local government have been adopted, one known as municipal government, to take care of conditions that are common only to the people of the town, the other for the people living in the rural sections. These two types of local government will be discussed separately.

County Government

NUMBER AND SIZE OF COUNTIES

In West Virginia there are fifty-five counties, the oldest being Hampshire (1754) and the newest Mingo (1895). When the state was admitted into the Union there were only fifty counties. Since then Grant, Mineral, Lincoln, Summers, and Mingo have been added. As most states run, the number of counties in West Virginia is not great, and since the day of easy communication has come, no increase in the number can be expected.

The state constitution forbids any county to be formed having less than four hundred square miles in area and six thousand inhabitants. Nor shall a new county be formed until a majority of the voters residing within the proposed boundaries give their consent. At present there exists some popular sentiment for the joining of two or more counties into one, but surely there is no public disposition to increase the number.

LEGAL STATUS

According to the laws of West Virginia, the legal status of the county cannot be changed without an amendment to the constitution. This unit of local government is altogether subordinate to the state. Its existence facilitates the administration of local finances, education, relief of the poor, roads, judiciary, and so forth. The county has a corporate status; it transacts business in the name of the people; it can sue and be sued as an individual.

The government of the county is outlined in the constitution, in which the officers are named by title, their duties are set forth, and the manner of their election is specified. The county exists as a branch of the sovereign state, for the administration of law and the maintenance of order. On the other hand the city government, or municipal corporation, is called into existence by the direct request of the people composing it. But its charter is granted under the general laws passed by the legislature and its power restricted in borrowing money, contracting debts, and levying taxes. The voters in each corporation having a population in excess of two thousand may make all laws and ordinances relating to their municipal affairs. The city government, therefore, functions for the convenience of the people living in it and has to do only with local conditions.

ORGANIZATION

The constitution requires that the voters shall elect certain officers of the counties. The county officers are sheriff, assessor (one or two), prosecuting attorney, and surveyor of lands, all of whom hold office for four years, and a clerk of the county court, a clerk of the circuit court, and a board of education, elected for terms of six years. Three commissioners constituting the county court are elected for each county for a term of four years, and justices of the peace and constables are chosen in the districts. Coroners and surveyors of roads are appointed by the county court. All these officers have definite duties assigned to them. Each may be removed from his office for the abuse of his official power.

This arrangement makes the county a definite unit for the administration of justice and the enforcement of state law. In the preceding chapter some of these offices have been discussed as parts of the judicial and administrative powers. In that connection it was seen that the circuit courts and the intermediate courts meet at the county seat several times each year, at which sessions both civil and criminal cases arising in the county may be presented for trial. At the same place meets the county court, whose duties are almost wholly administrative; it is there that the circuit clerk and the county clerk maintain their offices to which the people resort for the conduct of official business, and it is there that the assessor and superintendent of schools reside as agents of the public. There are also other public agents whose duties are confined to the county, of whom the sheriff is most important.

THE SHERIFF

The sheriff is the financial agent of the county and has in his possession funds collected from the people. He cannot serve two successive terms, nor is he allowed to be the deputy of his successor. He is not eligible to hold any other office for at least one year after the expiration of his term. So at the conclusion of his administration there must be a final settlement of his accounts kept for the people. The statement of settlement is made public, and if his accounts should be short he becomes liable to severe punishment. In his official duties the county sheriff is assisted by a deputy appointed by him. The sheriff retains responsibility not only for his own acts but for the conduct of his assistants.

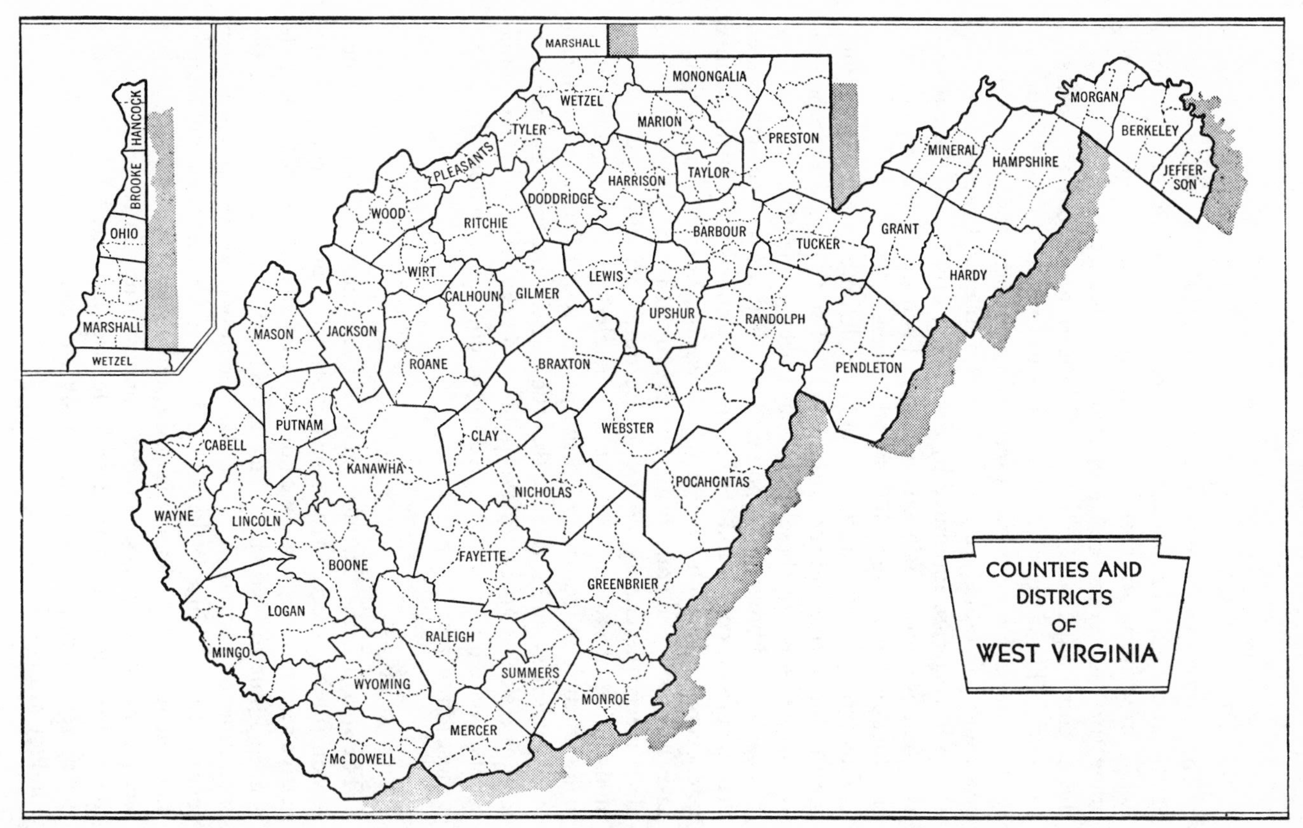
COUNTIES AND DISTRICTS OF WEST VIRGINIA
HANCOCK
BROOKE
OHIO
MARSHALL
WETZEL
MARSHALL
MONONGALIA
WETZEL
MARION
PRESTON
TYLER
PLEASANTS
TAYLOR
HARRISON
DODDRIDGE
WOOD
RITCHIE
BARBOUR
TUCKER
MINERAL
HAMPSHIRE
MORGAN
BERKELEY
JEFFERSON
GRANT
HARDY
WIRT
CALHOUN
GILMER
LEWIS
UPSHUR
RANDOLPH
MASON
JACKSON
ROANE
BRAXTON
PENDLETON
PUTNAM
CLAY
WEBSTER
CABELL
KANAWHA
NICHOLAS
POCAHONTAS
WAYNE
LINCOLN
BOONE
FAYETTE
GREENBRIER
LOGAN
RALEIGH
MINGO
SUMMERS
WYOMING
MONROE
MERCER
Mc DOWELL

Although elected by the voters of the county the sheriff attends to the enforcement of state laws and in that respect he acts as an official of the state. He may be appealed to by the governor and the attorney general for assistance in law enforcement; he is placed in charge of persons accused of law violation, is given custody of persons convicted in the courts of the state, and is a collector of state revenue. Therefore the sheriff is not in all respects a county officer.

The duties of the sheriff are manifold. He receives, collects, and disburses the funds for the county, and of these accounts he must keep a careful record. He collects taxes on property, biannually, on the first of November and the first of May. If any citizen defaults in his tax payments, his property becomes liable to be sold to satisfy the debt. In cases of this sort the sheriff makes the sale of the property at public auction.

In addition to his duties as treasurer of the county, the sheriff is also the keeper of the peace. He serves as jailer and attends to furnishing food to the inmates in prison. Under his charge prisoners are delivered from the jail to the courtroom or to the state prison. At the sessions of court he is in attendance, maintains good order, and carries into execution the orders of the judge. It is incumbent on him to make arrests and serve warrants and subpoenas. It may be added that the sheriff serves as a game protector of his county, although special wardens are appointed to enforce the game and fish and forestry laws.

The many duties assigned to the sheriff make his office an important one. The law prescribes that he shall pursue and take traitors, murderers, and other violators of the law, and commit them to prison. If danger in his county should become too great in times of disorder, he may appeal to the governor for assistance through the use of the national guard.

The sheriff is, therefore, the chief executive officer of the county. His salary is fixed by law and ranges in amount in the various counties from fifteen hundred dollars to five thousand dollars. The annual compensation of the deputies is fixed by the county court. Of course the sheriff is placed under heavy bond for the proper conduct of his office. Both oath and bond hold one who possesses such extensive power liable for the proper performance of his duties.

THE PROSECUTING ATTORNEY

The preceding chapter surveys the duties of the prosecuting attorney. He is elected by the voters of the county and is responsible to them, but his salary is fixed by law enacted by the legislature, and the length of his term is established by the constitution.

The duty of the prosecuting attorney is to aid in the administration of justice. Primarily he enforces the law, and his most important work is in criminal cases. He assists in calling witnesses before the grand jury to bring about indictments; he collects evidence and prepares the cases for prosecution. He is expected to treat the accused with fairness and justice, for public interest cannot be promoted by prosecuting the innocent.

Criminal prosecution he conducts in the name of the state and in this work he acts as the state's agent. But his most direct obligation relates to the people of the county in which he serves. It is they who elect him; it is in their courthouse that his office is kept and furnished; and it is they who deserve the protective hand of the law under his administration.

The prosecuting attorney represents the state and county in civil suits as well as in criminal actions. He acts as the lawyer for the public when its interests are threatened in any manner.

THE CORONER

For all purposes the coroner operates as a county officer and his jurisdiction stops at the county boundary. In most cases he is a physician, but the only specific requirement is that he shall be a resident citizen and legal voter.

He holds inquests on the bodies of persons whose death is supposed to have been due to violence or some other unlawful means, and attempts to determine the cause of the death. In this process the coroner summons a jury of six persons before whom witnesses testify. No counsel appears; consequently no cross-examination takes place. Usually the witnesses include a physician who gives expert testimony. By this procedure information may be promptly secured for the use of the prosecuting attorney in bringing to account the person guilty of the crime. The coroner's jury does not establish guilt or innocence – that fact has to be determined by trial in open court – but one accused by the jury of committing crime may be placed under arrest through the authority of a warrant issued by the coroner. Although the coroner's procedure is distinct from an ordinary trial in that the accused is not present, no counsel appears, and there is no cross-examination of witnesses, yet a jury is summoned, testimony given, and a verdict rendered. The coroner is therefore a judicial officer and his inquest has the status of a court.

The law of West Virginia requires that a coroner must be appointed for each county, but the law has been neglected to the extent that only thirty-four coroners are now serving in the state. In the absence of this officer a justice of the peace acts in his place.

CLERKS OF THE COURTS

The duties of the circuit clerk and the county clerk have already been explained. Here these officers are mentioned only to show their connection with the county government and the administration of the law. In three counties, Grant, Hardy, and Pendleton, one clerk serves both courts, circuit and county. In all the other counties there is one clerk for each court.

The clerk of the circuit court keeps a record of the proceedings of each session of the court. To his care are entrusted the seal, property, money, and records kept by the court in his county. He dockets the cases for the judge, keeps a careful record of all judgments rendered, and is subject to the command of the court in other matters.

As has already been seen, the county clerk is secretary to the county court. He records deeds, probates wills, issues licenses, keeps a record of the results of elections, and keeps a written account of the proceedings of the court. His office in the courthouse is kept open six days a week so that the citizens of the county may confer with him and consult the public records.

THE SURVEYOR

The law makes provision for a surveyor in each county of the state. When settlements were first established in western Virginia and land claims were new, it often happened that boundary lines became confused and the ownership of some tracts of land was uncertain. Moreover, land owned by the state was sold in farms to persons disposed to purchase a home. It became necessary, therefore, to have an officer authorized to make official surveys and establish definite boundary lines. As early as March, 1623, it was written in the laws of Virginia, "if there be any pettie differences betwixt neighbors about their devidents to be divided by the surveyor or if of much importance to be referred to the Governor and counsell; the surveyor to have 10 lbs. of tobacco upon every hundred acres." [1] From that early date to the present there has been need of an official land surveyor. But as our civilization grows older and boundary

[1] Hening, *Statutes at Large*, I, 125.

lines become more definitely established, the work of the surveyor shrinks in complexity.

It is the duty of the county surveyor, where a variance of opinion exists, to establish to the best of his skill and judgment the legal boundary lines of land. If the court should request a survey of land to be made, this officer obeys the order and makes written returns and plots of his measurements. The public records, books, and papers belonging to the county surveyor are delivered to the clerk of the county court and kept in his custody as a part of the public records.

The surveyor reports to the commissioner of school lands all waste, unappropriated, and forfeited lands, designating the location and situation of each tract. Land owned by the county, or that which is sold for taxes and unredeemed, may be measured by the official surveyor, and a copy of his survey filed with the county clerk.

It comes within the power of the county court to appoint a county engineer to survey roads and make measurements and calculations preparatory to the construction of bridges, public buildings, and other public works. If the county surveyor can qualify for that office there is no legal hindrance to his appointment. By experience it has been found that his work continues to be a necessary feature in county government.

THE ASSESSOR

The people of each county choose an assessor whose term is four years. He is eligible for re-election. His salary is fixed by law. The assessor comes to be known by every resident of the county, for he places a valuation on all private property and on this valuation taxes are based. Property tax is the principal source of revenue of the county. In the conduct of his work the assessor may with the consent of the county court appoint deputies to assist him.

The assessor prepares lists of properties in the names of the owners. In determining values of the long list of properties he has a difficult task and one requiring a high degree of ability. For this reason, if for no other, competent men are needed in this office. If an assessor should be so inclined he has a chance to give favors by reducing appraisal values. Honesty and integrity are, therefore, of first importance. In case his first purpose should be to win votes and the second to list property at its real and actual value, the taxpayer will suffer in proportion to the degree of dishonesty exercised by the assessor.

With the consent of the county court the assessor may appoint deputies ranging in numbers from one to nine, depending on county population. The salaries of the deputies are fixed by law; they vary from three hundred dollars to two thousand dollars annually.

On January first of each year the assessor and his deputies begin the round of assessment. They call on each taxpayer in the county, secure a correct description of his belongings, and determine to the best of their judgment the true and actual value of his real estate and personal property, that is, the price it would bring if voluntarily offered for sale. In his work of visiting every home, business, bank, store, and factory and placing a value on all property, the assessor stands in need of wisdom and experience.[2]

There are certain kinds of property exempt from assessment and taxation. This property includes public schools, colleges, cemeteries, churches, seminaries, homes for orphans and the infirm, property used for charitable purposes and that belonging to benevolent associations, and buildings and grounds owned by the state and by the national government.

On each adult male inhabitant there is levied by the state a capitation or head tax amounting to one dollar annually for the purpose of maintaining the public schools. The county court of each county places on every male inhabitant in its jurisdiction a capitation tax of one dollar for the support of the public roads. The same amount is levied by many of the town councils. The capitation tax thus totals three dollars in many municipalities and two dollars in the rural sections. Persons afflicted with physical infirmities may be exempt from the payment of the capitation tax.

REVIEW AND EQUALIZATION

At the regular session of the legislature held in 1933 the law concerning the review and equalization of the assessed value of property was amended. Previous to that time a special board, appointed by the Board of Public Works for each county, had this responsibility.

[2] For the purpose of local levies property is classified in four divisions:

Class I. All tangible personal property employed exclusively in agriculture, horticulture, and grazing; all products of agriculture, including livestock, while owned by the producer; all money, notes, bonds, bills, stocks, notes receivable, and other intangible personal property. Tax on these properties shall not exceed fifty cents on the hundred dollars assessed valuation.

Class II. All property owned, used, and occupied by the owner exclusively for residential purposes; all farms, including land used for horticulture and grazing, occupied and cultivated by the owner or bona fide tenants.

Class III. All real and personal property situated outside of municipalities, exclusive of Classes I and II.

Class IV. All real and personal property situated inside of municipalities, exclusive of Classes I and II.

The new law, however, abolished the board of review and equalization and placed its duties in the hands of the county court.

According to the present plan the county court meets annually, not later than July 5, for the purpose of reviewing and equalizing the values of property made by the assessor. The length of the session may not exceed twenty-five days. At this meeting the assessor and his assistants must be present and submit the property books for review. The court has power to add names to the list of property holders; it may cancel other names; it may increase and diminish property values, but it cannot change classifications. In case an increase in the value of a property is contemplated, the county court shall give the owner at least five days' notice before a change is authorized. If the owner makes no reply to the notice during that time, he is not privileged to call for another review during the year, unless he appeals to the circuit court for a correction. Whenever a tax payer becomes dissatisfied with the classification of his property he may file his objections with the assessor, who may either agree with the complaint or refuse to change his records. In the latter case appeal may be made to the state tax commissioner, whose decision may finally be referred to the circuit court for an adjustment.

If a property owner thinks that the county court has unduly increased his tax, he may appeal his case directly to the circuit court. On the other hand the state, through the office of the prosecuting attorney, may follow the same process if the county court should unjustly reduce the evaluation of property. Then the decision of the circuit court is expected to place a true and actual value on the property. It is important to note that usually the judgment of the county court is accepted by all parties concerned and thus appeals are quite infrequent.

THE BOARD OF EDUCATION

Until 1933 a board of education was elected for each magisterial district in the state, so that the district was the unit for the administration of education. In that year, however, the law was changed so as to make the county the unit for school purposes. Under the new law a county board of education is elected consisting of five members, each member serving for a term of six years. The members of the board must be residents of the county, and not more than two may be elected from the same district. Their salary is fixed by the legislature.

It is required that the board meet on the first Monday in July, on the first and third Tuesdays in August, and at any other time deemed proper by the members.[3] On the first Monday in May a meeting is held for the purpose of appointing teachers for the schools in the county and also a county superintendent of schools, who acts as secretary to the board.

The public schools of the county are under the administration of the board of education. It purchases land for the location of school buildings and for the agricultural interests connected with the educational program. It provides suitable buildings, furniture, and the other necessary supplies for the training, health, and cleanliness of the youth of the county. It attends to the transportation of children to and from school each day. All this would appear to be a big program but the board attends to other business in addition.

It fixes the length of the school term, the minimum of which is nine months if funds are available to continue that long. Free textbooks may be furnished to children whose parents are not able to purchase them. With respect to the health of the children, the board may arrange for medical and dental inspection for each pupil and employ a school nurse. The custodians of the buildings and the janitors are employed by the board of education.

The most important work of this authority is the employment of teachers and principals, the fixing of their salaries, and their dismissal when warranted. A special officer administers the compulsory attendance law.

Annually the board of education lays a levy on all taxable property in the county for the support of the schools. Collections and disbursements are made by the sheriff, but no money is paid for school purposes except by order of the board of education. The amount raised in the county is supplemented from a general school fund created from capitation taxes, fines, forfeitures, and so forth, set apart for the support of the public schools of the state. If this amount is not sufficient to maintain the schools and pay the minimum basic salaries to the teachers, a petition may be made to the state superintendent of schools to secure the necessary funds from the auditor. The definite object in the administration of the school law is to keep the schools of the state in session at least nine months in each year, and, by enforcing the compulsory attendance law, to reduce illiteracy to a minimum.

---

[3] In many counties the boards hold monthly sessions.

THE COUNTY SUPERINTENDENT OF SCHOOLS

In each county of the state the board of education appoints a superintendent of schools. His term shall not exceed four years. The board fixes the amount of his salary, which depends upon the total population of the county. A suitable office and secretarial help are provided for him by the board of education. An assistant or assistants to the superintendent may be appointed at the discretion of the board.

The primary duties of the superintendent are to serve as the chief executive officer and secretary to the board. He recommends teachers and supervises the educational program of the county. His duties are outlined in detail in the school law.

THE COUNTY AGRICULTURAL AGENT

The county is a convenient organization through which agencies, both state and national, may reach the people. One of these means of public service is the county agricultural agent. In cooperation with the farm bureau of the county and the extension division of the College of Agriculture of West Virginia University, the county court may appoint an agricultural agent for each county. At this writing there are only six counties in the state that do not have one of these officers.

The duty of the county agricultural agent is to encourage improved methods of farming. He gives practical instruction in cultivating and utilizing the land for the growing of crops and pasture and for conserving the timber and water supplies. From his office information is supplied concerning the selection of seed for planting and the best types of cattle, horses, hogs, sheep, and poultry. The agricultural agent makes soil analyses and recommends fertilizers for the farmers and stockmen. To stimulate interest in farming he directs the Four-H work, agricultural clubs, and groups in home economics. Much work of first-rate merit is being accomplished in the rural community through the leadership of the county agricultural agent.

THE HOME DEMONSTRATION AGENT

To promote the welfare of the people living in the rural regions of the county the law provides that the county court may employ a home demonstration agent. Like the agricultural agent, she must be highly trained in the work she is assigned to carry on. She organizes classes in cooking, sewing, and the proper furnishing and care of the home. She gives demonstrations in baking; in preserving vegetables, fruits, and meats; in quilting, weaving, and making clothing. She organizes clubs for girls and instructs in first aid and the work of the Red Cross. The home demonstration agent has a big program. It taxes wisdom and skill to carry on her work in a successful manner. Forty-two counties now employ home demonstration club agents.

THE COUNTY HEALTH OFFICER

On the recommendation of the county court the state public health council appoints in each county a qualified physician designated as the county health officer. On the recommendation of the council of a municipality the state council may choose a qualified person as municipal health officer. The county officer serves for a term of four years, while the town physician is appointed only for two years. The salaries are fixed by the county court and the town council respectively, and the money comes from the local treasury.

It is the duty of the local health officer to have charge over communicable and infectious diseases. The law requires every practicing physician to report promptly to the health officer any contagious diseases that come under his observation, so that the spread of the contagion may be curbed. The local health officer may procure from the state commissioner of health, free of charge, vaccine, antitoxin, and other forms of serum to prevent or combat disease. In order that all people may be treated, this medicine may be administered without charge to the indigent poor. It is now required that all children entering school for the first time shall be or shall have been immunized against smallpox and diphtheria.

The health officer may investigate any nuisance affecting the public health within his jurisdiction. He may order the discontinuance of the use of wells and springs if the water in them is found to be impure; he may place persons under quarantine who are afflicted with contagious disease; he may order the removal of any condition dangerous to the health of the people in the community. Persons who disobey his orders are liable to punishment by fine and imprisonment.

To further the health program the county court may employ a full-time health nurse. She must be legally qualified and suitably trained to do her work. Her duties in protecting the health and sanitation of the county are prescribed by the county court.

THE COUNTY BOARD OF HEALTH

The prosecuting attorney, the president of the county court, and the county health officer constitute the county board of health. This board administers the rules set forth by the state public health council. The county and municipal health councils are under the direction of the state council, which may supplant the local authorities if conditions should warrant such action.

If the local board should have reason to believe that any boat on the Ohio River or its tributaries, or a boat on any other river of the state, has people on board suffering with a communicable disease, such boat may be prevented from landing. Likewise, if any train or other conveyance within the borders of the state should have on board any person or persons afflicted with a contagious disease, or having in their possession disease-carrying matter, the board may order the conveyance to be detained. During the detention a thorough medical examination will be made to detect any danger so that proper treatment may be administered. As population grows in density and communication is made easier it becomes increasingly necessary to provide safeguards for the health and happiness of the people.

THE COUNTY ROAD SUPERVISOR

For each county the state road commissioner appoints a road supervisor and any assistants that are deemed necessary. The supervisor must be a resident of the county. His qualifications and duties are prescribed by the state commissioner.

Attention throughout the year has to be given to keeping the highways open and in repair. As the good road system of the state is extended, the duties of the supervisor become greater. He has charge over all primary and secondary roads in the county, including the county-district road system. The power once possessed by the county court over the highways of the state has been relinquished to the state road commission, except as to public landings and bridges and approach to bridges within municipalities.

Municipal Government

Many conditions in a town or city affect only those living within the corporation, and the residents should therefore have the power to regulate them. For this reason every town and city in West Virginia is granted a charter which confers on the inhabitants the privilege of self-government with respect to these local matters. Water supply, pavement of streets, levying and collecting taxes, maintaining good order and public health are some of the major concerns of the incorporated town. In West Virginia there are two hundred and three incorporated cities, towns, and villages known as municipalities.

THE HOME RULE AMENDMENT

At the general election held November 3, 1936, the voters of West Virginia made a change in the constitution of their state by passing the municipal home rule amendment. The purpose of this amendment was to give the inhabitants of each city greater freedom in forming and administering their own local government. It held true to the principle that government regulations should be kept near to the people and emanate from them.

During the meeting of the legislature next following the adoption of the home rule amendment, laws were passed to give effect to the new constitutional regulation. The laws passed by the legislature did not change any existing charter. All charters, laws and ordinances remained in operation and effect until modifications should be brought about by legal process.

By the enabling legislation passed in 1937, all the municipalities in the state were divided into four different classes: class one, municipalities having a population that exceeds 50,000; two, those having a population between 10,000 and 50,000; three, those having a population between 2,000 and 10,000; four, those having less than 2,000 inhabitants. After the passage of this enabling act, the voters in any city had authority to frame, adopt, or amend their charter after a new manner prescribed by law. Not only did the new amendment turn the matter of government back to the voters of the cities but the legislature devised certain plans of municipal government for them, any one of which the voters could adopt for their own charter.

(1) The first is the mayor-council plan. Here the mayor and council constitute the governing body. The mayor is elected by all the voters of the city, while the councilmen are chosen either by wards or at large. Other officers may be elected or appointed as the charter provides. (2) The second is the strong-mayor plan. The mayor is elected by the qualified voters of the city, and the administrative power is centered in his office. The council, which is elected by wards or at large, constitutes the legislative authority; that is to say,

it adopts the ordinances for the city and the mayor administers them. All the other officers, such as police and collectors, are appointed by the mayor. Their appointments may or may not be subject to approval by the council. (3) The third is the commissioner plan, which calls for the election at large of three or five commissioners. Their chief duties are assigned and divided as follows. One is a commissioner of public affairs; another attends to finances; the third to public safety. When there are five, the fourth attends to public works, the fifth to the opening, construction, and maintenance of streets. " A charter for a class III city shall, and a charter for a class I or class II city may, provide for a commission of three members: a commissioner of finance, a commissioner of public works, and a commissioner of public safety." The commissioners, who serve both as a governing body and as administrators, elect the mayor and the other necessary officers unless the charter states otherwise. (4) The fourth is the manager plan. Under this plan a council of several members is elected by the voters. In turn the council chooses from its own number a mayor, whose only special duties are to preside at council meetings and to represent the city on official occasions. The council, which is the governing body, appoints a city manager. The manager attends to the general affairs of the city and appoints subordinates to assist him. He is responsible to the council.

City elections under the home rule law are held on the first Tuesday in June, and the elected officers begin their official duties on the first day of July following.

When the constitution of the state was changed by the home rule amendment it was thought a rush might be made to adopt one of the new plans of city government. This has not happened. Only a few changes have been made from the old mayor-council plan to any of the new styles of government.

ORIGIN OF MUNICIPAL CHARTERS

It has been seen that municipalities having a population of less than 2,000 are styled towns or villages. How do they acquire their charters and plan their governments? In the first place the locality must have a population of one hundred or more, and a bounded territory of not less than a quarter of a square mile. After a survey of the land has been made and a census of the population taken, a petition for a certificate of incorporation is filed with the judge of the circuit court of the county in which the proposed town is located.

The petition contains a full description of the place to be incorporated and specifies a day on which the voters shall meet to vote upon the proposed question. On that day the voters cast ballots for or against incorporation. If the proposal is favored by a majority of the votes, the judge directs the circuit clerk to issue a certificate of incorporation.

In due time the citizens hold an election to choose officers for the new town — mayor, recorder, and at least five councilmen. These officers, acting together, form the town's council. They appoint a sergeant, health officer, street commissioner, and any other officers for whom there is need. This mayor-council type of government is the prevailing plan used in towns and villages, and continues to be used in many of the cities of West Virginia.

POWERS OF THE COUNCIL

If it is deemed in the interests of the people, the council has authority to rent, lease, or sell the electric light plant, waterworks, or any other publicly owned utility on condition that the proposed action is approved by a majority of the votes of the municipality. Councilmen are forbidden to be interested, directly or indirectly, in the sale of materials purchased for the use of the town.

To carry into effect the powers conferred upon it the council has authority to pass all needful ordinances, orders, and regulations that are not contrary to the constitution and the laws of the state. For violation of its own ordinances the council may prescribe fines and imprisonment. After a fair trial in the court of the mayor, or another officer authorized as police judge, punishment is imposed according to the degree of the crime committed.

Irrespective of the provisions of the charter the policemen of the town are bound by oath to aid in the enforcement of the criminal laws of the state. They may make arrests and bring the offenders before the justice of the peace. The jurisdiction of the town officers does not extend beyond the limits of the corporation. One who is convicted in a municipal court, if the fine exceeds ten dollars, may appeal his case to a circuit court or to a local intermediate court if one is available.

PUBLIC HEALTH AND SAFETY

To avoid congestion and provide greater safety from fire, panic, and other disorders, the council divides the town into wards or districts. To promote public health and safety the council is empowered to regulate the size of new buildings and other structures erected in the town, the area of yards, courts, and other open spaces, and the density of population. In order to avoid the danger of fire, noninflammable roofs can be specified for buildings, and water lines laid and hydrants placed at convenient points for use against fire hazards. As a matter of safety the council may purchase fire engines and employ skilled firemen to operate them. Equipment such as ladders, hose, and fire extinguishers is bought at public expense.

Any refuse or condition that threatens the health of the people must be removed. The health officer, appointed by the council, oversees this important work. He may quarantine homes in which there exists infectious or contagious disease, by vaccination and inoculation immunize people against contagion, and inspect water, milk, and other supplies of food. The general health of the town is his important responsibility. Suitable electric lights are furnished to facilitate travel and transportation and insure protection. Water and gas lines are extended to the homes. Schools, parks, town buildings, and streets are built and maintained at public expense. Good order and protection are under the care of the policemen and the town courts.

TOWN FINANCES

Advantages enjoyed by the inhabitants of towns are expensive. Electricity, gas, running water, and paved roads all have a price. Police protection, traffic regulation, and health preservation have a rate of charge. Therefore, the current expenses of the municipality have to be paid. In some cases payments amount to huge sums.

Based on the valuation of property made by the assessor and the volume of business transacted in the town, an annual municipal tax is levied by the council to defray all current expenses. Some towns levy an additional capitation tax of one dollar. Of course the supplies of gas, electricity, and water are usually furnished by incorporated companies, and the payments for these utilities do not go to the local government. However, it is altogether possible for the town to own its electric light system, its water supply, and its airport. In West Virginia eighty-nine towns own and operate their system of water supply; only three control their electric current.[4] In conclusion, it may be observed that citizens living in towns have their affairs regulated by local government to a greater degree than people living in the rural communities. For all their privileges and

[4] This statement is based on conditions as of January 1942.

restrictions the inhabitants of the town are required to pay in full measure.

SUMMARY

It has just been seen how a town may become incorporated and how it secures its charter, which in reality serves as its constitution. In American government the town has been allowed a great deal of freedom in forming its political system, since it has had no grand model to follow such as the colonial charters provided for the states in forming their constitutions. In changing the rules of town government from year to year too much stress has doubtless been placed on the form of the charter and not enough on the character of the men who are chosen to administer it. A government that fixes responsibilities on certain officers, and on them only, is likely to achieve more than one that is interested chiefly in the arrangement of its political system.

We have seen that several plans for town and city government have been established in West Virginia. It may be helpful to conclude this chapter with a brief analysis of their main features.

The mayor-council plan of local government is the oldest of the group, and is standard for towns having less than 2,000 population. There are two types, the centralized and the decentralized. The distinction rests chiefly on the degree of authority exercised by the mayor. In the centralized plan the executive power is centered in the authority of the mayor. He with the council appoints the police, health officer, boards, and commissions, makes contracts on behalf of the town, determines the rate of taxation, and often serves as the judge of the town court. In addition he and the council issue ordinances having the force of laws for the town, and he publicly represents the people of the town as their chief executive. This is the type used by most small towns in West Virginia.

On the other hand, the decentralized plan severely restricts the power of the mayor and council. Officers, boards, and commissions are elective; this arrangement takes the appointive power out of the hands of the executive officers and makes all officials directly responsible to the people rather than to the mayor and council. The mayor is left as the chief executive in name but not in fact. This form of town government experienced a rapid growth in the United States for a while, but for the last decade it has receded rather than advanced in popularity.

The other form of municipal government in West Virginia is

known as the city-manager type. In this form the administrative work is assigned to a special officer known as the city manager, who is appointed for an indefinite time by the council. The duties of the city manager are to plan and supervise all public works, such as erecting buildings and repairing streets, constructing airports and public buildings, issuing permits for private homes, caring for parks, and a multitude of other duties. On these matters he confers with the council and presents to it an annual budget to cover expenses. The council passes ordinances, forms the budget, levies taxes, and creates and abolishes departments. The power of the mayor is no greater than that of any member of the council, except that he presides at meetings of the council and represents the town on ceremonial occasions.

There is one form of city government that has not been adopted in West Virginia. It is known as the commission plan.[5] In this arrangement several commissioners, elected at large from the city, jointly assume all the duties of administration of the city government. They issue ordinances, make appointments, levy and collect taxes and are responsible for the construction of public buildings. This arrangement forms a plural executive in which is centered full authority to administer municipal government.

---

[5] The number of the commissioners is usually three, five, or seven.

CHAPTER 19

State Organization and Administration

The Complexity of Modern Government

As the population of the state increases and industry is enlarged and grows more complex, it becomes impossible for the governor and his staff of elected officers to administer all the public duties required by the general welfare. In order, therefore, to carry out the necessary functions of the government the legislature is obliged from year to year to create new departments for the purpose of administering various special lines of civic responsibility. And new departments call for new officers.

Down through the history of the state this method of expansion has been practiced, but within recent years the tempo of change has accelerated sharply. Life has become much more complex, and the activities of the government have expanded correspondingly. The manufacture of the automobile and the construction of a network of hard-surfaced roads have brought new conveniences and new problems. The airplane has taken a prominent place in the daily lives of the people. Invention, manufacturing, and mining also have brought with them problems of health, working hours, stream pollution, and a thousand others. Great corporations, with offices housed within elaborate edifices, have taken the place of the old single-track business. With the growth of cities have come water, gas, and electric power companies and supplies, and new aspects of police regulation, education, and health protection.

It is of paramount importance that every industry, with all its ramifications, should fit into the civil organization of the government wherein it exists. Investigation, regulation, and supervision have to be carried on by the state in order to provide adequate protection of the people, insure the security of the industry, and promote the honest interest of both industry and people. Hence the expansion of government agencies is accelerated.

Of course there is a danger that the government may grow too watchful in these matters and multiply agencies and personnel needlessly and extravagantly. Beginning with one officer, the agency may expand into a board or a commission. Some states have more than a hundred different units, acting separately, for the administration of public affairs. A condition of this kind is likely to drift into confusion, thence into disorder, unless amended. It is impossible for the governor to give these units proper supervisory attention; consequently the tendency will be for them to drift apart, without proper correlation. Such a condition becomes poor administration.

In West Virginia there are at present twenty-three main boards and commissions, and in addition fifty-four other branches of administrative government.

BOARDS, COMMISSIONS, AND DEPARTMENTS

It is necessary at the start to distinguish between the meanings of "board," "commission," and "department." Sometimes even state legislatures are remiss in their use and application of these words.

A board is a small group of persons who serve only part time in the administration of the work to which they are appointed. Usually the appointments come from the governor. Each year the members hold occasional meetings and are paid for the time actually spent in attending to their work. The daily details of their central office are cared for by a person, or persons, highly skilled in office practice and responsible to the board. The members of a board need not be technicians but just persons of sound judgment and good overseers. Examples are the Board of Public Works in the state and the board of education in the county.

A commission consists of several persons (usually three, five, or seven) appointed to full-time employment on a fixed annual salary. Each member needs to be well trained in his work. A typical example of this form of work may be found in the State Road Commission.

Different from either of these organizations is a department directed by a single head. The personnel under his direction are divided into divisions and bureaus, in which most of the detail is carried on. An example is the Department of Education.

In the creation of one of these bodies careful judgment must be exercised to determine whether it should be a board, a commission, or a department. If the group is to determine policies, perhaps the board or commission is best; but if action is needed, then a single-head department may be most efficient. When the unit is headed by more than one person, the group assembles to form policies, and sometimes it sits as a court, hears witnesses, and takes testimony. In general its decisions are subject to review by the regular courts. But it is possible to deliberate too long. While a board is delaying, an individual could be acting. He does not have to call a meeting or wait for a quorum. Yet in counsel there is wisdom. The counsel of three wise men is three times better than the opinion of one wise man.

THE MERIT SYSTEM

West Virginia has never adopted a merit system for the purpose of recruiting persons for state service; but such a system has been advocated from time to time, and in view of the fact that the number of full-time employees is increasing year by year its adoption would seem in line with progress. The ability of the individual employees of the state determines in a large measure the efficiency of the whole administrative system. The mode of selecting workmen, therefore, should be improved in every possible way. The business of the people should be conducted for the benefit of the people. For more than a century the spoils system has been in operation in national affairs and has also taken a place in state government. But it is decadent and detrimental to public interests. It is only reasonable that state employees should be selected from the standpoint of fitness, not favor. The highly trained, the honest, and the courageous should be invited to serve. Public office should be a model of efficiency. A number of states have adopted the merit, or civil service, system, usually with preference to the war veterans.

In the main, where it has been put into use, the civil service law is administered by a commission consisting of three persons. The power to appoint the commission is vested in the governor. A term of six years is most common.

Expenditures and the Budget

During the last decade there has been a notable increase in the rate of state expenditures. Several reasons may be cited for this condition – increase in population, rise in prices, more unemployment, and the assumption by the state of new functions of government. There are larger expenditures for the building of roads, conservation of streams and forests, education, pensions, public health, and poor relief. Of these public expenditures by the state, education takes about fifty per cent, health and public welfare about twenty per cent, and highways approximately seven per cent.

The only source of income at the command of the state is public taxation, and with mounting expenditures there is mounting taxation. The general revenue is now derived from the general property tax, the gross sales tax, the consumers sales tax, business profits, personal income tax, and several other levies.[1] Annually the expenditures of the state amount to many millions of dollars.[2] In order to administer this vast amount a fiscal plan has become necessary.

Every state in the Union has seen fit to adopt a budget system so that the collection and disbursement of funds may be properly correlated. In West Virginia the legislature meets only biennially;

---

[1] The different sources from which the revenue of the state is derived may be summed up as follows:

I. State Fund
1. Privilege tax
2. Consumers sale tax
3. Beer tax and licenses
4. Insurance tax and certificates
5. Charter tax
6. Personal income tax
7. Inheritance tax
8. Property tax
9. Business profits
10. Fees and Licenses
11. Institutional sales and services

II. General School Fund
1. Capitation, land, and chain store tax
2. Fees, fines, and licenses
3. Interest on investments
4. Sales of public lands
5. Federal aid

III. State Road Fund
1. Sales tax
2. Registration and license tax
3. Gasoline tax
4. Capitation tax
5. Sales of bonds
6. Federal aid
7. Miscellaneous income

[2] For the fiscal year 1949–50 the amount is estimated at about $180,000,000.

therefore plans for expenditures and for collecting revenue to meet them must be worked out for a period of two years. A budget is made for this whole period, itemizing proposed expenditures and expected revenue to cover them. Of course it lies within the power of the legislature to make extra appropriations, but such action would defeat the real purpose of the budget.

The budget is drafted by the Board of Public Works, which consists of the governor, secretary of state, treasurer, superintendent of schools, auditor, and commissioner of agriculture. In the process of drafting it, the board may require a statement from all the public officials and institutions, containing itemized estimates and other necessary information. It may provide also for public hearings and require attendance at them for the purpose of gaining needful information.

When all the information is gathered, a bill is formulated containing a complete plan of proposed expenditures and estimated revenue for each of the two fiscal years next succeeding. It includes the current assets, liabilities, reserves, and surplus or deficit; debts and funds; and an estimate of the financial conditions of the state at the beginning and end of each year covered by the budget.

Each budget is divided into two parts, the one consisting of governmental appropriations and the other of general appropriations. The first of these divisions embraces expenditures for the legislature, the executive department, the judiciary, interest on the public debt, salaries of officers, and aid to the public schools. The second division includes all other appropriations.

Within ten days after the convening of the legislature in its regular session the budget bill is submitted to it by the governor. A copy is delivered to the presiding officer of each house, who in turn causes the bill to be introduced in regular form. During the time the bill is being considered the legislature may summon the governor or any other member of the Board of Public Works and any official having authority to spend the public revenue, for the purpose of testifying as to the propriety of any item. Before its passage the Board of Public Works has the privilege of making corrections and amendments with the consent of the legislature.

While the budget bill is under consideration it cannot be amended so as to create a deficit, but the items relating to the legislature, the judiciary, and the executive departments may be increased or diminished. However, provision cannot be made for changing the compensation of any public officer during the time for which he is chosen. When the bill passes both houses it immediately becomes a law without the signature of the governor. No doubt the passing of the budget bill is the most important item on the program of legislation. Without its enactment there would be no funds to pay the officers or carry on public works, and the wheels of government would stop.

After the main bill has become a law it is legal for a supplementary bill to be passed if it is limited to some single purpose. If necessary this measure may levy a tax to meet certain necessary expense, providing revenue should not be available for this purpose. Unlike the regular measure, this bill must be signed by the governor. Of course during time of war or other emergency the legislature may make appropriations to care for the obligations of the state. And the governor may call a special session for the purpose of considering emergency appropriations.

The State Tax Commissioner

The tax commissioner serves as a central administrative officer for the state taxing system. He is appointed by the governor and serves for a term of six years at a salary of $6,000 annually. He resides in Charleston and maintains his office in the capitol.

The duty of the state tax commissioner is to see that the laws relating to assessments and collections of taxes in the state, counties, and municipalities are faithfully executed. During the year he or one of his deputies visits, for the purpose of making inspections of the tax-collecting agencies, each county and town, examines the work of the assessors, boards of review and equalization, justices, prosecuting attorneys, sheriffs, and clerks of the county courts. It comes within his duties to inquire into the proceedings of these officers and to impart to them information that will help in making a full and just assessment and collection of taxes. Sometimes he is requested to give assistance to boards of review and equalization in determining the value of property for the purpose of taxation.

Occasionally the governor requests the attendance of the state tax commissioner at the sessions of the Board of Public Works to help in arriving at the just value of property and to determine matters relating to the public revenue. In the commissioner's office the land books and the printed forms used for recording values of personal property are prepared and distributed to the assessors in the various counties. In addition to all these important duties, he renders help to the state auditor and treasurer in affairs relating to revenue and its collection. Reports and remittances for the state income tax are also submitted to his office.

Upon the conclusion of each year's business the state tax commissioner presents to the governor his annual report, covering the official operation of the tax laws of West Virginia. If he wishes he may include in his report recommendations for changing the laws concerning the assessment and collection of taxes; the governor at his discretion may reject such recommendations or initiate action on them. This annual report is submitted to the legislature at its next session and serves as a material aid in checking the values of taxable property. To consolidate his statewide duties the commissioner requires that an annual report be submitted to him by the assessor of each of the fifty-five counties.

The State Road Commission

MEMBERSHIP AND DUTIES

Since the state has largely assumed the responsibility of building our highways, it has become necessary to form an organization to give proper care to this important work. The legislature has established the State Road Commission, consisting of four regular members and a commissioner. The members of the commission are appointed by the governor for terms of four years. Regular meetings are held twice annually in the office of the commissioner, and other special meetings when the occasion demands them. The members receive ten dollars a day and expenses for the time actually served.

It is the chief purpose of the regular members to act as an advisory body to the state road commissioner. They make studies of the fields of legislation and administration with the object of recommending policies and practices to the commissioner relative to any duties required of him by law. In these investigations the members have open access to all books and documents of the state Department of Roads and Highways. The commission keeps the minutes of its own meetings, and these are filed as public records.

Perhaps the most important work of the State Road Commission is to fix a state policy as to the building of roads and highways. On this public matter it advises and makes recommendations to the governor and the legislature. Thus the work of improving public roads is very largely promoted by this agency.

THE STATE ROAD COMMISSIONER

The governor, with the advice and consent of the senate, appoints a road commissioner whose term of office is four years and who cooperates with the commission. Because of the serious responsibility of this officer he is forbidden by law to possess any invested interests in a corporation employed in the construction or repair of highways or in any materials used in such work, nor can he appoint subordinate officers who have such interests. The commissioner receives a salary of $7,500 annually and necessary traveling expenses.

For each county in the state the commissioner appoints a road supervisor and such assistants as are necessary. The supervisor and his assistants must be residents of the counties that they serve. Their duties and salaries are fixed by the commissioner.

The duties of the state road commissioner are manifold. First, he is obliged to supervise the construction and maintenance of all the primary and secondary roads of the state.[3] For the building and repairing of roads and bridges he signs the contracts as the legal agent of the State Road Commission and supervises its fiscal affairs. His further duties may be classified as follows:

1. Publishing information concerning the condition of roads.[4]
2. Administering the motor vehicle laws.
3. Issuing licenses for automobiles, trucks, and motorcycles.
4. Locating and relocating primary and secondary roads.
5. Supervising construction and maintenance of airports.
6. Discontinuing roads.
7. Constructing, repairing, and maintaining roads.
8. Adjusting damages caused by road construction.
9. Fixing standard widths for roads and bridges.
10. Testing materials used in road construction.
11. Acquiring and providing for the storage of road machinery.
12. Establishing road signs and markers.
13. Classifying and numbering roads.
14. Making an annual report of his work to the governor.

THE STATE ROAD FUND

The building and maintenance of roads has come to cost a vast sum of money, which must be raised by taxation levied by the legislature.

---

[3] At this writing (1950) there are 4,864 miles of primary and 28,323 miles of secondary roads in West Virginia.

[4] Each month a highly colored illustrated map of the roads is sent out free of charge from the office of the commissioner.

The road fund consists of the proceeds of all state license taxes imposed upon automobiles and other motor or steam driven vehicles; the registration fees levied on owners, operators, and dealers in automobiles; sums donated by the national government; bonds sold by the state for road purposes; appropriations made by the legislature; and fines collected for damages to the state roads. All this money is paid into the state treasury and credited to the state road fund. It amounts to several million dollars each year.

The State Military Forces

THE NATIONAL GUARD

The constitution declares the governor to be the commander-in-chief of the military forces of the state. It is his duty, therefore, to appoint and commission all officers of the military forces residing in West Virginia except those in the service of the United States. The organized militia is known as the national guard of West Virginia and may be called into active service at the summons of the President, being transferred by the governor from state to national duty. But the duty of training the national guard is left to the state, although the national government pays a large share of the expense. In personnel, arms, equipment, and training this agency of state and national defense rigidly adheres to federal laws issued by the Secretary of War.

The national guard consists of enlisted men and commissioned officers. The number of each is prescribed by federal law, and in time of imminent danger it may be increased by order of the national government. The officers of the staff, corps, and departments are appointed by the governor from soldiers who have had at least two years of military experience. The officers may retire at the age of sixty-four.

The uniforms of the soldiers are similar to those provided for the army of the United States. Necessary drill and target practice are ordered to keep the soldiers in at least a reasonably good condition. It is required by law that the guards shall be ordered to camp and participate in maneuvers five days or more annually. The duty of the governor is to order the national guard into active service when a riot, tumult, or other serious breach of the peace occurs.

THE ADJUTANT GENERAL

The chief commanding officer of the national guard, appointed by the governor, is the adjutant general, who holds the rank of brigadier in the national guard. His term of office is four years and his salary is $5,000 annually. With him are appointed six aides, whose rank may not exceed that of colonel. Besides being in chief command of drilling, he also has charge of the pay, quartermaster, and ordnance departments. He keeps a full record of the conduct of his office and annually makes a report to the governor.

MILITARY LAW

It is worth while to make a few observations concerning the regulations governing the army. Men enlisted in the ranks are under the rules of military law. This law applies to all persons in the military service of the state. When one enrolls in the national guard he takes an oath binding himself to perform certain duties relating to his work in the army and to refrain from disobedience to orders, disrespect to superior officers, mutiny, desertion, drunkenness, and any other act contrary to the military code. These regulations are styled military law and are designed to insure the maximum efficiency of the army.

To enforce the dictates of military law in West Virginia there are four special courts which have the same legal status as the civil courts of the state. These military courts consist of general courts-martial, special courts-martial, summary courts-martial, and courts of inquiry. The judges of these courts are appointed by the governor to try violations of military law. The United States government has published manuals of military law on which decisions in the courts are largely based.

MARTIAL LAW

The meanings of military law and martial law should not be confused. Military law has to do with life in the army during times of war and peace. It does not supplant the civil law. Martial law is invoked to repel invasion, quiet tumult, and subdue riot and breach of the peace. It is when the civil law fails to protect public safety that martial law, by order of the governor or the President, takes its place. The soldiers take over the duties of the civil officers and administer the government during the emergency.

Martial law is not a statutory law. It does not have prescribed rules; regulations are adopted by the officers in charge to take care of the situation demanding attention. These regulations must be rigidly obeyed, and the offenders must take the consequences, which are always severe. Sometimes this law is invoked to protect areas devastated by fire and flood, where it restores order out of confusion, protects homes from being looted, cares for the homeless and injured, and promotes orderly reconstruction. In instances of this kind the army takes charge of the situation and compels respect for authority until the civil officers can be safely restored to their former duties.

The Department of Public Safety

THE STATE POLICE

With the introduction of means of rapid transit, it became necessary to provide uniform rules for the protection of life and property on the highways. To enforce these rules the state police was created by an act of the legislature passed in 1919. The state police is under the direction of a superintendent who is appointed by the governor for a term of four years. The superintendent must not be less than thirty years of age or more than fifty-five. His present salary is $5,000 annually. The central office is kept in the capitol at Charleston.

The superintendent of the state police stands at the head of the Department of Public Safety. The department consists of four companies, A, B, C, and D, with headquarters established at Beckley, Charleston, Elkins, and Shinnston respectively. Detachment headquarters are located at seventeen other centrally situated places. Each company has a captain, a lieutenant, a first sergeant, sergeants, and corporals. The regular policemen are known as troopers. The number of troopers must not be less than thirty or more than fifty-five in any company. The total number of officers and troopers is about two hundred.

The members of the state police are supplied with uniforms, suitable equipment, and horses or other means of conveyance. In general their purpose is to preserve peace, protect property, prevent crime, and apprehend criminals, with jurisdiction extending throughout the state. But more particularly the duties of the state police may be summarized under the following headings:

1. Arresting anyone charged with violating a law of the state or the United States.
2. Serving criminal processes issued by any court or a justice of the peace. (They do not serve civil processes.)
3. Cooperating with local authorities in detecting crime and making arrests.

4. Serving in the capacity of forest patrolmen, game and fish wardens, and deputy prohibition officers.
5. Making complaint against and securing warrant for anyone violating the law.
6. Rendering assistance wherever called, under command issued by the governor or the sheriff. Of course the troopers are under the immediate command of their superintendent, who may order policemen to form an escort for a touring party, throw a protective guard around a wreck, direct traffic through crowds, or quell a riot.

THE BOARD OF PUBLIC SAFETY

In connection with this important work there is a Board of Public Safety, a bipartisan board consisting of two members appointed by the governor for a term of two years. Each member receives ten dollars a day for the time he actually spends in performing his official duties. The purpose of the board is to hear appeals from decisions of the superintendent of the department of public safety concerning charges brought against members of the constabulary. The board also hears evidence and renders decisions on charges brought against the superintendent or any of the inferior officers. These two board members, therefore, act in a large measure as a court.

The Public Health Department

As population increases and the density of cities becomes greater, there is always increased danger of contracting disease and spreading contagion. To combat this danger the state has established a Public Health Department with four divisions: (1) communicable disease; (2) sanitary engineering; (3) vital statistics; (4) child hygiene.

THE PUBLIC HEALTH COMMISSIONER

At the head of the department is a commission appointed for four years by the governor with the approval of the senate. The commissioner must be a physician and a graduate of a recognized medical college and must have had at least five years of medical practice. He appoints a director for each division of the department.

The duties of the commissioner are to administer the laws and rules relating to the department. He prepares regulations for the consideration of the health council and advises with this council. The state commissioner keeps in touch with the local health units maintained in the counties and cities and encourages their work. Under his supervision are kept the records of births and deaths in the state; he attends to curbing and blotting out epidemics; inspects the health conditions of public schools, theaters, auditoriums, etc.; inspects dairies, factories, hotels, and places of public gatherings. In his laboratories analyses are made of the water supply of towns and cities and of water from wells and springs. He oversees sewage disposal so that the public health is protected. He also promotes public health by encouraging the people to guard themselves against the invasions of preventable disease.

THE PUBLIC HEALTH COUNCIL

As a further protection to the health of the people there exists a Public Health Council consisting of the commissioner and six other members who are appointed by the governor for a term of four years. It is required by law that all the members of the council shall be graduates of medical colleges and shall have had at least five years of medical practice. This council maintains its office in the capitol, where it must hold at least two meetings annually.

The Public Health Council has to do with making rules and regulations for administering the work of the department. It advises with the commissioner, establishes qualifications for local health officers, and defines and amends public health regulations. A violation of the rules established by the health council constitutes a misdemeanor and is punishable by a fine and imprisonment.

HEALTH LABORATORIES

As a material aid in carrying out its duties the department of health has established laboratories. To these laboratories samples of water are sent for testing without expense. Other sources of disease are tested by analysis: for example, a scientific examination may be made of the head of a dog to determine whether he had hydrophobia. When a trouble spot is detected, preventive measures and remedies are prescribed. The health laboratories serve as a source of valuable information for the public, and they should be used when the need arises.

LOCAL HEALTH OFFICERS

To safeguard the public health it is not enough to have only a central department located at Charleston. On recommendation by the county court of any county in the state, the Public Health Council will appoint a legally qualified physician as the county health officer for a term of four years. In the same manner municipal health officers are appointed, but for terms of two years only. The salary of this local officer must not be less than $300 annually. In case a county does not have a health officer, the county court may employ a full-time public health nurse and provide for her payment. However, there is nothing to compel the county court to take this action.

The county health officer, the prosecuting attorney, and the president of the county court constitute the county board of health. Its jurisdiction extends throughout the county. The chief function of this board is to enforce the rules established by the state public health council.

It is the obligation of every practicing physician in the county or town to report any communicable or infectious disease discovered by him to the local health officer. Steps are immediately taken to eradicate the disease by treatment and quarantine or any other manner that prudence directs. The local health officer makes weekly reports to the state health department concerning the condition of the patients so afflicted. Places of detention may be established by the local health officer for the purpose of isolating people having infectious or communicable disease.

Vaccines and serums for curing and preventing disease are furnished by the state commissioner of health free of charge to the local health officer. Drugstores in the county may be used as depositories for these medicines if the local health officers so designate them.

THE DIVISION OF VITAL STATISTICS

In the division of vital statistics a registrar keeps a record of all births, deaths, and marriages in the state. Each incorporated town and each magisterial district constitutes a primary registration district for births and deaths, while each county is a designated district for marriage records. The state registrar appoints a registration officer for each district. The local health officer or any other officer may be designated to serve in this capacity.

THE INSPECTOR OF HOTELS

An inspector of hotels and restaurants is appointed by the governor. Rules are made by the Public Health Council to govern the sanitary condition of places of public lodging and eating. At least once annually the inspector makes a careful investigation of the kitchens, pantries, storage rooms, dining rooms, lunch counters, and all other places in which food is kept or prepared for public consumption. The inspector prohibits the use of any article that is not in a clean and sanitary condition, and the places where food is served must be clean and free from the danger of impairing the consumer's health. It comes within his range of duties to recommend changes in hotels and restaurants, and those in charge are required to comply with the orders.

All hotels and restaurants must be properly lighted, ventilated, and equipped with plumbing to safeguard health and provide at least reasonable comfort. A supply of pure water must be furnished to satisfy all necessities. Washrooms must be provided and towels supplied so that no two persons may use the same towel. The linens, after being used by one guest, are to be laundered before being used by another. Hotel rooms must be kept free of vermin. No person known to have an infectious or communicable disease may be employed in a hotel or restaurant.

Fire escapes and other necessary safeguards must be established.

PURE FOOD AND DRUGS

The law of West Virginia forbids the manufacture or sale of adulterated food or drugs in the state. If the local health officer has reason to doubt the genuineness or the purity of any article of food or any drug offered for sale he is empowered to enter the place where such article is kept and make an inspection of it. His jurisdiction in this case applies to stores, factories, creameries, drugstores, restaurants, hotels, laboratories, and any other places where he suspects that the law is being violated. If violations of the law are discovered, the goods are condemned and the owner becomes liable to prosecution.

It is the duty of the chief chemist in the state hygienic laboratory to make a scientific test of any foods or drugs sent to him. A careful record is made of the findings to the Department of Health and to the local health officer. Anyone found guilty of knowingly violating the law may be sentenced to prison for a period not exceeding one year or fined not more than $500, or both. Like any other good rule, the pure food and drug law is intended to protect the innocent and punish the guilty.

No person, firm, or corporation may sell or give away any poison unless the container is labeled with the emblem of the death's head and crossbones and the word "poison." The label shall also contain the name and the place of business of the seller and the name of one or more antidotes for the poison. The dispenser of poison must inform the purchaser as to its nature and the danger in its use. He must also be assured that it is to be used for a legitimate purpose. A careful record is kept of the name of the purchaser, the date of purchase, the quantity sold, and the purpose for which it was to be used.

It is unlawful for one to sell or dispense drugs without a license. Only persons properly trained may be licensed.

Again, for the protection of the healthy against the diseased, the common drinking cup and the common towel are forbidden. Anyone responsible for the contamination of a water supply is subject to severe punishment. Offensive matter may not be left near a roadside or on public grounds. The smoking of cigarettes in school buildings or school grounds while these places are being used for school purposes is forbidden by law.

THE STATE WATER COMMISSION

The State Water Commission is composed of the commissioner of health, the chairman of the Public Service Commission, and the chairman of the Game, Fish, and Forestry Commission, who serve without additional compensation. They elect one of their own number as chairman and choose a secretary who may or may not be a member of the commission.

The duties of the State Water Commission are to keep pure the water sources in the state, cause sources of pollution to be removed from rivers and creeks, and require the installation of water purifying plants. It is within the power of the commission to summon persons to testify why they caused the pollution of water courses. The method of the commission is to proceed upon inquiry before forming a decision.

The Department of Public Assistance

Because of the possibility of widespread public need growing out of an economic emergency the legislature in 1936 passed a public welfare law providing for administering general relief wherever necessary. The organization created under this law is known as the Department of Public Assistance. Its authority covers a wide range of interests. The department has to do with child welfare, with medical care of the indigent, and particularly with ill or crippled children. It was the certifying agency for the National Youth Administration and the Works Progress Administration and the selecting agency for the Civilian Conservation Corps. Through this legislation there is created a permanent system of public assistance in West Virginia.

To administer the law there is a bipartisan advisory board consisting of five members and a director, appointed by the governor. The director is paid an annual salary of $6,000; the members of the board receive ten dollars a day for the time actually occupied by official duties. The board, which is required by law to meet four times annually, serves as an advisory body to the director, and makes a careful study of needed legislation and of the administration of public assistance.

THE STATE DIRECTOR

The director maintains an office in the capitol, where he conducts his many and varied duties. He is the chief executive and the administrator of the department. In his office are made the rules and regulations pertaining to investigation and case supervision followed by the county organizations. With the approval of the state board, he forms agreements with the federal government on matters pertaining to public assistance in West Virginia. In addition to these duties he supervises the fiscal affairs of the department, makes reports, follows the directions of the state and federal law, keeps official records, exercises supervision over the county councils and directors, and creates boards of review to hear appeals from the county organizations.

THE COUNTY COUNCIL

Every county has a council for the local administration of public welfare. It is composed of five members, four of whom are appointed by the governor while the president of the county court serves as an ex-officio member. The term of the appointed members is three years, and they serve without compensation. A county director, who devotes all his time to his duties, is selected by the county board from a list of persons certified by the state board.

The county organization complies with instructions received from the state board and director, and performs all duties required by law. It has under its jurisdiction the administration of public welfare in the county. Its duty is to provide, from funds set apart for that purpose, protection for the indigent, aged, and blind, to care for dependent children whose situation conforms to conditions laid down in the federal social security law, and to rehabilitate adult persons who request and are qualified to receive public assistance or general relief.

WHO MAY RECEIVE PUBLIC ASSISTANCE

The law lays down certain conditions one must meet to qualify for public assistance; above all, it must be proved that the individual is in a state of actual need. The purpose of the law is to help those who cannot help themselves.

Persons in need of general relief may be classified as (1) those found by the county council to be public charges, or in danger of becoming public charges, (2) those needing physical or mental help, (3) those in need of medical or surgical care, (4) aged persons (sixty-five years or over) in need of food and shelter, and (5) dependent children.

Anyone in need of public assistance files an application with the county director, who investigates the case and submits his report with a recommendation to the county council. In turn the council reviews the case, and if it is approved the amount of help needed is specified and granted. The duty of the county council, after giving due deliberation to the matter, is to certify its findings to the state department, which may accept, modify, or reject the report. Persons in danger of becoming public charges may make application for general relief, care, or assistance to the county director, who reports the case to his county council. When necessity arises this help may include hospitalization and emergency aid. The matter is in the hands of the council for acceptance or rejection.

Separate units in the Department of Public Assistance are set apart for veterans' service, crippled children, child welfare, and medical service. These units are formed to facilitate administration and to take up the respective duties assigned to them.

The Public Service Commission

The Public Service Commission of West Virginia consists of three members appointed by the governor for terms of six years. The commission appoints a secretary and such other employees as are necessary to conduct the work on an efficient basis. Its office is maintained in the capitol at Charleston. Full and true records of all proceedings are kept by the secretaries. A seal is affixed to all papers issued by the commission. Since this organization is in charge of business for the state, the attorney general serves as its adviser on legal matters.

The function of the Public Service Commission is to supervise, in the interest of the people, the administration of the public utilities operated in the state, except vehicles operated on streets and roads. The supervision extends to all public utilities known as common carriers of passengers or goods, that is, railroads, street railroads, motor cars, ships, and airplanes. It has authority also over the transportation of oil, gas, and water by pipe line; the generation and transmission of messages by telephone, telegraph, and radio; the generation and transmission of electricity; and other utilities such as toll bridges, wharves, ferries, and the supply of water, gas, and electricity by a municipality.

The supervision of the Public Service Commission over utilities includes investigation of the conduct of their affairs relating to rates, charges, and tolls. If the fees are considered unjust, the commission may order them changed. In order to prevent undue discrimination or favoritism the commission may forbid or order changed practices, devices, or methods of service adopted by the utilities. If necessary it may compel obedience to its orders by a mandamus or an injunction. This commission has power to establish or change tariffs, rates, tolls, and schedules operated by utility companies. It keeps on file copies of rates, reports, classifications, schedules, and timetables used by the corporations transacting business in West Virginia. Its power extends to requiring them to establish and maintain adequate safety facilities for the convenience and protection of the public and the employees of the company. It prescribes systems of accounts, and requires the submission of reports covering the business transactions for each year.

The Public Service Commission hears complaints brought against the utilities. As a result of the evidence the rates may be lowered, they may be increased, or service may be altogether discontinued. If a railroad company desires to discontinue the use of a passenger train, it has to make formal application to the Public Service Commission for permission to do so. This commission has long since proved its worth as a fortress of protection to the interests of the people.

The Department of Banking

For the administration of the laws relating to banking, banking institutions, industrial loan companies, building and loan associations, and other legal corporations created to receive deposits and make loans, there is provided a Department of Banking. The superintendent of this department and his assistants make examinations of books, records, papers, and other evidence kept by banking institutions. The purpose of this inspection is to ascertain whether the corporation is observing all the laws relating to its particular business, and to cause the legal restrictions to be faithfully observed. But in the beginning an institution of this nature must file with the department a copy of its charter and by-laws showing that its business procedure complies with all legal requirements. Being satisfied of the legality of the proposed business, the commissioner issues a certificate permitting the organization to engage in business. It must be remembered, however, that the state commissioner does not have power of supervision over the banks organized under the laws of the United States.

The bank commissioner attends to seeing that these institutions follow just and equitable rules. Each year they are required to publish in a newspaper printed in the county in which they are located a statement setting forth their financial standing. Since so many people transact business in the banks the state has deemed it proper to exercise supervisory power over them, thus protecting the interests of the public.

The Director of Probation and Parole

In 1939 the legislature passed a law that authorizes a court of original jurisdiction of criminal action to place on probation any person convicted of crime if the sentence is less than life imprisonment. There is nothing in the law that compels the court to take such action, but if the character of the person convicted and the circumstances of the case satisfy the court that the punishment should be reduced, the judge can suspend the sentence and place the person on probation. It is also within the power of the court, in carrying out this procedure, to appoint a probation officer to whom the person paroled is responsible. Sometimes the sheriff of the county is appointed.

A regular officer known as the director of probation and parole is appointed by the governor for a term of four years. With the approval of the governor he has authority to release on parole any person eligible for that consideration. He must secure all available information in each case considered and form his own rules and regulations governing procedure. All persons sentenced under criminal charges come under his supervision. On various occasions the governor recommends to the director that he investigate applications for pardons, reprieves, and commutation. After the case has been thoroughly reviewed he makes a recommendation concerning it to the governor.

At present the director of probation has six assistants located in widely separated places in the state.

The Board of Control

MEMBERSHIP AND DUTIES

Preceding 1909 each institution maintained by the state had its own board which received a report from the head of the institution. This report was relayed to the governor or to some agency designated by him to receive it. Under this arrangement the institutions lacked a unified management. The legislature in 1909 created the Board of Control, a bipartisan group composed of three members. This board is appointed by the governor for a term of six years; members are eligible for reappointment. The present salary of each member is $6,000 annually. For the proper conduct of its affairs the members elect one of their number chairman and another treasurer-secretary. An office with the necessary clerical help is maintained in the capitol.

The duty of the Board of Control is to manage, control, and administer the business and financial affairs of the institutions owned and operated by the state. These institutions include the industrial schools, the sanitariums and hospitals, the penal institutions, and the schools of higher education. The plans for new buildings for these institutions and the supervision of their construction are under the administration of the Board of Control. This unification of management and administration under one responsible authority is to the advantage of the people who pay the bills.

The governor appoints a superintendent for each public hospital, sanitarium, home for children, and penal institution; the superintendent in turn selects the assistants needed to carry on the work of each institution. The salaries of all the officers are fixed by the board, which visits and inspects each of these centers when it is deemed prudent to do so.

In order to fulfill faithfully its legal obligations, the board purchases all supplies for the institutions under its charge. In its office is kept a complete financial account of the receipts and disbursements of each establishment. A complete itemized financial report of the same is made annually to the auditor of the state, and biennially a report of financial and other conditions is made to the governor. Thus the affairs of these institutions maintained by the public are open to public inspection.

PUBLIC PRINTING

The business of printing for the state is of far-reaching consequence. A superintendent of printing is appointed by the Board of Control. He asks for competitive bids and makes contracts for printing and binding. This material consists of blanks and forms for officials, of stationery, and of the decisions of the Supreme Court. But the legislature appoints a supervisor of printing who exercises oversight concerning the printing for both houses.

CENTRAL MAILING OFFICE

A central mailing office is maintained in the capitol for the convenience of the people employed there. It receives and distributes the incoming mail of the departments, bureaus, commissions, and other offices, and classifies and rates the outgoing mail before it leaves the capitol. This postal center is not rated as a post office, for it cannot issue money orders or receive postal savings.

The Department of Purchases

By an act passed by the legislature in 1935 a Department of Purchases was created for the purpose of limiting expenditures for commodities, for printing, and for contractual services for the state. The head of this department is a director who is appointed by the governor with the advice and consent of the senate and who remains in office during the will and pleasure of the governor. The office of the director is in the capitol. His present salary is $6000 annually, with traveling expenses incident to his official duties. He appoints his own assistants and other employees, of whom there are at present eighteen.

The director of purchases secures and contracts for the commodities needed by the various departments of the state governments. This includes negotiations for the purchase of grounds, buildings, offices, and other space needed to carry on public duties in Charleston. He also has charge of storerooms for supplies, sells the surplus, and keeps an inventory of all removable equipment belonging to the state. In order to maintain a high standard of efficiency the director establishes laboratories for the purpose of testing the qualities of commodities and prescribes methods of inspecting them.

With the approval of the governor the director may make purchases of commodities that are urgently needed or make contracts for their delivery. Further, it is within his power to authorize any department of the state government to purchase in the open market its supplies for immediate delivery. This regulation takes care of emergency cases when the work of an office could otherwise be delayed on account of a lack of supplies. Standards and classifications for buying goods are fixed by the director, and he requires sales-houses to deliver products that meet these specifications.

For the purpose of protecting the state the director requires each department to make a monthly report of the stock on hand. By enforcing this rule he avoids oversupplies or duplication of orders.

The Department of Archives and History

The Department of Archives and History is charged with the collection and permanent preservation of valuable papers, books, and documents relating to the settlement and development of this state. In the great collection that is kept in the capitol may be found rare books, records, and state papers – documents of the legislatures, the governors, and the courts, reports of boards and departments, and the like.

The head of the department, who is appointed by the governor, devises a system for recording, classifying, and preserving all the archives. He also keeps and protects the flags carried by the West Virginia regiments during the various wars. In connection with this department the West Virginia Historical and Antiquarian Society holds in trust documents, uniforms, guns, swords, and emblems pertaining to the history of this state. It has also set up a museum of history, science, industry, and social conditions with particular reference to the lives of our citizens.

The rooms of the library and the museum are kept open to the public. State and county officials and other persons may submit records, history, original papers, and official books to the department for protection and safekeeping. One may find in the Department of Archives a great depository of knowledge if he desires to seek it.

Other Agencies

The administrative agencies dealing with agriculture and conservation and those dealing with labor and compensation are treated in the next two chapters.

In addition, there are still other organizations in the state government that render valuable service and submit annual reports to the governor. Among these are the Geological Survey, the Commission for the Sale of Alcohol, the Negro Welfare Commission, the Sinking Fund Commission, and the Department of Buildings and Grounds. The duties of all are specified by law. All have potentialities for great service to the people, but their actual success and efficiency depends of course upon the genuine ability of the persons filling the offices.

CHAPTER 20

Agriculture and Conservation

Agriculture

INTRODUCTION

Although West Virginia has never been listed among the leading agricultural states, its farm resources have reached considerable proportions. From the earliest period of settlement until the present time the fertile soil, common in the valleys and the upland plains, has produced abundance for the people who have come here to live. The temperate climate and plenteous rainfall help to produce crops of choice quality as well as of wide variety. Another place can scarcely be found that surpasses, or even equals, the middle Allegheny region for the excellency of its agricultural products.

According to the most reliable sources of information, the Indians cultivated only a small portion of the soil of this state. Perhaps they grew corn in the Old Fields of the South Branch, along the Potomac, the Ohio, the Greenbrier, and the upper basins of the Kanawha and the Monongahela. The first settlers found open spaces in the forests that bore evidence of ancient primitive cultivation. When the white people crossed the mountains in greater numbers and began to dot the frontier with their log cabins, they turned to the soil to gain their daily bread. And the soil produced in plenty.

When the winter changed to spring in 1764 groups of surveyors camped at the mouth of the Little Kanawha, the Great Kanawha, and the Big Sandy and along the eastern shore of the Ohio. Carrying compass and chain, blazing trees to mark their courses, these runners of lines and makers of plats composed only the advance guard of the tide of emigration from the old East overflowing into the new West. They came on foot, or on packhorses, in the manner of the immigrants of their time, single file, with flocks and herds driven by day and corralled by night. The West had ample room to receive them.

As the population grew, regulatory laws drafted at Williamsburg and Richmond increased. First, trespass on farms and fields was forbidden. The fences made of new rails split by use of knotted maul and wooden wedge furnished warning enough to keep out. Land remained plentiful and cheap; when the fertility of one plot began to fail, another clearing opened a field of "new ground." By and by all the land suitable for cultivation came to be occupied and the pioneer period closed. Then successive seasons of cultivation eventually depleted the soil of its fertility, and the task of restoration was left to another generation learned in the science of agriculture.

FEDERAL ASSISTANCE

On July 2, 1862, Senator Benjamin F. Wade of Ohio succeeded in piloting through Congress his agricultural aid bill. President Lincoln promptly signed it.[1] By this measure the national government offered to set aside to the credit of the states 30,000 acres of its western lands for each of their representatives and senators in Congress. West Virginia came into the union with five members of Congress, two senators and three members of the House of Representatives. The people of the state were therefore entitled to 150,000 acres of land. The true purpose of the gift was to assist in establishing in every state, within five years, at least one agricultural, mechanical, and military college. The state of Virginia never supported an educational institution in the region west of the Alle-

[1] Senator Wade introduced this bill May 5, 1862, as Senate Bill No. 298. A measure embracing very similar principles had passed Congress two years previous to this time but had been vetoed by President Buchanan.

ghenies, so the new commonwealth did not delay in responding to the timely and generous offer.

West Virginia officially accepted the gift on October 3, 1863. On that day the legislature forwarded instructions to Governor Arthur I. Boreman to certify its decision to President Lincoln and his Secretary of the Interior. In due time West Virginia received its quota of land-script convertible into United States securities as an endowment for the establishment of the new school.

While a site for the new institution was under consideration the board of trustees of Monongalia Academy offered to the state (1866) their buildings, lands, and funds, including the property of Woodburn Seminary, on condition that the agricultural college should be located at Morgantown.[2] The official title of the new school was to be the Agricultural College of West Virginia. The offer was promptly accepted. In 1868, however, the legislature changed the name of the school to West Virginia University, which was to include a Department of Agriculture. Here began the study of scientific agriculture in West Virginia. For many years this new field of study had a struggle for existence, and it was not until after the turn of the century that the people of West Virginia became fully aware of the help to be gained from the school they so sorely needed. Although the state was young its statesmen had wisdom.[3]

THE DEPARTMENT OF AGRICULTURE

West Virginia was comparatively late in making agriculture one of its chief administrative branches of government. By special enactment the legislature in 1911 created the Department of Agriculture with headquarters at Charleston. Since that time much effort at public expense has been devoted to the promotion of interest in farming, gardening, and orcharding. The purpose of the department is to apply discovery and invention to the growing of crops and the breeding of domestic animals. Since 1900 interest in agriculture has had an amazing expansion in the state. That man may gain his living from the soil is a fact too important to be neglected in a state whose population is growing rapidly from year to year.

---

[2] The value of the property was estimated at $150,000.

[3] To encourage the people to give more attention to agriculture the legislature in 1863 declared, "Agricultural products grown directly from the soil, and the products and the increase in number of live stock produced within this state during the year preceding the first day of April, and remaining unsold on that day in the possession of the original owner or his agent" are not taxable. *Code of West Virginia*, 1870, p. 162.

For the purpose of administering the new department in the government there was created the office of commissioner of agriculture, which is now one of the main state executive offices. The office is filled by popular election for a term of four years at the same time and in the same manner as the other offices of the state. The law stipulates that the commissioner shall be a practical farmer, learned in the science of agriculture, and shall have made agricultural pursuits his chief occupation at least ten years preceding his election. The legislature decided that the office was too important to be undertaken by a novice.

The law wisely allowed the commissioner ample power to organize his department in the manner he deemed best. From a humble beginning the office has gradually developed into a complex administrative unit. Many duties have been added while few have been taken away. The commissioner appoints his assistants, agents, clerks, stenographers, botanists, pomologists, entomologists, and as many other helpers as he thinks are needed in this branch of government.

To increase efficiency the many duties of the office are classified, and each special field of work is assigned to a division. A director is placed at the head of each division. His assistants are chosen for their expert knowledge of the work placed in their care. For example, the division of administration possesses supervisory power over the general conduct of the whole department, and specifically attends to simplifying and coordinating the official duties of the employees. Here policies for the organization are fixed and put into practice.

The division of plant disease and control is of primary importance. So many crops are annually destroyed or injured by diseases and pests that the threat of greater loss cannot escape attention. Scientists give devoted care to these important matters, and in their laboratories remedies have been formulated that control or entirely eradicate the manifold dangers to both animal and vegetable life. Diseases affecting shrubs and trees come under the observation of the specialist. Sometimes these diseases and their remedies are not easy to ascertain. If necessary, the commissioner may issue orders for quarantine in order to stay the spread of contagion. Even that drastic measure does not always provide relief. The application of all known remedies failed to check the spread of the dreaded chestnut blight until it had completed its devastation. But the faithful application of sprays, dusts, and other preventives from the scientist's laboratories holds most destructive agents at least in check.

Perhaps even greater attention is paid to the safety of domestic animals and poultry. The discovery of the nature of disease and of the means of its cure has gone a long way toward the protection of the stockmen. Vaccines for cattle, hogs, and horses have proved to be of extreme value; there is no longer any need for fear of the death-dealing cholera if the proper preventive measures are exercised. So the scientist, armed with his test tube, carries the battle to the maladies that take from people their sources of food and clothing.

Again, quarantine may be applied to protect animals and poultry. There are two kinds of quarantine, general and special, both of which are administered by the commissioner of agriculture. The general quarantine covers towns, counties, or larger areas, while the special applies only to a farm, a building, coop, car, or field. Both efforts have the same purpose, to restrict the spread of disease.

The department also renders valuable service by gathering and testing seeds and fertilizers and by making the purity and effectiveness of both a matter of public information. Any person in the state may forward a sample of soil, seed, or plant food to the Agricultural Experiment Station at Morgantown, where a scientific analysis is made and a statement of the results returned to the interested person. The value to farmers of this beneficial service can scarcely be exaggerated, and from year to year more people profit from it.

The Department of Agriculture serves as a center from which information is distributed to the citizens of the state. Matter of interest to farmers, gardeners, and stockmen reaches them in printed form. The dissemination of this information affords the public an opportunity to profit by the accumulation of knowledge derived from investigation and other sources. For those who will read it this continuous flow of informative literature affords a source of knowledge not only concerning the matters already mentioned but also of the resources of counties, the kinds of soil, the location of minerals, and the adaptability of the various regions of the state to the production of vegetables, cereals, and domestic animals. The printing press is therefore one of the farmer's most helpful implements.

Thus far the duties of the Department of Agriculture have been explained as defensive or preventive. On the other hand, however, it possesses offensive or creative responsibilities. It has power to promote as well as to hinder, and in this realm of activity the department works through clubs and societies which have as their objective the growing of better crops and the raising of improved types of animals. In these efforts the United States Department of Agriculture cooperates with the state through the grading of farm products at collecting centers and shipping points. National agents also bring to the farmers the most modern methods of soil cultivation, harvesting, and the construction of buildings. This work is carried on at national expense.

THE AGRICULTURAL ADVISORY BOARD

To increase the efficiency of the agricultural program the legislature in 1923 created an advisory board composed of the governor, the commissioner of agriculture, and the director of the agricultural extension division of West Virginia University. Meetings are held quarterly at Charleston. The board conducts a survey of food production in the state and makes a study of the food-producing agencies. These data are accumulated in answer to requests sent out from the main office at Charleston.

After giving its attention to the summary reports received at the central office, the board may order an adjustment in the personnel of the Department of Agriculture. Such adjustment is designed to prevent overlapping or duplication or any interference in the commissioner's administration of his office. In short, the aim of the board is to secure competence and economy in this branch of our state government, a worthy aim which other officers can well afford to follow.

MARKETING

It is incumbent on the commissioner of agriculture to supervise the marketing of food in West Virginia. In the conduct of this duty he has the cooperation of the federal Department of Agriculture. Costs and sales prices of foods are ascertained. The organization of farm cooperatives and the establishment of assembling, grading, and storage plants have expert supervision. It is also one of the duties of this official to issue regulations governing the grading, packing, branding, and storing of food products and, if necessary, to enforce these regulations through the courts of the state. Because of the extensive activities of the fruit growers in the Eastern Panhandle this law chiefly applies to the packing and storage business in that region.

If he deems it advantageous to the public interest, the commissioner may establish auction markets for the disposition of foods and domestic animals. But in no way does this arrangement conflict with the establishment of markets by private interests. A public officer only intercedes in times of emergency or to dispose of products and choice animals raised on the farms owned by the state, such as those connected with the State University.

THE COLLEGE OF AGRICULTURE

Reference has previously been made to the establishment of the College of Agriculture, whose chief interest is to accumulate and impart knowledge in this special field. In this institution students pursue courses for the purpose of gaining knowledge to become successful farmers, stockmen, or teachers. As a part of the program of instruction experiments are conducted to discover ways and means for growing better fruit, vegetables, and flowers, and determine the quality of soils, the types of domestic animals, and their adaptability to conditions in West Virginia. The individuals who pursue these courses of study, which are carefully planned and classified, have access to the most recent and reliable knowledge with respect to successful farming. This information is gained both from experimentation at home and from other institutions which are interested in the same kind of work.

The leaders in the College of Agriculture design courses that cover both general and technical fields of study. Upon the completion of a course of specialized studies the individual is expected to be a capable farmer, entomologist, or dairyman or to have competence in some other branch of professional study. He should be able not only to carry on well in his own department but also to continue research leading to new discoveries. The people pay a goodly amount for maintaining the College of Agriculture and in return for these expenditures have a right to demand skilled knowledge and efficient services. As a result of these studies and researches standards inevitably improve.

THE AGRICULTURAL EXTENSION PROGRAM

The agricultural extension program is a division of the College of Agriculture of West Virginia University. The work committed to this division has a far-reaching effect on the industrial, social, and religious life of the people of the state. The primary object is to improve farming and home building. The program reaches its fulfillment through the organization and direction of clubs and associations which devote their interest to the study of methods of preparing and serving food, of maintaining cleanliness and beauty of the home, of raising and selling stock, and of planting, harvesting, and marketing of crops. These agencies reach people in all the rural regions and bring them into direct contact with the most modern methods and devices for making living more pleasing and convenient. Rural homes today have the advantages derived from the use of electricity, which is now being conveyed to the most remote sections, and are aided by modern appliances that relieve people from menial drudgery. This equipment applies to lighting, cooking, washing, refrigeration, heating, and work in the shop and in the field. To bring about these improvements private corporations cooperate with the state and nation.

But the extension program does not stop here. It brings to farmers a knowledge of how to grow and select better seed, of the uses of the proper kinds of fertilizers, of the rotation of crops, of methods of drainage of the soil, and of a thousand other things that improve the ways of rural life. The maintenance of a higher standard of human health should also be listed among the objectives of the extension program.

People cannot thrive unless they are happy. In addition to promoting physical conveniences, the agricultural extension program presents information that has to do with national and international affairs. This work breaks the narrow bounds within which so many people seem destined to live, and widens the horizon of their lives. The newspaper, the radio, and the moving pictures have added new luster to life, and, above all, the gasoline engine and hard-surfaced highways have permanently welded together rural and urban life in America. The use of the airplane only makes this association more complete.

So the constant interchange of travel from main street to main road makes neighbors of all our people. Yet the work for better living conditions goes on. The 4-H Clubs, the county farm agents, the home demonstration agents, the administration of social and civic centers, such as the one at Jackson's Mill, contribute to the success of the agricultural extension service, which has supervisory power over all these units.

If such a widely diversified program is to function well, it must be supported by a strong organization. In the administrative role the director assumes the leadership. From his office on the campus of West Virginia University instructions emanate to the various branches, such as the home demonstration agents, soil conservationists, club leaders, county agricultural agents, and many others. Each of these agencies serves as a nerve center from which effort radiates to make life happier. If people of other lands possessed vision and comprehension to follow this example, the distress in the world would be greatly relieved.

In free people there is an abiding power that impels them to go forward toward greater achievement, and their reward is found in a sense of greater happiness in the realizing of a worthy objective. So the agricultural extension program has set in motion an unfolding change in our civilization that tends toward a better way of life. It means better homes and churches, wider knowledge, and a more enlightened people.

A work so extensive has to have considerable financial support. All the money used directly or indirectly to maintain this program is derived from taxation, both national and state. Persons who think all these services are rendered without cost are greatly mistaken. Farmers and stockmen pay taxes like other businessmen. They pay taxes on their income, on their food, clothing, houses, and land, their medicine and their insurance. All services rendered to citizens are paid for by the citizens, and paid in proportion to the amount they receive and the quantity they produce.

Conservation

INTRODUCTION

From the time of the clearing of the first fields in western Virginia until within very recent years the decimation of forests, the pollution of streams, and the destruction of game went on at a rate that has brought no honor to those who wrought or permitted it. Only within the memory of the present generation have these gross mistakes been acknowledged and efforts set on foot to correct them. Practically all the virgin forests, protective home of bird and beast and defensive cover for the courses of streams, fell before the onslaught of rapacious lumbermen whose greed exceeded their judgment. The screen was torn from the earth and all life that had used the forests as a place of refuge was left exposed and doomed to perish. Even the streams of pure water, bereft of shade, gave up the life they had nourished so long. Raging forest fires in many places bared the soil down to the water's edge. Consequently, wildlife soon reached the verge of extermination.

Indeed, as far as West Virginia was concerned, certain species of birds and animals did not survive. The passenger pigeons, numbering millions in flight, which literally swarmed over the Allegheny Mountains at twilight to perch among the black forests of hemlock, spruce, and pine carpeting the Canaan Valley, ceased to exist when their places of refuge were torn down.[4] It is reliably recorded that hunters pursued and brought down the last wild elk in this state about 1843. This was also in the Canaan Valley. The American bison, beaver, otter, and deer almost reached the point of extinction before the period of restoration began. The restoration has been brought about only within recent years and by a people who recognize the glaring mistake of their predecessors.

THE FIRST CONSERVATION LAWS

It is to the everlasting credit of Governor W. E. Stevenson (1869–1871) that he recognized the evil and made an attempt to abate it. Upon his suggestion the legislature in 1869 passed a law which made it a violation to kill certain kinds of insectivorous birds and limited the open season on ruffed grouse, wild ducks, partridges, and rabbits.[5] The chief significance of this law is that it denoted the new trend of the legislative authorities toward protection. Surely popular sentiment supported them. In this same year a limitation was placed on fishing in Big Fishing Creek, Wetzel County.

Though the law was a move in the right direction, it was very limited in its application, and progress was painfully slow at first. But in 1875 the legislature strengthened the statute by extending the closed season and forbidding the destruction of the nests and eggs of all the birds placed on the protected list. It is reliably stated that this was the first law of its kind enacted in the United States. From that time down to the present, the lawmakers have given some attention to protective regulations over birds and animals. But until re-

---

[4] As late as the 1880's hunters living in the Upper Cheat basin resorted at night to the deep forests of Canaan for the purpose of killing pigeons. Under the cover of darkness, whose density was increased by the shadows of the giant evergreens, the birds were beaten and shot from the bending boughs where they sat in great coveys. Then, their way lighted with flaming torches of pitch, the marauders filled bags with the fallen birds and made off home to feast on their ill-gotten game.

[5] "It shall be unlawful for any person to kill or destroy pheasants, wild ducks, partridges, or rabbits at any time between the fourteenth day of February, and the fifteenth day of September, or to kill or destroy any other birds except crows, ravens, eagles, hawks, owls, jaybirds, woodpeckers, and blackbirds, or to hunt or catch rabbits with ferrets or snares, at any season of the year." *Acts of the Legislature of West Virginia*, 1869, p. 58.

cently they paid entirely too little heed to the saving of forests and streams. Apparently they did not know that one branch of the program was immutably joined to the other, and that the shelter and the sheltered survived or perished together.

THE COMMISSION OF FISHERIES

During that dark age man proved himself to be an unworthy custodian of his natural bounty. The brooks, once cooled by the shade of pine and rhododendron, gradually gave up their numerous trout. The mountain streams became increasingly used as channels for floating logs to the booms and mills. Mills for grinding grain barricaded the flow of the streams in every county in West Virginia. All this change served to impede the migration of the fish up and down the waterways. As industry increased, wildlife decreased in proportion.

This condition became so threatening that in 1877 the legislature created the Commission of Fisheries, composed of "three discreet and proper persons, one from each of the congressional districts of the state," appointed by the governor for a term of four years. Their duties were to establish hatcheries and pools for the propagation of fish, build fish ladders, remove obstructions in creeks and rivers, and stock designated streams. Only three thousand dollars was appropriated to administer the new program, a sum entirely inadequate for carrying out the provisions of this law. It appears that the governor and the legislature had no full conception of the magnitude of their undertaking. Moreover, the education of officials and public that was necessary to promote the undertaking was lacking. Officers failed to intercede effectively to prevent netting, trapping, and the dynamiting of streams. The general public remained too negligent of what was actually going on to rally effectively to the support of a policy of conservation and protection. All the while a second wilderness of denuded cliffs, eroded slopes and dried up water courses was rapidly taking the place of the forest wilderness through which the pioneers had made their painful way.

THE STATE GAME AND FISH WARDEN

In 1897 the legislature turned its attention once more to a constructive policy, and created the office of State Game and Fish Warden. But again the rule of too little and too late was sadly evident. At this time the country was in the midst of an upswing in industry, and West Virginia added to these activities by building railroads, mining coal, and manufacturing lumber. The forests fell fast.

The mode of compensating the warden greatly weakened his administration. He could receive an income only from the fines resulting from convictions for violating the game laws, and this amount could not exceed twelve hundred dollars with an additional twenty percent of the total sum accrued from the convictions. No part of the salary could be paid out of the treasury of the state. Certainly no need existed for such a penurious policy. There was every reason for a wider program and more definite principles of conservation of our natural resources. The lumber corporations then established in the state could have financed without difficulty a constructive program that would have stood as a monument to their memory for many years.

The law assigned new duties to the warden. Already he had too many responsibilities, more than should have been delegated to one officer, but he had no assistants or subordinates in office. The whole state was his realm to protect. Especially during the hunting and fishing seasons his labors were overwhelming. Consequently devastation continued without halt or hindrance. The cutting and burning of the forests went on, for he had no authority to check it.

It was not until 1901 that the warden gained the authority to appoint deputies, thus greatly strengthening the arm of protection. From this time on he could select as aides any persons he deemed capable, including sheriffs, deputy sheriffs, and assessors. But again the compensation of all the subordinates had to come from convictions for the violation of the game laws; moreover, no effort whatsoever was made by the legislature to limit the slashing of the forests. The warden and his deputies could no more rescue animals from perishing without the shelter of the forests than they could command the fish to survive while the exposed mountain streams dried in their courses. So the conditions developed into a paradox; laws were being made to protect while all the protected were being destroyed.

THE REFORM LAW OF 1909

Belatedly the legislature in 1909 awoke to the fact that the virgin forests might soon be completely depleted. It was like coming to the rescue of a besieged city after the enemy had taken possession of the walls, and wrecking crews, assisted by raging fires, were laying waste the buildings. In that very year the giant evergreens and hardwood trees of the Allegheny Mountains crashed day by day before the resounding ax and rasping saw drawn and redrawn by the brawny arms of the woodsmen. It was high time for the legislature to intercede.

The revised law of 1909 contained some laudable provisions. The statute continued the chief warden but gave him two deputies instead of one, and as many protectors in the several counties as he considered it wise to appoint. In addition, the regulation set forth that sheriffs, deputy sheriffs, and constables "shall be deputy wardens ex-officio in their respective counties." The chief of police of each municipality was also given the duty of protecting game.

A change was made in the duties of the chief warden. Henceforth his staff would make a collection of data relative to the annual destruction of forests and the extent of the virgin stands of timber. This information he would disseminate throughout the state for the enlightenment of the people. It also became incumbent upon the deputies in all the counties and towns to collect data and submit their reports to the central office at Charleston. Thus a much-needed campaign began to inform the public.

The law of 1909 placed greater restrictions on the hunter. Game taken in West Virginia could no longer be made an article of commerce; it could be sold neither within nor without the borders of the state. This regulation did not include the pelts of fur-bearing animals. Previous to this time hunting had been conducted on a somewhat commercial basis during the open season, and regular shipments had been made to the eastern markets. This was one of the main reasons why the point of complete extermination approached so soon.

The reform law of 1909 provided that every hunter must obtain a license, except owners of land when hunting on their own premises. For the first time the privilege of hunting was subject to a tax, which would assure an income for the development of a more complete program. The new law shortened the season for hunting, forbade the chasing of deer by dogs, required that bag limits be observed, banned hunting on Sunday, and abolished the profligate use of the plumage and bodies of birds for decorative purposes.

For the first time the forests were to have some protective attention. Under the new law, game wardens assumed the responsibility of fire marshals and were given authority to carry out an aggressive policy. They could deputize persons to help to confine and extinguish forest fires, hire volunteers, and summon residents living in the near-by region to assist in preventing fire hazards. Hereafter persons intentionally or carelessly setting fires made themselves liable to fine or imprisonment. He who willfully spread forest disaster had now become an offender against the state and his deeds recognized as criminal. At last justice was catching up with inequity. Railroad companies came under the same law as individuals. They were required to provide adequate protection against the spread of fire.

But the new law failed to fulfill the current needs. During those very years (1909–1921) the evergreens bordering Blackwater Falls disappeared, the region about the Sinks in Randolph County took on the appearance of desolation, and the whole Allegheny Plateau exchanged its coat of green for a desert gray.

THE REFORM LAW OF 1921

As time went on the need for a more positive policy widened. The legislature attempted in 1921 to bring about certain reforms. A commission composed of three members replaced the warden. The commission, appointed by the governor, named a chief warden and as many lieutenants as it deemed adequate to maintain safety. The new law gave this administrative body the power to create and establish reservations and refuges for animals and birds. At last the lawmakers were coming to see that they had on hand a real problem of conservation and were taking steps to meet it squarely.

By good fortune Mr. A. B. Brooks of French Creek, Upshur County, received the appointment to the office of chief game protector. This was a wise selection, for the new official was altogether competent to do the important work he was about to begin. He was well educated, highly intelligent, and deeply imbued with the principle of man's cooperation with the forces of nature to the end of protecting and improving the condition of forest, field, plants, birds, and wild animals in West Virginia. The wide understanding possessed by Mr. Brooks soon found an expression in his work.

To limit the destruction of the forests he built observation towers on the mountain tops, installed telephones in them, and manned them with experienced watchmen. With the aid of field glasses from these elevated positions the watchmen brought miles of the surrounding region under their observation. In this manner fires were detected at the starting point and aid was summoned so that they could be promptly extinguished. It is safe to state that during the five years following 1921 more was accomplished toward forest conservation than during the preceding fifty years.

But this was only the beginning of a progressive program. The warden set apart lands to be kept free from encroachment, lands which now have been developed into Watoga State Park. He established fish hatcheries and attended to a more faithful execution of the game laws. To extend his program he purchased a farm at French Creek and equipped it for the propagation of birds and animals.[6] The plan inaugurated by Mr. Brooks worked so well that more land was conserved, other parks were set apart, and laboratories for propagation were established in various sections of the state.[7]

The stage was now set for better things. The legislature in 1929 made a number of revisions in the law and changed the title of the governing body to the Game, Fish and Forestry Commission. This official designation was changed in 1933 to the Conservation Commission of West Virginia. No change in title has been made since that time.

The development of conservation in West Virginia has been slow, very imperfect, and at times discouraging. But one who thoughtfully traces the movement down through the years will be impressed with the gradual development of a greater and better program which keeps in step with the growth of other public enterprises and institutions. Such is the way of progress made by a people who are free to work out their own destiny in their own way – slow but ever moving forward toward the ideal of a happier life. The old soon becomes obsolete and falls away; the new today needs amending tomorrow. Through the whole succession of events is manifest the gradual achievement of progress.

PRESENT POLICY

The most recent law (1933) stipulates that an executive director of conservation shall be appointed by the governor. To cooperate with him there exists a bipartisan Conservation Commission, named by the governor, consisting of seven members, one from each con-

---

[6] "The Commissioner shall investigate the waters of the Gauley, Williams, Greenbrier, Elk, Cheat, Tygarts Valley, New, Bluestone, Coal and Gyandotte and report to the Governor what lands thereon are suitable for the purpose of a state park and game preserve." *Acts of the Legislature of West Virginia*, 1921, p. 432.

[7] In 1927 the State Forest and Park Commission was created. It consists of the governor, the commissioner of agriculture, the director of agricultural extension, the state geologist, and the executive director of the Conservation Commission. The duty of the commission is to determine the availability of state forests and parks. *Acts of the Legislature of West Virginia*, 1927, chap. 4.

gressional district and one at large. An executive secretary attends to current matters and is held responsible for the distribution of printed materials from the central office at Charleston. The commission advises with the director on policies and administration. Four regular meetings are held annually, and special sessions may be called at the behest of the director. The director is on a full annual salary but the commissioners serve without pay. The state defrays all traveling expenses.

In order to render the best service to the most people the commission has subdivided its duties into six units of administration, namely, education and publicity, law enforcement, fish management, forestry, game management, and state parks. Each division has assigned to it an important part in the conservation program. Although the duties have grown complex, administration is simplified by placing competent persons scientifically trained in charge of special fields of work. The task of balancing the development of the use of forests and streams and the lives of all the creatures that dwell in them with the manifold needs of man — economic, spiritual, and ethical — requires the work of the best intellect available.

The commission issues a monthly magazine, *West Virginia Conservation*, which brings to the public a knowledge of its work in general and in detail. This publication is an educational force which places before the people the needs for conservation and the best methods of attaining it. Through this medium of information is solicited the public cooperation which is essential. The main office also sends out a news letter which disseminates information to many people. It relates matters of recent interest, happenings on the range, interpretations of the law, notifications of the open and closed seasons, accounts of unusual events, etc.

Game wardens, appointed by the director, are located in every county, clothed with legal authority and the support of public sentiment to enforce the law. This manner of administration brings the activities of the commission near to the people and makes it a part of their daily interests. Each warden serves as an ambassador from the state house to the people and works jointly with every other interested person for the common weal. As long as the program gains public favor there will be a lessening need for the enforcement of legal restrictions, but while West Virginia increases its area of reservations careful protection will continue to be in order.

Under the direction of the division of fish and game management some streams and forests are closed throughout the year, and hunters and fishermen cannot acquire a license to enter them. Sometimes the period of closing lasts from one to five years, during which time the restoration of wildlife is promoted. From farm and hatchery new stock is transported to the woods and streams, where it is given adequate protection.

At present the state maintains four fish hatcheries, two for trout and two for bass. By this means of propagation these native species are being returned to the streams in which the pioneer settlers originally found them. The hatcheries supply thousands of fish annually to places suitable to receive them. The drainage from coal mines makes many of the streams unfit for animal life; this limits the number of water courses available for restocking. The number of polluted streams has increased during the last few years and will continue to do so as long as coal mining develops unless some way is found to purify the drainage. In parts of the state where coal mining does not exist the water courses are largely unpolluted and restocking is conducted with a large degree of success.

Under the direction of the division of game management six refuges are now in use. By means of these fully protected areas and the enforcement of the laws, several animals once extinct (or nearly so) have been restored to their native haunts and thrive there without unnecessary molestation. Among these are the deer, beaver, otter, and snowshoe rabbit. Each of the reserves is located at a place where the most favorable conditions exist for animals and birds to thrive. Here game multiplies and its predators are reduced in numbers. The establishment of reservations has proved to be one of the most successful means of perpetuating wildlife.

STATE PARKS AND FORESTS

Fifteen state parks, comprising about 35,000 acres of land, are now in use. Wild rugged scenery makes these parks places of grandeur and beauty. Areas of green are slowly taking form again and widening on the summits and slopes of the mountains. Many years will pass before their borders join to hide the bold exposure of the gray rocks and ledges. Sometimes it takes ages for the wisdom of nature to restore what the ignorance of man destroys in a few years. In some of the parks cabins, courts, and pools to be occupied during rest and recreation periods have been constructed at public expense. People are slowly learning that there is a certain solace to be found in the forests and mountains far away from the tumult and traffic so prevalent in the cities and along the arteries of commerce.

Eight state forests have now been acquired. They include approximately 60,000 acres. The strictest care is observed in preventing fire or other damage in these areas used not only for the natural growth of trees but as a place to replant some of the most valuable types of timber, such as chestnut and walnut.

The state nursery located at Lesage, in Cabell County, encourages the planting and growing of trees. From it seeds and plants are distributed to all parts of the state at a nominal cost. This work is largely promoted through clubs and individuals who manifest an interest in the objectives of the forestry program, not the least of which is educational. This nursery is a state institution, maintained at state expense, and conducted under the direction of experts trained in the science of forestry.

NATIONAL PARKS

It has pleased our federal government to establish in West Virginia the Monongahela National Forest and to extend the George Washington National Forest within the borders of the state. The Monongahela Forest occupies a section of the Allegheny region extending north from the central part of Greenbrier County to the Potomac River and including the major portions of five counties and lesser parts of several others. The George Washington Forest skirts the eastern border of the state, occupying parts of Pendleton, Hardy, and Hampshire counties. To prevent forest fires, towers stand at the most convenient places on the mountain crests, from which rangers keep vigilant watch. Roadways have been built to the most inaccessible places so that firemen may reach any part of the forest before a conflagration can gain destructive proportions. This precaution remains necessary although the careless starting of fire has become a criminal offense.

Watchfulness reduces destruction while nature restores. A great deal is done by the scientist to promote the growth of plants and trees. At the national nursery located at Parsons thousands of seedlings are grown annually and at the proper time planted in the highlands, where their growth comes under the protection of rangers. As a consequence of this work some of the denuded mountains are again slowly taking on a coat of green.

The same favorable results are attending the effort to restore wildlife. Two federal fish hatcheries are established in this state, one at White Sulphur Springs and the other at Leetown. The hatcheries serve not only West Virginia but other sections of the nation as well.

In this work we now have a unity of federal and state interest whose disposition is to preserve, protect, and develop with the help of public sentiment.

THE FORESTRY AMENDMENT

In 1946 a forestry amendment to the state constitution was ratified by the electorate. It is the result of an agitation for the reestablishment of our stock of timber. Reaction to the destructive process, carried on for two score years, set in with rather positive demands which now have found expression in the law recently enacted.

According to the provisions of the amendment a real estate owner may enter into a contract with the state to set aside a certain boundary of his land for the planting and harvesting of trees. During the time it takes the timber to mature, the land on which it grows is untaxed or taxed at a reduced rate. When the timber is sold, a certain percentage of the proceeds is paid to the state as a tax. The forming of such contracts is not compulsory but is left to the disposition of the owner of the real estate. Both large and small boundaries of land that cannot be utilized for any other purpose may now be used for growing timber without carrying a burden of taxation. Reforestation, soil conservation, and a greater supply of pure water may be realized through the wise administration of the forestry amendment.

CHAPTER 21

Labor and Compensation

The Department of Labor

In 1889 the legislature created the state Bureau of Labor, renamed in 1915 the Department of Labor. A commissioner administers the rules, regulations, and laws of this department. The commissioner, who is traditionally a person identified with the labor interests of the state, is appointed for a term of four years by the governor, subject to approval by the senate. He is responsible for selecting his clerks, stenographers, and assistants. Financially the department is supported by appropriations made by the legislature.

The neglect attending the general welfare of the laborer gave rise to the passage of the law creating the bureau; consequently the commissioner is given wide political powers. He may enter and inspect public institutions and any factory, workshop, or other place where labor is employed. This inspection has as its purpose the discovery of conditions that may threaten or endanger the health and safety of workmen. He is under legal compulsion to visit annually and inspect properly the factories and workshops of the state. He also sends blank forms to factory owners with the request that all questions be properly answered. Persons failing to comply with his recommendations are reported to the prosecuting attorney of the county in which the industry or condition is located, and he proceeds against the accused as in any other case of misdemeanor.

Annually the commissioner makes a report to the governor. This report embodies much statistical detail relating to the industrial interests located in the state. Particular attention is devoted to the financial, social, educational, and sanitary conditions common among the employees. Unsafe conditions and unjust impositions, from whatever source, never have been allowed, but only the right relations of man to man will avoid strife. In order to bring about greater industrial safety the commissioner makes recommendations for legislative action. By this means safe conditions may be required instead of being merely requested. Upon his request, county, district, and town officers assist the commissioner in accumulating the data for his annual report.

STATE EMPLOYMENT AGENCIES

In connection with his department the commissioner of labor maintains a state public employment agency. This agency seeks to find employment for idle workmen and to supply laborers to factories needing them. The federal government may cooperate with the department in order to promote employment. In carrying out his work the commissioner keeps in touch with various industries for the purpose of supplying all the manpower they need. No fees are charged for these services.

The law permits the establishment of private employment agencies, which charge fees for their services, but the commissioner of labor prescribes the regulations governing such agencies. Private agencies furnish information to employers enabling them to secure the services of workmen. It is strictly forbidden by law for any agency, public or private, to misrepresent the conditions surrounding employment or offer its services without an order from the employer.

To qualify as an employment agency the interested parties have to secure a license from the state tax commissioner and pay an annual license fee. The application for this privilege may be granted only to citizens of the United States and may be denied or revoked for just and legal cause. The employment agencies must keep a record of the names of all persons who appeal to them and the kind of work to which they are assigned. All this detail is reported monthly to the general office of the state commissioner, who may make an official inspection of the records kept by private agencies. Children of school age may not be employed in violation of the compulsory attendance law.

SAFETY AND WELFARE

There was a time in the history of industry when no great attention was given to the safety and welfare of workmen. That time has now passed, and the betterment of human conditions has become a matter of first consideration. Places where labor is employed, such as factories, mills, and workshops, have frequent inspections as a safeguard against the injury or accidental death of the employees. Most physical injuries caused in factories can and should be avoided. The law therefore requires that cogs, gearing, belts, and saws shall be so placed, covered, or otherwise arranged that the danger of human injury from them is kept at a positive minimum. Machinery known to be in dangerous disrepair cannot legally be kept in motion until repaired. In order to promote his program of safety the commissioner may adopt the protective code promulgated by the American Standard Association and adopted by the United States Department of Labor.

The law goes into great detail in specifying means of protection. Fire escapes, lighted stairways, handrails, etc., must be installed where safety requires their use. In certain places smoking is forbidden, and contact with noxious fumes, dusts, and gas must be reduced to a minimum. Where necessity dictates, washing and dressing rooms must be installed. At all times sanitary conditions must be maintained in all public works and first-aid equipment and fire extinguishers kept at hand for instant use.

HOURS OF LABOR AND WAGES

The standard legal work day has been fixed at eight hours. This regulation applies to employment on railroads and state public works projects but not to coal mining and other private industry. Exceptions may be made in case of emergencies. The hours of work for a calendar day in the coal mines are established by a mutual agreement made between the employers and the bargaining agents of the employees, but the time must not exceed the standard eight hours.[1]

Authorities contracting for public improvements, before advertising for bids for the construction of the same, determine on fair minimum wages to be paid to their employees. The amount is not necessarily uniform but depends very much on the kind of work,

[1] *Code of West Virginia,* 1943, p. 891.

skilled laborers generally receiving higher wages than unskilled. The minimum amount or rate of pay may be determined by taking the average paid in the locality where the work is to be done. The matter of the rate of wages is then made a part of the agreement between the contracting parties. Wages paid for public improvements usually set the standards for private employment.

The first child labor law in West Virginia was passed by the legislature in 1887. Since that date several revisions have been made but the principles of the law remain the same. Children under sixteen years of age cannot be employed in gainful occupations except in agriculture or domestic service in a private home.

In certain types of work the minimum age has been raised to eighteen years. Such employment includes mining, quarrying, manufacturing explosives, smelting, furnace operation, and other kinds of work specified in the state law. This regulation also applies to employment in pool rooms, billiard rooms, and places where beer is dispensed. The true purpose of the law is to protect the morals and health of the youth of the state, and conditions where doubt arises may be reviewed by the commissioner of labor, the commissioner of health, and the superintendent of schools.

The compulsory school attendance law applies to children from their seventh to their sixteenth birthday, but responsible persons under certain conditions may issue special work permits and vacation work permits to children under sixteen. This regulation affords protection for people in special need and an opportunity for youth to be occupied during the vacation period. At no place does the law exact labor, except as a punishment for crime, but it protects and respects labor.

The Department of Mines

A discussion of the laws relating to labor in West Virginia would be incomplete without particular reference to mines and mining, since coal mining is the state's biggest industry. Early in the development of the coal industry it was observed that people working in the mines needed special protection. Certain fatal disasters had emphasized this fact. In 1883 the legislature created the office of state mine inspector,[2] whose duties soon became too numerous for one person to perform. Four years later two inspectors took over this work, and in 1893 one more was added. In 1897 the legislature

[2] *Acts of the Legislature of West Virginia*, 1883, pp. 100–103.

again amended the original act by providing for a chief inspector and four assistants. The number of assistants has now been increased to eight. They are called inspectors-at-large, and each has a division assigned to his care. Other special assistants include quarry and electrical inspectors, an examining board, and the director of first-aid training.[3]

The chief inspector is an expert in his field of work; he must have had at least eight years' experience in working, ventilating, and draining mines. Annually he makes a report of his proceedings to the governor. This report contains a great deal of important information, such as the number of men employed, the number of mines in operation, and the quantity of coal and coke produced. His fund of knowledge is used in recommending legislation beneficial to the mining interests.

Care is exercised over the health and safety of the miners. The chief inspector attends to furnishing, equipping, and operating rescue cars suitable for use in mine disasters. When not in operation a car may be used for educational purposes and training for rescue work among the miners themselves. It is the endeavor of the Department of Mines never to lack a trained personnel for rescue work in time of emergency. Consequently mine rescue stations, with trained and well equipped crews, are placed in reach of all the coal operations. The chief of the department appoints a director of rescue work who is responsible for the safety program. But every precaution is taken to prevent disaster. Mines must use protective devices such as safety lamps, insulation of machines and wires, detectors of fire damp, ventilators, fans, etc.

Necessity also requires that protective measures be used in the operation of oil and gas wells. The place of drilling has to be designated by the State Geological Survey and the substructure of the earth noted so that the operation of wells shall not conflict with the mining of coal or create dangers and hazards in such mining. The Department of Mines also keeps on file all data relating to the drilling and operation of oil and gas wells, the amount of the products, their transportation by pipe lines and tank cars, storage tanks, the abandonment of wells, the disposal of wastes, etc. These are matters in which the public has concern and the government maintains a supervisory interest.

Within recent years the United Mine Workers union has made long strides toward the improvement of the welfare of the coal

[3] At present there are forty-one mine inspection districts in West Virginia.

miners. Some of these conditions pertain to the length of the work day, wages, health, and safety. The principle of collective bargaining is now recognized by law. It took years of persistent effort to achieve this objective which has promoted improved relations between employers and employees.

Although hours of labor and rates of wages have demanded much of the attention of the leaders of the unions and many improvements have been achieved in these respects, much remains to be done to guard the health and safety of the coal miners. Society must recognize the fact that the human body is the most valuable of all machines and therefore demands first attention.

Workmen's Compensation

In his message to the legislature in 1913 Governor Henry D. Hatfield recommended the passage of a workmen's compensation law. To the great satisfaction of the laborers and the governor, the legislators enacted the law at their next session. For many years a regulation of this kind had been needed and it now served as a source of relief in numerous cases.

The law is administered by a compensation commissioner appointed by the governor and approved by the senate. His term lasts six years. The legislature makes an appropriation for the maintenance of the office. Annually the commissioner makes a report to the governor, giving in detail a review of the work carried on by himself and his staff of assistants.

One of the special duties of the commissioner is to create a workmen's compensation fund from the premiums paid by employers for the benefit of employees and their dependents. The rate of the premium is based on a percentage fixed by the commissioner on the monthly payroll of the employers, the law having established a minimum of fifty cents. All sums so received are deposited in the state treasury to the credit of the workmen's compensation fund. The rate of the premiums is fixed at the lowest possible level consistent with the solvency of the fund, but where the hazards of a workman depend upon the type of his employment the commissioner may fix a rate for each individual.

If employers elect to do so they may create their own compensation fund by giving to the commissioner evidence of their ability to insure payments to injured employees at least equal to those under the state plan. In connection with the safety program the commissioner may require employers to adopt rules and regulations for the protection of employees, who, if disobedient to these rules, cannot legally claim compensation.

The legislature has carefully outlined the classification of benefits in cases of disability. Of these there are three, temporary partial disability, temporary total disability, and permanent disability. The degree of disability is determined by the facts of the case, and the award is made in accordance with the schedule determined by law. In case an injury causes death within four years after the accident, reasonable funeral expenses may be allowed, and a certain weekly sum paid to dependents for a limited time.

The commissioner exercises a great deal of power in adjudicating the various cases. He has full power and authority to hear and determine the questions that come within his jurisdiction, and his decisions are final unless dissatisfied parties file an appeal to the supreme court of appeals. There are certain rules to follow in making the appeal. The petition must be filed before the court within ninety days and all interested parties must have due notice of the proceedings. The intention in this instance is to dispense full and unqualified justice to all parties concerned.

CHAPTER 22

Taxation and Finance

Mounting Costs of Government

As political systems grow in complexity and the mass of governmental detail expands, the expense for administration inevitably increases. The growth of institutions in West Virginia and the increasing cost of their maintenance confirm this fact. In his address to the joint session of the legislature, January 8, 1947, the governor of West Virginia recommended that there be appropriated to defray our annual expense a sum which equals about thirty dollars for every man, woman, and child living in the state. In contrast, the appropriations for 1900 amounted to about two dollars per capita.

People pay for their own individual conveniences and comforts as well as for the general welfare. The increased demands on the public treasury are caused in a large measure by requests for better services in education, agriculture, road maintenance, health protection, police protection, and the like. It is quite true that society has been willing to pay the costs as long as the services improve in quality. But this fact will not permit one to draw the conclusion that the finest human skill, like the most precious jewel, can always be bought for the highest price.

The public often makes requests for special and general appropriations, but it seldom suggests where the money will come from, this matter being left solely to the resourcefulness of the governor and the legislature. Perhaps there never has been a meeting of the legislature at which a search has not been made for new sources of revenue. The search has been particularly urgent since the turn of the last century and shows every promise of continuing so.

We shall now trace briefly the history of West Virginia's fiscal development, giving special attention to the periods during which the greatest changes have occurred.

The State Revenue System in 1863

In February, 1863, the legislature of the reorganized government of Virginia, meeting in Wheeling, made sweeping changes in the laws relating to taxation. No doubt the leaders took action with the view that the new state, then in the process of formation, would in a short time profit from the reforms thus enacted. All these events took place in the midst of war, and those in authority strove to keep their political system alive, active, and efficient. This could only be done if money was available. Thus when West Virginia assumed the full status of statehood it inherited a code of laws providing for the laying and collecting of revenue. Moreover, the county and district officers, upon taking the required pledge, continued the administration of their official duties under the new commonwealth as if no change had taken place.[1] Thus the transition was accomplished quietly and easily.

The original monetary resources of the new state consisted largely of the revenue collected from the tax on real estate and personal property, but certain other items had not entirely escaped attention. Virginia had withdrawn the major amount of her revenue deposits from the banks in the western part of the state in 1863; consequently, West Virginia stood in desperate need of money to run its public affairs. In addition to the tax on land, houses, and personal property, the legislature fixed rates on boarding houses, ordinaries, bowling alleys, billiard tables, livery stables, distilleries, and mercantile establishments. License fees came also from theater proprietors, auctioneers, physicians, dentists, and lawyers.[2] Revenue collectors, stationed in booths at the terminals of bridges and hard by the turnpikes, gathered fees from the travelers whose gaze and steps were usually directed westward. West Virginians had struggled success-

1 *Acts of the Legislature of West Virginia,* June 26, 1863.

2 *Ibid.*

fully to achieve statehood, and now they were too wise to starve in a land of plenty. The whole plan of administering the finances soon took on a finished appearance even in the formative period of development.

Of course the legislature was vested with power to lay and collect taxes and make appropriations. The first session of the legislature of the new state clothed the Board of Public Works with the same powers and duties which it possessed on the nineteenth day of June, 1863, and continued its functions under the laws of the new state by adding to the personnel of the board the secretary of state.[3] Now it became the official obligation of this board to exercise supervision over public finances, including all works of internal improvement and that part of the Cumberland Road located in West Virginia. It appointed the collectors of tolls on the bridges and highways, supervised the building of roads, and fixed the rate of tolls that had not been regulated by legislative action.

The lawmakers had seen to the matter of fixing a maximum rate of fare on the turnpikes. For a single horse or mule on a section of the road covering a distance of five miles, the rate was three cents, one cent being added for each additional animal; for twenty sheep or hogs, five cents; for twenty cattle, ten cents; and for a cart or wagon, "if the tires of the wheels are not more than four inches wide, three cents for each animal drawing it." [4] The rate diminished as the width of the tires increased. And so the legislators had gone into much detail to specify the rates charged to drovers and travelers as they wearily trudged their way from the old east in search of an El Dorado in the west.

The arrangement for places to deposit the public revenues had not been neglected. The following institutions were declared to be state depositories: the Merchants and Mechanics Bank of Wheeling, and its branches located at Point Pleasant, Clarksburg, and Morgantown; the Northwestern Bank of Virginia at Wheeling, and its branches at Parkersburg and Wellsburg; and the Exchange Bank of Virginia at Weston. Nearly all the state deposits in these banks had been withdrawn before the establishment of the reorganized government.

---

[3] "Be it enacted by the Legislature of West Virginia, the same powers and duties which by the laws of the state of Virginia in force on the nineteenth of June last were vested in and required of the governor, auditor, and treasurer of the state as a board of public works, are hereby vested in and shall be exercised by the governor, auditor, treasurer, and secretary of state." *Acts of the Legislature of West Virginia*, First Session, 1863.

[4] *Code of West Virginia*, 1870, p. 414.

Public finances very much depended on local collections. The office of county sheriff remained unchanged, and he continued to be the local financial officer. He began collection of taxes on July first of each year. In some counties the sheriff at first met with serious opposition in the administration of his affairs, while in others he was undisturbed. Some of the county officers refused to take the oath of allegiance to West Virginia and the Union, thus causing civil government to cease until a reorganization could be effected. A terrible division among the people in this border state flared up during the war and continued until after Appomattox. During these years the collection of taxes was a burden, surely not a pleasure.[5]

The sheriff filed an annual report of his collections with the auditor, who was a member of the Board of Public Works. In view of the fact that during the war civil law was fully established in only about half the counties and all legislation in reference to the finances was made to fit that situation, it is not surprising that the total revenue fell far short of what it should have been, and that a proper balance in accounts could not be struck until civil government had been reestablished in the disorganized counties.[6]

The county boards of supervisors made up an estimate covering all debts and liabilities payable during the year, and laid adequate levies to meet the payments as they came due. Although times were hard and money was scarce, it was the object of the county government to keep its financial record clear. In order to establish a solid basis on which the system of taxation should stand, the supervisors placed a levy on the hundred dollars valuation of all taxable property according to the last assessment.[7]

In incorporated towns and villages taxes, fines, penalties, and license fees, prescribed by the council, provided funds for running the business of the municipality. It also came within the power of the council to require every male resident between twenty-one and fifty years of age to work on the streets, roads, or alleys of the town, or hire an acceptable substitute, or pay an amount fixed by the

[5] One may observe intimations of the situation by noting the rules adopted for paying the sheriff. In the first place he received 5% of the total amount of the taxes for which he was chargeable. In 1864 the rate was changed to 7½% if the total amount chargeable did not exceed $10,000. But if the sheriff happened to be a good collector and received the full amount for which he was responsible, he was paid an additional 2½%, which made the collection of taxes in West Virginia an expensive business in 1864.

[6] The amount of revenue received by the state during the year of 1865 was $381,382.92. *Auditor's Report*, 1865, p. 46.

[7] *Code of West Virginia*, 1870, p. 414.

council. The town sergeant made all financial collections for the municipal government.[8] West Virginia contained only a few incorporated towns in 1863.

Tax Revision of 1868

In this early period the inhabitants of the state were working out their own destiny after emerging from a devastating war. Scenes of battle were fresh in the memories of the soldiers who had so recently returned home to continue the conquest of the wilderness. The virgin forests remained almost undisturbed; explorations in the fields of coal, oil, and gas had scarcely begun. So the pioneer appealed to the newly cleared soil to yield its rich fruits and grains as the only source for the sustenance of a frugal, laborious life. The legislators, born on farms, left their plows in the furrows so that they might turn for a little while to meet in common council for the purpose of prescribing ways and means for healing the wounds and strengthening the body of the youthful state. Their trials had been heavy and their burdens needed to be lightened. There now came, however, the dawning of an industrial awakening that enlivened the people with a new vision of a better life. West Virginians now found themselves in possession of the richness of nature's stores long locked in the western piedmont region of the Alleghenies. But without delaying until this hope could be fulfilled the legislature, meeting in 1868, first set about lightening burdens by reducing taxes.

The first notable change in the revenue laws was the creation of a tax-free list of properties which included books, laboratory apparatus, furniture, and money belonging to the public schools. These exemptions were extended to all properties belonging to the state, county, or township, and to agricultural products "grown directly from the soil," and the natural increase of livestock less than one year old. Properties that belonged to incorporated academies, schools for the deaf and blind, asylums, and all "manufactured articles and products of mechanical skill and labor produced in the state during the year" were declared tax free. While in the mood for making changes, the legislature created a maximum rate of levy on real estate. This ceiling amounted to ten cents on the hundred dollars valuation for general purposes, and an additional ten cents to support public education.[9]

[8] *Code of West Virginia,* 1870, p. 330.

[9] *Acts of the Legislature of West Virginia,* 1868, pp. 60–62.

It has been mentioned that in certain counties the collection of revenues lapsed during the war. To amend this condition the legislature now instructed the sheriffs of the delinquent counties to make collections of all unpaid taxes back to 1861 – if necessary, "by the distress and sale of property." [10] These counties had not paid their taxes since the start of the war, and now that they had been incorporated in West Virginia it was only through the power of the new state that collections could be made. In obedience to the law the sheriffs set to work collecting delinquent taxes.

From the beginning of statehood male citizens had paid a capitation tax of sixty cents annually. The legislature of 1868 increased this amount to one dollar, and it has remained at that figure up to the present.

In the process of revision and change it was called to the attention of the lawmakers that there was no record of the lands that had been sold for taxes under the laws of Virginia prior to 1866. This situation had caused much confusion among the assessors, some of whom complained that they could not intelligently carry out the duties of their office without this information. Due notice being taken of this complaint, the legislature passed a joint resolution which instructed the auditor to secure the much-needed data from Richmond.[11] The information received after communication with the land office at the capital of Virginia eased the labors of our county assessors.

The progressive legislators went on to another new field of activity. In the previous year they had created two independent school districts, one in Clarksburg, the other in Wheeling. Now they added Morgantown and Weston to the number. The statute fixed the term at eight months and gave the boards of education authority to lay and collect taxes adequate to maintain the schools for the full session. The legislature took this action in the face of the fact that all the other public schools ran for only four months annually. However, the people in the incorporated towns having eight months of school had to pay for the advantage they enjoyed. Inequalities in the length of the school sessions remained until 1934, when the county unit system became operative.

---

10 *Acts of the Legislature of West Virginia*, 1868, p. 61.
11 *Ibid.*, pp. 64, 162.

Privilege and Franchise Taxes

Prior to the formation of the constitution of 1872 the state assembly lacked authority to levy taxes on privileges and franchises. In the new law the following provision was incorporated: "The legislature shall have power to tax, by uniform and equal laws, all privileges and franchises of persons and corporations."[12] It is a matter of more than incidental interest that this clause remained inoperative for nine years. Whether the omission was accidental cannot now be well made out. Finally in 1881 the legislature took action under the clause, and its action was directed at the railroads.

The railroads had undergone a period of great development in the '70's. The corporations came to wield quite as much influence politically as they did industrially. For several years common complaint had been heard that the owners of the railroads did not contribute their proper share to the public purse, and it was claimed that too many civil officers rode on passes. An assessment for county and district purposes had been made against the Baltimore and Ohio Railroad Company in 1877, but in the same year a preliminary order was obtained from the United States District Court that restrained and prohibited the auditor from certifying the taxes for collection to the sheriffs of the counties through which the railroad passed.[13] In the following year the court issued an injunction against the collection of these levies, but in the meantime the railroad company had paid its assessments in large measure. A state of confusion existed until the meeting of the legislature in 1881.

The new law of that year stipulated that railroad companies shall "list for taxation all their properties at the true and actual value in money, including all property, credits, money, and investments used or held in this state," and proportional values on locomotives and rolling stock passing in and out of the state. The tax on the property possessed by the railroads had to be at the same rate as on other property.

To make this law operative it was required that the chief officers of the railroad should file with the auditor a certified statement of the values of properties mentioned in the statute. In turn the auditor submitted this report to the Board of Public Works, and if it were satisfactory, the board directed the auditor to assess the properties for state, school, county, district and municipal purposes.

---

12 Constitution of West Virginia, Art. X, sec. 1.

13 *Auditor's Report*, 1878, pp. 5–6.

Should the companies deem the levy excessive, they could refer their grievance to the Board of Public Works for review.[14]

The sheriff collected the taxes from the railroad companies just as he did from other property holders, but the provision was included that the law applied to all railroad companies without exception and that the sheriff had no authority whatsoever to remit any collections he had made. This law of 1881 appeared to close the issue concerning the legality and propriety of laying a tax on railroads, which of course in time had an application to all other public utilities.

All through the decade following 1881 there was a tendency to bring about reforms. The state gave greatly needed attention to the building of roads and bridges. Previous to this time the roads, excepting the turnpikes, were merely trails, narrow, shaded, and rough; and bridges were practically nonexistent. When streams were flush, travel was delayed until the waters receded. The pioneering period was over. The age of the frontiersman who possessed the qualities of the warrior, hunter, and farmer, clad in the fringed frock, moccasins, and Indian leggings, had closed. Another turn in life had come. Now the descendants of these pioneers set themselves to develop and expand the riches that had been so dearly earned by exploration and occupation.

At this stage of affairs the county courts received instructions from the Board of Public Works to form estimates of the amounts of money needed in every magisterial district "to contract, put and keep in good repair" all the roads and bridges within the jurisdiction of the court. This program meant heavier levies, but if a property holder chose to do so, he could pay his road tax by contributing his daily labor, "and the price thereof, when performed by an able bodied man, as the law requires, shall be seventy-five cents per day." [15] As a result of this regulation the rights of way of many of the roads that now cross the hills and valleys of West Virginia were first located under the district system of making surveys. The importance of the work of the county surveyor during our period of development can scarcely be overestimated. His compass and chain were quite as useful as the trusted rifle and shot-pouch had been to his forefather. But the whole change meant a greater property tax, and since nearly every citizen owned his own house and field, he contributed directly to the keeping of his government and the building of his road.

---

[14] *Acts of the Legislature of West Virginia*, 1881, pp. 133–136.

[15] *Ibid.*, p. 158.

In 1885 a new regulation required any resident corporation, or one transacting business in West Virginia, to pay a privilege tax of ten dollars annually, and a nonresident company conducting affairs in the state to pay a yearly fee of five dollars. In view of this very moderate tax many business interests moved their headquarters from other states into West Virginia. During the following fifteen years the revenue from the levy on privileges and franchises increased about fiftyfold.

Signposts along the path of progress may be read in the revenue laws. It was in the same year (1885) that the salesman of the first sewing machines had to pay an annual tax of twenty dollars "if he traveled with one or more horses." By the same means of conveyance those persons who sold organs paid thirty dollars, and peddlers of lightning rods paid fifty dollars yearly. So peddlers and hawkers as well as the keepers of toll bridges and ferries felt the presence of the revenue collector, and as time went on with the rush of settlement, every newcomer made his contribution to the expense of his government.

Further Reforms

Owing to further industrial developments and the law requiring re-evaluations of property each decade, the legislature of 1891 turned its attention to the task of revising the laws governing taxation. In making preparation for this duty the Board of Public Works, in the meantime, had appointed a commissioner (a freeholder) in each assessment district to form a new estimate of property values. In this case the power to tax was making a strong effort to overtake, but not to hinder, industrial progress.

The statute instructed the commissioner to place "a fair cash value on all real estate within the district, including oil, gas, minerals, mineral water and coal." In the very year this work began, oil barges for the first time moved down the Little Kanawha River from Wirt and Wood counties to the Ohio. Gas and oil fields at Mannington and Sistersville had just begun operating, and a vigorous search was being made for other wells. At the same time workmen, blasting the rights of way for railroads through the virgin regions of coal and timber, broke the seclusion of the mountaineer and aroused him to the coming of a new age of industry. Stalwart lumbermen who had just completed their work of forest devastation in Maine, New York, and Pennsylvania followed the advance guard to the Blackwater,

Cheat, and Cherry rivers as well as to other places that abounded in the wealth of timber. The lumber camps of West Virginia also attracted Canadians, Swedes, and Norwegians, who generally entered this state via Pennsylvania. Sawmills, tanneries, and pulp mills followed in the wake of the slashing of the giant trees while alien labor, largely from southern Europe, operated the newly opened coal mines.[16]

The laws governing taxation could not remain static in the presence of such industrial activity. In an attempt to keep in step with the times, a board of equalization was created in 1899. This board consisted of one member from each congressional district and one at large. These officers, appointed by the governor, set to work to correct and equalize the assessment in every county. The task was most difficult. After making a persistent effort to complete its assigned task, the board filed its report with the auditor, who transferred it to the Board of Public Works. The report was received with a sense of dissatisfaction. The work was not all in vain, however, since these extensive investigations soon led to another undertaking in the same direction.

In the meantime wealth continued to grow, while the state failed to realize a revenue commensurate with its industrial developments. Eventually the legislature undertook to remedy this situation by making a change in the principle governing taxation on corporations. Hereafter the rate of levy would be based on the authorized capital invested and the increase of value in the shares of stock.

The passage of this act (1901) marked the beginning of a radical change in the license laws of West Virginia. Under the new law corporations would be required to pay at an equitable rate based upon the capital actually employed in the conduct of business instead of at a flat rate. This method had a strong tendency to squeeze the water out of corporation stocks but left open inducements for an increase in the actual value of investments in honest enterprise.

This reform measure, however, contained a serious fault. Corporations had only sixty days to comply with the new regulations. Not feeling able to meet the drastic demand, some companies forfeited their charters while others industriously labored to free them-

[16] It is reliably stated that some of the leaders of industry sent their agents to Italy, Austria, Hungary, and Poland for the purpose of bringing to America laborers to operate the coal mines and coke ovens. Alien labor was employed to a less extent in the cutting of timber and the manufacture of lumber.

selves from the imposed confusion. Two months was not long enough to re-evaluate all their properties. The old law levied a flat rate, regardless of the amount of invested capital, while under the new statute the tax varied in proportion to the value of the stock. The principle of taxing a privilege had changed to that of the taxing of property.

Some companies had made the mistake of placing excessive values on their property but now the time had come to do some sharp deflating. Thereafter, paper enterprise and indifferent business had to do a great deal of reorganizing to keep from folding up. It is a fact, however, that not all business firms could meet their tax obligations; consequently, the only thing left to do was to forfeit their charters and close their doors. Forfeitures numbered about twelve hundred annually during the next three years. This law also applied to telephone, telegraph, and express companies operating in West Virginia, and the tax imposed on those utilities amounted to a certain rate per mile which took into consideration the value of the investment and not the volume of business transacted.

In 1901 the governor, through a legislative grant of power, named a commission whose purpose was to make a comprehensive study of the laws relating to taxation and report its findings to the governor. In substance this report, and the recommendations made in it, would relate to valuations, assessments, and revenues and their disbursement. Although the laws with respect to rates and levies had undergone occasional changes, they had not sustained a thorough revision since 1863. The best-informed people attributed this morbid condition to the brief sessions of the legislature, lasting only forty-five days, which did not allow enough time for the revision of the laws relating to any department of the government.[17]

The new commission worked under legislative instructions to consider "changes in assessments and revenue laws, to reach property, persons, firms and corporations not now bearing their just proportion of the burden of taxation, and to raise the necessary amounts of revenue, with the least possible burden upon the people and property of the state, and to secure the proper disbursements of the same." [18] In addition, the report was to include the drafting of a bill to classify cities, towns, and villages, to incorporate municipalities

[17] The governor was pledged to a tax-reform policy.

[18] The members of the commission were W. P. Hubbard, H. G. Davis, L. J. Williams, John H. Holt and John K. Thompson. Alfred Phillips was the secretary.

having more than two thousand population, and to amend municipal charters that were then in operation.

The report presented by the commission was thorough and penetrating. It reached to the very bottom of the commercial and industrial life of the people. The high quality of this work demonstrated the rare ability of those who wrote it and who made another contribution to the fine records which they had already established.

In July, 1904, Governor Albert B. White called the legislature to meet in special session for the purpose of hearing the report of the tax commission and taking such action as was deemed right and proper. The legislators received the report with favor, and immediately began deliberations on the changes to be brought about in the system of taxation and its administration. Harmony prevailed in the government during the drafting of the new legislation; consequently the bills passed by the legislature were assured of a friendly reception in the chief executive's office.

Perhaps the greatest reform presented by the special session was the creation of the office of state tax commissioner,[19] an office whose importance and utility have never been questioned. As to his official obligations the law stated, "It shall be the duty of the state tax commissioner to see that the laws concerning the assessment and collection of taxes and levies, whether of the state or of any county, district or municipal corporation thereof, are faithfully enforced."

Each county now became one assessment district, in which all properties would be assessed at their true and actual values. The sheriff continued to be the tax collector, and ex officio the treasurer of the county. His manner of election and length of tenure in office did not undergo any change in the revised statute. The same conditions remained as before concerning the making of assessments, except that now the assessor was allowed one or more assistants.

Considerable change was made, however, in the kinds of properties to be entered on the tax list. Among these were included distributed shares of stock, inheritances, devises, and legacies. Although no change in the rate of levy had been attempted, the county court did have instructions to form its estimate of annual expenditures on or before the first day of August, leaving the fixing of the rate of levy until the first day of April. The durability of these laws has been duly tested now for more than forty years and they have remained the cornerstones of the revenue system of West Virginia.

[19] Governor White appointed Charles W. Dillon as the first state tax commissioner. His official duties began on November 28, 1904.

Heretofore it has been seen that when a new machine is invented or a discovery utilized it will not escape for long the observing eye of the levying power and the revenue collector. No better evidence of this truth may be found than in a law enacted February 27, 1907, which fixed our first license tax on automobiles.[20] Ten years followed before insurance companies could gain the privilege of writing policies that would cover automobiles and other motor vehicles. But the revenue laws followed surely in the wake of industrial improvement.

The State Budget Law

By the turn of the century the old irregular method of making appropriations for the administration of the government had served its time and was destined to give way to a more reliable manner of caring for the public purse. The old method had always caused much uncertainty and confusion in the mind of the treasurer of the state. Waste had developed in proportion to the increase of wealth, and the "pork-barrel" worked overtime. To remedy this situation that had already lasted too long, an amendment to the constitution was proposed by the legislature and ratified by the electorate in 1917.[21] This law is known as the budget amendment.

According to the terms of the amendment it became the duty of the Board of Public Works to form an estimate of the biennial expenditures of the state and of the revenue necessary to meet all debts and current expenses. In detail this report would indicate all the assets, liabilities, reserves, surpluses and public debts and provide means of meeting all liabilities. To form this report with a reliable degree of accuracy it became the obligation of all agencies that spent public funds to file itemized statements indicating the purposes and the amount of such expenditures. The board retained the authority, however, to modify and regulate these expenditures unless they were fixed by law. After making a detailed review of this accumulated data, increasing or diminishing amounts where it was deemed wise to do so, the board formulated the budget and made it ready for legislative action. Every proposed appropriation is shown in the budget bill which throws the financial accounts of the state open for public inspection. Not only does this plan reduce the hazards of wasteful spending but it greatly simplifies the keeping of the public accounts.

---

20 *Acts of the Legislature of West Virginia*, 1907.

21 The popular vote for the amendment was 51,405, against it 26,651.

There is nothing, however, to forbid the legislature from revising the budget bill upward or downward since the matter of raising and expending revenue is a prerogative of the lawmaking body.

The new law did not entirely close the door to the making of special appropriations which now may be brought about by the framing of a supplementary bill that follows the same course to become a law as the main bill. The supplement must, however, be devoted to a single purpose and must contain provisions for meeting expenses that were not listed in the original estimate. It may well be imagined that there is scarcely, if ever, a meeting of the legislature at which supplementary budget bills are not passed.

The budget amendment has definite virtues. It unifies the financial accounts of the state by placing them under the supervision of a director who devotes all his time and attention to his official duties, among which are the improvement of methods of making collections and disbursements, the accumulation of statistics used in the framing of the budget, and the administration of laws governing taxation. Through the offices of the budget director and the tax commissioner the revenue system of the state has come to correspond much more closely with the public welfare.

The Tax Limitation Amendment

From the time of the ratifying of the budget amendment until 1932 only slight changes were made in the principles of our revenue laws, but after the passing of three decades it had become quite apparent that both revision and reform were needed. Numerous changes in the industrial, commercial and professional life of the state had created new conditions that were uncomfortable under the restraint of old laws.

For the purpose of bringing about sorely needed changes, Governor William G. Conley called the legislature to meet in special session July 12, 1932. Pointing out specific reasons for his action the governor enumerated the following desiderata: the authorization of the payment of taxes in semiannual or quarterly installments, the passing of an emergency revenue law in order to balance the budget, the raising of a special fund for the relief of the unemployed, the placing of a limitation on levies, and the drafting of a constitutional amendment for the purpose of placing a ceiling on the tax on personal property and real estate.

The governor soon realized that he had on hand a rebellious legislature. He urgently recommended that a bill be passed placing a limit on the rate of taxation and that the legislative action remain in force until an amendment to the constitution definitely fixing the maximum rate of taxation could be ratified and become operative. But when the legislative mill began to grind, it passed over the governor's veto a bill which reduced the budget a flat twenty per cent below that which had been adopted by the previous assembly. This act carried with it a general reduction of public expenses, including the salaries of officers. Instead of creating new revenue the legislature adopted the policy of trimming expenses to lower levels.

The proposed constitutional amendment survived the ordeal of fire. It passed in time to be submitted to the electorate that year. The country was in the throes of an economic depression; the popular demand was for a reduction in public expenses, and the vote favoring the amendment reached landslide proportions.[22]

One of the outstanding provisions in the new amendment stated, "Taxation shall be equal and uniform throughout the state, and all property, both real and personal, shall be taxed in proportion to its value to be ascertained as directed by law." This statement leaves a broad range for legislative action, but later limitations changed the situation by placing ceilings on the tax rates. Here we have an expression of the sober second thought which usually precludes or at least modifies radical action in a popular government.

The aggregate of taxes assessed in any one year by all levying bodies could not exceed fifty cents on each one hundred dollars on the assessed value of property in Class I, one dollar on property in Class II, one dollar and fifty cents on property in Class III, and two dollars on property in Class IV.[23] All agricultural products in the possession of the producer and household goods to the value of two hundred dollars were placed on the list of exemptions. Henceforth taxes could be paid semiannually, a provision which was intended to reduce financial burdens.

The legislature did not fail to give attention to the needs of people who were actually in want. It consigned to county courts and municipal governments authority to transfer ten per cent of their road funds to be used for charity. In order to determine where charity was actually needed, the law set forth that two investigators and one overseer should be appointed by the governor in each magisterial

---

[22] The bill passed the legislature August 6, 1932. It was ratified by a majority of 335,482 to 43,931.

[23] Supplement (1934) to *Code of West Virginia* of 1932, p. 20.

district. This plan received a great deal of adverse criticism as having overdone public benevolence.

Governor Kump and Tax Reform

In view of the fact that the limitation amendment was ratified at the general election of 1932, it became necessary for the succeeding administration to put the principles of the amendment into operation. The legislature had recently extended the time limit after which property could be sold for the nonpayment of taxes. The new law reduced levies at the same time that the treasury faced special responsibilities for expenditures. The matter of decreasing revenues and increasing expenses confronted Governor H. G. Kump when he took the oath of office March 4, 1933. The new executive had had long and thorough training in legal matters, and he possessed wisdom and courage to carry on under adverse circumstances. It was obvious, he perceived, that new sources of revenue would have to replace those that had so recently dried up. With ability and discretion Governor Kump faced the situation squarely.

In his inaugural address the governor launched his first attack on a situation that was difficult if not embarrassing. He insisted that a sales tax should be levied which, in his opinion, would bring into the state treasury $15,000,000 annually. This amount would successfully take care of the deficit in the treasury and duly supplement the revenue set apart for the support of public education. From the first this recommendation met strong opposition from both political parties, the claim being that the burden of taxation would then be placed on the people who were least able to bear it.[24] In the face of all opposition the governor held steadily to his course, expanding rather than restricting his program. Vigorous action was needed. Vigorous executive action the legislature had.[25]

Being pressed by the insistence of the governor, the legislature soon set to work. In the first place it extended for one year the powers of the sheriffs whose terms had expired December 31, 1932, so that they might sell properties that had been returned delinquent for unpaid taxes prior to January 1, 1929. In too many instances properties had not been held as surety for taxes long overdue; under

[24] *Acts of the Extraordinary Session of the Legislature of West Virginia*, 1932, p. 1219.

[25] The *Wheeling Intelligencer*, March 17, 1933.

the new law sheriffs would be compelled to complete the business which they had evaded while in office.

Next the legislature turned its attention to a regulation often called the chain-store tax law. This tax was a progressive levy on the stores owned and operated in the state by corporations. Actually it was a privilege tax. In return for a certain fee the state tax commissioner issued a license to the owner of the establishment, which license enabled him to keep his store legally in operation. The amount of the fee ranged from two dollars for one store to two hundred and fifty dollars for each store in excess of seventy-five. The privilege tax was not new in West Virginia, but its use in this case furnished a rich source of revenue.

An enabling act passed by the legislature was necessary to make the tax limitation amendment operative. Owners of personal property and real estate needed relief from their disproportionate share in the payment of the public revenue. The legislators, alive to this situation, divided properties into four classes, on each of which a maximum levy could be fixed. The levy reduced the public income from these sources but the expense of running the government would constantly mount higher. Two ways were left open by which the embarrassment could be relieved, to borrow more or to tax more. The alternative chosen was more taxes.

At this juncture the finances of the state had reached a crisis, the kind that tests the statesmanship in a republic where the people rule and officers serve. On March 11, a bill was offered that was intended to change the date of making assessments from April 1 to January 1, so that the fiscal year would be the same as the calendar year. The advantage gained by the new arrangement was very largely to facilitate bookkeeping in the office of the treasurer and the state tax commissioner, but the law incorporated a more significant principle in that thereafter bank stock, national banking associations, and industrial loan companies were to be taxed at their true and actual values.

To bring clarity out of ambiguity the new law laid down methods for assessors to follow in the keeping of their records. Thereafter the office of the state tax commissioner was to be, more than ever before, the nerve center of the administration of all laws relating to the laying and collection of taxes. So assessors, sheriffs, and collectors for municipalities became the lieutenants of the central office at Charleston with which they filed their fiscal reports and from which they received directions for fulfilling the manifold duties of their offices.[26]

Another important change related to transient salesmen of goods. It was not an unusual business for citizens from other states to enter West Virginia for the purpose of selling merchandise to storekeepers and to other individuals. When the goods had thus been disposed of, the salesman recrossed the state boundary line as secretly as he had come without paying a privilege tax for the conduct of his business. But hereafter any person desiring to offer or furnish for sale goods or merchandise in West Virginia, "by auction or otherwise," must make an application to the assessor of the county in which he wishes to operate for the privilege of disposing of his goods. The assessor places a value and a tax on all articles offered for sale. Before any legitimate sale can be made the tax is due and payable. Transient salesmen who had used the boundary line of the state to protect them in evading the payment of taxes now faced the situation of paying taxes or fines. By putting all people engaged in the same business on a basis of equality the law had a solid foundation.

Attention was now turned to extending the privilege tax law. An amendment strengthened the old law so that it included the sale of coal, oil, gas, limestone, manufactured products, and electric power. Another rich source of revenue was thus uncovered, since all these products are abundantly produced in West Virginia. The privilege of transacting business in the state no longer was to go unnoticed, even by the legislators. These laws operated on the principle that a legitimate business enjoys safety under the protection of the state, and that it must pay for that protection.

The legislative mill kept grinding. Next came a levy on the gross incomes realized from the sale of tangible property, on banking, on contracting, on shows, moving pictures, and race tracks, and on the income derived from various businesses and professions. The privilege taxes required of railroads and steamship companies underwent a revision upward. Every motor vehicle carrier operating on the public highways, every railroad car corporation, express company, pipe line corporation, telephone and telegraph company, now bore a

---

[26] County clerks now were required to keep a certified list showing the transfer of titles to lands in the county prior to the first day of the fiscal year. In event of one person holding title to land and another person owning the subsurface of the same tract, as coal, oil, gas, and fireclay, the properties had to be listed separately on the tax records. And if it were found that buildings had been omitted from the tax list they were backtaxed for the full time of delinquency.

greater share of the public expense.[27] At the close of the fiscal year all these companies also paid a gross sales tax on their business. Surtaxes, labeled "emergency taxes," increased the rate on incomes and privileges, production, and business. Drugstores and taxicabs also paid their levies to the collectors, nor was any omission made with respect to inheritances and properties transferred in trust or otherwise.[28] In 1933 it really rained tax laws in West Virginia. To aid collections the legislature authorized the state tax commissioner to appoint twelve additional agents who would assist him in collecting present and delinquent levies.

The first session of the legislature, having completed a wide and comprehensive revenue program, adjourned June 3, 1933. Many people expressed satisfaction that the budget would be balanced, the deficit covered, old debts absorbed, and a reliable income left to carry on the ordinary affairs of administration. The governor pronounced the work a "splendid achievement." But complacence soon gave place to discontent.

On November 2, 1933, Governor Kump issued a call to the legislature to assemble in another extraordinary session. He stated, "I call you together at this time to counsel as to what can be done to restore and sustain orderly government, preserve the security of our people and maintain our free institutions." The trouble resulted largely from the demands of federal emergency relief and from a decision rendered by the state supreme court of appeals with respect to the administration of the recent constitutional amendment. The Federal Emergency Relief Administration had requested that West Virginia assume its proper share ($500,000 per month) of the federal allocation for human relief.[29] Moreover, the state supreme court of appeals had rendered a decision concerning the administration of the limitation amendment, a decision from which the governor sharply dissented. The court declared in the case of Bee vs. Huntington that debts owed by counties and municipalities had to be liquidated from the revenues obtained under the tax limitation amendment before any public funds could be expended to carry on

---

[27] *Acts of the Legislature of West Virginia,* 1933, p. 142. The income tax was abolished in 1944.

[28] *Acts of the Special Session of the Legislature of West Virginia,* 1933, p. 242.

[29] H. L. Hopkins, Federal Relief Administrator, gave notice to Governor Kump that 112,310 families in West Virginia were on relief, and that the state had furnished only 5 per cent of the amount necessary to keep them. Nevertheless there is strong justification for the opinion that the sum far exceeded the amount actually needed.

current expenses.[30] Most, if not all, of the units of local government were in debt, and in each of these cases that debt had to be paid off before funds could be applied to the payment of open business accounts. This judicial decision disarranged the financial plans of county and city governments, which had already formed their budgets.

Under the new rates of levy the annual income was estimated to be approximately $25,000,000. The yearly sum payable on the public debt would reach nearly $8,000,000, and about the same amount would be required to finance the program for education. In addition to these huge amounts $6,000,000 was needed for the relief of the poor. Now the grave question facing the administration was where to secure the funds to meet the running expense of the government. There was faith in the future but no money at present in the treasury and credit would soon be exhausted. The governor had only one course out of the situation — to call another meeting of the legislature. The idea had developed that a new constitutional convention should be summoned to change the supreme law of the state to harmonize with the recent decision of the supreme court of appeals, but this idea very soon met a severe popular negative reaction and disappeared as suddenly as it had appeared.

From the state house came the idea of proposing another constitutional amendment. This proposal also met a decisive negative reaction. Yet conditions were becoming desperate; there could be little further delay. In a short time the payment of the debts of the counties and municipalities would absorb all, or nearly all, the revenue collected from taxation, leaving the local governments with empty treasuries and without resources to maintain themselves. The matter of supporting local government and human relief had become so serious that the governor concluded that the constitutional guarantees to maintain the governments of cities and counties could no longer be maintained in the state.

Two problems had to be solved by the administration: (1) how to provide funds, at the request of the national government, for the relief of the poor; (2) how to continue orderly civil government under the laws of West Virginia. Stated in its simplest form the question was, How to raise more money? The legislature had to act.

Governor Kump called it into another extraordinary session. Both governor and legislators had a hard task, one which tested their

[30] W. E. Bee vs. City of Huntington, W. Va., *Reports* 114, p. 27.

originality but did not defeat it. Popular government cannot fail as long as the people are kept informed of their political condition and are free to work out their own destiny. They know full well they must rise or fall together, and rest assured, they will not fall. Here was a difficult situation facing a popular assembly.

The first major act of the legislature was to take $250,000 from the state road fund and devote it to human relief. Next $500,000 was taken from the state's general fund and set aside for the benefit of the schools, thus assuring a term of eight months. Soon there followed another appropriation of $3,000,000 as an additional relief fund. A series of appropriation bills followed in rapid succession. Money, however, could not be used until it became available. So a diligent search was made by the legislature for properties and privileges that could bear more taxes.

The new bills covered many civil interests. In the first place a levy of one and one-half per cent was placed on the net income of railroad car corporations and express companies. Next the tax drive struck at social clubs, dining cars, and the manufacturers and dispensers of beer. Then there came a rise of the privileges tax on the transacting of business in West Virginia. The general consumers sales tax followed, exacting two per cent, payable by the purchaser, on the retail price of goods sold in the state.[31] This new source of revenue came as an emergency measure but after the emergency had passed there was no disposition to remove the tax. Its administration was simple. Salesmen added two per cent to the purchase price of their goods, collected the amount from the purchaser, and periodically remitted the total to the office of the state tax commissioner.[32] Thus every merchant in the state became a tax collector.

And this was not all. The lawmakers went on to fix a fee of twenty dollars on all persons applying for registration as barbers and beauticians, with an annual renewal fee of five dollars. Resident junk dealers were required to pay an annual fee of twenty-five dollars, and nonresident dealers one hundred and fifty dollars. Sellers of spirituous liquors were likewise charged fees for the permits to carry on their business. All permits lasted only during the calendar year, and a charge was exacted for renewals.

With the purpose of easing financial conditions in the counties, the legislature authorized county courts and boards of education to trans-

---

[31] *Acts of the Legislature of West Virginia*, Second Extraordinary Session, 1933, p. 154.

[32] In 1933–34 the state received $1,076,343.20 for the consumer's sales tax.

fer money from one fund to another, and to borrow money from the national government. For example, the board of education of Doddridge County was given permission to secure a loan of $200,000 for the purchase of land and the construction of a high school building. Kanawha County had a different plan. In this case the board of education was given permission to convey land to the national government which in turn would construct school buildings on the land so conveyed. In this transaction it was agreed that the county would levy a tax adequate to make full payment for the buildings within the next thirty years. These methods amounted to borrowing from the federal government for the purpose of making local improvements and to paying the debt in long-time installments. Many municipalities and counties availed themselves of this source of revenue in order to build city halls, gymnasiums, market places, stadiums, etc. Huntington and Charleston revised their charters so that they could secure federal loans to build parks, new streets, and health centers. With the consent of the legislature Parkersburg secured a national loan in order to build an addition to the Camden-Clark Memorial Hospital.[33]

Miscellaneous Taxes

THE ALCOHOL TAX

Since 1920, the year in which the Prohibition Amendment was adopted, the revenue accruing from a tax on medicinal alcohol had not amounted to a great sum. But in 1934 this amendment was repealed, and in the following year the legislature created a commission to supervise the sale of alcohol in West Virginia. This commission set up dispensaries at which alcohol could be sold under the laws of the state. By paying a stipulated fee druggists, industries, and institutions could exercise this same privilege. Prices on alcohol are fixed by the commission, which exacts a heavy tax on each sale.

THE INSURANCE TAX

One of the greatest sources of revenue of the state is the insurance premium tax. Insurance companies are obligated under the present regulations to pay a sum equal to two per cent of the gross premiums received on policies issued in West Virginia, less the premium returned for collections. Annually each company pays the legal

[33] *Acts of the Legislature of West Virginia, Special Session*, 1933, p. 538.

rate to the state insurance commissioner, who deposits his collections with the auditor.

If an insurance company is incorporated under the laws of another state and is also licensed to transact business in West Virginia, the company must file an annual report to the state tax commissioner on or before the first day of March of each year, containing a summary of the business transacted. This report is also submitted to the office of the insurance commissioner. It includes a statement of the gross amount of premiums collected during the year and a remittance totaling two per cent of the collections. The remittance is made to the treasurer of West Virginia.

This law also applies to insurance companies incorporated under the laws of a foreign country that transact business in West Virginia, but only to the extent of the premiums collected in this state. All these companies, like other corporations, pay an annual license tax, the total of which, according to the most recent estimate, amounts to many thousands of dollars.

THE GROSS SALES TAX

The largest single source of revenue deposited in the public treasury comes from the gross sales tax. This money is derived from a small levy on the gross proceeds derived from the sale of coal, oil, gas, limestone, sand, and timber, and is paid by the producer. The rate varies according to the product, and is always subject to change. To extend this principle farther, the state at one time attempted to place an export tax on these products as they were transferred across the boundaries into other states, but the Supreme Court of the United States in the case of Pennsylvania vs. West Virginia declared the law void because it interfered with free commerce between the states.[34]

The gross sales tax has a wide application. It reaches persons engaged in businesses other than those mentioned above; it operates on every individual in West Virginia engaged in selling tangible property, whether real or personal. It is levied on contractors and on places of amusement such as theaters.

The most fruitful item on the whole list is the tax on gasoline. Every distributor, retailer, and importer has to pay an excise tax based on the quantity of gasoline he sells. The gallon measure, not the value, forms the unit for determining the tax. As gasoline flows

[34] Pennsylvania vs. West Virginia, 262 U.S., 553.

from one container to another, the revenue just as surely flows into the treasury of West Virginia.

THE INHERITANCE TAX

The legislature has deemed it proper to place a levy on property transferred or in trust, if the value is five hundred dollars or more. Whether the conveyance is made by deed, by will, or by the law that regulates descent and distribution, the tax must be paid. And it makes no difference whether or not the grantor is a resident or a nonresident of this state; if the property is within the laws of West Virginia, the inheritance tax directly applies to it.

When it is considered that approximately two million people live in West Virginia, it becomes evident that the revenue derived from the tax placed on property transferred in title, by will, or otherwise must be considerable. This law gives the public treasury a share in the large and small estates that pass from parents to children, the rate increasing as the value of the property rises.

THE PARI-MUTUEL TAX

Literally pari-mutuel means a reciprocal wager. In the present context the term refers to a tax levied on horse racing. First levied in West Virginia in 1935, it originally amounted to one per cent on the total poolings of the bets placed. A new law in 1947 raised the rate to three per cent on the first $100,000 and four per cent on amounts exceeding that sum.

In addition to these taxes there is a license fee that takes twelve per cent of the total pools. Besides this revenue all unredeemed moneys accumulated from the wagers won are deposited to the credit of the racing commission for one year. After public notice of this fact has been duly given, the amount remaining upon the expiration of the time limit is forfeited to the treasury of the state. Annually West Virginia receives a considerable sum from the pari-mutuel tax.

THE CIGARETTE STAMP TAX

The legislature of 1947 enacted a law placing a stamp tax, or an excise tax, on the sale of cigarettes. The rate now is one-half cent on each package of ten. Stamps are purchased and affixed to the packages by the manufacturer or the wholesale dealer, who is allowed ten per cent of the value of the stamps for purchasing them and placing them on the packages. This law became operative July 1, 1947.

INSTITUTIONAL CHARGES

A number of institutions maintained by the state render service without charge, while in others certain rates are fixed. Fees are required in the university and the colleges, and in certain hospitals and laboratories, but the amounts gathered revert to the institutions to help meet their expenses. Funds from such fees are not sufficient to meet the total expense of any school, hospital, or laboratory. The rest of the funds are acquired through appropriations made by the legislature. It is a fact, therefore, that some public institutions are run in part at public expense, in part by private funds.

OTHER SOURCES OF REVENUE

Only the main sources of our public revenue have been discussed in this chapter. It may be mentioned that among the many interests contributing to the public revenue are fees charged for the use of parks, the sale of books, examinations, registrations, and various other minor items.

CHAPTER 23

Public Education

Before 1863

INTRODUCTION

Public education was one of the chief interests of the people who first established homes in western Virginia. Although the skill to shoot superseded the skill to read during the rugged years on the frontier, the desire to acquire knowledge persisted in the pioneers, and eventually they found their way to learning just as surely as they marked their roads across the wilds of the Alleghenies to the sources of the rivers flowing west.

No doubt the first efforts made by the pioneers to teach an elementary knowledge in reading, writing, and ciphering occurred when they gathered their children about the hearthstone during that season of the year when the evenings are long and the firesides bright, to impart to them the rudiments of the primary branches. But in general the parents themselves had not gone far in the pursuit of academic knowledge. Before long, if not quite simultaneously with the founding of the first homes, a self-appointed teacher came into the community and canvassed the neighborhood in an effort to establish a subscription school. Although the term was short and the teacher's salary uncertain, this type of school, varying in fashion with the changes of the times, lasted more than a hundred years.

THE ALDERMANIC LAW

The state of Virginia exercised only a feeble effort to support public education in the west, having confined most of its assistance to the eastern region. However, in 1796 the legislature passed the aldermanic school law, which provided for the establishment of an elementary public school within a reasonable distance of every family, where the children might be taught the fundamentals of reading, writing, and arithmetic. This plan seemed to provide at least the outline of a definite school system, but because authority to set the time for the election of the school officials rested with the county court, whose members were often indifferent to public education, the aldermanic law in reality never became operative in western Virginia. There is some evidence, however, that schools were established here before the turn of the century. An interesting feature of the proposed system was the provision that the entire management of the schools should be in the hands of three county officers known as aldermen, who could divide the county into several districts, employ teachers, estimate the cost of building schoolhouses, pay the teachers, and lay a levy upon the property in the county to defray expenses.

THE LITERARY FUND

In response to an increasing demand for schools, the legislature in 1810 created the literary fund. According to this law, funds for supporting public education were to be derived from escheats, forfeitures, and confiscated properties. But these funds were to be devoted to the payment of the expenses of poor children who could not afford to attend the private and subscription schools.

The literary fund stimulated the establishment of elementary schools, but more people would have taken advantage of its provisions if the odium of "poor" had not applied to them. In fact the plan was sometimes called the "pauper system." Although the state applied a generous share of its revenue to the select schools, and later to the university, the literary fund in part was used to stimulate the growth of elementary education. In 1833 the total number of public schools in Virginia had reached 678, attended by 5816 poor children, a large majority of whom lived east of the Alleghenies. During this period the state had developed four types of schools, public primary, private, subscription, and the university.

THE REFORM OF 1846

Certain amendments had been made in the law of 1810 but the changes did not satisfy the advocates of public education. In answer to popular demands the legislature in 1846 passed an act establishing a uniform school system for the entire state. According to the new law the freemen in each county were to elect a board of education whose duty was to divide the county into districts, appoint teachers, construct buildings, and name trustees to care for each schoolhouse.

As had been the case in other instances, the manner of financing these uniform schools offered the greatest problem. The board of education drew part of its support from the literary fund, while the balance had to be supplied from a school tax levied on property by a two-thirds vote of the freemen in the county. Only five counties later to be incorporated in West Virginia accepted the provisions of this law, namely, Jefferson, Kanawha, Ohio, Cabell, and Wayne. Despite popular reluctance to adopt the new plan, it was actually the beginning of a public school system in Virginia and West Virginia.

A county board of education, consisting of one commissioner from each district, had the responsibility of administering the schools. The commissioners, elected annually, were a corporate body that inspected the schools, apportioned the funds among the districts, fixed the salaries of teachers, and named trustees for the several districts.

The district was in charge of three trustees whose duties included the purchase of sites, the building and supplying of schoolhouses, and the keeping of these houses enclosed and in proper repair. They appointed teachers and drew orders on the sheriff for the teachers' salaries as well as for other expenses, and they filed an annual report with the commissioners concerning conditions in the schools, operations, and expenses. The revenue was derived from a share of the literary fund, fines, forfeitures, donations, and taxation on all taxable property. The law was broad enough to remove from the tax-supported schools the odium of poverty, and the idea that public education is a public duty was becoming more evident.

At an election held in 1846 Jefferson County accepted the new public school system. A vote of 861 to 180 favored it, but the regulations were not put into effect by the county commissioners until the following year, when the legislature amended the law. The school system was put into operation in Jefferson County as fast as schoolhouses could be built. By 1861 there were twenty-seven schools in the county. Ohio and Kanawha counties also favored the new law and organized their first public schools in 1847. Although other counties in western Virginia voted in favor of establishing public schools, only five actually enjoyed those advantages prior to 1861, Cabell and Wayne having followed the examples of the other three. The agitation carried on for a public school system prepared the people to accept the regulation put into force by the new constitution of 1863.

Public Schools under the First Constitution

CONSTITUTIONAL PROVISIONS

The wise men who drafted the first constitution for West Virginia did not neglect to make ample provision for a system of public elementary schools. That was one of the issues about which the people of the West had contended with Richmond for many years, and they would not miss the chance when the power was placed in their own hands.

The Reverend Gordon Battelle, an ardent advocate of public schools, served as chairman of the committee on education in the constitutional convention. The chairman was wise and careful in his discriminations and basically sound in his decisions. Article X of the constitution surely left no doubt about the policy of the state on this matter. "The legislature shall provide, as soon as practicable, for the establishment of a thorough and efficient system of free schools." Obedient to this injunction the lawmakers hastened to comply with its demands, but they would not attempt to demolish completely the system inherited from Virginia. Rather they would graft a new branch to the old stem to make sure the plant would flourish. So it was written, "The school districts into which any township is now divided shall continue until changed by the board of education thereof." [1]

Not only did the constitution make a system of education a requirement in the state but it also outlined the method of its financial support and administration. It declared that a general superintendent was to have authority over all the schools, a state board of education was to be appointed by the governor, a superintendent and a board were to serve in each county, and the electors in every township

[1] *Code of West Virginia,* 1870, p. 290.

were to choose a board of school commissioners. One of the greatest improvements had to do with the raising of school funds. The literary fund was abolished and in the new state the finances were hereafter to be derived from fines, forfeitures, confiscations, and "general taxation on persons and property, or otherwise."

The constitution made it an obligation on the legislature to furnish educational advantages for the blind and the deaf-mutes, and to provide any other institutions of learning that would serve the best interests of the people. Here was a broad foundation on which a popular government could actually live and thrive, always supported by the people and administered for the general welfare.

ESTABLISHMENT OF THE SYSTEM

On December 10, 1863, the legislature passed an act establishing the first public school system in West Virginia. This act fulfilled the obligation exacted by the constitution. The aim of the lawmakers was to provide a means of instruction for all the youth of the state in such learning as would qualify them for the adequate discharge of their social and civil duties.[2]

The qualified voters in each township elected, according to the law, three commissioners for terms of three years. The three officers constituted a board of education for their township, a body corporate in law, which had the care, custody, and management of all property used for the public schools. They appointed a secretary who kept an official record of all proceedings of the board, and filed in his office all papers, contracts, and obligations as the board required.

In order to determine the number of schoolhouses needed in every township the board ordered (1864) the taking of an enumeration of all the youth residing within each school district. When this data had been gathered the board divided the township into subdistricts, allowing as nearly as possible fifty pupils for each subdivision. For this number of pupils the same authority provided for "one school for not less than six months in the year."

It was also incumbent on the board of education to appoint the teachers within its district, fix the amount of their salary, and dismiss them for general incompetency. This same authority fixed the branches of learning to be taught, selected the textbooks, and took any other action to promote the interests of education. Annually the board made a report to the county superintendent, covering in

[2] *Acts of the Legislature of West Virginia*, 1863, p. 245.

detail all matters relating to the teaching and administration of the schools.

HIGH SCHOOLS

Whenever, in the opinion of the board, the interest of education would be so promoted, a central union school of higher grade could be established. The board of education called a township meeting and if after full deliberation two-thirds of the qualified voters present and voting favored the proposition, the school would be established. Such institutions, however, did not at once become active. For many years the elementary grades filled the immediate needs of the general public. It is a matter of interest to note that the school of higher grade was referred to as a "union school."

SCHOOLS FOR COLORED CHILDREN

The legislature included in the law a provision for the education of colored children. The township board of education was authorized and required to establish schools for colored children wherever the whole number of enumeration exceeded thirty; if the number were less, the board cared for the education of the children in the way it thought best. Under the laws of Virginia no educational advancement had ever been promised to the colored people, but the progressive and humane attitude of the legislature of West Virginia may be marked in these acts. Early steps were taken to organize schools under this law. A separate school for the benefit of the colored youth of Wheeling was opened for the first time in November, 1866. Agents of the Freedmen's Bureau, upon learning what had been done for the interest of the colored people, visited the city and gave their approval.

THE COUNTY SUPERINTENDENT

On the same day on which the electorate chose the boards of education they also voted for a county superintendent of schools, whose term was two years. The law assigned to this officer a multitude of duties, among which was the examination of candidates for certificates in the primary and union schools. The certificates could be used only in the counties in which they were issued and were valid for only one year. At least three times during the term of six months the superintendent visited each school and made a thorough inspection of the manner of teaching and the condition of the school buildings and equipment. Through the organization of county teachers associations and teachers institutes he encouraged the development of skill in teaching.

Perhaps never before in the history of this country had any state struggled so valiantly to overcome a regional handicap as West Virginia did to organize a system of public schools, to improve the efficiency of teachers, and to elevate their profession. The effort included not only the improvement of a scientific profession but also the creating and fostering of popular interest in public schools sustained by public taxation. Much of the effort to impress upon the people the importance of public education was left in the hands of the county superintendents, and with them rested, very largely, the success or failure of the plan.

The county superintendent, in addition to making frequent visitations, kept in close touch with local conditions by receiving annual reports from the township boards. The reports contained such items as the number of schools in the township, the number of teachers and pupils, the salaries of teachers, and all other expenses. From these statements he secured the data contained in his annual report to the state superintendent.

THE STATE SUPERINTENDENT

At the head of the school system of the state was a general superintendent, elected by a joint vote of both branches of the legislature. He held office for a term of two years. On the third Tuesday in January, 1864, William R. White was chosen as the first man to fill this important office. The superintendent did not begin his official work until the first day of June following his election.

The chief obligation assumed by the superintendent was to see that the new school system became uniformly operative. This undertaking had many complications, one of the most perplexing of which was the interpretation of the school law as it applied to the powers and duties of township boards of education, school commissioners, and county superintendents. The legislature had called upon him to perfect the system of free schools it had so well outlined, and in his administrative duties he had a large degree of freedom.

It was expected that the superintendent would keep in communication with the school authorities in other states, keep informed on the most modern improvements in his field of work, and recommend sound principles of education. Annually, before the first day of August, he reported to the auditor the number of persons between the ages of six and twenty-one years in each county, the conditions of the schools, including the statistics compiled from the reports of the several county superintendents, and such plans as he might have matured for a more perfect organization of the public school system. In addition to these many duties the state superintendent signed all requisitions on the auditor for the payment of money into the county treasuries for the use of the public schools. He stood in a place of leadership to develop a popular sentiment for education in the state. The governor and legislature appealed to him for information relating to education and for proposals for legislation to further the advantages of learning.

THE SCHOOL FUND

The organization and administration of the public schools depended on an adequate appropriation of funds. A general school fund was formed from the proceeds realized from the sale of forfeited, delinquent, and unappropriated lands; from grants, devises, and bequests; and from sums of money appropriated by the legislature. All of this money, known as the school fund, was invested in interest-bearing securities and the amount of the accrued interest devoted to maintaining public education. The governor, auditor, treasurer, and superintendent of schools constituted the Board of the School Fund, which managed the finances used for public education according to the regulations prescribed by law.

In addition to the amount set aside by the legislature the district boards of education levied annually a tax on the property within their districts, sufficient to keep the schools in session for at least four months each year. The first report submitted by the state superintendent (1865) indicates that under this financial plan West Virginia started out with 133 schoolhouses, 431 schools, and 15,972 pupils. During the following year 935 schools were taught and the number of pupils increased to 34,219.[3]

Here in brief is given a sketch of the first school system in West Virginia. It was indeed a small beginning but the desire for more learning had sprung up. The movement traveled with such force that within the following decade schoolhouses stood by the side of every highway and within reach of all the youth of West Virginia.

[3] By 1876 we had 3137 schoolhouses and a youth enumeration of 184,760.

Public Schools under the Second Constitution

ORGANIZATION

The new constitution of 1872 reasserted the principle of its predecessor by declaring, "The legislature shall provide by general law for a thorough and efficient system of free schools." In the following year the legislature formulated a new school law which, with certain changes, remains the basis of the school system of today. Under the new code the school administration consisted of a state superintendent, county superintendents, district boards of education, and trustees for each precinct.

The state superintendent hereafter was to be elected by popular vote, a change the wisdom of which has been debated for many years. His term was four years and his general duties remained very much the same as before. The county superintendent was elected by the voters for two years only. He presided over the board of examiners that issued certificates to teachers, distributed funds to the boards of education, and annually submitted a report to the state superintendent.

The district board of education, composed of a president and two commissioners elected by popular vote, had fairly complete control of the local schools. The board, a corporation, fixed levies, located new schoolhouses and supervised their construction, supplied fuel and equipment, cared for the financial interests of the district, determined the number of subdistricts, and appointed three trustees for each school. This plan brought the administration of the elementary schools close to the people, particularly in the power exercised by the trustees, who were usually parents of some of the children placed under the care of the local teacher. The trustees, whose acts were subject to review by the board, appointed the teacher and assisted him in keeping the schoolhouse in repair and in comfortable condition. With certain amendments enacted from time to time, this organization continued in operation until 1933, when the county unit system came to be established.

The county unit system dispensed with the district and subdistrict officers and replaced them with a county board of education which took control of all the schools in the county. The county now constitutes one school district. At the general election the voters choose the five nonpartisan members of the board, whose term of office is four years.[4] The county board appoints the superintendent and takes

[4] *Acts of the Legislature of West Virginia*, 1933, p. 79.

charge of all public schools and properties devoted to educational interests in the county. It assures a minimum term of nine months or such part thereof as the maximum levy permits. It appoints teachers, lays the levy, secures sites for new buildings, and establishes high schools when and where public interest demands them.

To finance the new school system, under which the salaries of teachers were increased and the annual term lengthened, the board lays a uniform levy on the property within the county. In case the total amount accumulated from this source does not sustain all expenses, the state supplements the sum to a point where the state superintendent considers that a fair portion of available money has been extended to the needy county. The supplementary amount is taken from a general school fund accumulated from taxes, licenses, etc.

One of the outstanding features of the new law provides for the consolidation of schools and for payment at public expense for transportation of the youth to and from the school buildings. Taking advantage of this act and of the good roads that have made the change possible, the boards of education have conducted a definite program of consolidation since 1933.

INDEPENDENT SCHOOL DISTRICTS

The reform law of 1933 abolished the independent school districts, which had flourished in West Virginia from the time of the enactment of our first school law. The city of Wheeling had been made an independent school district as early as 1849, and when it became a part of West Virginia no change was made in the status of the schools. The example having been set, acts passed by the legislature in 1867 formed special districts in Clarksburg, Moundsville, and Morgantown. The concentration of taxable property in these cities made possible the higher levies necessary to maintain longer terms, to pay teachers higher salaries, and to build and equip better school buildings than the rural sections of the state could afford.

Out of the development of the independent district and the improved conditions in the elementary grades, there grew a demand for high schools in West Virginia. One can scarcely fix the time and place at which our first high school began. The state superintendent in 1892 reported seventeen such schools already in session. These were not district high schools, although in them grades above the elementary rank were taught. The high school movement did not begin in earnest until shortly after the turn of the century, when a campaign was begun to establish at least one secondary school in every county. From such a beginning the program has now reached its present state of development.

The Development of Academies

Long before West Virginia was formed the age of academies had begun, and from the number established one may measure the eagerness of the enterprising people for learning and more learning. So far as can now be ascertained, the first school of this rank in the state was Shepherdstown Academy, established about 1785, with Randolph Academy at Clarksburg, founded in 1787, running a close second. Extant records show that at least sixty-five of these schools were in operation in western Virginia before the Civil War.

Some of the earliest academies were established by acts of the legislature and in part supported by public funds. For instance, the school at Clarksburg received one-eighth of the surveyor's fees of the counties of Ohio, Harrison, Monongalia, and Randolph. Previous to that time such fees had gone to the support of William and Mary College. However, most of the academies had an altogether independent status. Some were denominational schools and were supported by friends and patrons; others were founded by diligent citizens interested in creating advantages for the youth of their region. Eventually a few of the academies became colleges which are still thriving.

Normal and Preparatory Schools

NORMAL SCHOOLS

Shortly after the inauguration of the first school system in West Virginia, Superintendent William R. White (1863–1869) observed that the lack of trained teachers was the greatest handicap to his work. He therefore turned his attention to inducing the legislature to establish teacher-training schools. In this effort he was notably successful. The year of 1867 witnessed the establishment of three normal schools designed for educating teachers. One of these institutions was established at Fairmont, one at West Liberty, and one at Guyandotte (later Huntington).[5] Their marked success created

[5] The school at Fairmont opened May 6, 1867. It continued in session five months, with an attendance of thirty-three "ladies and gentlemen." *Journal, Bills and Documents of the House,* 1868, p. 83.

a demand for others. In 1872 institutions were established at Shepherdstown, Glenville, and Concord.

All these schools have stood as safeguards to the school system in West Virginia. For many years they were styled normal schools, then they were renamed teacher colleges, and more recently colleges. They furnished not only training courses for teachers but also academic preparatory courses for entry to college and university. For many years most of our leaders in education began their preparatory work in the normal schools.

PREPARATORY SCHOOLS

The preparatory branch of the University had its beginning with the organization of the department of higher education and lasted until 1912, by which time the high schools had supplanted the need for it. To give other sections of the state better opportunities for entrance to the University, the legislature in 1895 established a preparatory school at Montgomery, in Fayette County, and in 1901 another at Keyser, in Mineral County. The second of these schools now has junior college rating as a branch of the University. The school at Montgomery has undergone several changes. In 1917 it became the West Virginia Trade School; in 1921 it was renamed New River State School, under which name it was made a degree-granting institution in 1928; in 1931 its title was changed to New River State College; and since 1941 it has been the West Virginia Institute of Technology.

Schools for Colored People

It has been seen that one of the first schools, if not the first, for the colored youth of the state opened in Wheeling, November, 1866. The board of education had purchased land and constructed a building of sufficient size for all the colored children. The cost of the property, which included a house for the janitor, amounted to nearly $2500. The school was soon visited by the agents of the Freedmen's Bureau, who found the conditions in agreement with their standards.[6]

At the same time that Wheeling District opened its school for colored children, preparations were made for establishing the same kind of school at Moundsville, where a sufficient number of pupils had been enumerated to meet the provision of the law. Other

---

[6] *Annual Report of the Superintendent of Free Schools*, 1867, p. 46.

counties fell in line with Ohio and Marshall. By 1892 Clarksburg had one hundred colored children in school, Martinsburg had a building in which two teachers were employed, Huntington had four teachers, and Parkersburg had an enumeration of one hundred seventy-seven pupils.[7]

Institutions of Higher Learning for Colored People

Through the influence of President John Cheney of Bates College, a gift was extended by John Storer of Maine to establish a college for the freed people of the South. The gift amounted to $10,000, with the provision that the same sum be raised by interested parties within the year 1867. Mission schools were being organized in the Shenandoah Valley and Mr. Storer came into that region for the purpose of locating his school. After careful investigation he decided that Bolivar Heights at Harpers Ferry would be most suitable for this purpose.

The matter having been taken up with Secretary Stanton of the War Department and General O. P. Howard of the Freedmen's Bureau, four buildings owned by the government were loaned for the use of the college. Largely through the influence of Senator Fessenden and General James A. Garfield in the House of Representatives, Congress made a gift of the property toward the founding of Storer College. The houses had been used as headquarters for the officers of the Union Army stationed at Harpers Ferry. By reason of these gifts the college opened its doors October 2, 1867. The institution secured a charter from the legislature of West Virginia two years later.

An act of Congress passed August 30, 1890, authorized that a portion of the proceeds realized from the sale of public lands be devoted to the more complete endowment of the agricultural and industrial arts. West Virginia received $18,000 from this source of revenue, and by act of the legislature an equitable portion of this sum was given to establish the West Virginia Colored Institute. The legislature, having fixed the location of the school in Kanawha County, set aside $10,000 to purchase a farm and construct a building. A committee appointed to find a suitable location for the school finally decided to purchase a site on the Kanawha River about eight miles west of Charleston. The school was chartered in 1891 and in the following year the first building was completed. In 1915

[7] Cork and Morgan, *Education in West Virginia* (Charleston, 1893).

the name was changed to West Virginia Collegiate Institute, and in 1929 it became West Virginia State College. This school has had a successful growth and has achieved a very creditable academic rating.

Another school of higher education for colored people is Bluefield State College. The legislature established this school in 1895 as Bluefield Colored Institute. In 1931 the name was changed to Bluefield State Teachers College and in 1943 to Bluefield State College.

Originally the institution was a high school. By authorization of the legislature, the Board of Regents in 1895 purchased four acres of land on an eminence overlooking Bluefield, and early in the following year let a contract for the construction of the first building on the campus. On December 6, 1896, students were admitted to classes. Through legislative appropriation classrooms, laboratories, and dormitories have been added. At the present time about one thousand students are enrolled.

This college, now offering both technical and teacher-training courses, has rendered outstanding service and merits a wide patronage. There is every reason to expect its continued growth.

School for the Deaf and Blind

West Virginia had no school for its deaf and blind people until 1870. Virginia had failed to establish a suitable institution west of the mountains for such unfortunate persons; and when the new state was formed it arranged with Virginia and Ohio for the education of its deaf and blind children. This arrangement soon proved entirely unsatisfactory, since very few availed themselves of the advantages offered.[8]

Largely through the influence of H. H. Johnson, supported by the interest of Governor Wm. E. Stevenson, the legislature on March 3, 1870, passed a bill to establish a school for the blind and deaf. Under the law the governor appointed one person from each senatorial district to constitute the Board of Regents of the West Virginia Institute for the Deaf and Dumb and Blind. This board of eleven members[9] had power to carry the provisions of the bill into effect. The amount appropriated to establish and administer the school for one year was $8,000.

After forming its organization the board invited various towns to

---

8 Deaf and blind children from West Virginia had attended school at Staunton, Va.

9 The number was later reduced to seven.

compete in offering inducements for the location of the school. The Literary Society of Romney, supported by the citizens of the town, offered the building of the Romney Classical Institute and fifteen acres of land as a site for the school. The board considered this offer the most favorable one received and at a meeting held in Parkersburg, June 23, 1870, it unanimously decided to locate the school at Romney in Hampshire County.

There was no delay in remodeling the building and preparing it for occupation. At a meeting of the board held at Romney, July, 1870, H. H. Hollister was elected as the first principal of the school, and on September 29 of the same year pupils were received in the new institution. The number of pupils totaled thirty, twenty-five mute and five blind. In addition to the principal three other teachers were appointed on the staff, Rosa R. Harris, Holdridge Chidester, and H. H. Johnson, the blind teacher who had been so active in the creation of the school.

The school met with popular favor at once, and in his first report Mr. Hollister requested an appropriation of $20,000 to increase the capacity of the building and to secure adequate equipment. His request was answered by a liberal appropriation, and soon two wings were added to the main structure, each thirty by seventy feet and three stories high.

From this humble beginning the institution has continued to grow in number of buildings, enrollment, and efficiency. The legislature has made generous appropriations for its maintenance. More than three hundred students are now enrolled in elementary, secondary, and vocational courses. In 1887 the legislature changed the name of the institution to the West Virginia School for the Deaf and Blind, a title which it still bears. In the organization of the curriculum separate schools are maintained for the deaf and blind pupils.

The West Virginia School for the Colored Deaf and Blind Children was chartered in 1925 and located about eight miles west of Charleston. Only about fifty pupils are now enrolled, but they enjoy the same advantages as those in the school at Romney.

Other State-controlled Institutions

Other publicly controlled institutions, including charitable, correctional, penal, and medical centers, are maintained by the state but cannot be considered as altogether educational. They operate at public expense so that proper care may be extended to the unfortunate. Each of these places is devoted to a special work, equipped with laboratories, and manned by highly trained technicians. The patients in the tubercular sanitariums at Hopemont and Pinecrest have the most skillful treatment for their affliction. On the other hand the industrial schools for boys and girls offer vocational and spiritual training for the inmates. The penal institutions give proper treatment to those persons convicted of crime who are segregated temporarily or permanently from civil society. The convict is taught a trade so that when he regains freedom he may re-establish himself in society and gain an honorable livelihood rather than continue to live as a public ward.

West Virginia University

By a legislative act passed December 4, 1868, West Virginia University was established. It superseded the West Virginia Agricultural College which originated from the National Land Grant Act passed by Congress July 2, 1862. The college, established in 1867, had absorbed the property of the Monongalia Academy and Woodburn Seminary, whose trustees had tendered the real estate and personal property of both schools to the state on condition that the land-grant college be located at Morgantown.

According to the Morrill Act passed by Congress in 1862, 30,000 acres of western public lands were allocated to each state for every senator and representative it had in the national Congress. The total area of land apportioned to West Virginia through this plan amounted to 150,000 acres, which the designated authorities very unwisely sold for only $90,000. This sum, increased from time to time by legislative appropriation, constituted a fund for the support of the school. According to the language of the original bill, the amount realized from the sale of the land shall constitute "a perpetual fund, the capital of which shall remain forever undiminished and the interest of which shall be inviolably appropriated to the endowment, support, and maintenance of at least one college, where the leading subjects shall be, without excluding other scientific and classical studies, and including military tactics, . . . such branches of learning as are related to agriculture and the mechanical arts." The transfer of the Agricultural College to the University did not violate the provision of the law.

Originally the institution was governed by a Board of Visitors, but upon its change to the University the governing body became the Board of Regents, consisting of one person from each senatorial district, appointed by the governor. This arrangement continued until 1919, when the governing power over the institution was given to the State Board of Education. Apparently the new plan did not work well enough to warrant its continuation. In 1927 the legislature vested the government of the University in a Board of Governors consisting of nine members appointed by the governor for a term of four years. Although some criticism has been made of this plan, it has given a high degree of satisfaction.

The Board of Governors has charge of the educational, financial, administrative, and business affairs of the University and its branch at Keyser. The board possesses full authority to employ all officers, teachers, and other employees of the University and fix their salaries, but the total amount of expenditures shall not exceed an aggregate fixed by the Board of Control. Under this plan of administration West Virginia University has experienced a period of great expansion.

In the beginning of the organization of the University the Board of Visitors, at a meeting held April 3, 1867, elected Dr. Alexander Martin as the first president. Since that time thirteen other administrators have filled the presidency of this institution, with an average tenure of about six years. Since the duties of administration have grown so numerous within the last years, the office of vice president and comptroller has been created to relieve the president somewhat of his burdens.

The method of financing has an important part in the history and administration of all institutions. It has been seen that West Virginia University draws a part of its support from the annual interest received from the land-grant endowment. Other revenues are derived from appropriations set aside by acts passed by the Congress of the United States for the support of special programs such as the Smith-Hughes and Smith-Lever funds. The major part of the revenue, however, comes from the biennial appropriations made by the state legislature, which are devoted to the purchase of grounds, construction of buildings, securing of apparatus and equipment, and payment of salaries. A considerable amount of financial support is derived from farms owned by the University, athletic games, and contributions made by private benefactors.

The Board of Governors appoints the president of the University and determines the amount of his salary. The length of his term is not limited to a fixed number of years, but, as has been noted above, the average tenure in office has not been very long.

The president's powers both general and particular are considerable. In the first place he is president of the general faculty and of the faculty of each college and department. He is the chief executive of all the various divisions and departments of the institution. His duties relate to administration and to the supervision of scientific investigations carried on in the University.

At the conclusion of each biennial period the president makes a report to the Board of Governors and the State Board of Control. In this report he relates in detail the conditions prevailing in the University and the progress it has achieved. At its discretion the board may request special information from the president, and he may relate such other details as he thinks it prudent to communicate.

In addition to the president the chief academic officers of the University are the deans and directors who are the administrative heads of the several colleges and schools. The business manager, the director of intercollegiate athletics, and the registrar also have important duties of administration. The University Senate is a legislative body composed of members of the faculty which exercises jurisdiction over academic matters relating to the University in general or to more than one college or division.

The University has kept in the van in its development and professional growth. From a small beginning it has expanded to embrace several colleges, schools, divisions, and an extension service that reaches every county in the state. Its physical plant, consisting of buildings, apparatus, farms, and equipment, is ever on the increase in order to accommodate an enrollment that now exceeds seven thousand students and a faculty that has risen from only five members [10] to approximately four hundred. The campus of sixty-six acres has been recently enlarged by purchase of another plot of about two hundred acres.

[10] The members of the first faculty were Alexander Martin, President; J. W. Scott, F. S. Lyon, S. G. Stevens and J. R. Weaver.

APPENDIX 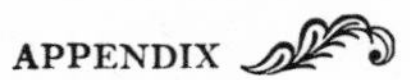

The Constitution of West Virginia

RATIFIED IN 1872

TABLE OF CONTENTS

ARTICLE I

RELATIONS TO THE GOVERNMENT OF THE UNITED STATES

1. The State of West Virginia is, and shall remain, one of the United States of America. The Constitution of the United States of America, and the laws and treaties made in pursuance thereof, shall be the supreme law of the land.

INTERNAL GOVERNMENT AND POLICE

2. The Government of the United States is a government of enumerated powers, and all powers not delegated to it, nor inhibited to the States, are reserved to the States or to the people thereof. Among the powers so reserved by the States is the exclusive regulation of their own internal government and police; and it is the high and solemn duty of the several departments of government, created by this Constitution, to guard and protect the people of this State from all encroachments upon the rights so reserved.

CONTINUITY OF CONSTITUTIONAL OPERATION

3. The provisions of the Constitution of the United States, and of this State, are operative alike in a period of war as in time of peace, and any departure therefrom, or violation, thereof, under the plea of necessity, or any other plea, is subversive of good government, and tends to anarchy and despotism.

REPRESENTATIVES TO CONGRESS

4. For the election of representatives to congress, the State shall be divided into districts, corresponding in number with the representatives to which it may be entitled, which districts shall be formed of contiguous counties, and be compact. Each district shall contain, as nearly as may be, an equal number of population, to be determined according to the rule prescribed in the Constitution of the United States.

ARTICLE II

THE STATE

1. The territory of the following counties, formerly parts of the Commonwealth of Virginia, shall constitute and form the State of West Virginia, viz:

The counties of Barbour, Berkeley, Boone, Braxton, Brooke, Cabell, Calhoun, Clay, Doddridge, Fayette, Gilmer, Grant, Greenbrier, Hampshire, Hancock, Hardy, Harrison, Jackson, Jefferson, Kanawha, Lewis, Lincoln, Logan, Marion, Marshall, Mason, McDowell, Mercer, Mineral, Mingo, Monongalia, Monroe, Morgan, Nicholas, Ohio, Pendleton, Pleasants, Pocahontas, Preston, Putnam, Raleigh, Randolph, Ritchie, Roane, Summers, Taylor, Tucker, Tyler, Upshur, Wayne, Webster, Wetzel, Wirt, Wood and Wyoming. The State of West Virginia includes the bed, bank and shores of the Ohio River, and so much of the Big Sandy River as was formerly included in the Commonwealth of Virginia; in all territorial rights and property in, and jurisdiction over the same, heretofore reserved by, and vested in, the Commonwealth of Virginia, are vested in and shall hereafter be exercised by the State of West Virginia. And such parts of the said beds, banks and shores as lie opposite, and adjoining the several counties of this State, shall form parts of said several counties respectively.

[All of the territory of West Virginia was taken from the Commonwealth of Virginia and in the first constitution forty-four of the above named counties were designated as forming the State of West Virginia, and in addition the counties of Berkeley, Hampshire, Hardy, Jefferson, Morgan and Pendleton were to be admitted should the constitution be adopted by a vote of the people of the districts comprising the counties. The districts adopted the constitution and these six counties became a part of the State.

The remaining five counties were created by acts of the legislature as follows: Mineral County, from Hampshire County, on February 1, 1866; Grant County, from Hardy County, on February 14, 1866; Lincoln County from parts of Cabell, Putnam, Kanawha and Boone Counties, on February 23, 1867; Summers County, from parts of Greenbrier, Monroe, Mercer and Fayette Counties, on February 27, 1871; and Mingo County, from Logan County, on February 23, 1895.]

POWERS OF GOVERNMENT IN CITIZENS

2. The powers of government reside in all the citizens of the State, and can be rightfully exercised only in accordance with their will and appointment.

REQUISITES OF CITIZENSHIP

3. All persons residing in this State, born, or naturalized in the United States, and subject to the jurisdiction thereof, shall be citizens of this State.

EQUAL REPRESENTATION

4. Every citizen shall be entitled to equal representation in the government, and, in all apportionments of representation, equality of numbers of those entitled thereto shall, as far as practicable, be preserved.

PROVISIONS REGARDING PROPERTY

5. No distinction shall be made between resident aliens and citizens as to the acquisition, tenure, disposition or descent of property.

TREASON, WHAT CONSTITUTES — PENALTY

6. Treason against the State shall consist only in levying war against it, or in adhering to its enemies, giving them aid and comfort. No person shall be convicted of treason, unless on the testimony of two witnesses to the same overt act, or on confession in open court. Treason shall be punished according to the character of the acts committed, by the infliction of one, or more, of the penalties of death, imprisonment or fine, as may be prescribed by law.

"MONTANI SEMPER LIBERI" — STATE SEAL

7. The present seal of the State, with its motto, "*Montani Semper Liberi*," shall be the great seal of the State of West Virginia, and

shall be kept by the Secretary of State, to be used by him officially, as directed by law.

WRITS, COMMISSIONS, OFFICIAL BONDS — INDICTMENTS

8. Writs, grants and commissions, issued under the authority of this State shall run in the name of, and official bond shall be made payable to the State of West Virginia. Indictments shall conclude, "Against the peace and dignity of the State."

ARTICLE III

BILL OF RIGHTS

1. All men are, by nature, equally free and independent, and have certain inherent rights, of which, when they enter into a state of society, they cannot by any compact, deprive or divest their posterity, namely: the enjoyment of life and liberty, with the means of acquiring and possessing property, and of pursuing and obtaining happiness and safety.

MAGISTRATES SERVANTS OF PEOPLE

2. All power is vested in, and consequently derived from the people. Magistrates are their trustees and servants, and at all times amenable to them.

RIGHTS RESERVED TO PEOPLE

3. Government is instituted for the common benefit, protection and security of the people, nation or community. Of all its various forms, that is the best which is capable of producing the greatest degree of happiness and safety, and is most effectually secured against the danger of maladministration; and when any government shall be found inadequate or contrary to these purposes, a majority of the community has an indubitable, inalienable and indefeasible right to reform, alter or abolish it in such manner as shall be judged most conducive to the public weal.

WRIT OF HABEAS CORPUS

4. The privilege of the writ of *habeas corpus* shall not be suspended. No person shall be held to answer for treason, felony or other crime, not cognizable by a justice, unless on presentment or indictment of a grand jury. No bill of attainder, *ex-post facto* law, or law impairing the obligation of a contract, shall be passed.

EXCESSIVE BAIL NOT REQUIRED

5. Excessive bail shall not be required, nor excessive fines imposed, nor cruel and unusual punishment inflicted. Penalties shall be proportioned to the character and degree of the offense. No person shall be transported out of, or forced to leave the State for any offense committed within the same; nor shall any person, in any criminal case, be compelled to be a witness against himself, or be twice put in jeopardy of life or liberty for the same offense.

UNREASONABLE SEARCH AND SEIZURE PROHIBITED

6. The right of the citizens to be secure in their houses, persons, papers and effects, against unreasonable searches and seizures, shall not be violated. No warrant shall issue except upon probable cause, supported by oath or affirmation, particularly describing the place to be searched, or the person or thing to be seized.

FREEDOM OF SPEECH AND PRESS GUARANTEED

7. No law abridging the freedom of speech, or of the press, shall be passed; but the Legislature may, by suitable penalties, restrain the publication or sale of obscene books, papers, or pictures, and provide for the punishment of libel, and defamation of character, and for the recovery, in civil actions, by the aggrieved party, of suitable damages for such libel, or defamation.

RELATING TO CIVIL SUITS FOR LIBEL

8. In prosecutions and civil suits for libel, the truth may be given in evidence; and if it shall appear to the jury, that the matter charged

as libelous is true, and was published with good motives, and for justifiable ends, the verdict shall be for the defendant.

PRIVATE PROPERTY, HOW TAKEN

9. Private property shall not be taken or damaged for public use, without just compensation; nor shall the same be taken by any company, incorporated for the purposes of internal improvement, until just compensation shall have been paid, or secured to be paid, to the owner; and when private property shall be taken, or damaged, for public use, or for the use of such corporations, the compensation to the owner shall be ascertained in such manner as may be prescribed by general law: *Provided*, That when required by either of the parties, such compensation shall be ascertained by an impartial jury of twelve freeholders.

SAFEGUARDS FOR LIFE, LIBERTY, AND PROPERTY

10. No person shall be deprived of life, liberty, or property, without due process of law, and the judgment of his peers.

POLITICAL TESTS CONDEMNED

11. Political tests, requiring persons, as a prerequisite to the enjoyment of their civil and political rights, to purge themselves by their own oaths, of past alleged offenses, are repugnant to the principles of free government, and are cruel and oppressive. No religious or political test oath shall be required as a prerequisite or qualification to vote, serve as a juror, sue, plead, appeal, or pursue any profession or employment. Nor shall any person be deprived by law of any right or privilege, because of any act done prior to the passage of such law.

MILITARY SUBORDINATE TO CIVIL POWER

12. Standing armies, in time of peace, should be avoided as dangerous to liberty. The military shall be subordinate to the civil power; and no citizen unless engaged in the military service of the

State, shall be tried or punished by any military court, for any offense that is cognizable by the civil courts of the State. No soldier shall, in time of peace, be quartered in any house, without the consent of the owner, nor in time of war, except in the manner to be prescribed by law.

RIGHT OF JURY TRIAL

13. In suits at common law, where the value in controversy exceeds twenty dollars exclusive of interest and costs, the right of trial by jury, if required by either party, shall be preserved; and in such suit before a justice a jury may consist of six persons. No fact tried by a jury shall be otherwise re-examined in any case than according to the rules of the common law.

[This section, prior to its amendment, read as follows: "In suits at common law, where the value in controversy, exclusive of interest and costs, exceeds twenty dollars, the right of trial by a jury of twelve men, if required by either party, shall be preserved; except that in appeals from judgments of justices, a jury of a less number may be authorized by law; but in trials of civil cases before a justice no jury shall be allowed and no fact tried by a jury shall in any case be otherwise re-examined than according to the rules of common law."

The amendment as set forth above was proposed by joint resolution of March 7, 1879, and was adopted at the general election in 1880. Vote on the amendment: For ratification, 56,482; against ratification, 34,073; majority, 22,409.]

TRIAL OF CRIMES — PROVISIONS IN INTEREST OF ACCUSED

14. Trials of crimes, and of misdemeanors, unless herein otherwise provided, shall be by a jury of twelve men, public, without unreasonable delay, and in the county where the alleged offense was committed, unless upon petition of the accused, and for good cause shown, it is removed to some other county. In all such trials, the accused shall be fully and plainly informed of the character and cause of the accusation, and be confronted with the witnesses against him, and shall have the assistance of counsel, and a reasonable time to prepare for his defense; and there shall be awarded to him compulsory process for obtaining witnesses in his favor.

RELIGIOUS FREEDOM GUARANTEED

15. No person shall be compelled to frequent or support any religious worship, place or ministry whatsoever; nor shall any man be enforced, restrained, molested or burthened, in his body or goods or otherwise suffer, on account of his religious opinions or belief, but all men shall be free to profess, and, by argument, to maintain their opinions in matters of religion; and the same shall, in no wise, affect, diminish or enlarge their civil capacities; and the legislature shall not prescribe any religious test whatever, or confer any peculiar privileges or advantages on any sect or denomination, or pass any law requiring or authorizing any religious society, or the people of any district within this State, to levy on themselves, or others, any tax for the erection or repair of any house for public worship, or for the support of any church or ministry, but it shall be left free for every person to select his religious instructor, and to make for his support such private contract as he shall please.

RIGHT OF PUBLIC ASSEMBLY HELD INVIOLATE

16. The right of the people to assemble in a peaceful manner, to consult for the common good, to instruct their representatives, or to apply for redress of grievances, shall be held inviolate.

COURTS OPEN TO ALL — JUSTICE ADMINISTERED SPEEDILY

17. The courts of this State shall be open, and every person, for an injury done to him, in his person, property or reputation, shall have remedy by due course of law; and justice shall be administered without sale, denial or delay.

CONVICTION NOT TO WORK CORRUPTION OF BLOOD OR FORFEITURE

18. No conviction shall work corruption of blood or forfeiture of estate.

HEREDITARY EMOLUMENTS, ETC., PROVIDED AGAINST

19. No hereditary emoluments, honors or privileges shall ever be granted or conferred in this State.

PRESERVATION OF FREE GOVERNMENT

20. Free government and the blessings of liberty can be preserved to any people only by a firm adherence to justice, moderation, temperance, frugality and virtue, and by a frequent recurrence to fundamental principles.

ARTICLE IV

ELECTIONS AND OFFICERS

1. The * male citizens of the State shall be entitled to vote at all elections held within the counties in which they respectively reside but no person who is a minor, or of unsound mind, or a pauper, or who is under conviction of treason, felony, or bribery in an election, or who has not been a resident of the State for one year, and of the county in which he offers to vote, for sixty days next preceding such offer, shall be permitted to vote while such disability continues; but no person in the military, naval or marine service of the United States, shall be deemed a resident of this State by reason of being stationed therein.

MODE OF VOTING BY BALLOT

2. In all elections by the people, the mode of voting shall be by ballot; but the voter shall be free to vote by either open, sealed or secret ballot, as he may elect.

---

* The woman suffrage amendment to the Constitution of the United States, declared in force August 26, 1920, provides that "the right of citizens of the United States to vote shall not be denied or abridged by the United States or by any State on account of sex."

VOTER NOT SUBJECT TO ARREST ON CIVIL PROCESS

3. No voter, during the continuance of an election at which he is entitled to vote, or during the time necessary and convenient for going to and returning from the same, shall be subject to arrest upon civil process, or be compelled to attend any court, or judicial proceeding, as suitor, juror or witness; or to work upon the public roads or except in time of war or public danger to render military service.

PERSONS ENTITLED TO HOLD OFFICE — AGE REQUIREMENTS

4. No person, except citizens entitled to vote, shall be elected or appointed to any State, county or municipal office; but the Governor and Judges must have attained the age of thirty, and the Attorney General and Senators the age of twenty-five years, at the beginning of their respective terms of service; and must have been citizens of the State for five years next preceding their election or appointment, or citizens at the time this Constitution goes into operation.

OATH OR AFFIRMATION TO SUPPORT THE CONSTITUTION

5. Every person elected or appointed to any office, before proceeding to exercise the authority, or discharge the duties thereof, shall make oath or affirmation that he will support the Constitution of the United States and the Constitution of this State, and that he will faithfully discharge the duties of his said office to the best of his skill and judgment; and no other oath, declaration or test shall be required as a qualification, unless herein otherwise provided.

PROVISIONS FOR REMOVAL OF OFFICIALS

6. All officers elected or appointed under this Constitution, may, unless in cases herein otherwise provided for, be removed from office for official misconduct, incompetence, neglect of duty, or gross immorality, in such manner as may be prescribed by general law, and unless so removed they shall continue to discharge the duties of their respective offices until their successors are elected, or appointed and qualified.

GENERAL ELECTIONS, WHEN HELD — TERMS OF OFFICIALS

7. The general elections of State and county officers, and of members of the legislature, shall be held on the Tuesday next after the first Monday in November, until otherwise provided by law. The terms of such officers, not elected, or appointed to fill a vacancy, shall, unless herein otherwise provided, begin, on the first day of January; and of the members of the Legislature, on the first day of December next succeeding their election. Elections to fill vacancies, shall be for the unexpired term. When vacancies occur prior to any general election, they shall be filled by appointments in such manner as may be prescribed herein, or by general law, which appointments shall expire at such time after the next general election as the person so elected to fill such vacancy shall be qualified.

[The original section provided, that the general election should be held on "the second Tuesday of October," and the change was made in order that the election of State officers would fall on the same day as the presidential election. The original section also provided that the terms of office of members of the legislature should begin on the first day of November next succeeding their election, but this amendment provided that the term should begin on the first day of December.

The amendment as set forth above was proposed by joint resolution of February 21, 1883, and ratified at the general election in 1884. Vote on the amendment: For ratification, 66,181; against ratification, 25,422; majority, 40,759.]

FURTHER PROVISIONS REGARDING STATE'S OFFICERS AND AGENTS

8. The Legislature, in cases not provided for in this Constitution, shall prescribe, by general laws, the terms of office, powers, duties and compensation of all public officers and agents, and the manner in which they shall be elected, appointed and removed.

IMPEACHMENT OF OFFICIALS

9. Any officer of the State may be impeached for maladministration, corruption, incompetency, gross immorality, neglect of duty, or any high crime or misdemeanor. The House of Delegates shall

have the sole power of impeachment. The Senate shall have the sole power to try impeachments and no person shall be convicted without the concurrence of two-thirds of the members elected thereto. When sitting as a court of impeachment, the President of the Supreme Court of Appeals, or, if from any cause it be improper for him to act, then any other judge of that court, to be designated by it, shall preside; and the Senators shall be on oath or affirmation, to do justice according to law and evidence. Judgment in cases of impeachment shall not extend further than to removal from office and disqualification to hold any office of honor, trust or profit, under the State; but the party convicted shall be liable to indictment, trial, judgment, and punishment according to law. The Senate may sit during the recess of the Legislature for the trial of impeachments.

FIGHTING OF DUELS PROHIBITED

10. Any citizen of this State, who shall, after the adoption of this Constitution, either in, or out of the State, fight a duel with deadly weapons, or send or accept a challenge so to do, or who shall act as a second or knowingly aid or assist in such duel, shall, ever thereafter, be incapable of holding any office of honor, trust or profit in this State.

SAFEGUARDS FOR BALLOTS

11. The Legislature shall prescribe the manner of conducting and making returns of elections, and of determining contested elections; and shall pass such laws as may be necessary and proper to prevent intimidation, disorder or violence at the polls, and corruption or fraud in voting, counting the vote, ascertaining or declaring the result, or fraud in any manner upon the ballot.

REGISTRATION LAW PROVIDED FOR

12. The Legislature shall enact proper laws for the registration of all qualified voters of this State.

[This section, prior to its amendment, read as follows: "No citizen shall ever be denied or refused the right or privilege of voting at an election because his name is not or has not been registered or listed as a qualified voter."

The amendment was proposed by joint resolution of February 22, 1901, and adopted at the general election in 1902. Vote on the amendment: For ratification, 55,196; against ratification, 25,379; majority, 29,817.]

ARTICLE V

DIVISION OF POWERS

1. The Legislative, Executive and Judicial Departments shall be separate and distinct, so that neither shall exercise the powers properly belonging to either of the others; nor shall any person exercise the powers of more than one of them at the same time, except that justices of the peace shall be eligible to the Legislature.

ARTICLE VI

LEGISLATURE

1. The legislative power shall be vested in a Senate and House of Delegates. The style of their Acts shall be, "Be it enacted by the Legislature of West Virginia."

COMPOSITION OF SENATE AND HOUSE OF DELEGATES

2. The Senate shall be composed of twenty-four, and the House of Delegates of sixty-five members subject to be increased according to the provisions hereinafter contained.

[The Senate is now composed of thirty-two, and the House of Delegates of one hundred members.]

SENATORS AND DELEGATES — TERMS OF OFFICE

3. Senators shall be elected for the term of four years, and Delegates for the term of two years. The Senators first elected shall divide themselves into two classes, one Senator from every district being assigned to each class; and of these classes, the first to be designated by lot in such manner as the Senate may determine, shall hold

their seats for two years, and the second for four years, so that after the first election, one-half of the Senators shall be elected biennially.

DIVISION OF STATE INTO SENATORIAL DISTRICTS

4. For the election of Senators, the State shall be divided into twelve Senatorial districts which number shall not be diminished, but may be increased as hereinafter provided. Every district shall elect two Senators, but where the district is composed of more than one county, both shall not be chosen from the same county. The districts shall be compact formed of contiguous territory, bounded by county lines, and, as nearly as practicable, equal in population, to be ascertained by the census of the United States. After every such census, the Legislature shall alter the Senatorial Districts, so far as may be necessary to make them conform to the foregoing provision.

[There are now sixteen senatorial districts, as provided by Acts of 1937, Ch. 128.]

SENATORIAL DISTRICTS DESIGNATED

5. Until the Senatorial Districts shall be altered by the Legislature as herein prescribed, the counties of Hancock, Brooke, and Ohio, shall constitute the first Senatorial District; Marshall, Wetzel and Marion, the second; Ritchie, Doddridge, Harrison, Gilmer and Calhoun, the third; Tyler, Pleasants, Wood and Wirt, the fourth; Jackson, Mason, Putnam and Roane, the fifth; Kanawha, Clay, Nicholas, Braxton and Webster, the sixth; Cabell, Wayne, Lincoln, Boone, Logan, Wyoming, McDowell and Mercer, the seventh; Monroe, Greenbrier, Summers, Pocahontas, Fayette and Raleigh, the eighth; Lewis, Randolph, Upshur, Barbour, Taylor and Tucker, the ninth; Preston and Monongalia, the tenth; Hampshire, Mineral, Hardy, Grant and Pendleton, the eleventh; Berkeley, Morgan and Jefferson, the twelfth.

[By the provisions of the reapportionment act of 1937 (Acts 1937, Ch. 128) the number of senatorial districts was increased to sixteen, the number of senators to thirty-two, and the counties rearranged in the various districts.]

PROVISIONS FOR DELEGATE REPRESENTATION

6. For the election of Delegates, every county containing a population of less than three-fifths of the ratio of representation for the House of Delegates, shall at each apportionment, be attached to some contiguous county or counties, to form a Delegate District.

[Each county now has at least one delegate.]

DELEGATE APPORTIONMENT AFTER CENSUS

7. After every census the Delegates shall be apportioned as follows: The ratio of representation for the House of Delegates shall be ascertained by dividing the whole population of the State by the number of which the House is to consist and rejecting the fraction of a unit, if any, resulting from such division. Dividing the population of every Delegate District, and of every county not included in a Delegate District, by the ratio thus ascertained, there shall be assigned to each a number of Delegates equal to the quotient obtained by this division, excluding the fractional remainder. The additional Delegates necessary to make up the number of which the House is to consist, shall then be assigned to those Delegate Districts, and counties not included in a Delegate District, which would otherwise have the largest fractions unrepresented; but every Delegate District and county not included in a Delegate District shall be entitled to at least one Delegate.

DESIGNATION OF DELEGATE DISTRICTS

8. Until a new apportionment shall be declared, the counties of Pleasants and Wood shall form the first Delegate District, and elect three Delegates; Ritchie and Calhoun the second, and elect two Delegates; Barbour, Harrison and Taylor the third, and elect one Delegate; Randolph and Tucker the fourth, and elect one Delegate; Nicholas, Clay and Webster the fifth, and elect one Delegate; McDowell and Wyoming the sixth, and elect one Delegate.

[There are now no delegate districts, each county having at least one member.]

FURTHER APPORTIONMENTS

9. Until a new apportionment shall be declared, the apportionment of Delegates to the counties not included in Delegate Districts, and to Barbour, Harrison and Taylor counties, embraced in such districts, shall be as follows:

To Barbour, Boone, Braxton, Brooke, Cabell, Doddridge, Fayette, Hampshire, Hancock, Jackson, Lewis, Logan, Greenbrier, Monroe, Mercer, Mineral, Morgan, Grant, Hardy, Lincoln, Pendleton, Putnam, Roane, Gilmer, Taylor, Tyler, Upshur, Wayne, Wetzel, Wirt, Pocahontas, Summers and Raleigh counties, one Delegate each.

To Berkeley, Harrison, Jefferson, Marion, Marshall, Mason, Monongalia and Preston counties, two Delegates each.

To Kanawha County, three Delegates.

To Ohio County, four Delegates.

[Many changes have been made in this apportionment. Kanawha County, the largest in population, now has eleven Delegates.]

ARRANGEMENT OF SENATORIAL AND DELEGATE DISTRICTS

10. The arrangement of the Senatorial and Delegate Districts, and apportionment of Delegates, shall hereafter be declared by law, as soon as possible after each succeeding census, taken by authority of the United States. When so declared they shall apply to the first general election for members of the Legislature, to be thereafter held, and shall continue in force unchanged, until such Districts shall be altered, and Delegates apportioned, under the succeeding census.

ADDITIONAL TERRITORY MAY BE ADMITTED INTO STATE

11. Additional territory may be admitted into, and become part of this State, with the consent of the Legislature and a majority of the qualified voters of the State, voting on the question. And in such case provision shall be made by law for the representation thereof in the Senate and House of Delegates, in conformity with the principles set forth in this Constitution. And the number of members of which each house of the Legislature is to consist, shall thereafter be increased by the representation assigned to such additional territory.

RESIDENCE REQUIREMENTS FOR SENATORS AND DELEGATES

12. No person shall be a Senator or Delegate who has not for one year next preceding his election, been a resident within the District or County from which he is elected; and if a Senator or Delegate remove from the District or County for which he was elected, his seat shall be thereby vacated.

ELIGIBILITY TO SEAT IN LEGISLATURE

13. No person holding a lucrative office under this State, the United States, or any foreign government; no member of Congress; no person who is a salaried officer of any railroad company, or who is sheriff, constable, or clerk of any court of record, shall be eligible to a seat in the Legislature.

BRIBERY CONVICTION FORFEITS ELIGIBILITY

14. No person who has been, or hereafter shall be convicted of bribery, perjury, or other infamous crime, shall be eligible to a seat in the Legislature. No person who may have collected or been entrusted with public money, whether State, county, township, district, or other municipal organization, shall be eligible to the Legislature, or to any office of honor, trust, or profit in this State, until he shall have duly accounted for and paid over such money according to law.

SENATORS AND DELEGATES NOT TO HOLD CIVIL OFFICE OF PROFIT

15. No Senator or Delegate, during the term for which he shall have been elected, shall be elected or appointed to any civil office of profit under this State, which has been created, or the emoluments of which have been increased during such term, except offices to be filled by election of the people. Nor shall any member of the Legislature be interested, directly or indirectly, in any contract with the State, or any county thereof, authorized by any law passed during the term for which he shall have been elected.

OATH OF SENATORS AND DELEGATES

16. Members of the Legislature before they enter upon their duties, shall take and subscribe the following oath or affirmation: "I do solemnly swear (or affirm) that I will support the Constitution of the United States, and the Constitution of the State of West Virginia, and faithfully discharge the duties of Senator (or Delegate) according to the best of my ability"; and they shall also take this further oath, to-wit: "I will not accept or receive, directly or indirectly, any money or other valuable thing, from any corporation, company, or person for any vote or influence I may give or withhold, as Senator (or Delegate), on any bill, resolution, or appropriation, or for any act I may do or perform as Senator (or Delegate)." These oaths shall be administered in the hall of the house to which the member is elected, by a Judge of the Supreme Court of Appeals, or of a Circuit Court, or by any other person authorized by law to administer an oath; and the Secretary of State shall record and file said oaths subscribed by each member; and no other oath or declaration shall be required as a qualification. Any member who shall refuse to take the oath herein prescribed, shall forfeit his seat; and any member who shall be convicted of having violated the oath last above required to be taken, shall forfeit his seat and be disqualified thereafter from holding any office of profit or trust in this State.

MEMBERS OF LEGISLATURE PRIVILEGED FROM CIVIL ARREST

17. Members of the Legislature shall, in all cases except treason, felony, and breach of the peace, be privileged from arrest during the session, and for ten days before and after the same; and for words spoken in debate, or any report, motion or proposition made in either House, a member shall not be questioned in any other place.

TIME OF ASSEMBLY OF LEGISLATURE

18. The Legislature shall assemble at the seat of government biennially, and not oftener, unless convened by the Governor. The first session of the Legislature, after the adoption of this Constitution,

shall commence on the third Tuesday of November, 1872; and the regular biennial session of the Legislature shall commence on the second Wednesday of January, 1875, and every two years thereafter, on the same day.

CONVENING OF LEGISLATURE BY GOVERNOR

19. The Governor may convene the Legislature by proclamation whenever, in his opinion, the public safety or welfare shall require it. It shall be his duty to convene it, on application in writing, of three-fifths of the members elected to each House.

SEAT OF GOVERNMENT

20. The seat of government shall be at Charleston, until otherwise provided by law.

PROVISIONS FOR ASSEMBLING OF LEGISLATURE OTHER THAN AT THE SEAT OF GOVERNMENT

21. The Governor may convene the Legislature at another place, when, in his opinion, it can not safely assemble at the seat of Government, and the Legislature may, when in session, adjourn to some other place, when in its opinion, the public safety or welfare, or the safety of the members, or their health, shall require it.

* LENGTH OF LEGISLATIVE SESSION

22. All sessions of the Legislature, other than extraordinary sessions, shall continue for a period of sixty days from the date of beginning. But all regular sessions may be extended by the concurrence of two-thirds of the members elected to each House.

* This section originally read as follows: "No session of the Legislature, after the first, shall continue longer than forty-five days, without the concurrence of two-thirds of the members elected to each House."

Under the provisions of Senate Joint Resolution No. 3, adopted February 12, 1919, and ratified at the general election in 1920, the section was amended to read as follows: "All sessions of the Legislature other than extraordinary sessions, shall continue in session for a period not exceeding fifteen days, from date of convening, during which time no bill shall be passed or re-

CONCERNING ADJOURNMENT

23. Neither House shall, during the session, adjourn for more than three days, without the consent of the other. Nor shall either, without such consent, adjourn to any other place than that in which the Legislature is sitting.

RULES GOVERNING LEGISLATIVE PROCEEDINGS

24. A majority of the members elected to each House of the Legislature shall constitute a quorum. But a smaller number may adjourn from day to day, and shall be authorized to compel the attendance of absent members, as each House may provide. Each House shall determine the rules of its proceedings and be the judge of the elections, returns and qualifications of its own members. The Senate shall choose, from its own body, a President; and the House of Delegates, from its own body, a Speaker. Each House shall appoint its own officers, and remove them at pleasure. The oldest delegate present shall call the House to order at the opening of each new House of Delegates, and preside over it until the Speaker thereof shall have been chosen and have taken his seat. The oldest member of the Senate present at the commencement of each regular session thereof shall call the Senate to order, and preside over the same until a President of the Senate shall have been chosen and have taken his seat.

---

jected, unless the same shall be necessary to provide for a public emergency, shall be specially recommended by the Governor and passed by a vote of four-fifths of the members elected to each house; whereupon, a recess of both houses must be taken until the Wednesday after the second Monday of March following. On reassembling of the Legislature, no bills shall be introduced in either house without a vote of three-fourths of all the members elected to each house taken by yeas and nays. The regular session shall not continue longer than forty-five days after reconvening, without the concurrence of two-thirds of the members elected to each house." Vote on the amendment: For ratification, 160,929; against ratification, 122,744; majority, 38,185.

Under Joint Resolution No. 9, adopted in 1927, and ratified at the general election in 1928, the section was again amended to read as set forth in the text. Vote on the amendment: For ratification, 275,374; against ratification, 85,123; majority, 190,251.

AUTHORITY TO PUNISH MEMBERS

25. Each House may punish its own members for disorderly behavior, and with the concurrence of two-thirds of the members elected thereto, expel a member, but not twice for the same offense.

PROVISIONS FOR UNDISTURBED TRANSACTION OF BUSINESS

26. Each House shall have power to provide for its own safety and the undisturbed transaction of its business, and may punish, by imprisonment, any person not a member, for disrespectful behavior in its presence; for obstructing any of its proceedings, or any of its officers in the discharge of his duty, or for any assault, threat or abuse of a member, for words spoken in debate. But such imprisonment shall not extend beyond the termination of the session and shall not prevent the punishment of any offense, by the ordinary course of law.

ACCOUNTING FOR STATE MONIES

27. Laws shall be enacted and enforced, by suitable provisions and penalties, requiring sheriffs, and all other officers, whether State, county, district or municipal, who shall collect or receive, or whose official duty it is or shall be to collect, receive, hold or pay out any money belonging to, or which is, or shall be, for the use of the State or of any county, district, or municipal corporation, to make annual account and settlement therefor. Such settlement, when made, shall be subject to exceptions, and take such direction, and have only such force and effect, as may be provided by law; but in all cases such settlement shall be recorded, and be open to the examination of the people at such convenient place or places as may be appointed by law.

ORIGINATION OF BILLS

28. Bills and resolutions may originate in either House, but may be passed, amended or rejected by the other.

REQUIREMENT FOR READING OF BILLS

29. No bill shall become a law until it has been fully and distinctly read, on three different days, in each House, unless in case of urgency, by a vote of four-fifths of the members present, taken by yeas and nays on each bill, this rule may be dispensed with: *Provided,* in all cases, that an engrossed bill shall be fully and distinctly read in each House.

ACTS TO EMBRACE BUT ONE OBJECT — TIME OF EFFECT

30. No act hereafter passed shall embrace more than one object, and that shall be expressed in the title. But if any object shall be embraced in an act which is not so expressed, the act shall be void only as to so much thereof as shall not be so expressed, and no law shall be revived, or amended, by reference to its title only; but the law revived, or the section amended, shall be inserted at large, in the new act. And no act of the Legislature, except such as may be passed at the first session under this Constitution, shall take effect until the expiration of ninety days after its passage, unless the Legislature shall by a vote of two-thirds of the members elected to each House, taken by yeas and nays, otherwise direct.

HOW BILLS MAY BE AMENDED

31. When a bill or joint resolution, passed by one House, shall be amended by the other, the question on agreeing to the bill, or joint resolution, as amended, shall be again voted on, by yeas and nays, in the house by which it was originally passed, and the result entered upon its journal; in all such cases, the affirmative vote of a majority of all the members elected to such house shall be necessary.

"MAJORITY" DEFINED

32. Whenever the words, "a majority of the members elected to either House of the Legislature," or words of like import, are used in this Constitution, they shall be construed to mean a majority of the whole number of members to which each House is, at the time, entitled, under the apportionment of representation, established by the provisions of this Constitution.

COMPENSATION OF MEMBERS

33. The members of the Legislature shall each receive for his services the sum of five hundred dollars per annum and ten cents for each mile traveled in going to and returning from the seat of government by the most direct route. The Speaker of the House of Delegates and the President of the Senate, shall each receive an additional compensation of two dollars per day for each day they shall act as presiding officers. No other allowance or emolument than that by this section provided shall directly or indirectly be made or paid to the members of either House for postage, stationery, newspapers, or any other purpose whatever.

[The amendment of sections 22 and 33, Art. VI, was proposed by Senate Joint Resolution No. 3, adopted February 12, 1919, and ratified at the general election November 2, 1920. The only change made in section 33 was to strike out the words "four dollars per day" and insert "five hundred dollars per annum." Vote on the amendment: For ratification, 160,929; against ratification, 122,744; majority, 38,185.]

DISTRIBUTION OF LAWS AND JOURNALS PROVIDED FOR — CONTRACTS FOR PRINTING

34. The Legislature shall provide by law that the fuel, stationery and printing paper, furnished for the use of the State; the copying, printing, binding and distributing the laws and journals; and all other printing ordered by the Legislature, shall be let by contract to the lowest responsible bidder, bidding under a maximum price to be fixed by the Legislature; and no member or officer thereof, or officer of the State, shall be interested, directly or indirectly, in such contract, but all such contracts shall be subject to the approval of the Governor, and in case of his disapproval of any such contract, there shall be a reletting of the same in such manner as may be prescribed by law.

STATE NOT TO BE MADE DEFENDANT IN ANY COURT

35. The State of West Virginia shall never be made defendant in any court of law or equity, except the State of West Virginia, including any subdivision thereof or any municipality therein, or any

officer, agent, or employee thereof, may be made defendant in any garnishment or attachment proceeding, as garnishee or suggestee.

[This section, prior to its amendment, read as follows: "The State of West Virginia shall never be made defendant in any court of law or equity." The amendment as above set forth was proposed by House Joint Resolution No. 3, adopted March 8, 1935, Acts 1935, p. 662, and was ratified at the general election in 1936.]

LOTTERIES PROHIBITED

36. The Legislature shall have no power to authorize lotteries or gift enterprises for any purpose, and shall pass laws to prohibit the sale of lottery or gift enterprise tickets in this State.

TERMS OF OFFICE NOT TO BE EXTENDED AFTER ELECTION

37. No law shall be passed after the election of any public officer, which shall operate to extend the term of his office.

SALARIES OF OFFICIALS NOT TO BE INCREASED DURING OFFICIAL TERM

38. No extra compensation shall be granted to any public officer, agent, servant or contractor, after the services shall have been rendered or the contract made; nor shall any Legislature authorize the payment of any claim or part thereof, hereafter created against the State, under any agreement or contract made, without express authority by law; and all such unauthorized agreements shall be null and void. Nor shall the salary of any public officer be increased or diminished during his term of office, nor shall any such officer, or his or their sureties be released from any debt or liability due to the State: *Provided*, The Legislature may make appropriations for expenditures hereafter incurred in suppressing insurrection, or repelling invasion.

LOCAL LAWS NOT TO BE PASSED IN ENUMERATED CASES

39. The Legislature shall not pass local or special laws in any of the following enumerated cases; that is to say, for

Granting divorces;

Laying out, opening, altering and working roads or highways;

Vacating roads, town plats, streets, alleys and public grounds;

Locating, or changing county seats;

Regulating or changing county and district affairs;

Providing for the sale of church property, or property held for charitable uses;

Regulating the practice in courts of justice;

Incorporating cities, towns or villages, or amending the charter of any city, town or village, containing a population of less than two thousand;

Summoning or impaneling grand or petit juries;

The opening or conducting of any election, or designating the place of voting;

The sale or mortgage of real estate belonging to minors, or others under disability;

Chartering, licensing, or establishing ferries or toll bridges;

Remitting fines, penalties or forfeitures;

Changing the law of descent;

Regulating the rate of interest;

Authorizing deeds to be made for land sold for taxes;

Releasing taxes;

Releasing title to forfeited lands.

The Legislature shall provide, by general laws, for the foregoing and all other cases for which provision can be so made; and in no case shall a special act be passed, where a general law would be proper, and can be made applicable to the case, nor in any other case in which the courts have jurisdiction, and are competent to give the relief asked for.

39-(a). No local or special law shall hereafter be passed incorporating cities, towns or villages, or amending their charters. The Legislature shall provide by general laws for the incorporation and government of cities, towns and villages and shall classify such municipal corporations, upon the basis of population, into not less than two nor more than five classes. Such general laws shall restrict the powers of such cities, towns, and villages to borrow money and contract debts, and shall limit the rate of taxes for municipal purposes, in accordance with section one, article ten of the Constitution of the State of West Virginia. Under such general laws, the electors of each municipal corporation, wherein the population exceeds two thousand, shall have power and authority to frame, adopt and amend the charter of such corporation, or to amend an existing charter thereof, and through its legally constituted authority, may pass all laws and ordinances relating to its municipal affairs: *Provided*, That any such charter or amendment thereto, and any such law or ordinance so adopted, shall be invalid and void if inconsistent or in conflict with this Constitution, or the general laws of the State then in effect, or thereafter from time to time enacted.

[This section (39-a), added to Art. VI, was proposed by Senate Joint Resolution No. 3, adopted March 9, 1935, Acts 1935, p. 706, and was ratified at the general election in 1936.]

LIMITING POWERS OF COURT OR JUDGE

40. The Legislature shall not confer upon any court, or judge, the power of appointment to office, further than the same is herein provided for.

EACH HOUSE TO KEEP JOURNAL OF PROCEEDINGS

41. Each house shall keep a journal of its proceedings, and cause the same to be published from time to time, and all bills and joint resolutions shall be described therein, as well by their title as their number, and the yeas and nays on any question, if called for by one-tenth of those present, shall be entered on the journal.

APPROPRIATION BILLS TO BE SPECIFIC

42. Bills making appropriations for the pay of members and officers of the Legislature, and for salaries for the officers of the government, shall contain no provision on any other subject.

BOARD OR COURT OF REGISTRATION OF VOTERS PROHIBITED

43. The Legislature shall never authorize or establish any board or court of registration of voters.

VIVA VOCE VOTE NECESSARY IN ELECTION OF CERTAIN OFFICERS

44. In all elections to office which may hereafter take place in the Legislature, or in any county, or municipal body, the vote shall be *viva voce*, and be entered on its journals.

BRIBERY AND ATTEMPT TO BRIBE — PUNISHMENT

45. It shall be the duty of the Legislature, at its first session after the adoption of this Constitution, to provide, by law, for the punishment by imprisonment in the penitentiary, of any person who shall bribe, or attempt to bribe, any executive or judicial officer of this State, or any member of the Legislature in order to influence him, in the performance of any of his official or public duties; and also to provide by law for the punishment by imprisonment in the penitentiary of any of said officers, or any member of the Legislature, who shall demand, or receive, from any corporation, company or person, any money, testimonial, or other valuable thing, for the performance of his official or public duties, or for refusing or failing to perform the same, or for any vote or influence a member of the Legislature may give or withhold as such member; and also to provide by law for compelling any person, so bribing or attempting to bribe, or so demanding or receiving a bribe, fee, reward, or testimonial, to testify against any person or persons, who may have committed any of said offenses; *Provided,* That any person so compelled to testify, shall be exempted from trial and punishment for the offense of which he may have been guilty, and concerning which he is compelled to testify; and any person convicted of any of the offenses specified in this section, shall, as a part of the punishment thereof, be forever disqualified from holding any office or position of honor, trust, or profit in this State.

MANUFACTURE AND SALE OF LIQUORS

46. The Legislature shall, by appropriate legislation, regulate the manufacture and sale of intoxicating liquors within the limits of this State, and any law authorizing the sale of such liquors shall forbid

and penalize the consumption and the sale thereof for consumption in a saloon or other public place.

[This section, prior to its amendment, read as follows: "On and after the first day of July, one thousand nine hundred fourteen, the manufacture, sale and keeping for sale of malt, vinous or spirituous liquors, wine, porter, ale, beer or any intoxicating drink, mixture or preparation of like nature, except as hereinafter provided, are hereby prohibited in this State: *Provided, however,* That the manufacture and sale and keeping for sale of such liquors for medicinal, pharmaceutical, mechanical, sacramental and scientific purposes, and the manufacture and sale of denatured alcohol for industrial purposes may be permitted under such regulations as the Legislature may prescribe. The Legislature shall, without delay, enact such laws, with regulations, conditions, securities and penalties as may be necessary to carry into effect the provisions of this section."

The amendment as set forth above, which became effective March 1, 1935, was proposed by Senate Committee Substitute for Engrossed House Joint Resolution No. 1, adopted March 9, 1933, Acts Regular Session, 1933, p. 532, and was ratified at the general election in 1934. Vote on the amendment: For ratification, 276,978; against ratification, 237,559; majority, 39,419.]

INCORPORATION OF RELIGIOUS DENOMINATIONS PROHIBITED

47. No charter of incorporation shall be granted to any church or religious denomination. Provisions may be made by general laws for securing the title to church property, and for the sale and transfer thereof, so that it shall be held, used, or transferred for the purposes of such church, or religious denomination.

HOMESTEAD EXEMPTION

48. Any husband or parent residing in this State, or the infant children of deceased parents, may hold a homestead of the value of one thousand dollars, and personal property to the value of two hundred dollars, exempt from forced sale subject to such regulations as shall be prescribed by law: *Provided,* That such homestead exemption shall in no wise affect debts or liabilities existing at the time of the adoption of this Constitution; and *Provided, further,* That no property shall be exempt from sale for taxes due thereon, or for the payment of purchase money due upon said property, or for debts contracted for the erection of improvements thereon.

PROPERTY OF MARRIED WOMEN

49. The Legislature shall pass such laws as may be necessary to protect the property of married women from the debts, liabilities and control of their husbands.

PLAN OF PROPORTIONAL REPRESENTATION

50. The Legislature may provide for submitting to a vote of the people at the general election to be held in 1876, or at any general election thereafter, a plan or scheme of proportional representation in the Senate of this State; and if a majority of the votes cast at such election be in favor of the plan submitted to them, the Legislature shall, at its session succeeding such election rearrange the Senatorial Districts in accordance with the plan so approved by the people.

* THE BUDGET SYSTEM

51. The Legislature shall not appropriate any money out of the treasury except in accordance with the following provisions:

SUB-SECTION A

Every appropriation bill shall be either a budget bill, or a supplementary appropriation bill, as hereinafter mentioned.

SUB-SECTION B

First: Within ten days after the convening of the Legislature, unless such time shall be extended by the Legislature for the session at which the budget is to be submitted, the Board of Public Works, which shall consist of the Governor, Secretary of State, Auditor, Treasurer, Attorney General, Superintendent of Free Schools and Commissioner of Agriculture, shall submit to the Legislature two

* This section, known as "The Budget Amendment," added to Article VI, was proposed by Senate Joint Resolution No. 1, adopted May 23, 1917, (Acts 1917, Extraordinary Session), and was ratified at the general election in 1918. Vote on the amendment: For ratification, 51,405; against ratification, 26,651; majority, 24,754.

budgets, one for each of the ensuing fiscal years. Each budget shall contain a complete plan of proposed expenditures and estimated revenues for the particular fiscal year to which it relates; and shall show the estimated surplus or deficit of revenues at the end of such year. Accompanying each budget shall be a statement showing: (1) the revenues and expenditures for each of the two fiscal years next preceding; (2) the current assets, liabilities, reserves and surplus or deficit of the State; (3) the debts and funds of the State; (4) an estimate of the State's financial condition as of the beginning and end of each of the fiscal years covered by the two budgets above provided; (5) any explanation the Board of Public Works may desire to make as to the important features of any budget and any suggestion as to methods for the reduction or increase of the State's revenue.

Second: Each budget shall be divided into two parts, and the first part shall be designated "Governmental Appropriations" and shall embrace an itemized estimate of the appropriations: (1) for the Legislature as certified to the Board of Public Works in the manner hereinafter provided; (2) for the Executive Department; (3) for the Judicial Department, as provided by law, certified to the Governor by the Auditor; (4) to pay and discharge the principal and interest of any debt of the State of West Virginia hereafter created in conformity with the Constitution and all laws enacted in pursuance thereof; (5) for the salaries payable by the State under the Constitution and laws of the State; (6) for the aid of the public schools in conformity with the laws of the State; (7) for such other purposes as are set forth in the Constitution and laws made in pursuance thereof.

Third: The second part shall be designated "General Appropriations," and shall include all other estimates of appropriations.

The Board of Public Works shall deliver to the presiding officer of each House the budgets and a bill for all proposed appropriations of the budgets clearly itemized and classified; and the presiding officer of each House shall promptly cause said bill to be introduced therein, and such bill shall be known as the "Budget Bill." The Board of Public Works may, before final action thereon by the Legislature, amend or supplement either of said budgets to correct an oversight or in case of an emergency, with the consent of the Legislature by delivering such an amendment or supplement to the presiding officers of both Houses; and such amendment or supplement shall thereby become a part of said budget bill as an addition to the items of said bill or as modification of or a substitute for any item of said bill such amendment or supplement may affect.

The Legislature shall not amend the budget bill so as to create a deficit but may amend the bill by increasing or diminishing the items therein relating to the Legislature, and by increasing the items therein relating to the judiciary, but except as hereinbefore specified, may not alter the said bill except to strike out or reduce items therein: *Provided, however,* That the salary or compensation of any public officer shall not be increased or diminished during his term of office; and such bill when and as passed by both Houses shall be a law immediately without further action by the Governor.

Fourth: The governor and such representatives of the boards, officers and commissions of the State expending or applying for State's money as have been designated by the Board of Public Works for this purpose, shall have the right, and when requested by either House of the Legislature it shall be their duty to appear and be heard with respect to any budget bill during the consideration thereof, and to answer inquiries relative thereto.

SUB-SECTION C — SUPPLEMENTARY APPROPRIATION BILLS

Neither House shall consider other appropriations until the budget bill has been finally acted upon by both Houses, and no such other appropriations shall be valid except in accordance with the provisions following:

(1) Every such appropriation shall be embodied in a separate bill limited to some single work, object or purpose therein stated and called herein a supplementary appropriation bill; (2) each supplementary appropriation bill shall provide the revenue necessary to pay the appropriation thereby made by a tax direct or indirect, to be laid and collected as shall be directed in said bill unless it appears from such budget that there is sufficient revenue available; (3) no supplementary appropriation bill shall become a law unless it be passed in each House by a vote of a majority of the members present, and the yeas and nays recorded on its final passage. Each supplementary appropriation bill shall be presented to the Governor of the State as provided in section fourteen of article seven of the Constitution and thereafter all the provisions of said section shall apply.

Nothing in this amendment shall be construed as preventing the

Legislature from passing in time of war an appropriation bill to provide for the payment of any obligation of the State of West Virginia within the protection of section ten of article one of the Constitution of the United States.

SUB-SECTION D — GENERAL PROVISIONS

First: If the "Budget Bill" shall not have been finally acted upon by the Legislature three days before the expiration of its regular session, the Governor may, and it shall be his duty to issue a proclamation extending the session for such further period as may, in his judgment, be necessary for the passage of such bill; but no other matter than such bill shall be considered during such extended session except a provision for the cost thereof.

Second: The Board of Public Works for the purpose of making up its budgets shall have the power, and it shall be its duty, to require from the proper State officials, including herein all executive departments, all executive and administrative officers, bureaus, boards, commissions and agencies expending or supervising the expenditure of, and all institutions applying for state monies and appropriations, such itemized estimates and other information, in such form and at such times as said board shall direct. The estimates for the legislative department, certified by the presiding officer of each House, of the judiciary, as provided by law, certified by the Auditor, and for the public schools, as provided by law, shall be transmitted to the Board of Public Works, in such form and at such times as it shall direct, and shall be included in the budget.

The Board of Public Works may provide for public hearings on all estimates and may require the attendance at such hearings of representatives of all agencies, and all institutions applying for state monies. After such public hearings, it may, in its discretion, revise all estimates except those for the legislative and judiciary departments, and for the public schools as provided by law.

Third: The Legislature may, from time to time, enact such laws, not inconsistent with this section, as may be necessary and proper to carry out its provisions.

Fourth: In the event of any inconsistency between any of the provisions of this section and any of the other provisions of the Constitution, except amendments thereto heretofore made and ratified by the people, the provisions of this section shall prevail. But nothing herein shall be construed as preventing the Governor from calling extraordinary sessions of the Legislature, as provided by section seven of article seven, or as preventing the Legislature at such extraordinary sessions from considering any emergency appropriation or appropriations.

If any item of any appropriation bill passed under the provisions of this section shall be held invalid upon any ground, such invalidity shall not affect the legality of the bill or of any other item of such bill or bills.

MOTOR FUEL AND MOTOR VEHICLE REVENUE

52. Revenue from gasoline and other motor fuel excise and license taxation, motor vehicle registration and license taxes, and all other revenue derived from motor vehicles or motor fuels shall, after the deduction of statutory refunds and cost of administration and collection authorized by legislative appropriation, be appropriated and used solely for construction, reconstruction, repair and maintenance of public highways, and also the payment of the interest and principal on all road bonds heretofore issued or which may be hereafter issued for the construction, reconstruction or improvement of public highways, and the payment of obligations incurred in the construction, reconstruction, repair and maintenance of public highways.

[This section was proposed by House Joint Resolution No. 6, (Acts, Regular Session, 1941, p. 589) and ratified at the General Election November 3, 1942. Vote on the amendment: For ratification, 228,828; against ratification, 38,651; majority, 190,177.]

FORESTRY

53. The Legislature may by general law define and classify forest lands and provide for cooperation by contract between the State and the owner in the planting, protection, and harvesting thereof. Forest lands embraced in any such contract may be exempted from all taxation or be taxed in such manner, including the imposition of a severance tax or charge as trees are harvested, as the Legislature may from time to time provide. But any tax measured by valuation shall not exceed the aggregate rates authorized by section one of article ten of this Constitution.

[This section was proposed by House Joint Resolution No. 7, (Acts, Regular Session, 1945, p. 640) and ratified at the General Election November 5, 1946. Vote on the amendment: For ratification, 179,150; against ratification, 148,104; majority, 31,046.]

ARTICLE VII

EXECUTIVE DEPARTMENT

1. The Executive Department shall consist of a Governor, Secretary of State, State Superintendent of Free Schools, Auditor, Treasurer, Commissioner of Agriculture and Attorney General, who shall be, *ex-officio*, reporter of the Court of Appeals. Their terms of office shall be four years, and shall commence on the first Monday after the second Wednesday of January next after their election. They shall reside at the seat of government during their terms of office, and keep there the public records, books and papers pertaining to their respective offices, and shall perform such duties as may be prescribed by law.

[This section, prior to its amendment, read as follows: "The Executive Department shall consist of a Governor, Secretary of State, State Superintendent of Free Schools, Auditor, Treasurer and Attorney General, who shall be *ex-officio* Reporter of the Court of Appeals. Their terms of office, respectively shall be four years, and shall commence on the fourth day of March, next after their election. They shall, except the Attorney General reside at the seat of government during their terms of office, and keep there the public records, books and papers pertaining to their respective offices and shall perform such duties as may be prescribed by law.

The amendment as set forth above was proposed by House Joint Resolution No. 7, adopted June 3, 1933, Acts First Extraordinary Session, 1933, p. 506; and was adopted at the general election in 1934. Vote on the amendment: For ratification, 251,965; against ratification, 145,787; majority, 106,178.]

ELECTION

2. An election for Governor, Secretary of State, State Superintendent of Free Schools, Auditor, Treasurer and Attorney General, shall be held at such times and places as may be prescribed by law.

[This section, prior to its amendment, read as follows: "An election for Governor, State Superintendent of Free Schools, Auditor, Treasurer, and Attorney General, shall be held at such times and places as may be prescribed in this Constitution or by general law."

The amendment as set forth above was proposed by House Joint Resolution of February 15, 1901, and adopted at the general election in 1902. Vote on the amendment: For ratification, 59,509; against ratification, 22,022; majority, 37,487.]

CERTIFICATION OF ELECTION RETURNS — CONTESTS

3. The returns of every election for the above named officers shall be sealed up and transmitted by the returning officers to the Secretary of State, directed to "the Speaker of the House of Delegates," who shall, immediately after the organization of the House, and before proceeding to business, open and publish the same, in the presence of a majority of each House of the Legislature, which shall for that purpose assemble in the Hall of the House of Delegates. The person having the highest number of votes for either of said offices, shall be declared duly elected thereto; but if two or more have an equal and the highest number of votes for the same office, the Legislature shall, by joint vote, choose one of such persons for said office. Contested elections for the office of Governor shall be determined by both Houses of the Legislature by joint vote, in such manner as may be prescribed by law.

[The amendment of this section was proposed by House Joint Resolution of February 15, 1901 (Acts 1901, p. 460) and ratified at the general election in 1902. The effect of the amendment was to strike out the following at the end of the original section: "The Secretary of State shall be appointed by the Governor, by and with the advice and consent of the Senate, and shall continue in office, unless sooner removed, until the expiration of the official term of the Governor by whom he shall have been appointed." For the vote on the adoption of the amendment, see note following section 2.]

ELIGIBILITY

4. None of the executive officers mentioned in this article shall hold any other office during the term of his service. The Governor shall not be eligible to said office for the four years next succeeding the term for which he was elected.

[The amendment of this section was proposed by House Joint Resolution of February 15, 1901 (Acts 1901, p. 460) and ratified at the general election in 1902. The section, prior to being amended, read as follows: "Neither the Governor, State Superintendent of Free Schools, Auditor, Treasurer, nor Attorney General, shall hold any other office during the term of his service. The Governor shall be ineligible to said office for the four years next succeeding the term for which he was elected." For the vote of the adoption of the amendment, see note following section 2.]

CHIEF EXECUTIVE — POWERS

5. The chief executive power shall be vested in the Governor, who shall take care that the laws be faithfully executed.

GOVERNOR'S MESSAGE

6. The Governor shall at the commencement of each session, give to the Legislature information by message, of the condition of the State, and shall recommend such measures as he shall deem expedient. He shall accompany his message with a statement of all money received and paid out by him from any funds, subject to his order, with vouchers therefor; and at the commencement of each regular session, present estimates of the amount of money required by taxation for all purposes.

EXTRAORDINARY LEGISLATIVE SESSIONS

7. The Governor may on extraordinary occasions convene, at his own instance, the Legislature; but when so convened it shall enter upon no business except that stated in the proclamation by which it was called together.

GOVERNOR TO NOMINATE CERTAIN OFFICERS

8. The Governor shall nominate, and by and with the advice and consent of the Senate, (a majority of all the Senators elected concurring by yeas and nays) appoint all officers whose offices are established by this Constitution, or shall be created by law, and whose appointment or election is not otherwise provided for, and no such officer shall be appointed or elected by the Legislature.

RECESS VACANCIES — HOW FILLED

9. In case of a vacancy, during the recess of the Senate, in any office which is not elective, the Governor shall, by appointment, fill such vacancy, until the next meeting of the Senate, when he shall make a nomination for such office, and the person so nominated, when confirmed by the Senate (a majority of all the Senators elected concurring by yeas and nays) shall hold his office during the remainder of the term, and until his successor shall be appointed and qualified. No person, after being rejected by the Senate, shall be again nominated for the same office, during the same session, unless at the request of the Senate; nor shall such person be appointed to the same office during the recess of the Senate.

GOVERNOR'S POWER OF REMOVAL

10. The Governor shall have power to remove any officer whom he may appoint in case of incompetency, neglect of duty, gross immorality, or malfeasance in office; and he may declare his office vacant and fill the same as herein provided in other cases of vacancy.

REMISSION OF FINES AND PENALTIES BY GOVERNOR

11. The Governor shall have power to remit fines and penalties in such cases and under such regulations as may be prescribed by law; to commute capital punishment and, except when the prosecution has been carried on by the House of Delegates, to grant reprieves and pardons after conviction; but he shall communicate to the Legislature at each session the particulars of every case of fine or penalty remitted, of punishment commuted and of reprieve or pardon granted, with his reasons therefor.

GOVERNOR COMMANDER-IN-CHIEF OF MILITARY FORCES

12. The Governor shall be commander-in-chief of the military forces of the State, (except when they shall be called into the service of the United States) and may call out the same to execute the laws, suppress insurrection and repel invasion.

OFFICIAL BOND OF STATE OFFICERS

13. When any State officer has executed his official bond, the Governor shall, for such causes and in such manner as the Legislature may direct, require of such officer reasonable additional security; and if the security is not given as required, his office shall be declared vacant, in such manner as may be provided by law.

HOW BILLS BECOME LAWS

14. Every bill passed by the Legislature shall, before it becomes a law, be presented to the Governor. If he approve, he shall sign it, and thereupon it shall become a law; but if not, he shall return it, with his objections, to the House in which it originated, which House shall enter the objections at large upon its journal, and proceed to reconsider it. If, after such reconsideration, a majority of the members elected to that House agree to pass the bill, it shall be sent, together with the objections to the other House, by which it shall likewise be reconsidered, and if approved by a majority of the members elected to that House, it shall become a law, notwithstanding the objections of the Governor. But in all such cases, the vote of each House shall be determined by yeas and nays to be entered on the journal. Any bill which shall not be returned by the Governor within five days (Sundays excepted) after it shall have been presented to him, shall be a law, in like manner as if he had signed it, unless the Legislature shall, by their adjournment, prevent its return, in which case it shall be filed with his objections in the office of the Secretary of State within five days after such adjournment, or become a law.

RESPECTING APPROPRIATIONS OF MONIES

15. Every bill passed by the Legislature making appropriations of money, embracing distinct items, shall before it becomes a law, be presented to the Governor; if he disapproves the bill, or any item or appropriation therein contained, he shall communicate such disapproval with his reasons therefor to the House in which the bill originated; but all items not disapproved shall have the force and

effect of a law according to the original provisions of the bill. Any item or items so disapproved shall be void, unless re-passed by a majority of each House according to the rules and limitations prescribed in the preceding section in reference to other bills.

VACANCY IN GOVERNORSHIP, HOW FILLED

16. In case of the death, conviction or impeachment, failure to qualify, resignation, or other disability of the Governor, the President of the Senate shall act as Governor until the vacancy is filled, or the disability removed; and if the President of the Senate, for any of the above named causes, shall become incapable of performing the duties of Governor, the same shall devolve upon the Speaker of the House of Delegates; and in all other cases where there is no one to act as Governor, one shall be chosen by joint vote of the Legislature. Whenever a vacancy shall occur in the office of Governor before the first three years of the term shall have expired, a new election for Governor shall take place to fill the vacancy.

VACANCIES IN OTHER EXECUTIVE DEPARTMENTS

17. If the office of Secretary of State, Auditor, Treasurer, State Superintendent of Free Schools, or Attorney General, shall become vacant by death, resignation, or otherwise, it shall be the duty of the Governor to fill the same by appointment, and the appointee shall hold his office until his successor shall be elected and qualified in such manner as may be prescribed by law. The subordinate officers of the executive department and the officers of all public institutions of the State shall keep an account of all monies received or disbursed by a semi-annual report thereof to the Governor under oath or affirmation; and any officer who shall wilfully make a false report shall be deemed guilty of perjury.

[The amendment to this section was proposed by House Joint Resolution of February 15, 1901 (Acts 1901, p. 460) and ratified at the general election in 1902. The only change in the original section was the insertion of the words "Secretary of State" in the first line and by substitution of the words "prescribed" for the word "provided." For the vote on the adoption of the amendment, see note following section 2 of this article.]

EXECUTIVE HEADS TO MAKE REPORTS

18. The subordinate officers of the Executive Department and the officers of all the public institutions of the State, shall, at least ten days preceding each regular session of the Legislature, severally report to the Governor, who shall transmit such report to the Legislature; and the Governor may at any time require information in writing, under oath, from the officers of his department, and all officers and managers of State institutions, upon any subject relating to the condition, management and expenses of their respective offices.

SALARIES OF OFFICIALS

19. The officers named in this article shall receive for their services a salary to be established by law, which shall not be increased or diminished during their official terms, and they shall not, after the expiration of the terms of those in office at the adoption of this amendment, receive to their own use any fees, costs, perquisites of office, or other compensation, and all fees that may hereafter be payable by law, for any service performed by any officer provided for in this article of the Constitution, shall be paid in advance into the State treasury.

[This section, prior to amendment, read as follows: "The Governor shall receive for his services a salary of twenty-seven hundred dollars per annum and no additional emolument, allowance or perquisite shall be paid or made to him, on any account. Any person acting as Governor shall receive the emoluments of that office. The Secretary of State shall receive one thousand; the State Superintendent of Free Schools, fifteen hundred; the Treasurer, fourteen hundred; the Auditor, two thousand; and the Attorney General, thirteen hundred dollars per annum; and no additional emolument or allowance except as herein otherwise provided, shall be paid or made out of the treasury of the State to any of the foregoing executive officers on any account."

The amendment as set forth above was proposed by House Joint Resolution adopted February 13, 1901 (Acts 1901, p. 459) and was ratified at the general election in 1902. Vote on the amendment: For ratification, 56,280; against ratification, 23,513; majority, 32,767.]

ARTICLE VIII

JUDICIAL DEPARTMENT

1. The judicial power of the State shall be vested in a supreme court of appeals, in circuit courts and the judges thereof, in such inferior tribunals as are herein authorized and in justices of the peace.

[The amendment of this entire article was proposed by joint resolution of March 6, 1879 (Acts 1879, p. 175) and ratified at the general election in 1880. Vote on the amendment: For ratification, 57,941; against ratification, 34,270; majority, 23,671.]

SUPREME COURT OF APPEALS

2. The Supreme Court of Appeals shall consist of * four judges, any three of whom shall be a quorum for the transaction of business. They shall be elected by the voters of the State and hold their office for the term of twelve years, unless sooner removed in the manner prescribed by this Constitution, except that the judges in office when this article takes effect, shall remain therein until the expiration of their present term of office.

SCOPE OF JURISDICTION

3. It shall have original jurisdiction in cases of *habeas corpus*, *mandamus*, and prohibition. It shall have appellate jurisdiction in civil cases where the matter in controversy, exclusive of costs, is of greater value or amount than one hundred dollars; in controversies concerning the title or boundaries of land, the probate of wills, the appointment or qualification of a personal representative, guardian, committee or curator; or concerning a mill, road, way, ferry or landing; or the right of a corporation or county to levy tolls or taxes; and, also in cases of *quo warranto*, *habeas corpus*, *mandamus*, *certiorari*, and prohibition, and in cases involving freedom or the constitutionality of a law. It shall have appellate jurisdiction in criminal

---

* The Supreme Court of Appeals now consists of five judges, under the provisions of the "Judicial Amendment" set forth at the end of the Constitution, and Acts 1903, ch. 19, amending and reenacting section 1 of chapter 113 of Warth's Code of 1899.

cases where there has been a conviction for felony or misdemeanor in a circuit court, and where a conviction has been had in any inferior court and been affirmed in a circuit court, and in cases relating to the public revenue, the right of appeal shall belong to the State as well as the defendant, and such other appellate jurisdiction, in both civil and criminal cases, as may be prescribed by law.

BINDING AUTHORITY OF DECISIONS

4. No decision rendered by the supreme court of appeals shall be considered as binding authority upon any of the inferior courts of this State, except in the particular case decided, unless such decision is concurred in by at least three judges of said court.

REVERSAL OF AFFIRMANCE OF JUDGMENTS

5. When a judgment or decree is reversed or affirmed by the supreme court of appeals, every point fairly arising upon the record of the case shall be considered and decided; and the reasons therefor shall be concisely stated in writing and preserved with the record of the case; and it shall be the duty of the court to prepare a syllabus of the points adjudicated in each case concurred in by three of the judges thereof, which shall be prefixed to the published report of the case.

WRIT OF ERROR, SUPERSEDEAS AND APPEAL

6. A writ of error, *supersedeas*, or appeal shall be allowed only by the Supreme Court of Appeals, or a judge thereof, upon a petition assigning error in the judgment or proceedings of the inferior court and then only after said court or judge shall have examined and considered the record and assignment of errors, and is satisfied that there is error in the same, or that it presents a point proper for the consideration of the Supreme Court of Appeals.

PROVISIONS FOR FILLING SUPREME COURT VACANCIES

7. If from any cause a vacancy shall occur in the Supreme Court of Appeals, the Governor shall issue a writ of election to fill such

vacancy at the next general election for the residue of the term, and in the meantime he shall fill such vacancy by appointment until a judge is elected and qualified. But if the unexpired term be less than two years the Governor shall fill such vacancy by appointment for the unexpired term.

OFFICERS OF SUPREME COURT

8. The officers of the Supreme Court of Appeals, except the reporter, shall be appointed by the court, or in vacation by the judges, thereof, with the power of removal; their duties and compensation shall be prescribed by law.

TERMS OF SUPREME COURT

9. There shall be at least two terms of the Supreme Court of Appeals held annually at such times and places as may be prescribed by law.

CIRCUIT COURTS

10. The State shall be divided into * thirteen circuits. For the circuit hereinafter called the first, two judges shall be elected, and for each of the other circuits one judge shall be elected by the voters thereof. Each of the judges so elected shall hold his office for the term of eight years unless sooner removed in the manner prescribed in this Constitution. The judges of the circuit courts in office when this article takes effect, shall remain therein until the expiration of the term for which they have been elected in the circuit in which they may respectively reside, unless sooner removed as aforesaid. A vacancy in the office of a judge of the circuit court shall be filled in the same manner as is provided for in the case of a vacancy in the office of a judge of the Supreme Court of Appeals. During his continuance in office the judge of a circuit court shall reside in the circuit of which he is judge. The business of the first circuit may be apportioned between the judges thereof, and such judges may hold courts in the same county or in different counties within the circuit at the same time or at different times as may be prescribed by law.

* Now twenty-four.

TERMS OF CIRCUIT COURT

11. A circuit court shall be held in every county in the State at least three times in each year, and provisions may be made by law for holding special terms of said court. A judge of any circuit may hold the courts in another circuit.

CIRCUIT COURT JURISDICTION

12. The circuit court shall have the supervision and control of all proceedings before justices and other inferior tribunals, by *mandamus*, prohibition and certiorari. They shall, except in cases confined exclusively by this Constitution to some other tribunal, have original and general jurisdiction of all matters at law where the amount in controversy, exclusive of interest, exceeds fifty dollars; of all cases of *habeas corpus*, *mandamus*, *quo warranto* and prohibition; and of all cases in equity, and of all crimes and misdemeanors. They shall have appellate jurisdiction in all cases, civil and criminal, where an appeal, writ or error or *supersedeas* may be allowed to the judgment or proceedings of any inferior tribunal. They shall also have such other jurisdiction, whether supervisory, original, appellate or concurrent, as is or may be prescribed by law.

DIVISION OF STATE INTO CIRCUITS

13. Until otherwise provided by law, the State shall be divided into the following circuits: The counties of Brooke, Hancock, Ohio and Marshall shall constitute the first circuit; the counties of Monongalia, Marion and Harrison, the second; the counties of Preston, Taylor, Barbour, Tucker and Randolph, the third; the counties of Wetzel, Tyler, Ritchie and Doddridge, the fourth; the counties of Wood, Wirt and Pleasants, the fifth; the counties of Clay, Gilmer, Jackson, Roane and Calhoun, the sixth; the counties of Putnam, Kanawha and Mason, the seventh; the counties of Cabell, Wayne, Lincoln and Logan, the eighth; the counties of McDowell, Mercer, Raleigh, Wyoming and Boone, the ninth; the counties of Greenbrier, Monroe, Summers, Fayette and Pocahontas, the tenth; the counties of Upshur, Lewis, Braxton, Nicholas and Webster, the eleventh; the counties of Grant, Hardy, Hampshire, Mineral and

Pendleton, the twelfth; the counties of Jefferson, Berkeley and Morgan, the thirteenth.

[By various acts of the Legislature authorized by section 14 following, the division of the State into circuits has been changed and the number increased to twenty-four.]

REARRANGEMENT OF STATE INTO CIRCUITS

14. The Legislature may rearrange the circuits herein provided for at any session thereof, next preceding any general election of the judges of said circuits, and after the year one thousand eight hundred eighty-eight, may, at any session, increase or diminish the number thereof.

SPECIAL TERMS AND JUDGES OF CIRCUIT COURTS

15. The Legislature shall provide by law for holding regular and special terms of the circuit courts, where from any cause the judge shall fail to attend, or, if in attendance, can not properly preside.

SALARIES OF AND LIMITATION ON JUDGES

16. All judges shall be commissioned by the Governor. The * salary of a judge of the Supreme Court of Appeals shall be two thousand two hundred dollars per annum, and that of a judge of the circuit court shall be one thousand eight hundred dollars per annum; and each shall receive the same mileage as members of the Legislature: *Provided*, That Ohio county may pay an additional sum per annum to the judges of the circuit court thereof; but such allowance shall not be increased or diminished during the term of office of the judges to whom it may have been made. No judge, during his term of office, shall practice the profession of law or hold any other office, appointment or public trust, under this or any other government, and the acceptance thereof shall vacate his judicial office. Nor shall he, during his continuance therein, be eligible to any political office.

* The "Judicial amendment" proposed by House Joint Resolution No. 15, adopted by the Legislature in 1901, providing that the Supreme Court of Appeals shall consist of five judges, who shall receive such salaries as shall be fixed by law, was ratified at the general election in 1902. Vote on the amendment: For ratification, 54,676; against ratification, 24,710; majority, 29,966.

HOW JUDGES MAY BE REMOVED

17. Judges may be removed from office by a concurrent vote of both Houses of the Legislature, when from age, disease, mental or bodily infirmity or intemperance, they are incapable of discharging the duties of their office. But two-thirds of all the members elected to each House must concur in such vote, and the cause of removal shall be entered upon the journal of each House. The judge against whom the Legislature may be about to proceed shall receive notice thereof, accompanied with the cause alleged for his removal, at least twenty days before the day on which action is proposed to be taken therein.

CLERK OF CIRCUIT COURTS

18. The voters of each county shall elect a clerk of the circuit court, whose term of office shall be six years; his duties and compensation and the manner of removing him from office shall be prescribed by law; and when a vacancy shall occur in the office, the circuit court or the judge thereof in vacation shall fill the same by appointment until the next general election. In any case in respect to which the clerk shall be so situated as to make it improper for him to act, the said court shall appoint a clerk to act therein. The clerks of said courts in office when this article takes effect, shall remain therein for the term for which they were elected, unless sooner removed in the manner prescribed by law.

COURTS OF LIMITED JURISDICTION

19. The Legislature may establish courts of limited jurisdiction within any county, incorporated city, town or village, with the right of appeal to the circuit court, subject to such limitations as may be prescribed by law; and all courts of limited jurisdiction heretofore established in any county, incorporated city, town or village, shall remain as at present constituted until otherwise provided by law. The municipal court of Wheeling shall continue in existence until otherwise provided by law, and said court and the judge thereof, shall exercise the powers and jurisdiction heretofore conferred upon them; and appeals in civil cases from said court shall lie directly to the supreme court of appeals.

REGARDING PARTICIPATION IN CIVIL WAR

20. No citizen of this State who aided or participated in the late war between the government of the United States and a part of the people thereof, on either side, shall be liable in any proceeding, civil or criminal; nor shall his property be seized or sold under final process issued upon judgments or decrees heretofore rendered, or otherwise, because of any act done in accordance with the usages of civilized warfare in the prosecution of said war. The Legislature shall provide, by general laws, for giving full force and effect to this section.

PARTS OF COMMON LAW EFFECTIVE

21. Such parts of the common law, and of the laws of this State as are in force when this article goes into operation, and are not repugnant thereto, shall be and continue the law of the State until altered or repealed by the Legislature. All civil and criminal suits and proceedings pending in the former circuit courts of this State, shall remain and be proceeded in before the circuit courts of the counties in which they were pending.

COUNTY COURTS

22. There shall be in each county of the State a county court, composed of three commissioners, and two of said commissioners shall be a quorum for the transaction of business. It shall hold four regular sessions in each year, and at such times as may be fixed upon and entered of record by the said court. Provisions may be made by law for holding special sessions of said court.

TERMS OF OFFICE OF COUNTY COMMISSIONERS

23. The commissioners shall be elected by the voters of the county, and hold their office for the term of six years, except at the first meeting of said commissioners they shall designate by lot, or otherwise, in such manner as they may determine, one of their number, who shall hold his office for the term of two years, one for four years, and one for six years, so that one shall be elected every two

years. But no two of said commissioners shall be elected from the same magisterial district. And if two or more persons residing in the same district shall receive the greater number of votes cast at any election, then only the one of such persons receiving the highest number shall be declared elected, and the person living in another district, who shall receive the next highest number of votes, shall be declared elected. Said commissioners shall annually elect one of their number as president, and each shall receive two dollars per day for his services in court, to be paid out of the county treasury.

POWERS OF COUNTY COURTS

24. The county courts, through their clerks, shall have the custody of all deeds and other papers presented for record in their counties, and the same shall be preserved therein, or otherwise disposed of, as now is, or may be prescribed by law. They shall have jurisdiction in all matters of probate, the appointment and qualification of personal representatives, guardians, committees, curators, and the settlement of their accounts, and in all matters relating to apprentices. They shall also, under such regulations as may be prescribed by law, have the superintendence and administration of the internal police and fiscal affairs of their counties, including the establishment and regulation of roads, ways, bridges, public landings, ferries and mills, with authority to lay and disburse the county levies: *Provided*, That no license for the sale of intoxicating liquors in any incorporated city, town or village, shall be granted without the consent of the municipal authorities thereof, first had and obtained. They shall in all cases of contest judge of the election, qualification and returns of their own members, and of all county and district officers, subject to such regulations, by appeal or otherwise, as may be prescribed by law. Such courts may exercise such other powers, and perform such other duties, not of a judicial nature, as may be prescribed by law. And provision may be made under such regulations as may be prescribed by law, for the probate of wills, and for the appointment and qualification of personal representatives, guardians, committees and curators during the recess of the regular sessions of the county court. Such tribunals as have been heretofore established by the Legislature under, and by virtue of the thirty-fourth section of the eighth article of the Constitution of one thousand eight hundred seventy-two, for police and fiscal purposes, shall, until other-

wise provided by law, remain and continue as at present constituted in the counties in which they have been respectively established, and shall be and act as to police and fiscal matters in lieu of the county court created by this article until otherwise provided by law. And, until otherwise provided by law, such clerk as is mentioned in the twenty-sixth section of this article, shall exercise any powers and discharge any duties heretofore conferred on, or required of, any court or tribunal established for judicial purposes under the said article and section of the Constitution of one thousand eight hundred seventy-two, or the clerk of such court or tribunal respectively, respecting the recording and preservation of deeds and other papers presented for record, matters of probate, the appointment and qualification of personal representatives, guardians, committees, curators, and the settlement of their accounts, and in all matters relating to apprentices.

REMOVAL OF CAUSES

25. All actions, suits and proceedings not embraced in the next preceding section, pending in a county court when this article takes effect, together with the records and papers pertaining thereto, as well as all records and papers pertaining to such actions, suits and proceedings, as have already been disposed of by said courts, shall be transmitted to and filed with the clerk of the circuit court of the county, to which office all process outstanding at the time this article goes into operation shall be returned; and said clerk shall have the same power and shall perform the same duties in relation to such records, papers and proceedings as were vested in and required of the clerk of the county court on the day before this article shall take effect. All such actions, suits and proceedings so pending as aforesaid, shall be docketed, proceeded in, tried, heard and determined in all respects by the circuit court, as if such suits and proceedings had originated in said court.

CLERK OF COUNTY COURT

26. The voters of each county shall elect a clerk of the county court, whose term of office shall be six years. His duties and compensation and the manner of his removal shall be prescribed by law. But the clerks of said courts, now in office, shall remain therein

for the term for which they have been elected, unless sooner removed therefrom, in the manner prescribed by law.

DISTRICTING OF COUNTY — ELECTION OF JUSTICES OF THE PEACE

27. Each county shall be laid off into districts, not less than three nor more than ten in number, and as nearly equal as may be in territory and population. There shall be elected in each district containing a population not exceeding twelve hundred, one justice of the peace, and if the population exceeds that number, two such justices shall be elected therein. Every justice shall reside in the district for which he was elected and hold his office for the term of four years, unless sooner removed in the manner prescribed by law. The districts as they now exist shall remain till changed by the county court.

JURISDICTION OF JUSTICE OF THE PEACE

28. The civil jurisdiction of a justice of the peace shall extend to actions of assumpsit, debt, detinue and trover, if the amount claimed, exclusive of interest, does not exceed three hundred dollars. The jurisdiction of justices of the peace shall extend throughout their county; they shall be conservators of the peace and have such jurisdiction and powers in criminal cases as may be prescribed by law. And justices of the peace shall have authority to take the acknowledgment of deeds and other writings, administer oaths, and take and certify depositions. And the Legislature may give to justices such additional civil jurisdiction and powers within their respective counties as may be deemed expedient, under such regulations and restrictions as may be prescribed by general law, except that in suits to recover money or damages, their jurisdiction and powers shall in no case exceed three hundred dollars. Appeals shall be allowed from judgments of justices of the peace in such manner as may be prescribed by law.

REFORMATION OF COUNTY COURTS

29. The Legislature shall, upon the application of any county, reform, alter or modify the county court established by this article

in such county, and in lieu thereof, with the assent of a majority of the voters of such county voting at an election, create another tribunal for the transaction of the business required to be performed by the county court created by this article; and in such case all the provisions of this article in relation to the county court shall be applicable to the tribunal established in lieu of said court. And when such tribunal has been established it shall continue to act in lieu of the county court until otherwise provided by law.

COUNTY COURT TO FILL VACANCIES

30. The office of commissioner and justice of the peace, shall be deemed incompatible. Vacancies in the office of commissioner, clerk of the county court and justices of the peace, shall be filled by the county court of the county until the next general election.

ARTICLE IX

COUNTY ORGANIZATION

1. The voters of each county shall elect a surveyor of lands, a prosecuting attorney, a sheriff, and one and not more than two assessors, who shall hold their respective offices for the term of four years.

CONSTABLES, CORONERS AND OVERSEERS OF THE POOR

2. There shall also be elected in each district, of the county, by the voters thereof, one constable, and if the population of any district shall exceed twelve hundred, an additional constable, whose term of office shall be four years, and whose powers as such shall extend throughout the county. The assessor shall, with the advice and consent of the county court, have power to appoint one or more assistants. Coroners, overseers of the poor, and surveyors of roads shall be appointed by the county court. The foregoing officers, except the prosecuting attorneys, shall reside in the county and district for which they shall be respectively elected.

SHERIFFS — CONSECUTIVE TERMS PROHIBITED

3. The same person shall not be elected sheriff for two consecutive full terms; nor shall any person who acted as his deputy be elected successor to such sheriff, nor shall any sheriff act as deputy of his successor; nor shall he during his term of service, or within one year thereafter, be eligible to any other office. The retiring sheriff shall finish all business remaining in his hands, at the expiration of his term; for which purpose his commission and official bond shall remain in force. The duties of the office of sheriff shall be performed by him in person, or under his superintendence.

MALFEASANCE AND MISFEASANCE IN OFFICE

4. The presidents of the county courts, the justices of the peace, sheriffs, prosecuting attorneys, clerks of the circuit and of the county courts, and all other county officers shall be subject to indictment for malfeasance, misfeasance, or neglect of official duty and upon conviction thereof, their offices shall become vacant.

COMMISSIONING OF OFFICERS NOT OTHERWISE PROVIDED FOR IN CONSTITUTION

5. The Legislature shall provide for commissioning such of the officers herein mentioned, as it may deem proper, not provided for in this Constitution, and may require any class of them to give bond with security for the faithful discharge of the duties of their respective offices.

COMPENSATION — DEPUTIES

6. It shall further provide for the compensation, the duties and responsibilities of such officers, and may provide for the appointment of their deputies and assistants by general laws.

CONSERVATORS OF THE PEACE

7. The president of the county court and every justice and constable shall be a conservator of the peace throughout his county.

FORMATION OF NEW COUNTIES

8. No new county shall hereafter be formed in this State with an area of less than four hundred square miles, nor in population below six thousand; nor shall any county from which a new county, or part thereof shall be taken, be reduced in area below four hundred square miles, nor in population below six thousand. Nor shall a new county be formed without the consent of a majority of the voters residing within the boundaries of the proposed new county and voting on the question.

ARTICLE X

TAXATION AND FINANCE

1. Subject to the exceptions in this section contained, taxation shall be equal and uniform throughout the State, and all property, both real and personal, shall be taxed in proportion to its value to be ascertained as directed by law. No one species of property from which a tax may be collected shall be taxed higher than any other species of property of equal value; except that the aggregate of taxes assessed in any one year upon personal property employed exclusively in agriculture, including horticulture and grazing, products of agriculture as above defined, including live stock, while owned by the producer, and money, notes, bonds, bills and accounts receivable, stocks and other similar intangible personal property shall not exceed fifty cents on each one hundred dollars of value thereon and upon all property owned, used and occupied by the owner thereof exclusively for residential purposes and upon farms occupied and cultivated by their owners or bona fide tenants, one dollar; and upon all other property situated outside of municipalities, one dollar and fifty cents; and upon all other such property situated within municipalities, two dollars; and the Legislature shall further provide by general law for increasing the maximum rates authorized to be fixed by the different levying bodies upon all classes of property by submitting the question to the voters of the taxing units affected, but no increase shall be effective unless at least sixty percent of the qualified voters shall favor such increase, and such increase shall not continue for a longer period than three years at any

one time, and shall never exceed by more than fifty percent the maximum rate herein provided and prescribed by law; and the revenue derived from this source shall be apportioned by the Legislature among the levying units of the State in proportion to the levy laid in said units upon real and other personal property; but property used for educational, literary, scientific, religious or charitable purposes, all cemeteries, public property, the personal property, including live stock, employed exclusively in agriculture as above defined and the products of agriculture as so defined while owned by the producers may by law be exempted from taxation; household goods to the value of two hundred dollars shall be exempted from taxation. The Legislature shall have authority to tax privileges, franchises and incomes of persons and corporations and to classify and graduate the tax on all incomes according to the amount thereof and to exempt from taxation incomes below a minimum to be fixed from time to time, and such revenues as may be derived from such tax may be appropriated as the Legislature may provide. After the year nineteen hundred thirty-three, the rate of the state tax upon property shall not exceed one cent upon the hundred dollars valuation, except to pay the principal and interest of bonded indebtedness of the State now existing.

[This section, prior to its amendment, read as follows: "Taxation shall be equal and uniform throughout the State, and all property, both real and personal, shall be taxed in proportion to its value, to be ascertained as directed by law. No one species of property, from which a tax may be collected, shall be taxed higher than any other species of property of equal value; but property used for educational, literary, scientific, religious or charitable purposes, all cemeteries and public property may, by law, be exempt from taxation. The Legislature shall have power to tax, by uniform and equal laws, all privileges and franchises of persons and corporations."

The amendment as above set forth was proposed by House Joint Resolution No. 3, adopted August 6, 1932 (Acts Ex. Sess., 1932, p. 16) and was ratified at the general election in 1932. Vote on the amendment: For ratification, 335,482; against ratification, 43,931; majority, 291,551.]

CAPITATION TAX

2. The Legislature shall levy an annual capitation tax of one dollar upon each male inhabitant of the State who has attained the age of twenty-one years, which shall be annually appropriated to the sup-

port of free schools. Persons afflicted with bodily infirmity may be exempted from this tax.

RECEIPTS AND EXPENDITURES OF PUBLIC MONIES

3. No money shall be drawn from the treasury but in pursuance of an appropriation made by law, and on a warrant issued thereon by the Auditor; nor shall any money or fund be taken for any other purpose than that for which it has been or may be appropriated or provided. A complete and detailed statement of the receipts and expenditures of the public monies shall be published annually.

LIMITATION ON CONTRACTING OF STATE DEBT

4. No debt shall be contracted by this State, except to meet casual deficits in the revenue, to redeem a previous liability of the State; to suppress insurrection, repel invasion or defend the State in time of war; but the payment of any liability other than that for the ordinary expenses of the State, shall be equally distributed over a period of at least twenty years.

POWER OF TAXATION

5. The power of taxation of the Legislature shall extend to provisions for the payment of the State debt, and interest thereon, the support of free schools, and the payment of the annual estimated expenses of the State, but whenever any deficiency in the revenue shall exist in any year, it shall, at the regular session thereof held next after the deficiency occurs, levy a tax for the ensuing year, sufficient with the other sources of income, to meet such deficiency, as well as the estimated expenses of such year.

CREDIT OF STATE NOT TO BE GRANTED IN CERTAIN CASES

6. The credit of the State shall not be granted to, or in aid of any county, city, township, corporation or person; nor shall the State ever assume, or become responsible for the debts or liabilities of any county, city, township, corporation or person; nor shall the State

ever hereafter become a joint owner, or stockholder in any company or association in this State or elsewhere, formed for any purpose whatever.

DUTIES OF COUNTY AUTHORITIES IN ASSESSING TAXES

7. County authorities shall never assess taxes, in any one year, the aggregate of which shall exceed ninety-five cents per hundred dollars valuation except for the support of free schools; payment of indebtedness existing at the time of the adoption of this Constitution; and for the payment of any indebtedness with the interest thereon, created under the succeeding section, unless such assessment, with all questions involving the increase of such aggregate, shall have been submitted to the vote of the people of the county, and have received three-fifths of all the votes cast for and against it.

BONDED INDEBTEDNESS OF COUNTIES, ETC.

8. No county, city, school district, or municipal corporation, except in cases where such corporations have already authorized their bonds to be issued, shall hereafter be allowed to become indebted, in any manner, or for any purpose, to an amount, including existing indebtedness, in the aggregate, exceeding five per centum on the value of the taxable property therein to be ascertained by the last assessment for State and county taxes, previous to the incurring of such indebtedness; nor without, at the same time, providing for the collection of a direct annual tax, sufficient to pay, annually, the interest on such debt, and the principal thereof, within, and not exceeding thirty-four years: *Provided*, That no debt shall be contracted under this section, unless all questions connected with the same, shall have been first submitted to a vote of the people, and have received three-fifths of all the votes cast for and against the same.

MUNICIPAL TAXES TO BE UNIFORM

9. The Legislature may, by law, authorize the corporate authorities of cities, towns and villages, for corporate purposes, to assess and collect taxes; but such taxes shall be uniform, with respect to

persons and property within the jurisdiction of the authority imposing the same.

ARTICLE XI

CORPORATIONS

1. The Legislature shall provide for the organization of all corporations hereafter to be created, by general laws, uniform as to the class to which they relate; but no corporation shall be created by special law: *Provided*, That nothing in this section contained, shall prevent the Legislature from providing by special laws for the connection, by canal, of the waters of the Chesapeake with the Ohio River by the line of the James River, Greenbrier, New River and Great Kanawha.

CORPORATE LIABILITY AND INDEBTEDNESS

2. The stockholders of all corporations and joint stock companies, except banks and banking institutions, created by laws of this State, shall be liable for the indebtedness of such corporations to the amount of their stock subscribed and unpaid, and no more.

EXCLUSIVE PRIVILEGES PROHIBITED

3. All existing charters or grants of special or exclusive privileges under which organization shall not have taken place, or which shall not have been in operation within two years from the time this Constitution takes effect, shall thereafter have no validity or effect whatever: *Provided*, That nothing herein shall prevent the execution of any *bona fide contract* heretofore lawfully made in relation to any existing charter or grant in this State.

RIGHTS OF STOCKHOLDERS

4. The Legislature shall provide by law that in all elections for directors or managers of incorporated companies, every stockholder shall have the right to vote, in person or by proxy, for the number

of shares of stock owned by him, for as many persons as there are directors or managers to be elected, or to cumulate said shares, and give one candidate as many votes as the number of directors multiplied by the number of his shares of stock, shall equal, or to distribute them on the same principle among as many candidates as he shall think fit; and such directors or managers shall not be elected in any other manner.

STREET RAILROADS

5. No law shall be passed by the Legislature, granting the right to construct and operate a street railroad within any city, town or incorporated village, without requiring the consent of the local authorities having the control of the street or highway proposed to be occupied by such street railroad.

BANKS

6. The Legislature may provide by general law for the creation, organization and regulation of banking institutions.

[This section, prior to its amendment, read as follows: "The Legislature may provide, by general banking law, for the creation and organization of banks of issue or circulation, but the stockholders of any bank hereafter authorized by the laws of this State, whether of issue, deposit or discount, shall be personally liable to the creditors thereof over and above the amount of stock held by them respectively to an amount equal to their respective shares so held, for all its liabilities accruing while they are such stockholders."

The amendment as set forth above was proposed by House Joint Resolution No. 3, adopted February 16, 1937 (Acts 1937, p. 581), and was ratified at the general election in 1938. Vote on the amendment: For ratification, 139,985; against ratification, 62,241; majority, 77,744.]

RAILROADS

7. Every railroad corporation organized or doing business in this State shall annually, by their proper officers, make a report under oath, to the auditor of public accounts of this State, or some officer to be designated by law, setting forth the condition of their affairs,

the operations of the year, and such other matters relating to their respective railroads as may be prescribed by law. The Legislature shall pass laws enforcing by suitable penalties the provisions of this section.

ROLLING STOCK CONSIDERED PERSONAL PROPERTY

8. The rolling stock and all other movable property belonging to any railroad company or corporation in this State, shall be considered personal property and shall be liable to execution and sale in the same manner as the personal property of individuals; and the Legislature shall pass no law exempting any such property from execution and sale.

RAILROADS, PUBLIC HIGHWAYS

9. Railroads heretofore constructed, or that may hereafter be constructed in this State, are hereby declared public highways and shall be free to all persons for the transportation of their persons and property thereon, under such regulations as shall be prescribed by law; and the Legislature shall, from time to time, pass laws, applicable to all railroad corporations in the State, establishing reasonable maximum rates of charge for the transportation of passengers and freights, and providing for the correction of abuses, the prevention of unjust discrimination between through and local or way freight and passenger tariffs, and for the protection of the just rights of the public, and shall enforce such laws by adequate penalties.

STATIONS TO BE ESTABLISHED

10. The Legislature shall, in the law regulating railway companies, require railroads running through, or within a half mile of a town or village, containing three hundred or more inhabitants, to establish stations for the accommodation of the trade and travel of said town or village.

COMPETING LINES — LEGISLATIVE PERMISSION

11. No railroad corporation shall consolidate its stock, property or franchise with any other railroad owning a parallel or competing

line, or obtain the possession or control of such parallel or competing line, by lease or other contract, without the permission of the Legislature.

RIGHT OF EMINENT DOMAIN

12. The exercise of the power and the right of eminent domain shall never be so construed or abridged as to prevent the taking, by the Legislature, of the property and franchises of incorporated companies already organized, and subjecting them to the public use, the same as of individuals.

ARTICLE XII

EDUCATION

1. The Legislature shall provide, by general law, for a thorough and efficient system of free schools.

STATE SUPERINTENDENT OF FREE SCHOOLS

2. The State Superintendent of Free Schools shall have a general supervision of free schools, and perform such other duties in relation thereto as may be prescribed by law. If in the performance of any such duty imposed upon him by the Legislature he shall incur any expenses, he shall be reimbursed therefor: *Provided:* The amount does not exceed five hundred dollars in any one year.

COUNTY SUPERINTENDENTS

3. The Legislature may provide for county superintendents and such other officers as may be necessary to carry out the objects of this article and define their duties, powers and compensation.

EXISTING PERMANENT AND INVESTED SCHOOL FUND

4. The existing permanent and invested school fund, and all money accruing to this State from forfeited, delinquent, waste and unap-

propriated lands; and from lands heretofore sold for taxes and purchased by the State of Virginia, if hereafter redeemed or sold to others than this State; all grants, devices or bequests that may be made to this State, for the purposes of education or where the purposes of such grants, devises or bequests are not specified; this State's just share of the literary fund of Virginia, whether paid over or otherwise liquidated; and any sums of money, stocks or property which this State shall have the right to claim from the State of Virginia for educational purposes; the proceeds of the estates of persons who may die without leaving a will or heir: and of all escheated lands; the proceeds of any taxes that may be levied on the revenues of any corporation; all monies that may be paid as an equivalent for exemption from military duty; and such sums as may from time to time be appropriated by the Legislature for the purpose, shall be set apart as a separate fund to be called the "School Fund," and invested under such regulations as may be prescribed by law, in the interest-bearing securities of the United States, or of this State, or if such interest-bearing securities can not be obtained, then said "School Fund" shall be invested in such other solvent, interest-bearing securities as shall be approved by the Governor, Superintendent of Free Schools, Auditor and Treasurer, who are hereby constituted the "Board of the School Fund," to manage the same under such regulations as may be prescribed by law; and the interest thereof shall be annually applied to the support of free schools throughout the State, and to no other purpose whatever. But any portion of said interest remaining unexpended at the close of a fiscal year shall be added to and remain a part of the capital of the "School Fund": *Provided*, That all the taxes which shall be received by the State upon delinquent lands, except the taxes due to the State thereon, shall be refunded to the county or district by or for which the same were levied.

[This section is modified by the "Irreducible School Fund Amendment" set forth at the end of the Constitution.]

SUPPORT OF FREE SCHOOLS

5. The Legislature shall provide for the support of free schools by appropriating thereto the interest of the invested "School Fund," the net proceeds of all forfeitures and fines accruing to this State under the laws thereof; the State capitation tax, and by general

taxation of persons and property or otherwise. It shall also provide for raising in each county or district, by authority of the people thereof, such a proportion of the amount required for the support of free schools therein as shall be prescribed by general laws.

SCHOOL DISTRICTS

6. The school districts into which any county is now divided shall continue until changed in pursuance of law.

LEVIES FOR SCHOOL PURPOSES

7. All levies that may be laid by any county or district for the purpose of free schools shall be reported to the clerk of the county court, and shall, under such regulations as may be prescribed by law, be collected by the sheriff, or other collector, who shall make annual settlements with the county court, which settlements shall be made a matter of record by the clerk thereof, in a book to be kept for that purpose.

MIXED SCHOOLS PROHIBITED

8. White and colored persons shall not be taught in the same school.

CERTAIN ACTS PROHIBITED

9. No person connected with the free school system of the State, or with any educational institution of any name or grade under State control, shall be interested in the sale, proceeds or profits of any book or other thing used, or to be used therein, under such penalties as may be prescribed by law: *Provided*, That nothing herein shall be construed to apply to any work written, or thing invented, by such person.

CREATION OF INDEPENDENT FREE SCHOOL DISTRICTS

10. No independent free school district, or organization shall hereafter be created, except with the consent of the school district

or districts out of which the same is to be created, expressed by a majority of the voters voting on the question.

APPROPRIATION FOR STATE NORMAL SCHOOLS

11. No appropriation shall hereafter be made to any State normal school, or branch thereof, except to those already established and in operation, or now chartered.

LEGISLATURE TO FOSTER GENERAL SCHOOL IMPROVEMENTS

12. The Legislature shall foster and encourage moral, intellectual, scientific and agricultural improvement; it shall, whenever it may be practicable, make suitable provision for the blind, mute and insane, and for the organization of such institutions of learning as the best interests of general education in the State may demand.

ARTICLE XIII

LAND TITLES

1. All private rights and interests in lands in this State derived from or under the laws of the State of Virginia, and from or under the Constitution and laws of this State prior to the time this Constitution goes into operation, shall remain valid and secure and shall be determined by the laws in force in Virginia, prior to the formation of this State, and by the Constitution and laws in force in this State prior to the time this Constitution goes into effect.

LAND ENTRY PROHIBITED

2. No entry by warrant on land in this State shall hereafter be made.

FORFEITED LANDS

3. All title to lands in this State heretofore forfeited, or treated as forfeited, waste and unappropriated, or escheated to the State of

Virginia, or this State, or purchased by either of said States at sales made for the non-payment of taxes and become irredeemable, or hereafter forfeited, or treated as forfeited, or escheated to this State, or purchased by it and become irredeemable, not redeemed, released or otherwise disposed of, vested and remaining in this State, shall be, and is hereby transferred to, and vested in any person (other than those for whose default the same may have been forfeited or returned delinquent, their heirs or devisees), for so much thereof as such person has, or shall have had, actual continuous possession of, under color or claim of title for ten years, and who, or those under whom he claims, shall have paid the State taxes thereon for any five years during such possession; or if there be no such person, then to any person (other than those for whose default the same may have been forfeited, or returned delinquent, their heirs or devisees), for so much of said land as such person shall have title or claim to, regularly derived, mediately or immediately from, or under a grant from the Commonwealth of Virginia, or this State, not forfeited, which but for the title forfeited would be valid, and who, or those under whom he claims has, or shall have paid all State taxes charged or chargeable thereon for five successive years, after the year 1865, or from the date of the grant, if it shall have issued since that year; or if there be no such person, as aforesaid, then to any person (other than those for whose default the same may have been forfeited, or returned delinquent, their heirs or devisees), for so much of said land as such person shall have had claim to and actual continuous possession of, under color of title for any five successive years after the year 1865; and have paid all State taxes charged or chargeable thereon for said period.

WASTE AND UNAPPROPRIATED LANDS

4. All lands in this State, waste and unappropriated, or heretofore or hereafter for any cause forfeited, or treated as forfeited, or escheated to the State of Virginia, or this State, or purchased by either and become irredeemable, not redeemed, released, transferred or otherwise disposed of, the title whereto shall remain in this State till such sale as is hereinafter mentioned, be made, shall by proceedings in the circuit court of the county in which the lands, or a part thereof, are situated, be sold to the highest bidder.

FORMER OWNER'S PRIVILEGE

5. The former owner of any such land shall be entitled to receive the excess of the sum for which the land may be sold over the taxes charged and chargeable thereon, or which, if the land had not been forfeited, would have been charged or chargeable thereon, since the formation of this State, with interest at the rate of twelve per centum per annum, and the costs of the proceedings, if his claim be filed in the circuit court that decrees the sale within two years thereafter.

LAND BOOKS — TAXES

6. It shall be the duty of every owner of land, or of an undivided interest therein, to have such land, or such undivided interest therein entered on the land books of the county in which it, or a part of it, is situated, and to cause himself to be charged with taxes legally levied thereon and pay the same. When, for any five successive years, the owner of any tract of land, or undivided interest therein, shall not have been charged on such land books with State, county and district taxes thereon, then, by operation hereof, the land, or undivided interest therein, shall be forfeited and the title vested in the State. But if, for any one or more of such five years, the owner of such land, or of any undivided interest therein, shall have been charged with State, county, and district taxes on any part of such land, such part thereof, or undivided interest therein, shall not be forfeited for such cause. And any owner of land so forfeited, or of any interest therein, at the time of the forfeiture thereof, who shall then be an infant, married woman, or insane person, may, until the expiration of three years after the removal of such disability, have the land, or such interest, charged on such land books, with all State and other taxes that shall be, and but for the forfeiture would be, chargeable on the land, or interest therein, for the year one thousand eight hundred sixty-three, and every year thereafter, with interest at the rate of ten per centum per annum, and pay all taxes and interest thereon for such years, and thereby redeem the land or interest therein: *Provided*, That such right to redeem shall in no case extend beyond twenty years from the time such land was forfeited.

[This section, prior to its amendment, read as follows: "It shall be the duty of every owner of land to have it entered on the land books of the county in which it, or a part of it, is situated, and to cause himself to be charged with the taxes thereon, and pay the same. When for any five successive years after the year 1869, the owner of any tract of land containing one thousand acres or more, shall not have been charged on such books with State tax on said land, then by operation hereof, the land shall be forfeited and the title thereto vested in the State. But if, for any one or more of such five years, the owner shall have been charged with State tax on any part of the land, such part thereof shall not be forfeited for such cause. And any owner of land so forfeited, or of any interest therein at the time of the forfeiture thereof, who shall then be an infant, married woman, or insane person, may, until the expiration of three years after the removal of such disability, have the land, or such interest charged on such books, with all State and other taxes that shall be, and but for the forfeiture would be, chargeable on the land, or interest therein for the year 1863, and every year thereafter with interest at the rate of ten per centum per annum; and pay all taxes and interest thereon for all such years and thereby redeem the land or interest therein: *Provided*, Such right to redeem shall in no case extend beyond twenty years from the time such land was forfeited."

The amendment as set forth above was proposed by House Joint Resolution No. 4, adopted January 22, 1934 (Acts Second Ex. Sess. 1933, p. 583) and was ratified at the general election in 1934. Vote on the amendment: For ratification, 257,090; against ratification, 177,796; majority, 79,294.]

ARTICLE XIV

AMENDMENTS

1. No convention shall be called, having the authority to alter the Constitution of the State, unless it be in pursuance of a law, passed by the affirmative vote of a majority of the members elected to each House of the Legislature and providing that polls be opened throughout the State, on the same day therein specified, which shall not be less than three months after the passage of such law, for the purpose of taking the sense of the voters on the question of calling a convention. And such convention shall not be held unless a majority of the votes cast at such polls be in favor of calling the same; nor shall the members be elected to such convention until at least one month after the result of the vote shall be duly ascertained, declared and published. And all acts and ordinances of the said convention shall be submitted to the voters of the State for ratification or rejection, and shall have no validity whatever until they are ratified.

HOW AMENDMENTS ARE MADE

2. Any amendment to the Constitution of the State may be proposed in either House of the Legislature; and if the same, being read on three several days in each House be agreed to on its third reading, by two-thirds of the members elected thereto, the proposed amendment, with the yeas and nays thereon, shall be entered on the Journals, and it shall be the duty of the Legislature to provide by law, for submitting the same to the voters of the State for ratification or rejection at the next general election thereafter, and cause the same to be published at least three months before such election in some newspaper in every county in which a newspaper is printed. And if a majority of the qualified voters, voting upon the question at the polls held pursuant to such law, ratify the proposed amendment, it shall be in force from the time of such ratification, as a part of the Constitution of the State. If two or more amendments be submitted at the same time, the vote on the ratification or rejection shall be taken on each separately.

Amendments to the Constitution

THE JUDICIAL AMENDMENT

[Proposed by House Joint Resolution No. 15 (Acts 1901, p. 462). Ratified in November, 1902. Vote on the amendment: For ratification, 54,676; against ratification, 24,710; majority, 29,966.]

The Supreme Court of Appeals shall consist of five judges. Those judges in office when this amendment takes effect shall continue in office until their terms shall expire, and the Legislature shall provide for the election of an additional judge of said court at the next general election, whose term shall begin on the first day of January, one thousand nine hundred five, and the Governor shall, as for a vacancy, appoint a judge of said court to hold office until the first day of January, one thousand nine hundred five. The judges of the Supreme Court of Appeals and of the circuit court shall receive such salaries as shall be fixed by law, for those now in or those hereafter to come into office.

THE IRREDUCIBLE SCHOOL FUND AMENDMENT

[Proposed by House Joint Resolution No. 28 (Acts 1901, p. 465). Ratified in November, 1902. Vote on the amendment: For ratification, 56,694; against ratification, 24,763; majority, 31,931.]

The accumulation of the school fund provided for in section four of article twelve, of the Constitution of this State, shall cease upon the adoption of this amendment, and all money to the credit of said fund over one million dollars, together with the interest of said fund, shall be used for the support of the free schools of this State. All money and taxes heretofore payable into the treasury under the provisions of said section four, to the credit of the school fund shall be hereafter paid into the treasury to the credit of the general school fund for the support of the free schools of the State.

THE GOOD ROADS AMENDMENT OF 1920

[Proposed by Senate Joint Resolution No. 15 (Acts 1919, p. 502). Ratified November 2, 1920. Vote on the amendment: For ratification, 248,689; against ratification, 130,569; majority, 118,120.]

The Legislature shall make provision by law for a system of state roads and highways connecting at least the various county seats of the State, and to be under the control and supervision of such state officers and agencies as may be prescribed by law. The Legislature shall also provide a state revenue to build, construct, and maintain, or assist in building, constructing and maintaining the same and for that purpose shall have power to authorize the issuing and selling of state bonds, the aggregate outstanding amount of which, at any one time, shall not exceed fifty million dollars.

When a bond issue as aforesaid is authorized, the Legislature shall at the same time provide for the collection of an annual state tax sufficient to pay annually the interest on such debt, and the principal thereof within and not exceeding thirty years.

THE GOOD ROADS AMENDMENT OF 1928

[Proposed by House Joint Resolution No. 17 (Acts 1927, p. 361). Ratified November 6, 1928. Vote on the amendment: For ratification, 360,597; against ratification, 92,885; majority, 267,712.]

The Legislature shall have power to authorize the issuing and selling of state bonds not exceeding in the aggregate thirty-five million dollars in addition to the state bonds which were authorized to be issued and sold by the amendment to the Constitution proposed by Senate Joint Resolution No. 15, adopted February 15, 1919, and afterwards ratified by a vote of the people. The proceeds of said additional bonds hereby authorized to be issued and sold shall be used and appropriated solely for the building and constructing or for assisting in building and constructing the system of state roads and highways provided for by the amendment to the Constitution above mentioned.

When a bond issue as aforesaid is authorized, the Legislature shall at the same time provide for the collection of an annual state tax sufficient to pay annually the interest on such debt and to pay the principal thereof within and not exceeding thirty years.

For the "Budget Amendment" of 1918, see Art. VI, § 51, page 425.

For the "Legislative Amendments" of 1920 and 1928, see Art. VI, §§ 22, 33, pages 415, 416.

For the "Tax Limitation Amendment" of 1932, see Art. X, § 1, page 449.

For the "Lame Duck Amendment" of 1934, see Art. VII, § 1, page 430.

For the "Land Book Assessment Amendment" of 1934, see Art. XIII, § 6, page 461.

For the "Prohibition Repeal Amendment" of 1934, see Art. VI, § 46, page 423.

For the "Garnishee Amendment" of 1936, see Art. VI, § 35, page 419.

For the "Municipal Home Rule Amendment" of 1936, see Art. VI, § 39-(a), page 421.

For the "Banking Institutions Amendment" of 1938, see Art. XI, § 6, page 454.

CONSTITUTIONAL AMENDMENTS SUBMITTED
1880–1948

1880

Judicial system amendment, providing for the reorganization of the judicial system. Adopted. Vote for, 57,941; against, 34,270.

Jury and justices' courts amendment, relating to trial by jury in justices' courts. Adopted. Vote for, 56,482; against, 34,073.

1884

General elections amendment, providing for the holding of general elections on the Tuesday after the first Monday in November, instead of on "the second Tuesday in October." Adopted. Vote for, 66,181; against, 25,422.

1888

Jury and justices' courts amendment, relating to right of trial by jury. Rejected. Vote for, 47,963; against, 62,443.

Prohibition amendment, prohibiting forever the manufacture and sale of all intoxicating liquors within the State. Rejected. Vote for, 41,668; against, 76,555.

Legislative amendment, providing that no session of the Legislature should continue longer than sixty days without the concurrence of two-thirds of the members elected to each House. Rejected. Vote for, 30,445; against, 79,631.

1902

Registration law amendment, providing for the enactment of registration laws by the Legislature. Adopted. Vote for, 55,196; against, 25,379.

Executive Department amendment, providing for the election and qualification of a Secretary of State. Adopted. Vote for, 59,509; against, 22,022.

Salary amendment, providing for the payment of such salaries to officials as may be established by law. Adopted. Vote for, 56,280; against, 23,513.

Judicial amendment, providing that the Supreme Court of Appeals shall consist of five judges, who shall receive such salaries as shall be fixed by law. Adopted. Vote for, 54,676; against, 24,710.

Irreducible school fund amendment, relating to the permanent and invested school fund. Adopted. Vote for, 56,694; against, 24,763.

1908

Qualification amendment, eliminating appointive officials from the provisions of section 4, Article IV of the Constitution. Rejected. Vote for, 39,162; against, 40,626.

Salary increase amendment, providing for an increase in compensation for county commissioners. Rejected. Vote for, 31,059; against, 51,445.

1910

Qualification amendment, providing for the appointment of female citizens to certain offices within the State. Rejected. Vote for, 44,168; against, 45,044.

Supreme Court amendment, increasing the number of Supreme Court judges to seven. Rejected. Vote for, 36,427; against, 52,578.

1912

Prohibition amendment, prohibiting the manufacture and sale of intoxicating, malt, vinous or spirituous liquors. Adopted. Vote for, 164,945; against, 72,603.

1916

County court amendment, providing for increase in compensation for county commissioners. Rejected. Vote for, 80,674; against, 130,023.

1918

Budget amendment, providing for adoption of a budget system. Adopted. Vote for, 51,405; against, 26,651.

1920

Good roads amendment, providing for a fifty million dollar bond issue for the construction and maintenance of good roads. Adopted. Vote for, 248,689; against, 130,569.

1922

Legislative amendment, providing for a split session of the Legislature, and for payment to each member of five hundred dollars per annum. Adopted. Vote for, 160,929; against, 122,744.

1926

Budget amendment, providing for amendment to section 51 of Article VI. Rejected. Vote for, 126,125; against, 134,842.

Property qualification amendment, providing for collection of taxes on money, notes, accounts receivable, and bonds, at a rate not to exceed fifty cents on each one hundred dollars actual value. Rejected. Vote for, 111,927; against, 159,653.

1928

Good roads amendment, providing for a bond issue of thirty-five million dollars for the construction of good roads. Adopted. Vote for, 360,597; against, 92,885.

Legislative amendment, providing for a legislative session of sixty days. Adopted. Vote for, 275,374; against, 85,123.

1930

Lieutenant-governor amendment, providing for the election of a lieutenant-governor. Rejected. Vote for, 48,781; against, 172,703.

Probate commissioner amendment, providing for the appointment of a probate commissioner in each county. Rejected. Vote for, 50,674; against, 173,447.

Budget amendment, providing for an amendment to section 51. Article VI. Rejected. Vote for, 50,226; against, 171,464.

Circuit Court amendment, providing for the division of the State into circuits by the Legislature. Rejected. Vote for, 49,902; against, 170,220.

1932

Tax limitation amendment, providing for the classification of property for taxation purposes. Adopted. Vote for, 335,482; against, 43,931.

1934

Prohibition amendment, providing for the repeal of the prohibition amendment. Adopted. Vote for, 276,978; against, 237,559.

Capitation tax amendment, providing that the payment of capitation tax may be made a qualification for voting in elections. Rejected. Vote for, 124,232; against, 313,330.

Lame duck amendment, providing that terms of the Governor and other members of the Executive Department shall commence on the first Monday after the second Wednesday of January next after their election. Adopted. Vote for, 251,965; against, 145,787.

Land book assessment amendment, providing for the separate assessment of individual interests in lands. Adopted. Vote for, 257,090; against, 177,796.

1936

Garnishee amendment, providing for the garnishment of wages of officers, agents, or employees of the State, including any subdivision thereof and municipality therein. Adopted. Vote for, 161,386; against, 61,472.

Municipal home rule amendment, providing uniform law for incorporation of municipalities with population in excess of two thousand, and for amendment of existing charters by municipal corporations. Adopted. Vote for, 150,370; against, 59,580.

1938

Banking institutions amendment, providing for the creation, organization and regulation of banking institutions. Adopted. Vote for, 139,985; against, 62,241.

1940

Judiciary amendment, providing for the establishment by the Legislature of a summary court in each county in the State. Rejected. Vote for, 133,256; against, 300,979.

Elective Officers amendment, providing for the election of Governor, Auditor and Attorney General and for appointment by the Governor of the heads of such executive departments as may be established by law. Rejected. Vote for, 86,402; against, 311,096.

Budget bill amendment, relating to the biennial budget bill. Rejected. Vote for, 95,094; against, 298,333.

1942

Good Roads amendment, limiting the use of all revenue derived from motor vehicles and motor fuels to road purposes. Adopted. Vote for, 228,828; against, 38,651.

1946

School amendment, removing State Superintendent of Schools from Board of Public Works. Rejected. Vote for, 174,156; against, 181,606.

Forestry amendment, providing classification and contract between State and owner in the planting, protection and harvesting of forest lands. Ratified. Vote for, 179,150; against, 148,104.

1948

Road bond amendment, providing for the issuance and sale of $50,000,000.00 of bonds for the construction of secondary roads. Ratified. Vote for, 475,272; against, 163,579.

SUGGESTIONS FOR FURTHER READING

BEFORE 1863

The student who wishes to make a detailed study of the government of West Virginia must first of all examine the early political structure of Virginia, which contains the roots of West Virginia's political institutions. Of primary importance here are W. W. Hening, *The Statutes at Large; Being a Collection of All the Laws of Virginia from 1619 to 1792* (13 vols., New York, 1819–23), and Samuel Shepherd, *The Statutes at Large of Virginia from 1792 to 1806* (3 vols., Richmond, 1835–36), together with the acts of the legislature following the period covered by Shepherd. Unfortunately, Hening and Shepherd are both comparatively rare and are not available in the ordinary library.

Various important secondary works are more easily accessible. Of first-rate value for the early period is Percy Scott Flippin, *The Royal Government of Virginia* (New York, 1919). An excellent special study is O. P. Chitwood, *Justice in Colonial Virginia* (Baltimore, 1905). The debt of Virginia's political institutions to English models may be studied by means of George B. Adams's *Constitutional History of England* (New York, 1927) and F. W. Maitland's book of the same title (Cambridge, 1926).

Virginia's role in the whole story of American colonial history will be found described in any good American history. The present author has been especially indebted to Edward Channing, *History of the United States* (6 vols., New York, 1905–25); Edward Eggleston, *Beginners of a Nation* (New York, 1896); H. L. Osgood, *The American Colonies in the Seventeenth Century* (3 vols., New York, 1907) and *The American Colonies in the Eighteenth Century* (4 vols., New York, 1924); and C. M. Andrews, *The Colonial Period of American History* (New Haven, 1938).

The part played by Virginia in the period between the Revolution and the Constitution is described in A. C. McLaughlin, *The Confederation and the Constitution* (New York, 1905). For her share in the framing and adoption of the Constitution, see especially the following works: Max Farrand, *The Framing of the Constitu-*

tion (New Haven, 1913), *The Fathers of the Constitution* (New Haven, 1921), and *The Records of the Federal Convention of 1787* (4 vols., New Haven, 1937); Jonathan Elliot, *The Debates in the Several State Conventions on the Adoption of the Federal Constitution* (revised ed., 5 vols., 1836–45 and later reprints); David Robertson, *Debates and Other Proceedings of the Convention of Virginia* (Richmond, 1805); and Hugh Blair Grigsby, *The History of the Virginia Federal Convention of 1788* (Richmond, 1890).

Study of the preceding topic reveals at once the importance of the conflicting interests of the east and west. On this topic C. H. Ambler, *Sectionalism in Virginia from 1776 to 1861* (Chicago, 1910), is invaluable, both for exposition and for the citation of other books which should be consulted. For the events leading up to the formation of West Virginia, W. P. Willey, *Inside View of the Formation of the State of West Virginia* (Wheeling, 1901), and Granville D. Hall, *The Rending of Virginia* (Chicago, 1902), admirably serve the same twofold purpose.

SINCE 1863

There are rich collections of source materials, as well as secondary works, in the Archives of West Virginia University and in the State Department of Archives and History at Charleston. Various lists of the books and papers in these two depositories have been issued from time to time. The fullest bibliography of materials relating to West Virginia is in the biennial report of the State Department of Archives and History for the period ending June 30, 1938. Since this excellent list is available, we content ourselves here with mention of a few types of material that the student should investigate.

For study of West Virginia's government the printed records of the two constitutional conventions, of 1861–62 and 1872, are indispensable. Not only in various libraries but also in the offices of many lawyers may be found complete collections of the acts of the legislature from the first session to the present time. The journals of the senate and the house of delegates, and the messages of the governors, together with the reports of the various administrative departments, are generally accessible.

Of the general works, J. M. Callahan's *History of West Virginia* (Chicago, 1923) contains full information. No book detailing the structure of our state government has appeared since R. E. Fast and

Hu Maxwell, *History and Government of West Virginia* (Morgantown, 1901); the present work is designed to fill this gap. Various good texts, however, treat comparatively the political structures of the several states; among them may be singled out F. A. Ogg and P. O. Ray, *Introduction to American Government* (9th ed., 1948).

Regional and county histories contain much valuable material on political institutions. As examples may be mentioned Hu Maxwell's histories of Tucker, Randolph, and Barbour counties (1884, 1898, 1899) and Oren F. Morton's histories of Pendleton, Preston, and Monroe counties (1910, 1914, 1916). Such local histories as J. M. Callahan's *History of Morgantown* (Morgantown, 1926) and W. S. Laidley's *History of Charleston and Kanawha County* (Chicago, 1911) should not be neglected. The student should also become acquainted with the rich potentialities of the files of newspapers contained in many libraries.

Concomitant with the growth of political government is the development of such other areas of activity as education, industry, transportation, health protection, etc. Secondary works on these subjects may easily be located by means of the bibliography mentioned above.

Index